REPRESENTING THE

Bryan Burns
1945–2000

REPRESENTING THE HOLOCAUST

In Honour of Bryan Burns

Editor
SUE VICE

VALLENTINE MITCHELL
LONDON • PORTLAND, OR

First published in 2003 in Great Britain by
VALLENTINE MITCHELL
Crown House, 47 Chase Side, Southgate,
London N14 5BP

and in the United States of America by
VALLENTINE MITCHELL
c/o ISBS, 920 NE 58th Avenue, #300,
Portland, OR 97213-3786

Website: www.vmbooks.com

Copyright © 2003 Vallentine Mitchell

British Library Cataloguing in Publication Data

Representing the Holocaust: in honour of Bryan Burns
1. Holocaust, Jewish (1939–1945) 2. Holocaust, Jewish (1939–1945), in literature 3. Holocaust, Jewish (1939–1945) – Historiography
I. Vice, Sue II. Burns, Bryan III. Immigrants & minorities
940.5'318

ISBN 0 8530 3496 6 (cloth)
ISBN 0 8530 3495 8 (paper)

Library of Congress Cataloging-in-Publication Data

Representing the Holocaust: in honour of Bryan Burns / editor, Sue Vice.
  p. cm.
ISBN 0-85303-496-6 (cloth) – ISBN 0-85303-495-8 (pbk.)
1. Holocaust, Jewish (1939–1945) – Influence. 2. Holocaust, Jewish (1939–1945), in literature. 3. Holocaust, Jewish (1939–1945), in motion pictures. 4. Holocaust survivors – Great Britain. 5. Refugees, Jewish – Great Britain. I. Burns, Bryan. II. Vice, Sue, 1961–

D804.3 R474 2003
940.53'18 – dc21

2003005827

This group of studies first appeared in a Special Issue on 'Representing the Holocaust' of *Immigrants & Minorities* (ISSN 0261-9288) 21/1 & 2 (March/July 2002) published by Frank Cass.

All rights reserved. No part of this publication may be reproduced, stored in or introduced into a retrieval system, or transmitted, in any form or by any means, electronic, mechanical, photocopying, recording or otherwise without the prior written permission of Vallentine Mitchell.

Typeset in 10/12pt Zapf Calligraphica by Vallentine Mitchell
Printed in Great Britain by Antony Rowe Ltd

Contents

Foreword by Bryan Cheyette   vii

In Memoriam
Bryan Burns (1945–2000)   **Sue Vice**   1

History

1. The Holocaust and the Museum World in Britain: A Study of Ethnography   **Tony Kushner**   13

2. Britain's Holocaust Memorial Days: Reshaping the Past in the Service of the Present   **Donald Bloxham**   41

3. Holocaust Refugees in Great Britain and the Research Centre for German and Austrian Exile Studies in London   **J.M. Ritchie**   63

Film

4. Fiction of the Real: *Shoah* and Documentary   **Bryan Burns**   81

5. Public Memory and Active Recall in Two Holocaust Films: *Partisans in Vilna* (1986) and *Come and See* (1985)   **Ben Smith**   89

Cultural Approaches

6. Ghetto Journals: The Case of Kovno   **Bryan Burns**   111

7. Identification and the Genre of Testimony   **Robert Eaglestone**   117

Biography

8. Breaking Free from 'A Scottish Shetl': The Life, Times and Jewishness of C.P. Taylor   **Avram Taylor**   143

9. Sidney Pollard: The Refugee Historian **David Renton** 184

Literature

10. Selfhood in Descent: Primo Levi's
    The Search for Roots and *If This is a Man* **Rachel Falconer** 203

11. Sylvia Plath and Holocaust Poetry **Gillian Banner** 231

12. Binjamin Wilkomirski's *Fragments* and
    Holocaust Envy: 'Why Wasn't I There Too?' **Sue Vice** 249

Bryan Burns: Curriculum Vitae 269

Notes on Contributors 275

Index 277

Foreword

BRYAN CHEYETTE

I first encountered Bryan Burns when I was an undergraduate and, subsequently, postgraduate student in the Department of English Literature at Sheffield University during the years 1977 to 1986. Bryan, I now realize, had only taken up his post as lecturer in English Literature three years before I arrived as a fresh-faced and remarkably naive eighteen-year-old. From a distance Bryan was a somewhat exotic figure, with his unmistakably sonorous voice and his cultural reach which, from the first, had a range of reference far beyond our diminutive shores. The non-celtic spelling of his first name was particularly noticeable to a fellow member of the 'awkward Bryan squad'.

In 1977, Bryan was one of the youngest lecturers in a department from which the august William Empson had recently retired, and where such notable figures as Brian Morris and Roma Gill were my teachers. In fact, the department boasted a group of colleagues – John Bull, Neil Corcoran, Shirley Foster, Kenneth Graham, Frances Gray, John Haffenden, Christopher Heywood, Sandy Lyle, Ian MacKillop, Mick Mangan, Neil Roberts, Philip Roberts, Robin Robbins and Derek Roper – who were all skilled communicators. It was in this company that Bryan was given full rein to take pleasure in his teaching, to the delight of generations of his undergraduate and postgraduate students.

At the same time, Bryan was a free spirit in the department and, to my eyes, appeared to be a perennial outsider. I was aware that he visited Poland quite regularly – especially Krakow and Lodz (where my paternal grandmother was born) – and I remember being disturbed at the time by those colleagues who travelled to the killing fields of Poland merely to teach English literature. These were, of course, my youthful prejudices and I was sensible enough to leave such thoughts unexpressed. The department was rightly committed to its strong links with Polish universities and there were regular stories about trips to Poland, from Bryan among others, during my time at Sheffield. What is clear is that these cultural exchanges did leave their mark both on

Bryan and the department as a whole. The appointment of Sue Vice as a lecturer in English Literature in 1989 acted as a catalyst in this regard. Her interest in Holocaust literature coincided with Bryan's own deepening cultural involvement with East-Central Europe and, out of this happy conjunction, two popular undergraduate courses took shape: 'Jewish Writing: Prelude to the Holocaust' and 'Representing the Holocaust'. These courses began in 1993 and the MA in Holocaust Studies soon followed in 1996.

When I returned to Sheffield as the external examiner of the Holocaust Studies MA in 1996, I was to reflect on a department that had developed a good deal since my student days. To some extent, these changes mirrored the evolving nature of English studies in the 1980s and 1990s with its turn away from English literary texts towards theory, other media and other cultural contexts. As the Englishness of the literary canon came under scrutiny, minority voices and the complicity of English literature with histories of oppression of all kinds began to determine much new research in the discipline. My own research in both the English Literature department and the Department of Economic and Social History, under Kenneth Graham and Colin Holmes, is part of the story. I was fortunate enough to be a postgraduate student at the same time as Tony Kushner, who also worked under Colin Holmes and has contributed to this volume. The sea-change in both Jewish studies and English studies in the past two decades has a distinct Sheffield dimension, as the essay on Sidney Pollard in the collection makes plain. That Bryan's doctoral students, as well as his old and new colleagues, have contributed to the volume testifies to his considerable role in the 'Sheffield school' of immigrant and minority studies.

The fact that Bryan and Sue were given *carte blanche* to teach and research Jewish and Holocaust literature is in part a response to the opening up of English literary studies, but it also cannot simply be reduced to this moment. What characterizes Bryan's work, more than anything else, is a staunch refusal to be merely fashionable or modish. Although Holocaust and Jewish literature courses began to be taught in several English departments in the 1980s and 1990s – in Leeds, London, Manchester and Southampton as well as Sheffield – it is significant that this development is not part of the received accounts concerning the changing face of English literary studies. Bryan, in other words, chose an area that remains difficult and unclassifiable and I suspect that this was one of its main attractions.

What is clear from his essays in the present collection is that all of Bryan's writing on the Holocaust is essentially a product of his teaching. Most academics turn their research into university courses whereas Bryan seems to have taken a less instrumental and more humane view. His thoughts on ghetto diaries or films on the Holocaust have been distilled in the seminar room over many years before being published. This is one reason for their modest yet resonant understanding and for the confidence of their intellectual ambition. Another reason for the adeptness of these essays is precisely the refusal to play the identity card. By focusing on European Jewish writing before the Holocaust Bryan, from the start, was to refuse the language of victimhood (an inevitable component of contemporary identity) which has tended to deform much of our thinking. It is not a coincidence, in this regard, that many of the essays in the volume are exemplary meditations on the meaning of victimhood in contemporary memorialization or museum or literary culture; a victimhood which has culminated in the fraudulent but once universally celebrated Binjamin Wilkomirski.

Not unlike Geoffrey Hartman, Bryan Burns began his career writing on William Wordsworth. What could be more different than the death camps of Eastern Europe and the English countryside of Wordsworth's poetry? George Steiner, in his *Language and Silence: Essays 1958-1966* (1967), long ago challenged English literary studies to bring together these two worlds: 'The ultimate of political barbarism grew from the core of Europe ... This is of obvious and appalling relevance to the study or teaching of literature. It compels us to ask whether knowledge of the best that has been thought and said does, as Matthew Arnold asserted, broaden and refine the resources of the human spirit.'[1] It is my honour to write the foreword to an outstanding volume dedicated to an exceptional individual who, through his writing and teaching, did insist on the always tenuous Arnoldian task of broadening and refining the 'resources of the human spirit.'

NOTE

1. George Steiner, *Language and Silence: Essays 1958–1966* (Harmondsworth, 1979 [1967]), p.23.

In Memoriam

Bryan Burns (1945–2000)

SUE VICE

I found it hard to begin the biographical introduction to this collection of essays in memory of Bryan Burns, which is called *Representing the Holocaust* after the undergraduate course that he and I taught for several years. It was hard partly because in my head I kept hearing Bryan's voice: the phrase 'No fuss!' was his invariable response to any attempt to praise or honour him, or even give out detailed information during his illness. On the other hand, I know that Bryan would, alongside his self-contained modesty, have been very pleased by the present collection. We both often lamented the absence of a more recent version of Berel Lang's excellent edited volume, *Writing the Holocaust* (1988), which we could recommend to our students; I think the present collection goes some way to filling that gap. It includes contributions by friends, colleagues and former students of Bryan. Colin Holmes, whose input to the volume in terms of commissioning and organizing has been equal to that of a co-editor, met Bryan during discussions in 1995 about setting up what turned out to be Britain's first Holocaust Studies MA; Hamish Ritchie went on to teach on that degree. Rachel Falconer and I were Bryan's colleagues in the Department of English Literature at Sheffield; Gillian Banner's Ph.D. thesis was co-supervised by Bryan and me, and it has been published as *Holocaust Literature* by Vallentine Mitchell (2000). Ben Smith has recently completed the Ph.D. he began under Bryan's enthusiastic supervision. Other contributors met Bryan at Holocaust-related conferences and meetings.

Despite the fact that he fought shy of any extreme emotional displays, Bryan had a long-standing and profound interest in the

---

The Editor's thanks are due to all those who offered reminiscences and information about Bryan; and also to Mark Anstee, John Haffenden, Debby Hyuams, Lydia Linford, Sue Owen, Derek Roper, Dan Stone, and all the staff in the office of the Department of English Literature, University of Sheffield, especially Sue Turton.

Holocaust, with which he was first confronted in a material way on trips to Poland in the 1970s. Robert Hope, who met Bryan when both were five years old, says of their first Polish trip that, 'walking through Krakow's empty, wrecked ghetto with its sad, battered, padlocked synagogue produced all his work on the Holocaust, Jewish writing and his extended love affair with Eastern Europe'. Bryan once recounted the story of a visit to a small exhibition in Vienna on the Holocaust, at which he became suddenly so shaken by a display of identity cards owned by long-dead Jewish workers that he had to be led outside. I imagine this moment to have been a watershed in Bryan's engagement with the Holocaust. But this kind of epiphany was rare with Bryan, and he would have regarded repetitions of this foundational confrontation with the detail of mass death as self-indulgent.

Bryan's background would not lead a biographer to predict his personal or professional interest in Holocaust Studies. He was born in Berwick-upon-Tweed on 18 June 1945, and attended the local grammar school; he maintained a strong attachment to Berwick and his family there – his widowed mother and his aunts – throughout his life. Bryan graduated with a BA in English Language and Literature from the University of Durham in 1966, then took a Dip. Ed. at the University of Bristol in 1968. He returned to Durham in 1970 and completed an MA dissertation entitled, 'The Revisions of Wordsworth's *Yarrow Revisited* Volume of 1835 and the Form of Wordsworth's Later Poetry'. This project set the scene for Bryan's specialization in Romantic poetry and prose. His Ph.D., awarded by King's College, University of London, in 1980, was on 'Moods and Themes in the Writings of Thomas Love Peacock', and formed the basis for his first book, *The Novels of Thomas Love Peacock* (1985).

Between his MA and Ph.D., however, Bryan decided to live and work abroad. Anyone who knew him would agree that one of Bryan's most profound pleasures was overseas travel; his last trip, in the summer of 2000, was to the Canary Islands, and he had planned to visit Bulgaria and Lithuania in the near future. He was Lecturer in English at the University of Teheran in 1970–71, and Lecturer in English at the University of Zagreb in 1971–72. After taking a decision to go for permanence over the exotic, he took up a post as Lecturer in English Literature at the University of Sheffield in 1974; he was appointed when the late Brian Morris (who became the Labour peer Lord Morris of Castle Morris) was Head of Department. Bryan had long been interested in film as a personal pastime, and as it was listed on his curriculum vitae, he was asked about this at his Sheffield interview. Ian MacKillop, who was on the appointment panel, remembers asking

Bryan if he would be interested in developing this interest in film into some teaching: 'He responded with a broad smile and said yes. We then planned a course after visiting Victor Perkins at Warwick and talking about how they taught it there.' In 1980–81 Bryan was Visiting Professor of English at the University of Southern California in Los Angeles; one of the attractions of USC for him was, according to Shirley Foster, that he was able to see at least one film every day. Bryan was also invited to be a visiting lecturer, for periods of up to two weeks, at a variety of foreign universities, including Łódź, Oviedo, Malaga, Sofia, and, in 2000, Szeged.

In 1998 Bryan was promoted to Senior Lecturer at Sheffield; as the list of his publications at the end of this volume shows, he had a sudden surge of writing and publishing in the 1990s. This productiveness was partly the result of his taking a significant step in abandoning the plans he had held for over 15 years to write a book on the novels of Tobias Smollett. Instead, Bryan moved decisively into the area of film studies. In doing so, he mirrored the shifts simultaneously taking place in the English literature departments of British universities – they too showed signs of a broadening move away from a focus solely on conventional literary criticism, to other kinds of narrative, textual, hermeneutic and cultural studies, including film.

Bryan's book *World Cinema: Hungary* came out in 1996, and his study of Pal Gabor's 1978 film *Angi Vera* was sent to the publisher just before his illness was diagnosed in June 2000. He had plans, described in his curriculum vitae and sketched out in documents and research folders, to write his next book on the ghetto diaries of the Holocaust years, focusing on the Kovno Ghetto. The contribution included in the present volume on that topic is a fragment of preliminary work, and was the basis of a paper Bryan gave at a CCUE conference at the University of Loughborough in 1996.

It seems that Bryan's engagement with the Holocaust emerged from his cosmopolitan interests: in travel, in twentieth-century European fiction (Leonardo Sciascia and Giorgio Pressburger were firm favourites), and in European cinema. Equally, his Holocaust interests affected his view of film, as the essay on Claude Lanzmann's epic *Shoah*, included in this volume, suggests. Bryan taught a wide range of Holocaust films within the undergraduate and MA courses at Sheffield, including István Szabó's *Confidence* (1980), of which he noted that 'in Eastern Europe, only the Hungarian cinema has as yet dealt with the Holocaust in anything other than a cursory way'; Imre Gyöngyössy and Bárna Kabay's *The Revolt of Job* (1983), which Bryan described as 'the most thoroughgoing attempt to deal with the Holocaust in the

Hungarian cinema'; Alan Adelson and Kathryn Taverna's documentary *Łódź Ghetto* (1988); Alain Resnais' *Night and Fog* (1955); and, an especial favourite, the Quay Brothers' animated version of Bruno Schulz's stories *The Street of Crocodiles* (1986). In 1995, Bryan organized a day-conference on Holocaust film, at which the speakers included Guy Austin from Sheffield; Bryan Cheyette – a former student – from London; Patrick Finney from Lampeter; and Bryan himself, speaking on *Shoah*.

Bryan's cinematic interests were especially those of genre and technique, and how the content of Holocaust and inter-war European film could threaten to overwhelm its form. In 1999 Bryan published an article on the little-known Goskind Brothers' films of pre-war Jewish life in five cities. He included this arcane but fascinating material in his classes, and inspired fine written work on it. Bryan argues in this article that despite their apparent 'artlessness', the Goskinds' travelogues are put together with purposeful idiosyncrasy in terms of their shot construction and *mise-en-scène*. This formal disruptiveness is the key to the films' covert political agenda: to urge their (Jewish) viewers to emigrate to Palestine.

During the 1980s, inspired by visiting Budapest on holiday, Bryan began researching Hungarian cinema with a view to writing a book on the subject. He visited Hungary four times between 1985 and 1995 for this purpose – thus, incidentally, adding Hungarian to the list of languages of which he had 'reading knowledge' (the others were Latin, Dutch and Portuguese; he was fluent in French, German, Spanish, Italian, Serbo-Croat and Farsi). Bryan was funded by the Hungarian Ministry of Culture and the British Council for these trips to the Budapest Film Archives, where he watched a large corpus of films – beginning with those of Miklós Jancsó – with the help of an interpreter. Bryan was well aware that he had been granted unusual access for a foreigner to what he called the 'riches of Hungarian cinema', and he also noted the high regard for his interest held by his Hungarian hosts.

Gyula Gazdag's *That was a Hungarian Fairy Tale* (1987) was one of the set films on the Sheffield undergraduate film course 'Memory and the Cinema'; although it was never quite an unqualified hit with the students, it did register Bryan's commitment to art cinema. He was overjoyed when the Showroom Arts Cinema opened in Sheffield in 1995, and never went anywhere else to see films; the inclusion of Hollywood films in the 'Memory and the Cinema' course, even one so venerable as Alfred Hitchcock's *Marnie* (1964), caused him some good-humoured disquiet. More to Bryan's taste were films like Ingmar Bergman's *Wild Strawberries* (1957) and Bernardo Bertolucci's *The Conformist* (1970).

Bryan was interested not only in the Holocaust, the effective end of Jewish life in Europe, but also in pre-war Jewish European life – and, perhaps more unusually, in Jewishness itself. In a sense this interest requires some explanation, given that Bryan came from a non-practising Protestant background. As well as turning to Bryan's multicultural and worldly interests for an answer, colleagues speculated whether his apparent philosemitism constituted a displaced interest in gay history and suffering. I think Bryan would have found this an amusing but erroneous effort to explain away an engagement which he developed because, quite simply, he found the subject to be so interesting on so many levels: in intellectual, emotional, literary and moral terms. Bryan's optional course 'Jewish Writing' ran at undergraduate and MA levels; he subtitled it 'Prelude to the Holocaust', partly to signal its historical focus, and also so that it could be seen as part of an informal 'Holocaust track' leading to the course he and I shared, 'Representing the Holocaust'. Many students did choose both.

The inter-war focus and selection of texts for Bryan's course 'Jewish Writing' made it strikingly unusual among British university departments of English literature. In the words of Bryan's module description,

> This course examines the representation of pre-Holocaust Jewish experience in novels, short stories, travel books and films, and aims to show some of the characteristic features of Jewish life in the early decades of this century, to point to the development of antisemitism before the Second World War and to examine the ways in which antisemitic feeling is expressed during the period.

Bryan included on this course Osip Mandelstam's *The Noise of Time* and Nadezhda Mandelstam's *Hope Abandoned*; a section on golem narratives, including I.L. Peretz's and Jorge Luis Borges' stories, both entitled 'The Golem', and Henrik Galeen and Paul Wegener's film *The Golem* (1914); Alfred Döblin's *Journey to Poland* and Israel Joshua Singer's *Of a World That Is No More*; Jacob Wassermann's *My Life as German and Jew* and Sholom Aleichem's *Marienbad*; and Giorgio Bassani's novel *The Garden of the Finzi-Continis*. Bryan spent many hours scouring second-hand bookshops for Joseph Roth's then-unobtainable novel *Job* for this course; he would have been amazed and delighted to know that Granta have recently reissued not only *Job* but all of Roth's novels and his essays in paperback.

I often co-marked the students' work for Bryan's 'Jewish Writing' course, and was struck by their unmistakeable signs of expertise and engagement. Across all our teaching on these subjects – an undergraduate and an MA Holocaust literature course; a Jewish writing undergraduate and MA course; several Ph.D. students – the vast majority of the students were non-Jewish. This is another distinctive and positive feature of the Jewish and Holocaust studies teaching at Sheffield: a demographic pattern has become an asset. The very presence of such students, and Bryan's own non-Jewishness, gives the lie to Norman Finkelstein's attribution of the increased focus on the Holocaust to entrenched Jewish interests. Of course, to demand any particular ethnic or religious affiliations to work in this area would suggest that Jewish and Holocaust Studies are solely the province of 'identity politics'; this is fortunately not the case, as the work of many Holocaust scholars testifies.

Bryan was diagnosed as having the form of cancer known as non-Hodgkin's lymphoma in June 2000. He planned to take early retirement on grounds of ill-health; but the various kinds of treatment he underwent were ineffective, and he died on 8 November 2000. Bryan and I had planned to teach our undergraduate 'Representing the Holocaust' course together, but in the event he could only take one seminar – this was on *Shoah*, just ten days before his death. By this time Bryan appeared very frail, but when asked by Erica Sheen if he was all right after the exertion of the class, simply replied that he realized how much he would miss teaching. One of the students in that class, Chris Leary, describes her impressions in a paragraph she read out at the memorial event in December 2000:

> Even the most apathetic student would look forward to a lecture or tutorial taken by Bryan. He inspired such respect and affection, having the rare ability to transfer his boundless enthusiasm to his students, and his last seminar, just a week before he died, was no exception. Bryan spoke about the Holocaust film *Shoah* with an energy and commitment that appeared to miraculously resonate from his fragile frame. His illness may have ravaged his body, but his voice, that incredible, captivating voice, was as potent as ever.
>
> Bryan made us laugh with his self-deprecating anecdotes. He motivated us to radically question our own way of thinking, and he was ever attentive to our, perhaps not always ingenious, responses. Typically, at the end of the seminar, Bryan deflected enquiries regarding his own health, focusing instead on the well-being of his students. He said he looked forward to seeing us in two weeks' time. Tragically it was not to be. But what we are left with is the knowledge that we were honoured to be taught by

such an exceptional teacher, and privileged to have known such an exceptional man.

Bryan's aptitude and enthusiasm for teaching were legendary within the Department of English Literature at Sheffield and outside it. However, it was something that took place strictly between him and the students; he was never keen to allow colleagues into a classroom once he had started a seminar. His success was attributable to what seem like simple features: he treated students with gentleness and respect; he could draw out even the most timid; and he relied on the positive effects of humour. Above all, he allowed himself to come across as human too. Chris Leary has described attending one of Bryan's lectures on Romantic poetry when snow began to fall outside. 'Oh', said Bryan, 'what a good thing I didn't hang out my washing' – at which the whole audience burst out laughing.

Bryan was also a first-rate supervisor of research students; as his curriculum vitae shows, their subjects were very varied but many of those who wanted to had their theses published as monographs and gained academic jobs. Suzanne Speidel is one of these; she completed her Ph.D. on film adaptation just before Bryan's death, and has since been appointed to a lectureship in film at Sheffield Hallam University. Suzanne read out this testimony to Bryan's supervisory habits at his memorial event:

> One particularly memorable correction I had from Bryan on my Ph.D. work was in response to the fact that for long time I was persistently unable to use the correct spelling of the word 'principal'. After correcting the same word in my work over and over again for a period of about five years, Bryan finally resorted to ringing the mistake, and writing in the margin 'My heart is broken'. I have to say, it was an extremely effective piece of marking, in that I don't think I've misspelled the word 'principal' since.

Suzanne also mentions a striking aspect of Bryan's role in the university, which was his extremely positive view of a profession that many now feel is increasingly stressful and bureaucratic. This was partly the result of Bryan's disposition; for him, the cup was always half full. He took pleasure in a variety of things, including strong friendships with both men and women; walking to work through Sheffield's Botanical Gardens; and zealously throwing out most pieces of paper that appeared on his desk. Robert Hope adds, 'He had a strong nose for the ridiculous and for humbug. He liked to laugh.' Bryan loved opera, and made regular visits to the Buxton Festival Opera and to hear Opera North with Shirley Foster; she notes that, 'Bryan looked for political message and theme, as well as for the more filmic elements of staging and physical movement; I tended to respond more to the music itself': but they managed to share these differing expertises.

The memorial event in celebration of Bryan's life took place in Sheffield on 14 December 2000 in St George's Lecture Theatre, which is a converted church. It was attended by many of Bryan's friends, present and former colleagues and students, and was introduced by Erica Sheen. The selection of readings and performances aimed to include as many of Bryan's interests as possible, and so featured Neil Roberts' reading from Jane Austen's *Pride and Prejudice*, Neil Corcoran's of C.P. Cavafy's poem 'The Horses of Achilles', and a shared reading (by Emma Denny, Frances Gray, John Haffenden, Mick Hattaway and Derek Roper) of a play by Thomas Love Peacock. The readings were ordered in such a way that they described a descent towards death – Shirley Foster showed one of Bryan's favourite passages, the final scene from Joseph Losey's film of *Don Giovanni*; Ben Smith and Sue Vice showed the opening of *Shoah*. However, the second half of the memorial event traced an upward trajectory, starting with Emily Macnamara's reading of Thomas Hardy's poem 'The Going', and culminating in brief extracts from Bryan's 'Top 25 Films' (compiled by Martin Flanagan, Suzanne Speidel and Rob Speranza); and a staged reading, arranged by Frances Gray, of Angela Carter's *Puss in Boots* (Bryan had befriended Carter while she was a creative writing fellow at Sheffield in the 1970s). Bryan's lifelong friend Robert Hope gave a personal reminiscence; music was provided by Rosie Brown and Elsie Walker; and Sally Shuttleworth announced the Bryan Burns Prize for Achievement, to be awarded annually for the best undergraduate work on film or the Holocaust.

I will conclude with a simple but moving nineteenth-century epitaph which Neil Roberts read at Bryan's funeral, having chanced upon it on a gravestone during a visit to Berwick. It seems uncannily also to describe the more secular, but equally dignified and enlightened Bryan Burns:

Epitaph for Dr Balmer, Vicar of Berwick

a man of high endowments
attainments and worth
an accurate and elegant scholar
a faithful and affectionate pastor

Bryan Burns (1945–2000)

an able and skilful tutor
an enlightened and ardent friend
of liberty, order and peace
firm yet liberal in his principles
kind and generous in his dispositions
bland yet dignified in his demeanour
and in the discharge of all his duties
most conscientious
though dead yet he lives in the fruits
of his labours.

History

1

The Holocaust and the Museum World in Britain: A Study of Ethnography

TONY KUSHNER

The Imperial War Museum's (IWM) permanent Holocaust exhibition opened in June 2000 to general acclaim in the media. Subsequently the exhibition, like the United States Holocaust Memorial Museum in Washington, DC, has proved immensely successful in generating visitors (over a quarter of a million in its first twelve months) and it appears to have elicited positive instant responses from them. In contrast to its American counterpart, however, there has been little questioning of the scope of the IWM exhibition or at a more basic level, whether it was appropriate in the first place. This contribution is an attempt to open up dialogue about the nature of the IWM Holocaust exhibition including the validity or otherwise of some of its items of display. It desires to situate the exhibition in wider debates than those focusing more narrowly on Holocaust commemoration. First, it places the exhibition in the context of collective memory and identity in Britain, especially in relation to the outside world and more specifically, Germanness and Jewishness. Second, it examines how other forms of atrocities and racism have been represented in order to provide a comparative framework.

In *Making Representations: Museums in the Post-Colonial Era*, Moira Simpson has suggested that

> In Europe, the tradition of museums as institutions both reflecting and serving a cultural elite has been long established and, in many, is still maintained. The museum, the 'cabinet of curiosities', is the storeroom of a nation's treasures, providing a mirror in which are reflected the views and attitudes of dominant cultures, and the material evidence of the colonial achievements of the European cultures in which museums are rooted. The colonial origins of the museum remain an enduring influence upon these institutions and upon public perceptions of them.[1]

Simpson's work is part of a fast-growing literature on the role of 'collecting' and display in the imperial story and its later legacy.[2] While this new emphasis inside and beyond museum studies is necessary and important, it has potential dangers if it obscures, through the desire to highlight the fundamental dichotomy between the 'west' and its colonial 'others', the construction of hierarchies and the existence of prejudices *within* European society.

The history of anti-Semitism and the representation of the 'Jew' more generally is one obvious subject that would be missed out of accounts focusing solely on the polarisation of Europe and its colonies. The work of Bryan Cheyette on representation of Jews in imperial British literature in the nineteenth and early twentieth century reveals the limitations of more 'reductive simplicities' in explaining racism solely through a crude understanding of colonialism, especially through Edward Said's narrow use of the concept of orientalism. In a study focusing on the figure of the Jew in the imperial fiction of John Buchan, Rider Haggard and Rudyard Kipling entitled 'Neither Black Nor White', Cheyette 'specifically opposes postcolonial theorists who maintain that there was, historically, a homogenous and dominant white "Western Judeo-Christian" culture'.[3]

The need to compare and connect racisms aimed at Jews and blacks is slowly gaining recognition.[4] There is still, however, a lacuna in respect to the racisms generated within Europe towards various national groupings. In Britain, for example, although Germans in nineteenth-century race science typologies were often constructed on a similar level and indeed with the same roots – as good Aryans/nordics/teutons/Anglo-Saxons (a connection cemented by Royal marriage) – alongside the 'best' of the English population, this did not stop them being perceived and treated as a racial threat throughout the twentieth century. Indeed, anti-Germanism remains one of the most respectable forms of prejudice in modern British politics and society leading to the failure to confront its historical roots.[5]

In April 2002, for example, Leeds United, a football team with a strong reputation for racism among its players as well as supporters, was generally reprimanded for employing a comedian, Stan Boardman, who told a deeply offensive anti-Pakistani/Indian joke at an official dinner. The club spokesman acknowledged that 'Booking Boardman had been a mistake'. He added, candidly revealing the hierarchy of acceptability of intolerance in British society, that the club 'had not been aware that Boardman's set contained racist material, other than that directed at "the Germans"'.[6]

It is thus not surprising that the manifestations of the largely uncontested force of anti-Germanism in contemporary British culture remain to be explored. The suggestion made by the commentator

Simon Hoggart that the 'British people ... are not particularly anti-German these days, but we are just hard-wired to make German jokes' is perhaps reassuring to the national mythology of inherent fairness, tolerance and decency. It is, however, hardly convincing.[7] Linda Colley has argued that national identity was defined in the long eighteenth century in many ways by Francophobia: 'Imagining the French as their vile opposites, as Hyde to to their Jekyll, became a way for Britons ... to contrive for themselves a converse and flattering identity.'[8] A similar process has been at work, it will be argued here, in relation to Germany during the twentieth century – a process that is still ongoing.

The journalist and novelist Julie Burchill has acknowledged the depths of her hostility to the Germans. She writes of her exposure, aged nine, to 'a picture of people in a concentration camp staring through barbed wire at the camera. I seem to remember to this day that I literally felt the world shift on its axis as I stared into those hollow eyes, and frankly that was it for me and Fritz.' She adds that 'I nursed my loathing over the years, and it's fair to say that Not Being German – in fact, being The Opposite of German – did in some way define my life.'[9] However disturbing, Burchill's honest self-reflection, in contrast to Hoggart's less convincing denial of prejudice, reveals much of widespread attitudes and responses in post-1945 Britain. Indeed, animosity had much longer roots.

Hatred of the 'Hun' and all things German was intense during the First World War and its immediate aftermath.[10] Not surprisingly, Germanophobia revived during the Second World War,[11] growing towards a genocidal collective mentality after the disclosures from Belsen and Buchenwald in spring 1945. One young man, a scientific researcher, wrote in his diary:

> Now we can really imagine what the German concentration camps were like. The sickening pictures which have now been published proved that they were veritable slaughterhouses. Two men I was speaking to about it argued that the only way to prevent such things happening again would be to exterminate the Germans. 'They're certainly not fit to live', said one.[12]

Such views were not isolated.[13] Whilst declining thereafter, anti-Germanism has never disappeared nor been seriously confronted as a prejudice worth removing. It will be argued that it is the processes by which Germany and Germanness have been constructed and reconstructed that provide the key to understanding the dynamics and the success of the Imperial War Museum's permanent Holocaust exhibition. As will also emerge, it indirectly explains the exhibition's

...dency to at best marginalize and at worst objectify the place of the Jew within the European experience.

A recent report suggested that two-thirds of the British population had no language other than English. Checking to find out whether Britain's command of foreign languages was indeed the worst in Europe, a reporter for *The Guardian* newspaper telephoned a range of national bodies and heritage sites using a range of European languages. The call to the Imperial War Museum was in German, enquiring what was showing there. After several transfers and the use of a dictionary, public relations at the Museum, with some embarrassment and hesitation, stumbled a reply that there was an exhibition on the Holocaust.[14]

The Imperial War Museum's Holocaust Exhibition, which cost £5 million, funded by private sponsorship and a Heritage lottery grant of £12 million for the museum as a whole, was officially opened by the Queen in June 2000. Just two years later, it has already become well established within the Museum's displays, yet the creation of the Holocaust exhibition marked a radical departure in the history of the Museum.[15] The Imperial War Museum was founded in 1917 to collect and display material relating to the Great War. Subsequently it has broadened and redefined itself as 'Britain's National Museum of Twentieth Century Conflict', incorporating also 1939–45, the Falklands and other post-1945 wars.[16]

In the absence of a national museum of Britain, it has been suggested that the Imperial War Museum, for all its uneven development in the twentieth century, fulfilled that role. As Sue Malvern has argued, 'The Imperial War Museum displays its collections to tell stories and to represent the nation to "itself"'. She goes further and suggests that with its strange mixture of artefacts, 'The museum was an ethnographic collection whose ethnographic subject was the nation-in-arms'. Malvern highlights how in

> ethnographical museums cultural artefacts are very frequently labelled as anonymous and undated, in contrast to European art collections, where works of art are always assigned an author and a date. European cultures are not represented, unless they can be classified as belonging to folk traditions, as for example at the Pitt Rivers Museum, Oxford. War museums such as the Imperial War Museum, however, which also house extensive collections of artefacts, curios and memorabilia, arguably function as these missing ethnographic collections of European nations ... .[17]

From the start, the Imperial War Museum faced criticism for

representing items of destruction rather than technology that revealed mankind's ability to improve the world. By including German and Turkish weapons it emphasized a national democratic victory over a defeated enemy and added to the demonization of the common foe. Britishness could be defined by homogeneity, at the exclusion of marginal groups such as women, those of colour, and aliens at home, but also in opposition to the 'other' in the form of the 'Hun'. Malvern concludes that 'In 1920, the Imperial War Museum became less a museum for the study of war than an ethnographic collection for the display of the British nation-in-arms, a display which defined nationhood by the martial prowess of its citizen army'.[18]

It is not surprising that within this framework there was no consideration of the violence inflicted by Britain on its imperial people. Nor did the Second World War fundamentally change its approach to display – in essence more military hardware was added and the war, as with the parallel genre of 1950s films, novels and memoirs, was represented as a traditional conflict with Britain, of course, as the triumphant victors.[19] That the continent of Europe also represented an epicentre of genocide and ethnic cleansing was hardly mentioned. Again a nationalist approach dominated, with the myth of 'Britain alone' defeating the evils of Nazism to the fore.[20] It was as late as 1991 that the small display 'Belsen 1945' was added to the permanent exhibition on the Second World War in the Imperial War Museum and even then the Anglocentric focus to the overall museum narrative failed, ultimately, to be challenged.[21]

The Museum's 'Belsen 1945' concentrated on the British liberation of this notorious camp and the subsequent relief work carried out there. Most of the photographs and films used displayed the confrontation of British soldiers and then medical workers with the dead and dying of Belsen. These are appalling images, including the huge mounds of bodies and the bulldozing of them into mass graves.[22] They have been used frequently since 1945 and it has been suggested 'most closely define the Holocaust in popular images today',[23] but their meaning at particular points in time and place has been far from static.[24] As Cornelia Brink suggests,

> The pictures from 1945 have been and still are viewed as 'icons of extermination' in many countries. Only an analysis of the photographs within the specific contexts in which they have been published will reveal which memories they preserve, which they curtail, what different meanings they assign to the events, what kind of knowledge they transmit and how meanings change over longer periods of time.[25]

The rest of this contribution will highlight the use made of these liberation images and others depicting atrocities at the Museum, querying whether the representation of the body of the victims of Nazism can, in essence, humanize the impact of genocide or whether it perpetuates the dehumanization process at the core of the perpetrators' project.

It has been highlighted how while trophy-gathering practices such as scalping and head-hunting have long been regarded by Europeans as the barbaric practices of savage peoples, the gathering of body parts as trophies, along with weapons, clothing and jewellery, was not uncommon among European and American settlers' and others. As Moira Simpson states, 'Examples of such items have found their way into some museum collections'. Regarded now by some as repulsive, there has been pressure for their removal, but that process, as Simpson adds, 'also serves to remove such items of unsavoury history from the public consciousness and the actions of their collectors from the public conscience.'[26] There is clearly a dilemma here when representing man-made horrors that many would prefer not to confront.

In the Pitt Rivers Museum, 'at the request of Maori visitors, the Maori tattooed heads have been taken off display' but 'the "other", the "different", in particular perhaps many of the dark and ghoulish manifestations of humanity, such as shrunken heads and skull racks, remain on display to challenge us'.[27] It is far from clear how these items challenge, for example, young visitors who vote the shrunken heads their 'firm favourite' of all the Museum's exhibits.[28] As we shall see, the aims of curators and the prejudices of museum visitors are often in conflict. It is significant, however, that Simpson does not feel that these dilemmas of representation are applicable to the crimes of the Nazis: 'While such histories [of colonial collecting of body parts] should be told, display is not always the most appropriate method: one would not wish, for example, to see the remains of Jewish holocaust victims of Auschwitz or Belsen displayed for all to see, as they were found in the gas chambers and incinerators.'[29]

The reality is that such remains *have* been displayed and images of them feature regularly in exhibitions and documentaries but with little thought to their impact or self-reflexivity of why they are being employed. As early as December 1945 in Nuremberg, Thomas Dodd, an assistant prosecutor, produced a shrunken head, that of a Pole who had been hanged at Buchenwald as an 'exhibit' to strengthen the moral repugnance against the accused as well as to 'prove' the nature of Nazi crimes against humanity. As Lawrence Douglas writes, 'it signified an understanding and materialized a very particular representation of

Nazi atrocities before the Nuremberg Tribunal'. Such items, however, would, as he adds, have been familiar in a different context and with different meaning to Sir Geoffrey Lawrence, chief judge of the Tribunal, who in the early 1930s had acquired two shrunken heads for display at the Pitt Rivers Museum, Oxford.[30]

The newspaper photographs and newsreel footage of Belsen and other liberated western concentration camps, just as the shrunken head at Nuremberg, were used to serve various ends by the British and American state apparatus at the end of the war. First, they were used as 'proof positive', as a contemporary newsreel in Britain put it, of Nazi atrocities.[31] Second, and as a corollary of the first, they showed the absolute moral rectitude of the western Allied war effort. As General Eisenhower stated, after visiting Ohrdruf, a Nazi concentration camp in Germany, 'We are told that the American soldier does not know what he was fighting for. Now, at least he will know what he is fighting against.' Eisenhower's words, alongside a huge photograph of dead inmates at the camp, introduce visitors to the United States Holocaust Memorial Museum's main exhibition, opened in 1993.[32]

For many years after the war, the western camps, especially Belsen for the British, and Buchenwald and Dachau for the Americans, represented the evils of Nazism.[33] All had complex individual histories but none represented the purer type of extermination camp of eastern Europe – that is, centres where the major purpose was mass murder with little or no slave labour or internment function. In fact, only four camps can be said to clearly fit into that category – Chelmno, a mobile killing centre, and the first to be used to gas Jews, and three others which formed the basis of Aktion Reinhard, Sobibor, Treblinka and Belzec, created in 1942 to destroy the three million plus Jews of Poland under Nazi control. Well over two million Jews were gassed in these four camps.[34] Auschwitz, in which it is now estimated 1.1 million Jews were murdered, alongside several hundred thousand Gypsies, non-Jewish Poles, and others, was an enormous and much more complex site, incorporating vast slave labour camps.[35]

When, particularly through the war crimes trials in the later 1940s, awareness of gas chambers became more widespread, it was assumed that these must have operated in the western camps, that is, those such as Belsen, liberated by the western Allies rather than those captured earlier by the Soviet Union such as Majdanek and Auschwitz, a perception that still continues to this day.[36] In fact, those that died in Belsen, for a brief while a camp for privileged Jews, did so due to punishment, disease, starvation and general neglect.[37]

A problem of representation exists. The Reinhard camps were

levelled to the ground by the Nazis in 1943 in an attempt to erase all evidence to mass murder. In Auschwitz all the surviving gas chambers were blown up. The speed of the Soviet advance was such that some evidence of mass murder, including the leaving behind of ill survivors such as Primo Levi, was exposed.

For the Soviet liberators in January 1945, the scenes of mass murder were horrific, but partly due to the time of the year, on one level the scenes and smells were less intensive than the western camps. There was the evidence of medical experiments and the piles of belongings, piles of human hair and so on to show the scale of destruction, which for both reasons of ideology and miscalculation, were overestimated at some four million victims, three times more than the total accepted today. But the revelations from Auschwitz, anticipating the ideological impact of the cold war, received little or no publicity in the west, and it did not become a widely used metaphor until the 1960s for the Holocaust specifically or, more generally, the destructive potential of modernity (for secularists) and evil (for those of a theological bent).[38]

The focus on concentration camps in early memory of what would later become known as the Holocaust, and specifically those liberated by the western allies, not only led to the marginalization of the eastern camps, although the sheer scale and efforts made by the Polish government to make it into an national site of mourning made Auschwitz a partial exception.[39] It also obscured the so-called Einsatzgruppen murders, in which at least two million Jews were shot, or more basically clubbed to death. As Richard Wright has shown, techniques of forensic archaeology have recently proved important in reconstructing the detail of such murders.

Wright was employed by the Australian government to find evidence of war crimes relating to individuals who after the war made Australia their home. He excavated a mass grave in Serniki in the Ukraine which revealed some 550 bodies. The mass murder was carried out in 1942 and the excavation some 50 years later. The archaeology confirmed local testimony:

> An awful scene unfolded. As the eyewitnesses had said, they were mostly women and children. The men were old men. They had been herded down a ramp into the grave. One lot had gone to the left and been shot while lying down within the grave; the others had gone to the right. The majority had entry and exit wounds of bullets in their skulls. Some of them had been clubbed.[40]

In many cases, however, the lack of evidence due to the Nazis burning bodies or the subsequent obscurity of sites has proved too problematic. Indeed, as Richard Wright points out in relation to Serniki, which is on the southern margins of the Pripet marshes, 'The area of the grave is now an ominous-looking dark pine forest, but feelings of that sort are illusory. At the time of the killings this was open country.'[41] Intense skill and luck are required to find the places of mass murder, even in recent cases as with former Yugoslavia where again the talents of Richard Wright have been employed in war crimes trials in the Hague. For the Holocaust, as bystander memory fades, hundreds if not thousands of sites of destruction have been lost to posterity.

In essence, therefore, the extermination of over six million Jews remains largely a crime of mass murder without the presence of the victims' bodies, contrasting, for example, to the Armenian genocide or more recent mass murder in Cambodia and Rwanda. It is for that reason that the images from Belsen became so important as a symbol of what the Nazis had done. An appealing but deceptive symmetry has developed – the enormity of the crime is matched by the sheer horror of the images even if the latter are not generally representative of the former.[42] It is telling, for example, that in Roberto Benigni's Oscar-winning film, *Life is Beautiful* (1998), intended by its director as a fable and 'not a story about the Holocaust. It's a story about a father who is trying to protect a child',[43] the one moment where an attempt is made to allude to the horror of the concentration camp is when the hero glimpses a mountain of corpses, even if they appear through 'a sort of bluish mist'.[44]

It remains that the photographs and films of the liberated western camps were, and continue to be, even with our greater understanding of the detail of the destruction process, potentially problematic both in respect of the perpetrators and the victims. With regard to the perpetrators, the images tend to confirm that the perpetrators must have been monsters, sub-human, in fact animals, 'the bitch and beast of Belsen',[45] rather than ordinary men and women fully capable of such crimes (or, as Daniel Goldhagen would have it, anti-Semitic sadists who were ordinary Germans).[46]

In respect of the victims, few contemporaries in 1945 were willing to make the effort to find out their background. One small group who did were the army cameramen who created the images for the newsreels of the camps. One of them, Sergeant Oakes, recorded in his notes (or dope sheets) on one part of his film: 'An inmate tells the world. Helen Goldstein, a Pole – Her crime: being born from Jewish extraction. Four years in concentration camps, but was only here two weeks before the British arrived.' Many assumed that those liberated in 1945 would not survive or if they did they would be too damaged to have a meaningful future. For complex reasons, their ethnic-religious identity was downplayed or ignored in their media representation in Britain. Oakes' dope sheet comments, for example, as with similar comments from other cameramen, were 'edited out'. The government was 'concern[ed] about how the story would be received by the British public'.[47]

In short, it did not matter who the victims were, or who they had been. They were a people without a past or a future, used almost solely to illustrate the inhumanity of the Nazis/German people.[48] One image of an individual in Belsen, for instance, taken shortly after liberation, has been and continues to be labelled in different ways – as a dead *or* a dying man. The image was/is used to shock, not to create any sense of empathy.[49] For many survivors, the images of liberation remain highly disturbing. In Boston during the 1980s, the idea of reproducing a form of Nathan Rapoport's statue 'Liberation' from Liberty Park in New York, which features an American GI carrying a tiny survivor, was rejected by the survivors because they feared in the words of James Young that 'a millennium of Jewish civilization would be reduced to the one degrading moment they shared with American liberators'.[50]

These early images of liberation remain, therefore, deeply problematic. How then does the Imperial War Museum's new exhibition, the largest and most expensive in Britain dealing with *any* form of mass murder, deal with Jewish life and culture? Initially the exhibition was to focus on 'man's inhumanity to man' as a history of genocide in the twentieth century.[51] Undoubtedly if this had been carried out then the Jews and other groups would simply have been represented as victims, as people to whom something was done, without any attempt to explain their complex and diverse histories, or for that matter the specific context of each genocide.[52] Due to lobbying, the focus of the proposed exhibition changed, and its finished form represents something of a compromise, allowing for the particular dynamics of the Holocaust to be explored at great length but where the narrative structure is driven by a chronology created by the Nazis rather than their victims.

The overall tendency to focus on Nazi actions is partially countered by the use of powerful video and oral testimony of survivors. Such testimony, however, is frustratingly brief and used ultimately to illustrate what the Nazis did, and even then never on its own as a form of evidence that can be relied upon as 'proof positive' – in this sense, the exhibition follows the example of the post-war trials which marginalized eye-witness accounts in favour of 'hard' written and, as with the shrunken head, physical evidence.[53] In the immediate post-war period the objective was to secure convictions and also to educate for the present and the future. The emphasis on 'proof' over half a century later is driven by somewhat different dynamics. The need to educate is still there, although with a much more focused agenda of meeting the needs of the British national school curriculum in which the Holocaust is now relatively prominent and, as a result, taught widely.[54]

There is also the awareness of the presence of Holocaust deniers and the desire to either counter it or at least not provide them with any ammunition through by ensuring that, as Suzanne Bardgett, director of the project, put it, 'irrefutable historical evidence is plac[ed] before the visitor'.[55] Here, the Imperial War Museum was following the example of Washington. Michael Berenbaum, the US Holocaust Memorial Museum's project director, explained before it opened in April 1993, that the transfer and display of a barrack from Birkenau was necessary 'to refute the lies of Holocaust negationists'.[56] Although impressive life story interviews were carried out with the survivors for the Imperial War Museum exhibition, the use of this material is fragmentary and its integrity as a whole is not maintained. Indeed, at the early stages of planning for the exhibition it had not been intended to use such testimony so extensively: the narrative was to be driven almost exclusively by fully authenticated artefacts, documents and photographs.[57]

Throughout discussions when it was suggested that partly following the example of Washington there was a need to explain Jewish life and culture before the Holocaust, the response was firmly that the Imperial War Museum was not and could not become a museum of ethnography. As we have seen, this is not necessarily true – it has functioned from the start implicitly if not explicitly as a, if not *the*, museum attempting to represent the nature of Britishness, or more narrowly, Englishness, to the people of the nation.

In relation to the Second World War, for example, the atrium, at the heart of the building, is known, according to Anne Karpf, 'as the biggest boys' bedroom in London'. Tanks and other military hardware, especially airplanes, including the iconic Spitfire and Hurricane, dominate the physical space. As Karpf adds, their presence is not simply physical but represents an ideological (and one could add, cultural) statement: 'It points to the obsession with technology which, along with triumphalism and the much mythologised spirit of defiant optimism, for so long characterised the war in British popular imagination.'

The presence of many veterans and their families, both individually and collectively in organised reunions in the atrium, attests to the continuing memorial function of the Imperial War Museum and the status of the little ships from Dunkirk and the Spitfire as anthropologically central items in the construction of Englishness. The Museum certainly has not focused centrally on representing the diversity of, and power relations within, the British empire, still commemorated in its title, new or whatever. This lacuna continues to this day. As Malvern points out: 'Representations of black veterans are conspicuous by their absence.'[58]

For the Imperial War Museum to attempt to display the rich, contested lives of the European continents' Jews would have been a remarkable change in approach and direction. Yet under pressure from its historical advisors and, it has to be said, from its funders, the final exhibition, through the life story of survivors, along with some artefacts, does provide something of a history of Jews from central and eastern Europe. But as James Young argues in relation to many Holocaust museums, 'these artifacts ... force us to recall the victims as the Germans have remembered them to us: in the collected debris of a destroyed civilization'.[59] Ultimately, the original anthropological approach of the Imperial War Museum is kept in place. Its Holocaust exhibition is, indirectly, an exhibition on Britishness, one that focuses on what it is not – Nazism/Germanness.

There is a fetishisation of Nazi memorabilia in the exhibition, including a pristine SS uniform, and items, all painstakingly authenticated, relating to the destruction process, including a dissection table from a euthanasia centre and a bonecrusher from Mauthausen concentration camp which was a particularly prized acquisition amongst the exhibition project team.[60] Throughout the exhibition nothing is left to the visitors' imagination: a handcart from the Warsaw ghetto, used to carry the dead from the street, is thus substantiated by a photograph of a similar handcart in action. Likewise, personal testimony, clearly regarded as a 'soft' source on the authentication front, is used alongside 'harder' evidence such an artefact or film so that an experience or object could not have been possibly imagined.[61] Everyday Jewish items are scarce in comparison, and, at the start of the exhibition, bizarrely mixed with anti-Semitica and Nazi material. The first display case thus includes antisemitic propaganda from all over the world alongside Jewish religious items. The visitor is immediately alienated from these strange exotic creatures – Jews on the one hand – and anti-Semites on the other.

The inability to place Jewish culture in a suitable context at the Imperial War Museum as a whole or the Holocaust exhibition in particular is not simply limited because of its specific focus on modern conflict. David Weiss relates finding tefillin at the Pitt Rivers Museum in Oxford:

> They were lying among a rather disordered assortment of tribal philtres, talismans and amulets in a glass-enclosed case bearing the simple legend 'Asian and African Fetishes' ... I wondered how they came to rest here, in the image-choked vaulted hall of the Oxford University Museum's anthropological collection ... Bending over the case, I saw yellowed slips of heavy paper describing each of the fetishes. The one placed at the side of the tefillin explained that these are a representative specimen of the phylacteries ritually worn in the past at worship by males of certain Jewish sects, a phallic archetype of the Israelitic Jehovah cult and ... to ward off the evil eye.[62]

Tefillin in Britain are thus displayed under the glass case as either representing an ancient and 'uncivilized' tribe or alongside propaganda images of Jews which present them as sub-humans. Items which are in fact part of the everyday material culture of ordinary religious (male) Jews both in the past *and* today, are displayed in the British heritage world, with the exception of its marginalized Jewish museums, as utterly alien and 'other' and inevitably confined to the past. Moreover, as James Young puts it: 'That a murdered people remains known in Holocaust museums anywhere by their scattered belongings, and not their spiritual works, that their lives should be recalled primarily through the images of their death, may be the ultimate travesty.'[63]

The exhibition proper ends with a scale model of Auschwitz, some 12 metres long and 2 metres wide. It shows the arrival of a transport at Auschwitz in May 1944 – a time when the gas chambers were working at full capacity – depicting the arrival of some 2,000 Hungarian Jews awaiting selection at the ramp.[64] Alongside it are a few items of clothing and shoes from the stores at Majdanek.[65] The scale model is similar to that at the US Holocaust Museum and again at Yad Vashem and the original such example at Auschwitz itself.[66] These models, including their tiny figures, are totally white. What is the purpose of these representations?

The Chapman Brothers, in their installation 'Hell' in the Royal Academy of Art's Apocalypse exhibition, parody such concentration camp models.[67] Their version of Auschwitz is in colour, and with deliberate and somewhat childish provocation, the Chapmans show SS officers being pushed into the crematoria and thus deliberately attempt to undermine the pious awe that now accompanies the Holocaust. The reverential approach to the Holocaust was illustrated at the opening of the Imperial War Museum exhibition and in media and other responses to it. As Jim Garret, then curator of the Manchester Jewish Museum admonished in the *Museums Journal*, 'This exhibition deserves to be seen – and remembered'.[68]

A sense of duty, among Jewish and non-Jewish visitors has been present. One synagogue group reported back after a day trip to see it, 'No one looks forward to a visit to a Holocaust exhibition as it will not be a bundle of joy, but the Imperial War Museum exhibition *should* [my emphasis] be visited'.[69] As Jake Chapman puts it: 'People become very sincere when you show them this sort of thing. It becomes a kind of moral potty training for adults.' Such overstated sincerity was particularly evident in the official and televised ceremony for the first Holocaust Memorial Day in Britain on 27 January 2001.[70]

The Chapman Brothers also attack the voyeurism that has been constantly connected to Holocaust imagery. Whether the public will deconstruct the images in the Chapman Brothers' diorama is far from certain – postmodern irony is not a familiar genre in Holocaust commemoration – but problematizing the representation of the Jewish and other victims' bodies at the Imperial War Museum and other Holocaust exhibitions is essential if the tendencies towards, at best, sentimentality and, at worst, mawkishness are to be avoided.

But what sort of anthropological function is at work, explaining why it seems no major national Holocaust exhibition can be complete without a death camp model? Is it a matter, in the case of the Imperial War Museum, of boys with toys – a hangover from 'airfix' model plane kits from childhood and a link, however bizarre, with the Museum's atrium? This is undoubtedly an element, especially within the world of military heritage representation where it is normal to represent the battlefield with appropriate scale model soldiers. But beyond this, there is the obsession still with the organized, but still highly marginal, world of Holocaust denial, to *prove* the Holocaust to new generations.

Liberated Auschwitz retained its massive scale and the remains of humans, but not many complete bodies. Somewhat ironically, given their tinyness compared to the original, although they are huge by museum standards, the models are meant to show the vastness as well as the specific function of Auschwitz. Jim Garret has defended the example within the Imperial War Museum: 'To dismiss the 40-foot-long representation of Auschwitz as simply "a model" is to miss its *raison d'être*' – that there is an almost total absence of photographs of the arrival at the ramp of such transports. 'This solid representation of an actual event [the selection of Jews from the Berehevo ghetto] enables an appreciation of scale to be imparted'.[71]

The Museum team in the planning stages expressed themselves as 'sensitive to the views of those who claim that the Holocaust cannot be represented'. The model is the only major re-creation in the exhibition, the only point in which the documentary approach is compromised. Ultimately, its colour, size and form highlight artifice. One thinks somewhat cruelly of the Stonehenge model in the spoof rock documentary, *Spinal Tap* (1984), when the replica demanded by the heavy metal band to accompany one of their songs on stage ends up, through a drafting mistake, being 18 inches tall rather than the 18 feet demanded: it is 'dwarfed by dwarfs'. As one of 'Spinal Tap' puts it: the model 'understates the hugeness of the thing'.[72] The human figures of the Imperial War Museum's Auschwitz model in their endless rows, according to the designer, are astonishingly 'clinical and graphic'.[73] In fact, as the Chapman Brothers' alternative version highlights, they are, as the model as a whole, aestheticized and sanitized.

The final image at the museum is that of a British soldier, with neck scarf round his mouth, bulldozing the grotesque and filthy figures in Belsen. Naked and tangled, it is hard to tell when one body starts and another ends, let alone if they are male or female, young or old. This is by far the biggest photograph in the whole exhibition. Are we doomed then to see the dead victims only as piles of corpses, nameless and without any form of identity other than that inflicted on them by the Nazis and their allies?

The Imperial War Museum does not engage in any depth with the place of Britain, as a bystander nation, in the Nazi era.[74] By such absence of discussion, the exhibition sits oddly in the London borough of Lambeth – it is ultimately about the perpetrators, and, in an English/British context, that is, still fundamentally about Germany and in turn 'our', that is the British, glorious role in the Second World War. It does not encourage the British visitor, for example, towards self-reflection – on the importance of place, for example, and the role of the site, formerly Bethlem Royal Hospital (Bedlam), in the incarceration and appalling treatment of those classified as mentally ill, or for that matter of the racial violence, including most notoriously, the murder of black teenager Stephen Lawrence, in an adjacent south London district.

Indeed, the exhibition ends with Belsen, confirming the righteousness of the British war effort. In his *Body Horror: Photojournalism, Catastrophe and War*, John Taylor argues that 'Death is rarely seen in ragged human remains unless they are foreign.' He adds that

Reports of horrors overseas concentrate on the essential strangeness of victims, whether they invoke revulsion or invite compassion. Even in those stories which spark moral debate, the press uses stereotypes of alien life: they include refugees, corpses and even skeletons in the streets. These pictures contrast with idealised British systems of value, care and order. They imply that outside Britain, chaos is the norm, and life is cheap.[75]

They are, in short, 'unBritish'. Within the Imperial War Museum's Holocaust Exhibition the victims specifically highlight the duality of Britishness/Germanness. Out of this matrix of understanding and representation, can the body of the victim as individual ever be recovered?

The Aktion Reinhard camps today remain largely neglected and unvisited, in stark contrast to Auschwitz and some of the western camps. The physical archaeology remaining is fragmentary, but at Belzec particularly, recent digs have helped build up a more detailed picture of what happened there. Up to a million people were gassed at Belzec, the first purpose-built Nazi death camp. There are no records of the camp, which were destroyed alongside the buildings and any human remains – almost all the bodies were exhumed and burnt by the Nazis.

Recently bodies have been discovered in digs, raising the question of what should be done with them. Orthodox Jewish leaders have refused permission to dig in areas where it is known that the ashes of Jewish victims are present. The digging that has revealed bodies has been near an SS hut. It is not clear who the people were – they could have been Jewish victims, less likely (simply through the numbers of those killed at the camp) Gypsies or indeed the local SS. It has been assumed that they were Jewish and they have been buried according to Jewish orthodox tradition.

Similar issues have emerged at another Aktion Reinhard camp, Sobibor.[76] Whether orthodox Jews have a right to speak for all such victims is far from clear. More locally the same has been true at the York Archaeological Trust dig in the medieval Jewish cemetery.[77] Related issues of ownership of human remains which have found their way into university collections and museums have for groups such as Aborigines and Native Americans proved even more controversial.[78]

There is a tension between the growing sensitivity towards orthodox Jews and their fears of disturbing the mass graves at sites such as Belzec and Sobibor, on the one hand, and the absence of such consideration given to the representation of the victims' bodies in the museum and media world on the other. Archaeology may be able to reveal far more about, for example, Belzec, known only through a handful of documents and post-war testimonies. The excavation carried out on the site has certainly shown it to be much bigger than was previously recognized but beyond that the knowledge gained has been limited, as those involved have been in a constant struggle with the local authorities, Jewish orthodox religious leaders and funding restraints.

A genuine dilemma is posed between the need to know (although the scientific claims of accuracy of modern archaeological techniques should not be accepted without some degree of scepticism) and the need to respect a (mass) burial site. In contrast, the frequent use of graphic images of the victims, naked and without any decency, to show the nature of Nazism, has evoked far too little soul-searching.

Digs such as those carried out by Richard Wright can reveal much about the identity of the individuals. They also connect mass murder to ordinary and easily forgotten local sites. It is significant, however, that the Einsatzgruppen murders have been portrayed in museums through the tiny amount of surviving film footage and photographs of naked people, especially women, about to be shot. Such images have been shown regardless of the offence caused, especially to orthodox Jews, by images of naked women. More generally, the individuality of the victims is lost sight of in the desire to educate.

In the Mauthausen camp museum there are four poster-sized photographs of a victim of the Nazis, the first in striped prisoner uniform, the second and third naked from front and rear and the fourth as a skeleton. The caption states that prisoner 13992 had been subject to medical experiments. The images also appear in the United States Holocaust Memorial Museum. Prisoner 13992 was the father of Alphons Katan who discovered the photographs by accident when visiting the museum at Mauthausen. Subsequently he has been campaigning for the removal of these photographs from public display. Katan told the Washington museum that 'You are humiliating my father even in his death by presenting his pictures'.[79]

It is possible that Alphons Katan will succeed in his mission to get these images of his father removed and his father's body to be buried. As Cressida Fforde has illustrated in relation to Aboriginal human remains, there is a greater chance of repatriation for burial (and in this case removal of the offensive images) once the body concerned has a name and thus becomes less a 'thing' and more an individual.[80] But, given the intensity of the Nazi murder machine, many victims will never be given a name and the cases in which surviving relatives and friends can identify images of the dead or those about to be killed will be exceptional. That should not, however, be an excuse for those responsible for museum displays and other visual representations of the Holocaust not to examine closely the ethical considerations of showing such images as well as contextualizing (that is, who took the photograph and why) and problematizing such images (making the viewer aware of the dilemmas of such re-production) when they are deemed absolutely necessary.

John Taylor argues that in the name of civility, the horrors of war and atrocity can be disguised, with a potential for public debate, especially national self-criticism, to be avoided or suppressed. He concludes that

> civility sits uneasily with war – unless it is known to be describing official histories, censored reports and popular victories. How would the Holocaust be remembered if it existed only in 'civil' representations – those which were most discreet? What would it mean for knowledge if the images ceased to circulate, or were never seen in the first place? What would it mean for civility if representations of war crimes were always polite? If prurience is ugly, what then is discretion in the face of barbarism?[81]

In the cases of slavery,[82] lynchings,[83] genocide, and the destructive side of imperialism there is still a need to confront the lack of general empathy for the horrors inflicted, and appalling visual imagery makes an *initial* impression. Yet the absence of such representation in regard to 'us', which Taylor himself emphasizes, is not matched by the lack of care in representing the 'other' as victim, and the dichotomy in standards is clearly related.

The Imperial War Museum exhibition, for example, includes a photograph of a semi-naked terrified young Jewish girl who has been subject to sexual abuse through a local 'action' in Lvov. Jim Garret talks of this image and others of naked victims: 'Those who suffered never gave their consent to be looked at over 60 years later.' Surely Garret, now curator of the Pump House in Manchester, a major museum illustrating the lives of ordinary people in Britain, is asking a major question that requires agonizing reflection. His answer, however, like that of the Imperial War Museum project team, is straightforward and lacking any sense of ambiguity. 'But this is evidence. There is no other way of presenting the realities of a government-led systematic, premeditated persecution and extermination of millions of innocent people.'[84]

In other words, the utter removal of dignity of the victims by the Nazis has to be permanently reproduced in order to 'prove' the scale and horror of humiliation and mass murder. As with such other images of death and nakedness, the Museum is taking the chance that the victims or their relatives did/do not survive and cannot come to the exhibition to object. If they did, is it conceivable that the images would not be removed? In the particular case of the young girl from Lvov, there is also naivety in how such images will be consumed.

Joan Smith has written of William Styron's novel *Sophie's Choice* (1979) and D.M. Thomas's *The White Hotel* (1981) that their success is the juxtaposition of 'sex and the Holocaust ... dressed up as art'. She goes further and suggests that 'The model of female sexuality constructed by Thomas and Styron has nothing to do with real women but exists to legitimize masculine sexual fantasies which are violent, vicious and ultimately lethal'.[85] Alternative readings of the motivation of both writers are possible.[86] Nevertheless, Smith is right to point out that the books' success is at least in part due to their eroticized narratives. 'The rapturous reception of their books, and their status as bestsellers, suggest that a significant proportion of the reading public is receptive to such fevered imaginings.'[87]

From the 1950s at least, Nazi horror has been consumed as a form of pornography to the extent that books such as the salacious *The Scourge of the Swastika* (1954), which featured photographs of naked women being paraded at a concentration camp, as well as standard atrocity material such as the shrunken heads of Buchenwald and the mass open graves of Belsen, were stored in bookshops in the backroom section of 'forbidden' literature.[88] Early forms of printed testimony from survivors published by newly emerging pocket paperback companies such as Digit Books and Badger Books, while often subtle and important in themselves, were also marketed in the form of 'sexploitation'. Their covers featured pictures of vulnerable and often exposed young women in concentration camps with brutal SS thugs in the background.[89]

The crude appeal of sado-masochism in relation to Nazism and its victims extended beyond the sexually repressed 1950s, perhaps most famously played out in Liliana Cavani's *The Night Porter* (1974).[90] The film came out the same year as David Friedman's *Ilsa, She-Wolf of the SS* which is perhaps more typical of the less artistic attempts which fill this ever popular and quite diverse genre. Even serious novels dealing with the Holocaust, such as Sherri Szeman's *The Kommandant's Mistress* (1993), have been marketed by their mainstream publishers with titles and covers to titillate the reader.[91] As Joseph Slade has argued, 'The public is outraged when Nike, the athletic supplier, markets a T-shirt decorated with swastika, but accepts as "normal" the eroticizing of

National Socialism.' He concludes that

> It would be nice to think that we are actually trying to defile fascism – to distance ourselves from it – by eroticizing it... or that we are trying to dramatize Nazi cruelty – to mark it as unmistakably the expression of alien 'others' – as a way of keeping our collective memory of the Holocaust alive ... Neither seems likely ... Unable to comprehend a mass ideological commitment to extermination, we focus on individual acts of psychotic cruelty.[92]

In total contrast to the creators of cheap movies and videos, it was not the intention of those responsible for the Imperial War Museum's Holocaust exhibition to provide titillating material. Indeed, they were aware from the start of the potential danger of voyeurism. Nevertheless, intentions can sometimes lead to the opposite impact of that desired. Catherine MacKinnon has written of media and other coverage of sexual violence in the former Yugoslavia during the early 1990s and how it provides a pornographic scripting of rapes. Yet her descriptions are so horrific in their detail that it has been argued by Rose Lindsey that 'the effect is one of voyeuristic hard-core porn, ironically closer in style to the pornography that MacKinnon lambasts, than to an academic text'.[93]

It may at this point be useful to return to John Taylor's statement about atrocity images and what he views as the impossibility of 'discretion in the face of barbarism'. Taylor reproduces a newspaper photograph by Mark Edwards of a man carrying his wife who is dying of cholera in the streets of Calcutta. He suggests that Edwards' photograph 'of the dying woman is remarkable for her nakedness and beauty'.[94] That even academic analyses of the representation of atrocities can lead to their sexualization is an indication of the fundamental instability of such images and the danger of relying on the reader or viewer to distance themselves from the voyeurism inescapably linked to pornography. Discretion *can* have its place. It is, however, largely absent in the Imperial War Museum's Holocaust exhibition because of the overriding and well-intentioned desire to provide evidence.

The exhibition, with its insistence on proof, is unwilling to allow its narrative structure to be in anyway undermined by self-reflexivity. More specifically, in the case of the photograph of the young girl from Lvov, it fails to provide any context whatsoever in which to place sexual violence against the victims of Nazism. As these are underplayed and sometimes even denied in many forms of writing on the Holocaust, the reproduction of the image might possibly have been justified. But without any form of reflection, it, alongside other problematic images of the victims in the exhibition, reflects the lack of progress in Holocaust representation that has occurred since the end of the war.

To conclude, we need to move beyond the need to prove the Holocaust, which almost inevitably belittles the victims, presenting them as humiliated bodies without a past or a future. Sue Malvern's analysis of how the Imperial War Museum 'displays its collections to tell stories and to represent the nation to "itself"' concluded by pondering how the then to be completed Holocaust exhibition would change its focus. 'It will bring into question again who and what the museum represents and to whom.'[95] For the foreseeable future at least, however, I would argue that the Holocaust exhibition, while being on the surface more inclusive of the small number of survivors and Britain and the greater part of British Jewry, does not, as a whole, shift its overall narrative thrust of 'us' and 'them' or 'here' and 'there'.[96]

James Young has written of the dangers of the United States Holocaust Memorial Museum that it 'will enshrine not just the history of the Holocaust, but American ideals as they counterpoint the Holocaust. By remembering the crimes of another people in another land, Americans will recall their nation's own idealized reason for being.' If in national mythology the USA is the home for the oppressed, within the Museum's representation, those liberated at Buchenwald and Dachau by GIs were 'potential Americans ... the Holocaust was the beginning of their becoming American, making the Holocaust an essentially American experience'.[97]

In a specifically British context where the memory of the Second World War as a reference point of collective identity is so profound,[98] the 'here' and 'there', defined in America as itself against the diseased continent of Europe, is made more geographically specific. In Britain in the short and probably also the medium term, it is almost inevitable that the categories Nazi and German will be blurred through the continuing power of Germanophobia. Instead of opening up self-exploration of national intolerance towards minority groups, it is possible and indeed likely that Holocaust representation that focuses on the 'there' carried out by foreigners will add further ammunition to those who argue for British exceptionalism in a world of many racisms. Furthermore it continues to present the victims as exotic 'others' with little past and certainly no future. Denying its past tradition of immigration, it was hard if not impossible for Britain, in contrast to America, to imagine those liberated from Belsen as future citizens. Indeed, only one or two thousand survivors at most were allowed entry to Britain after the war.[99]

Instead of the reassuring linear narrative chosen by the Imperial War Museum, there has to be much greater awareness of the problems of Holocaust representation and that the well-meaning goal of authenticity, which privileges artefacts, documents, films and photographs over testimony, is misplaced. James Young writes in relation to the sites of Auschwitz and Majdanek,

> In confusing these ruins for the events they now represent, we lose sight of the fact that they are framed for us by curators in particular times and places ... we must continue to remind ourselves that the historical meanings we find in museums may not be proven by artifacts, so much as generated by their organization.[100]

Similarly, Marcus Wood critiques the 'Transatlantic Slavery' gallery, by far the largest on its subject matter in Britain, in the Merseyside Maritime Museum in Liverpool and its attempt to 'come to terms' with the past. It displays items of horror, such as branding irons and slave collars, but 'Their patina of age, their elegant forms, the clean stands they are placed upon, the neat labels with their dates and matter of fact descriptions place them comfortably within an aesthetics of museum display which can cover any old object from any culture'. Through objects of torture and destruction, and the re-creations of the middle passage in Liverpool and the Auschwitz model in the Imperial War Museum, both exhibitions fail to recognize the limits of representation.[101] Moreover, they both share a tendency, even though this was not intended, to represent the victims as 'something alien and exotic'. In the case of the Transatlantic Slavery gallery, representations of Africa conform 'to the conventions of anthropological and ethnographic exhibits ... There is the peculiar sense that these exhibits are timeless.'[102]

When the anthropological collection of General Pitts Rivers was transferred to the Bethnal Green branch of the South Kensington Museum in 1874 it was arranged into four sections: 'skulls and hair'; 'weapons'; 'miscellaneous arts of modern savages including navigation' and the 'prehistoric series'.[103] In a curious way, the Imperial War Museum, now with the Holocaust exhibition neatly integrated into its whole, replicates these categories.

First, actual skulls and hair may not be, for reasons of taste, included, but the graphic representation of the victims' bodies is reproduced throughout. Second, the means of mass destruction are reproduced through artefacts and images. Third, Nazi civilization is displayed, and within it the images the Nazis made themselves of their victims. Fourth, the victims' own culture is represented as 'prehistory'.

The Pitt Rivers Museum, now in Oxford, is venerated by some as a 'museum of museums'. The Imperial War Museum's history is nearly half a century shorter than Pitt Rivers' but it shares its slowly evolving nature, one in which the Holocaust exhibition, while initially controversial, is, on an ideological and cultural level and taking the long view, not a major new departure.

Is a different approach possible? One counter-strategy would be the embracing of testimony, because of and not in spite of its complex relationship to evidence. It would allow for no obvious narrative structure, but its very absence would point to the diversity, fullness and contested nature of the Jewish experience before the Shoah as well as the chaos caused by the Nazi onslaught. It can enable not a coming to terms with the past but the possibility of greater inclusivity when both history and memory are brought together in a form of constructive tension.[104] Some elements of representation are revealed in the Polish documentary, *Birthplace* and the story of the Grynberg family.

In 1993, Henryk Grynberg returned to the village in which he and his parents lived before the war and were in hiding during it. His father was murdered by a local farmer. Remarkably some 50 years later the villagers returned to the exact spot where he was buried and exhumed his remains, as well as a milk bottle which he carried around trying to find sustenance for his family. The rootedness as well as the marginality of Grynberg's family as Jews became clear in the short documentary. It is a bleak film, and the only redemption is in the finding of the shallow grave. The body, however, as well as his father's dignity, is regained. The rootedness of his family in Poland before the war, the empathy as well as the antipathy of the local non-Jews during it, the closeness of the family as fugitives within their own village, and how the murder, some 50 years later, was still traumatizing local memory, are all evocatively portrayed. Overall, *Birthplace* showed how the Holocaust, as represented by the killing of one man, continued to problematize individual and group identity in relation to a place called home.[105]

We are a long way here from the piles of dead bodies Belsen and other concentration camps so casually illustrated by the Holocaust museum in Washington and the permanent exhibition in London. We remain, however, intimately connected through life story to the very normalcy of Jewish life in Europe as well as the human impact of the Holocaust. We are also shown the everyday nature of mass murder, whether in the killing fields of colonial massacres or among the better-known genocides of the twentieth century: the Armenians, Cambodians, Bosnians and Rwandans.

NOTES

1. Moira Simpson, *Making Representations: Museums in the Post-Colonial Era* (London, 1996), p.1.
2. For the British case, see, for example, Annie Coombes, *Reinventing Africa: Museums, Material Culture and Popular Imagination* (New Haven, CT, 1994) and more generally George W. Stocking, Jr. (ed.), *Objects and Others: Essays on Museums amd Material Culture* (Madison, WI, 1985) and I. Karp and S. Lavine (eds), *Exhibiting Cultures* (Washington, DC, 1991).
3. Bryan Cheyette, 'Neither Black Nor White: The Figure of "the Jew" in Imperial British Literature', in Linda Nochlin and Tamar Garb (eds.), *The Jew in the Text: Modernity and the Construction of Identity* (London, 1995), pp.31, 41.
4. See, for example, the work of Paul Gilroy, especially his *Between Camps: Race, Identity and Nationalism at the End of the Colour Line* (London, 2000). See also Tony Kushner, 'Antisemitism', in David Goldberg and John Solomos (eds), *A Companion to Racial and Ethnic Studies* (Malden, MA, 2002), pp.64–72.
5. See, however, the extensive work of Panikos Panayi, especially his *The Enemy in Our Midst: Germans in Britain during the First World War* (Oxford, 1991). On the impact of contemporary anti-Germanism, see the 'Everyman' documentary 'Two World Wars and One World Cup', BBC 1, 25 April 1993.
6. Vikram Dodd, 'Racist Jokes Make Leeds United Sorry', *The Guardian*, 3 May 2002.
7. Simon Hoggart, 'Hard-Wired to be Beastly to the Germans', *The Guardian*, 17 May 2002. More generally on the myth of fairness, see Colin Holmes, *A Tolerant Country: Immigrants, Refugees and Minorities in Britain* (London, 1991).
8. Linda Colley, *Britons: Forging the Nation 1707–1837* (London, 1994 [orig. 1992]), p.368.
9. Julie Burchill, 'Thinking the Wurst', *The Guardian*, 22 Sept. 2001.
10. Panayi, *The Enemy in Our Midst*.
11. See Margaret Kertesz, 'The Enemy: British Images of the German People during the Second World War' (unpublished Ph.D., University of Sussex, 1992), p.175 which utilizes a November 1944 Mass-Observation directive to reveal 'a continued hardening of opinion' since 1942. The more subjective and detailed Mass-Observation material is confirmed by opinion poll data from September 1943 carried out by Gallup. Answering 'What are your feelings at the present time towards the German people?', 45 per cent expressed 'hatred, bitterness, anger', 14 per cent 'dislike', six per cent that they 'deserve what they are getting', five per cent 'contempt'. Only seven per cent expressed 'friendly' feelings, and even then only for some Germans. In George Gallup (ed.), *The Gallup International Public Opinion Polls: Great Britain 1937–1975*, Vol.1 *1937–1964* (New York, 1976), p.82.
12. Mass-Observation Archive: Diarist S5205, 20 April 1945, University of Sussex.
13. Mass-Observation Archive: File Report 2248, May 1945 'German Atrocities'. See also Diarist C5270, 21 April 1945.
14. 'Can You Say That in English?' *The Guardian*, 21 Feb. 2001.
15. See Imperial War Museum, *The Holocaust: The Holocaust Exhibition at the Imperial War Museum* (London, 2000) and Tony Kushner, 'Oral History at the Extremes of Human Experience: Holocaust Testimony in a Museum Setting', *Oral History*, Vol.29, No.2 (Autumn 2001), pp.83–94.
16. Imperial War Museum, *The New Imperial War Museum* (London, 1992).
17. Sue Malvern, 'War, Memory and Museums: Art and Artefact in the Imperial War Museum', *History Workshop Journal*, No.49 (2000), pp.179, 188, 198 note 4.
18. Ibid, p.188.
19. See Geoff Hurd (ed.), *National Fictions: World War Two in British Films and Television* (London, 1984).
20. Tony Kushner, '"Wrong War Mate": Fifty Years After the Holocaust and the Second World War', *Patterns of Prejudice*, Vol.29, Nos.2 and 3 (1995), pp.3–13.
21. Imperial War Museum, *The Relief of Belsen* (London, 1991). See also Joanne Reilly *et al.* (eds.), *Belsen in History and Memory* (London, 1997), pp.12–13, 197–8 on the

background to this exhibition.
22. For the most detailed analysis of the creation of this visual material see Hannah Caven, 'Horror in Our Time: images of the concentration camps in the British media, 1945', *Historical Journal of Film, Radio and Television*, Vol.21, No.3 (2001), pp.205–53.
23. Ibid., p.205.
24. Ibid.
25. Cornelia Brink, 'Secular Icons: Looking at Photographs from Nazi Concentration Camps', *History and Memory*, Vol.12, No.1 (Spring/Summer 2000), p.145.
26. Simpson, *Making Representations*, p.177.
27. Julia Cousins, *The Pitt Rivers Museum* (Oxford, 1993), p.28.
28. Simpson, *Making Representations*, p.174.
29. Simpson, *Making Representations*, p.177.
30. Lawrence Douglas, 'The Shrunken Head of Buchenwald: Icons of Atrocity at Nuremberg', *Representations*, No.63 (Summmer 1998), pp.41–3. For the ongoing legacy and appeal of such material see Walter Poller, *Medical Block Buchenwald* (London, 1988 [orig. 1960]) which on the cover emphasizes that it is 'illustrated' and not surprisingly the photographic images emphasize torture.
31. Paramount News newsreel available in Imperial War Museum film archive. See more generally Nicholas Pronay, 'Defeated Germany in British Newsreels: 1944–45', in *Hitler's Fall: The Newsreel Witness* (London, 1988), pp.42–4.
32. See Edward Linenthal, *Preserving Memory: The Struggle to Create America's Holocaust Museum* (New York, 1995), pp.1–2, 193–4; Michael Berenbaum, *The World Must Know: The History of the Holocaust as Told in the United States Holocaust Memorial Museum* (Boston, MA, 1993), p.8 and for more critical comment on the use of these images and the Eisenhower quotation, Philip Gourevitch, 'Nightmare on 15th Street', *The Guardian*, 4 Dec. 1999.
33. See Tony Kushner, *The Holocaust and the Liberal Imagination: A Social and Cultural History* (Oxford, 1994), Ch.7.
34. Yitzhak Arad, *Belzec, Sobibor, Treblinka: The Operation Reinhard Death Camps* (Bloomington, IN, 1987).
35. Robert Jan Van Pelt and Deborah Dwork, *Auschwitz: 1270 to the Present* (New Haven, CT, 1996).
36. See my contribution to the introduction in Reilly *et al.*, *Belsen in History and Memory*, pp.6–7.
37. Jo Reilly, *Belsen: The Liberation of a Concentration Camp* (London, 1998).
38. On Auschwitz in the immediate post-war trials see Donald Bloxham, *Genocide on Trial: War Crimes Trials and the Formation of Holocaust History and Memory* (Oxford, 2001).
39. Van Pelt and Dwork, *Auschwitz*, Epilogue: 'Owning and Disowning Auschwitz'.
40. Richard Wright, 'Uncovering Genocide: War Crimes: The Archaeological Evidence', *International Network on Holocaust and Genocide*, Vol.11, No.3 (1996), p.9.
41. Ibid., p.9.
42. Hannah Arendt, *The Origins of Totalitarianism* (3rd edition, London, 1967 [orig. 1951]), p.446 in a footnote commented:

> It is of some importance to realize that all the pictures of concentration camps are misleading insofar they show the camps in their last stages, at the moment the Allied troops marched in. There were no death camps in Germany proper, and at that point all extermination equipment had already been dismantled. On the other hand, what provoked outrage of the Allies most and what gives the films their special horror – namely, the sight of human skeletons – was not at all typical for the German concentration camps; extermination was handled systematically by gas, not by starvation.

43. Melanie Wright, '"Don't Touch My Holocaust: Responding to *Life is Beautiful*', *Journal of Holocaust Education*, Vol.9, No.1 (Summer 2000), pp.19–32 esp. p.29.
44. J. Hoberman, 'Dreaming the Unthinkable', *Sight and Sound*, Feb. 1999.

45. Raymond Phillips (ed.), *Trial of Josef Kramer and Forty-Four Others (The Belsen Trial)* (London, 1949), p.xxxix who comments that Kramer was depicted as 'a sadistic beast in human form thirsty for the blood of his tortured victims'. See also Caven, 'Horror in Our Time', pp.220–22 on representations of Irma Grese and Josef Kramer.
46. Daniel Goldhagen, *Hitler's Willing Executioners: Ordinary Germans and the Holocaust* (Boston, MA, 1996).
47. Caven, 'Horror in Our Time', pp.209, 225, 227.
48. Kushner, *The Holocaust and the Liberal Imagination*, passim.
49. The image is reproduced in The Imperial War Museum, *The Relief of Belsen*, p.5 and labelled as 'A man, dying of starvation'. More generally on the sloppy approach in the use of presenting Holocaust-related photographs see Bryan Lewis, 'Documentation or Decoration? Uses and Misuses of Photographs in the Historiography of the Holocaust' (unpublished M.Phil., University of Birmingham, 1999).
50. James Young, *The Texture of Memory: Holocaust Memorials and Meaning* (New Haven, CT, 1993), p.323.
51. See Suzanne Bardgett, 'Man's Inhumanity to Man: A New Museum within the Imperial War Museum' (unpublished proposal, May 1995).
52. In fact the final stage of the project is a much smaller exhibition on genocide in the twentieth century which employs a video supplemented by interactive educational material which opened in 2002.
53. Douglas, 'The Shrunken Head of Buchenwald', p.39; Donald Bloxham, *Genocide on Trial: War Crimes Trials and the Formation of Holocaust History and Memory* (Oxford, 2001), pp.58–63.
54. See Philip Rubinstein and Warren Taylor, 'Teaching about the Holocaust in the National Curriculum', *Journal of Holocaust Education*, Vol.1, No.1 (Summer 1992), pp.47–54; Anita Ballin, 'The Imperial War Museum as Educator', *Journal of Holocaust Education*, Vol.7, No.3 (Winter 1998), pp.38–43. The interest of teachers and students as well as the availibility of source material also explain the 'popularity' of the Holocaust in the classroom.
55. Suzanne Bardgett, 'The Imperial War Museum Holocaust Exhibition Project', *Journal of Holocaust Education*, Vol.7, No.3 (Winter 1998), p.37; Pierre Vidal-Naquet, *Assassins of Memory: Essays on the Denial of the Holocaust* (New York, 1992).
56. Quoted by Young, *The Texture of Memory*, p.346.
57. Kushner, 'Oral History at the Extremes of Human Experience', pp.83–94.
58. Malvern, 'War, Memory and Museums', p.198, note 4.
59. Young, *The Texture of Memory*, p.132.
60. More generally see David Phillips, *Exhibiting Authenticity* (Manchester, 1997). For an exploration of the use of objects in relation to the United States Holocaust Museum and other museums see Julian Spalding, *The Poetic Museum: Reviving Historic Collections* (London, 2002). Suzanne Bardgett, 'The Holocaust Exhibition at the Imperial War Museum', *News of Museums of History* (forthcoming), talks of the 'ironic situation' of the acquisition of distressing artefacts being 'a source of professional satisfaction'.
61. The Imperial War Museum, *The Holocaust*, p.2.
62. David Weiss, *The Wings of the Dove* (Washington, DC, 1987), p.159 quoted by Colin Richmond, 'Parkes, Prejudice and the Middle Ages' in Sian Jones et al (eds), *Cultures of Ambivalence and Contempt* (London, 1998), p.219.
63. Young, *The Texture of Memory*, p.133.
64. Stephen Greenberg and Gerry Judah, 'Death in the Detail', *Jewish Chronicle*, 2 June 2000. Judah built the Auschwitz model from a design by Greenberg.
65. Kathy Jones, 'The Shoes of Majdanek Come to London', *Imperial War Museum Holocaust Exhibition Report* (Summer 2000). The shoes are featured in the initial leaflet for the exhibition and on the cover of its catalogue.
66. Linenthal, *Preserving Memory*, p.205, on the models built in Auschwitz by Mieczyslaw Stobierski.

67. James Hall *et al.* (eds.), *Apocalypse* (London, 2000).
68. Jim Garret, 'A Hell on Earth', *Museums Journal*, Aug. 2000.
69. The visit was by the Third Age group of Cheshire Reform Congregation. See Joan Rose, 'Visit to the Imperial War Museum', *Shofar*, Vol.29, No.2 (Oct. 2000), p.18.
70. Jonathan Jones, 'Shock treatment', *The Guardian*, 7 Sept. 2000. On Holocaust Memorial Day in Britain see Donald Bloxham's contribution in this volume.
71. Garret, 'A Hell on Earth'. For a reproduction of detail from the model showing the selection, see The Imperial War Museum, *The Holocaust*, p.46.
72. Directed by Rob Reiner, released in 1984 and re-released in 2000.
73. Gerry Judah in *Jewish Chronicle*, 2 June 2000.
74. For more general discussion on this point see Tony Kushner, '"Pissing in the Wind"? The Search for Nuance in the Study of Holocaust "Bystanders"', in David Cesarani and Paul Levine (eds.), *'Bystanders' to the Holocaust: A Re-evaluation* (London, 2002), pp.63–4.
75. John Taylor, *Body Horror: Photojournalism, Catastrophe and War* (Manchester, 1998), p.129.
76. Robin O'Neil, 'Belzec Extermination Camp: Report, July 1998' (unpublished typescript); 'Row Over Mass Grave Excavations at Sobibor', *Jewish Chronicle*, 21 Dec. 2001.
77. See Jane Hubert, 'A Proper Place for the Dead: A Critical Review of the "Reburial" Issue', in Robert Layton (ed.), *Conflict in the Archaeology of Living Traditions* (London, 1989), pp.132–3. For the assessment of the evidence, see Jane McComish, 'The Medieval Jewish Cemetery at Jewbury, York', *Jewish Culture and History*, Vol.3, No.2 (Winter 2000), pp.21–30.
78. Simpson, *Making Representations*, Ch.7.
79. Yehuda Koren, 'In Pursuit of Dignity', *Jewish Chronicle*, 31 Aug. 2001.
80. Cressida Fforde, 'Controlling the Dead: an Analysis of the Collecting and Repatriation of Aboriginal Human Remains (unpublished Ph.D. thesis, University of Southamtpon, 1997), esp. pp.152–3.
81. Taylor, *Body Horror*, pp.195–6.
82. See Marcus Wood's superb *Blind Memory: Visual Representations of Slavery in England and America 1780–1865* (Manchester, 2000).
83. James Allen *et al.*, *Without Sanctuary: Lynching Photography in America* (Santa Fe, NM, 2000).
84. Garret, 'A Hell on Earth'.
85. Joan Smith, *Misogynies: Reflections on Myth and Malice* (London, 1989), pp.127, 137.
86. See, for example, Sue Vice, *Holocaust Fiction* (London, 2000), Ch.2 and esp. p.66 on D.M. Thomas and the claim of pornography.
87. Smith, *Misogynies*, p.137.
88. Lord Russell of Liverpool, *The Scourge of the Swastika* (London, 1954), photographs opposite pp.180, 196, 197, 213.
89. See Micheline Maurel, *Ravensbruck* (London, 1958) published by Digit Books with the plug on the cover from a *Sunday Times* review: 'a coarse, savage book'. The imagery and approach was even extended to a Badger Books account of the life of Sue Ryder by A.J. Forrest entitled *But Some There Be* (London, 1957).
90. Annette Insdorf, *Indelible Shadows: Film and the Holocaust* (Second Edition, New York, 1989), pp.136–8.
91. Sherri Szeman, *The Kommandant's Mistress* (London, 1994 [orig. 1993]), published by Minerva in paperback. Szeman was not happy with the title and even less so the cover which has a woman in a Jewish camp uniform with her breasts exposed.
92. Joseph Slade, 'Nazi Imagery in Contemporary Culture: The Limits of Representation', *Dimensions*, Vol.11, No.2 (1997), pp.9, 14–15.
93. Catherine MacKinnon, 'Turning Rape into Pornography: Postmodern Genocide', in Alexandra Stiglmayer (ed.), *Rape: The War Against Women in Bosnia-Herzogovina* (London, 1994), pp.73–81 quoted in Rose Lindsey, 'Nationalism and Gender: A Study of War-Related Violence Against Women' (unpublished Ph.D., University of

Southampton, 2000), pp.139–40 and idem, 'From Atrocity to Data: Historiographies of Rape in Former Yugoslavia and Their Effects on the Study of the Gendering of Genocide', *Patterns of Prejudice*, Vol.36, No.4 (2002), pp.59–78.
94. Taylor, *Body Horror*, pp.132–3.
95. Malvern, 'War, Memory and Museums', pp.179, 197.
96. Most organized survivor groups in Britain, including the Hendon Holocaust Survivor Centre and the '45 Aid Group, have been enthusiastic about the exhibition. Their lack of critical comment in contrast to survivors in the USA and Washington museum reflects perhaps their greater marginality and sense of gratitude that a national museum was at last recognizing the Holocaust.
97. Young, *The Texture of Memory*, pp.337, 345.
98. Paul Gilroy, *There Ain't No Black in the Union Jack: The Cultural Politics of Race and Nation* (London, 1987), pp.131–5; Patrick White, *On Living in an Old Country: The National Past in Contemporary Britain* (London, 1985); Angus Calder, *The Myth of the Blitz* (London, 1991).
99. Tony Kushner and Katharine Knox, *Refugees in an Age of Genocide: Global, National and Local Perspectives during the Twentieth Century* (London, 1999), Ch.6.
100. Young, *The Texture of Memory*, p.128.
101. Wood, *Blind Memory*, pp.297–9; Anthony Tibbles (ed.), *Transatlantic Slavery: Against Human Dignity* (London, 1994).
102. Wood, *Blind Memory*, p.299.
103. Cousins, *The Pitt Rivers Museum*, p.5; David van Kevren, 'Museums and Ideology: Augustus Pitt-Rivers, Anthropological Museums and Social Change in Britain', *Victorian Studies*, Vol.28, No.1 (Autumn 1984), pp.171–89, esp. 175–6 and 183–4 for the early Pitt-Rivers Museum in Bethnal Green and South Kensington and its representation of 'races'.
104. Such an approach was to be adopted by the Manchester Shoah project, set up in the 1990s and which was finally abandoned, largely though not exclusively for reasons of finance, in 2001.
105. 'Birthplace' (1993) and shown on BBC 2, Timewatch, 23 March 1994.

2

Britain's Holocaust Memorial Days: Reshaping the Past in the Service of the Present

DONALD BLOXHAM

The tension between the historical specificity and the universal implications of the Holocaust is not a new one for scholars of the subject. In many forms over the last thirty years, the ritual question has been posed as to whether the supposed 'uniqueness' of the Holocaust precludes the drawing from it of relevant comparisons, warnings and 'lessons'. The debate has periodically spilled over into the public arena as, for instance, around the establishment of the United States Holocaust Memorial Museum in the 1990s or the Imperial War Museum's Holocaust exhibition in London.

This essay argues that the conceptual confusions around why the Holocaust is deemed worthy of special commemoration have extended into the annual British Holocaust Memorial Day (HMD), first commemorated on 27 January 2001, the fifty-sixth anniversary of the liberation of Auschwitz concentration camp. It suggests that the day may have the potential to achieve the ends it espouses, but not in the way in which it is currently organized. Unfortunately, a reorganization along the lines that would be required is unlikely under the prevailing political and cultural circumstances. It concludes by suggesting that the intellectual inconsistencies and even mild hypocrisies that mark the day must be seen within the context of a conservative statement about British 'national' identity in the twenty-first century, and one that is not actually concerned with addressing the serious questions that the Holocaust poses.

I

The author must at the outset place his own convictions within the 'uniqueness' debate. I do not accept the contention of the uniqueness of the Holocaust. I recognize it as a particularly extreme case of

.t this is a distinction of degree rather than nature. is not a word that historians should be comfortable with, ity is to examine every historical event in its specificity. this matter the term has acquired such value-laden status that .. very use diminishes, whether intentionally or not, other instances of genocide or indeed of state-sponsored mass murder that have not, by often arbitrary standards, been deemed worthy of the label 'genocide'. The concept of 'uniqueness' should be recognized for what it originally was before it became an article of faith for some historians and many survivors: a device emerging out of politicized, ahistorical debate.[1]

On the other hand, I would contend that owing to its colossal scale, its chronological and geographical proximity, the Holocaust *is* of enormous *significance* for western society. But to put it in a category of significance all of its own is in itself a culturally-laden statement, informed by western narcissism. For if Hitler turned European imperialism in upon Europe, the devastations and exploitations introduced outside the continent in every corner of the globe by that imperialism have yet to register on our post-imperial consciences. Like the proverbial bad driver who had never been in an accident but had seen dozens, European civilization had bequeathed rich legacies of mass murder and intercommunal strife to its extra-European subject societies.

Whatever the efforts around the first two HMDs to make the days relevant by connecting Britain to the events of the Holocaust with reference to the refugees and survivors who came here, to the war effort itself and the 'liberation' of Belsen concentration camp,[2] in terms of actual perpetrator agency, the British linkage with mass atrocity and death is much more direct in the record of interference, settlement and exploitation in north America, Africa, Australasia and the Indian subcontinent. That these happened outside Europe should not shroud the fact that they were manifestations of European ideologies and/or chauvinisms, power politics or economic agendas. No matter how much more 'important' we might perceive the Holocaust to be than, for instance, the British role in the total destruction of the small population of Tasmania, the fact remains that the Tasmanian episode was the only one of the two which was of British commission, and it is representative of a much more historically common form of genocidal atrocity than was the Holocaust.

The destructive potential of 'the west' was manifest long before the Second World War, but only when the European continent erupted at its own core were some of its cultural underpinnings gradually brought into question. Zygmunt Bauman's important *Modernity and the Holocaust* raises important universal questions about the exclusionary potential of 'rationalized', post-enlightenment societies.[3] It is relevant to the imperial crimes of the 'west', as indeed to the more 'ordinary' discriminations and exclusions within European society before the First World War and even up to the present – with the ongoing treatment of Romanies a prime example. His conclusion that the Holocaust is a 'legitimate resident in the house of modernity' of course indicates his splendid grasp of the wider dysfunctions of that 'modernity', but the fact remains that it took the Holocaust to give force to this truth, when, had 'the west' displayed any self-reflection about its capacity for destruction, this might already have been plain to see. Thus in this most bold attempt at contextualizing the Holocaust within broader patterns of human development, it is still, paradoxically, *de facto* attributed a 'unique' position.

On a much less refined intellectual level than any of the above was the bill proposing 'a day to learn about and remember the Holocaust', introduced to the House of Commons on 30 June 1999 by the Labour MP for Hendon, Andrew Dismore (though he is by no means alone, even among scholars who should possess a greater breadth of historical understanding). In the aftermath of a visit to Auschwitz organized by one of the organizations that was to become involved at an advisory level in HMD, he had realized 'how unique the Holocaust was', and how, as such, it was worthy of special commemoration.[4] There is no evidence that this declaration was the result of extensive comparative enquiry into the history of other genocides and of visits to other sites of mass killing from other periods and in other regions.

There is also no evidence that at any time during the conceptualisation and planning of the first HMD was the 'uniqueness'/'exceptionality' of the Holocaust brought properly into question, which is surely related to the fact that no advisory groups concerned primarily with genocides perpetrated by other regimes than the Nazis were brought in to help shape the concept. Moreover, even within that range of Nazi genocide, most of the advisory groups were overwhelmingly interested in the Jewish catastrophe.[5] This is also related to the crude question of whether HMD is just to be a 'Jewish' concern or a concern for everybody. Much hot air has been expended over this and analogous questions pertaining to the purported 'Holocaust industry' in the USA.[6]

It is not my intention to enter any of those often bad faith debates. Nevertheless, it is clear that the Holocaust is not and should not be just a 'Jewish' concern, as most of the HMD advisory groups would also argue, and this is self-evidently the view of the Home Office and the Labour leadership. HMD would not have got government endorsement had it not been intended to make some sort of statement of universal relevance, and indeed with the Stockholm conference of foreign ministers in January 2000 at which the project was announced in line with parallel developments elsewhere in Europe, this was the direction that the wind was blowing across the continent as a whole. (Although it is still not clear why Britain could not have followed the European Union's example and designated 27 January as a more inclusive 'Genocide Remembrance Day'.) Nevertheless, if we distinguish the broad relevance of the Holocaust from the narrower memorialization of the Holocaust, and also from the proprietorship of that memorialization, it would have been preferable had a much wider range of groups and intellectuals been involved in the original planning of the concept.

However ill-advised it may be, whatever the arguments for and against the notion of the 'uniqueness' of the Holocaust, if indeed these were actually given much thought at all, we have now to accept that that purported exceptionality is enshrined within HMD. Such must be the rationale for the official singling out of the Holocaust for annual contemplation, and thus instantly the tension between uniqueness and universality has been introduced to the collective consciousness of Britain. The challenge for those running HMD now is less to continue to emphasize its specificity and more to emphasize its universality. This is no easy task, given the sensitivity with which Holocaust survivor organizations in particular view close 'comparisons' between the Holocaust and other historical events. (As an example of this unfortunate tendency, the question of refugees is often the subject of remarkable, spurious distinctions – both among the public and former victims themselves – between refugees from Nazism/Fascism as innocent and apolitical and those seeking safe European havens today as somehow 'different' and less worthy of sympathy.) As I shall later try to illustrate, the limited attempts so far to give the Holocaust a wider 'relevance' have, far from drawing out its universal 'lessons' in a meaningful way, instead been manifested as rather safe and politically acceptable, not to say convenient, messages.

II

If the uniqueness/universality question problematizes the whole concept of a specifically Holocaust-oriented memorial day, then a key problem internal to HMD as it has been established is its victim-led nature. In the original proposal for the HMD, the first stated objective was to 'commemorate the communities who suffered as a result of the Holocaust'. The desire to 'provide a national mark of respect for all victims of Nazi persecution and demonstrate understanding with all those who still suffer its consequences' is to be juxtaposed with the imperative to 'recognise that the Holocaust was a tragically defining episode of the 20th Century, a crisis for European civilization and a universal catastrophe for humanity'.[7] The latter statement gives force to the former: the victims of the Nazis are to be singled out for special commemoration because they were victims of a particularly special event, 'a defining episode of the 20th Century, a crisis for European civilisation'. On the surface this is fair, but, for reasons I shall try to elucidate, the commemorative function has effectively overwhelmed any prospect of meaningful *education*.

This is a sensitive subject, and it seems heretical even to raise it given that this historian, like so many others in the field, was introduced to the Holocaust through survivor testimony. Moreover, one of the most important objectives of recent scholarship has been to rescue the particularity of individual experience from the vast scale of the Holocaust, to personalize the story, not just to do justice to the victims as autonomous human beings but also to make the catastrophe comprehensible at a human level for the audience.[8] But, and here is another tension between the particular and the universal, it is on the collective level that the 'uniqueness' of the Holocaust is held to lie. More specifically, it is supposed to reside in the Nazi intent to murder, with a few minor exceptions, all Jews everywhere.[9]

The issue of 'intent' is at the heart of the United Nations' definition of genocide,[10] heavily influenced as that definition is by the occurrence of the Holocaust. Nazi intent has been used to mark out the murder of the Jews from other instances of state-sponsored mass killing, including the destruction of non-Jewish groups by the Nazis, which have involved similar numbers or proportions of murdered among the victim group. There is an assumption in this distinction which has not been properly enunciated. The assumption is that apart from allowing a common factor of mass death in each case or contested case of genocide, the experience of the victims is actually irrelevant to the categorization of the crime. In this logic of 'uniqueness', if the Holocaust itself is unique, the suffering of its victims is not. Indeed, personal instances of pain and deprivation between cases of genocide or other types of extreme human rights abuse may not really be contrasted, nor a hierarchy discerned of suffering on a personal level, given that any given case of genocide features a broad spectrum of torments which overlap with those inflicted in any other given case.

The problem is not simply a philosophical one. It is also a highly practical matter. The dean of Holocaust historians, Raul Hilberg, made one important mistake in his seminal work *The Destruction of the European Jews*; he generalized without sufficient substantiation about the passive behaviour of the Jews during the Holocaust.[11] For this he was strongly criticized,[12] and the criticism had merit at the time, as Hilberg reflected early approaches to the Holocaust from the Nuremberg trials onwards in ignoring the victims. But much has now changed, and survivors have become perhaps the most prominent public interpreters of the Holocaust, establishing a significant proprietorship over the subject.[13]

Hilberg's rationale for concentrating on the perpetrators would have been recognized by Raphael Lemkin, inspirer of the genocide convention, and it remains entirely appropriate today to anyone capable of seeing past the horrors of what the Nazis did to understanding why they did it – the 'lessons of the Holocaust', as it were. Hilberg was concerned with 'the storm that caused the wreckage'.[14] He was concerned above all with the mechanics of the 'final solution of the Jewish question'. Just as to understand the recent spate of train disasters is to understand the workings and failings of the British rail system, from high management to unscrewed bolts at points, to understand, to gain insight into the Holocaust is to understand the ways in which tens of thousands of Germans and others found themselves prepared to participate in a spectrum of roles in the mass murder of Jews and others.

Naturally it would be absurd and distasteful to have HMD without survivors, a crime without victims. Anyway a 'memorial' day has as its chief function commemoration of loss (and it is also too late now to contend the appropriateness of the whole 'memorial day' concept). To ignore the survivors would also be an ironic perpetuation of the lack of interest in the immediate post-Holocaust period in their experiences, and of British governmental responses from 1933–45, with their reluctance to embrace Jewish victims *qua* Jewish victims. Yet the day has explicitly been assigned as a day of education also, and it is vital to get the balance right. Further, and of which more later, the victim profile presented in HMD is still very partial and exclusive, even in the narrow terms of the crimes of Nazism.

The danger of the present approach, and what might lead to marginalization of HMD as a particularist venture, is emphasizing the tragedy of the experience of (select groups of) victims at the expense of understanding how they came to face those experiences. The former might result in increased knowledge and awareness of some aspects of the Holocaust *per se*, but that, in isolation, is insufficient to fill what we are told is the broad educational remit of HMD, and it would indeed be unfortunate if the day simply boiled down to stating that it was important to know about the Holocaust without establishing precisely why. The latter has more to tell us about the general human 'condition' (or particular cultural variants of that mythical state), breakdowns in 'civilized' values, and about the structures, discriminations and pressures that actually led to the crime.

The understandable natural responses of horror and pity, and the oft-accompanying pieties of 'never again', can overwhelm the need for forensic investigation and real explanation. Equally importantly, if the logic is accepted that the singularity of the Holocaust rests on the perpetrators' not the victims' side, repeated focus upon the victims looks like a veneration with no clear justification of one particular instance of suffering among many. If 'lessons' of the Holocaust are to be found at all, they are to be found on the side of the perpetrators, not in the lighting of candles of remembrance. The latter act shows decency in the desire to remember and may show the conviction of 'never again', but it does nothing concrete about ensuring 'never again', and is often carried out while 'again' is indeed recurring, if not generally in the west.

The 'pathos approach', as I shall call it, has established dominance both in the first two HMD ceremonies and in the education packs that have accompanied each day. The ceremonies were replete with survivor readings and discussions, and musical and choral recitals, the packs with photographs of victims, children to the fore. We search in vain in them for anything which feeds off the large body of historical scholarship about how men and women became murderers. In this pathos approach, 'the Holocaust' is left hanging in the air as an ill-defined metaphor of terrible evil. Yet explaining or 'understanding' the events as we are constantly enjoined to do is not primarily a matter of identifying with the victims and the tragedy of their experiences, which must, to a certain extent, be taken as a given. It is much more to do with understanding what institutional and personal pressures, what precise belief systems and circumstances, allowed the idea of genocide to be accepted and acted upon by tens of thousands of people.

In short, we must try to do what Andy Charlesworth has long advocated,[15] and turn the mirror around. We must perform that least tasteful task of trying to identify with the perpetrators, as well as those more-and-less active bystanders in close proximity to the crimes. Only with this approach do we have any chance of ensuring 'that the horrendous crimes, racism and victimisation committed during the Holocaust are neither forgotten nor repeated',[16] for the perpetrators and those who are prepared to become directly involved with or against that perpetration are the people who determine whether or not genocide happens.[17]

Trying to understand the perpetrators does not require vast erudition. One straightforward text which does a reasonable job of assessing the behaviour of a prime perpetrator without glorifying or sensationalizing his behaviour is Gitta Sereny's interview-based study of the former Treblinka commandant Franz Stangl.[18] Christopher Browning's work on the 'Jewish bureau' in the German Foreign Office remains a fairly accessible, seminal English-language study of how and why the so-called 'desk murderers', the middle rank of bureaucrats essential in 'oiling the wheels' of the 'final solution', did their job.[19] Perhaps most significant of all, in terms of its brevity, simplicity-of-style, insight and relevance, is Browning's study of the so-called 'ordinary men', a group of un-remarkable, non-Nazified police reservists called upon to murder Jews in occupied Poland because of a shortage of hardened killers.[20] Kill these men did, and again and again, for the most part without question, though not without some qualms at first. Browning's analysis of their motivations and actions is not uncontested – indeed, the juxtaposition of contrary interpretations would fortify the educational process by providing the 'debate' beloved of didactic exercises[21] – but it might be thought to be an unparalleled starting point for discussion.

On the macro level, over and above the question of individual motivations, historians would in the main concur that the Holocaust is as much about the rise of ethnic nationalism and scientific racism in Europe, the exclusionary and destructive potential of the modern state, and the particular dynamics of the Hitler state, as about the historical legacy of anti-Judaism/anti-Semitism. Maintaining the language of economics, the latter factor was the necessary one for the Holocaust to happen to the Jews, the former factors were the sufficient ones for the Holocaust to happen at all. For the present day political agenda, these historically-specific fields of enquiry – the development of ethnic nationalism and scientific racism and so on – have been replaced with the vaguer, more abstract and hence universal mantra of the fight against 'discrimination', 'prejudice' or 'racism'. If simplistic, even banal (who outside the extreme right would openly promote a reverse case?), this is on the surface fine, for it would be impossible to translate the circumstances of the Holocaust precisely into 'lessons' for today, and could it possibly be wrong to make official pronouncements in this direction?

HMD must needs play a little fast and loose with the historical record, and perhaps we might accept even imprecise appropriations of the past that seem to serve laudable goals for the future. Could one criticize HMD if informing about the Holocaust could be shown to have prevented even one racist assault? Yet apart from the difficulty of showing that learning about Nazi genocide actually affects current behaviour – indeed a bold recent study from the University of Nevada bucks the general unproved trend towards assuming the benefits of 'Holocaust education' to show that it makes no such difference[22] – this emotive question is the wrong one. A more appropriate question might ask: why use the Holocaust at all to illustrate the evils of contemporary discrimination and intolerance when other less extreme or unusual examples might be more appropriate?

As an oft-invoked case, the murder of Stephen Lawrence has much more to tell us about the problems and manifestations of extreme racism in a liberal democracy than do the actions of a totalitarian and self-confessedly racist state where racism was the state-endorsed social norm, not a target of official disapprobation. The point is that reducing the Holocaust entirely to its concrete core of racism and discrimination is to ignore what made it 'special', and thereby to undermine the implicit rationale for the day. Part of what made the Holocaust special, of what makes genocide special, is that genocide is almost by definition a state crime.

Theories of exclusion giving rise to different forms of discrimination can be legitimated by a range of ideologies, not just biological racism; but what provides the potential for any exclusionary ideology to be translated to genocide is the far-reaching power of the state: its perceived legitimacy; its ability to call upon the loyalty of its citizens and mobilize and unify their efforts; its control of the means of violence and coercion in pursuit of that mobilization and unity. This is not the whole story, naturally. All manner of circumstances have to interact before the most extreme course is taken, but only the state and its workings – both as instrument and instrumentalizer – can empower and impel individuals to genocide. How is a state-established memorial day to confront the difficult questions raised in this section? How is the state effectively to interrogate both itself and its citizenry?

III

This section must begin with a caveat. I have great sympathy for those arguments positing in criticism of HMD that the state is an inappropriate sponsor of remembrance for a state-sponsored atrocity;

that it is incapable, effectively, of addressing for the better its own potentialities.[23] Parts of this line of argument are pursued below. However my sympathy is limited in terms of the rather Holocaust-centric way this criticism has evolved. As in the 'Shoah business' as a whole, with its colossal corpus of philosophical, theological, literary and cultural studies-based scholarship of varying quality, over and above that increasingly small proportion of rigorous historical research, these protests seem rather intellectually precious, especially given that at the same time as they are being made elsewhere state-sponsored atrocities (not their representations five decades later) are actually in progress un-addressed. The impression given is that the Holocaust is 'uniquely' difficult to represent,[24] again in the absence of anywhere near the same volume of thought on the representation of other genocides, and thus the 'uniqueness' of the Holocaust is again indirectly substantiated.

The state's role in 'representation' needs to be concretized in terms of today's issues rather than left as a rather abstract intellectual argument – it is a political as much as philosophical matter. Indeed it should have a greater political immediacy than ever at this moment. Since we have entered a period of so-called asymmetric warfare – predicted since the end of the cold war with its bipolar opposition – and particularly since 11 September 2001, the officially endorsed focus on violent threats within the international system has been placed on non-state organizations, primarily terrorists, alongside so-called rogue states whose practices can conveniently be depicted as antithetical to the 'norms' of civilized statehood. This rhetoric may or may not be appropriate, notwithstanding that realpolitik dictates who is to be labelled a terrorist or rogue state, but the fact remains that, as observed, states of many colourings remain the most likely agents of the supreme international transgression: genocide. The increasing veneration of the state, almost in a return to the pre-Second World War days of the primacy of legal positivism, ignores those who have perished *en bloc* in the process of state formation, and nation-state formation in particular, as Mark Levene has illustrated.[25]

But the argument of the state's inappropriateness to confront acts of state can tend to a *reductio ad absurdum*, precluding it from doing anything but bolstering or increasing its own authority. The state is inherently a bearer of authority and thus to some extent authoritarian, with a lower-case initial, though the insidiousness of that authority can vary greatly. We must allow that while it exists it is capable of making authoritative statements to the good as well as the bad – it is, after all, a normatively neutral mechanism (hence its propensity to be instrumentalized for either good or bad indifferently).

It is at those points where present-day state mechanisms of discrimination do come unavoidably into play, for instance, in the parallels that might be made between British refugee policy and refugee policy in the Nazi era, that the logic of state-sponsored reflection directly undermines the possibility of real self-criticism. Yet there are sufficient points of very significant historical divergence for this not to be a crippling problem for the day as a whole. Besides, beyond the central HMD ceremonies and the nationally-distributed educational materials, there is scope at the local level for differing interpretations and approaches to the day which could at least in theory undermine any narratives imposed from the 'top downwards'. Further to this argument, it is possible that the administration of the day will be delegated at some point to a non-governmental organization, so expanding its potential freedom.

Thus I would contend that the state is capable of promoting or at least allowing a self-critical civic culture, albeit within variable restraints. This is not to say that HMD has so succeeded. It remains to see what difference a decentralization of the day's administration will have on its ability to ask difficult questions of the state and of the policy of the government of the day. So far even on the individual level, when HMD has encouraged the examination of individuals who are not from the victims' side, difficult questions have been avoided, only the more comfortable ones addressed.[26]

It is actually another convenient anti-totalitarian liberal myth – given the self-understanding of liberalism as ideologically moderate – that 'evil' resides in the force of big ideas. It is straightforward to stigmatize the ideological rationales for discrimination, since, whatever the ordinary prejudices of the average citizen, quasi-scientific doctrines of exclusion are generally the preserve of the extreme and can be associated with forces against which liberalism instinctively opposes itself. It is much more difficult to locate potential for gross wrongdoing in the weakness of that average citizen, in his or her susceptibility to group or institutional pressures, or his or her ambition, greed, fear of criticism, or subscription to the everyday myths by which every nation(-state) perpetuates and justifies itself. It is almost as difficult to locate the potential for extreme elements to do harm in the moral vacuum left by the self-interested indifference of that average citizen.

It is hardly a good idea electorally to preach the capacity of most people for participation or acquiescence in murder, however indirectly, under certain circumstances. Thus our attention is inevitably drawn to the tiny, unrepresentative minority of 'bystanders' who bucked the trend and intervened to save or succour the victims – these are the examples of physical and moral courage which it is hoped we will follow with our civic behaviour, and represent one of the key 'lessons' of the Holocaust as they are handed down to us. ('A touchstone of the human capacity for good in the face of evil'.)[27] Yet the stated desire of British politicians for greater popular participation in democracy[28] really only extends to increased voter turnout in the interests of legitimating an increasingly moribund bi-party rotation of power. More direct expressions of democratic freedom are as actively opposed as they always have been, including, for instance, the clamp-down on protests against human rights abuses in Tibet, launched at the Chinese premier on his last visit to London, just, incidentally, at the time when the form of HMD was being finalized.

The work of Nechama Tec on Christian rescuers of Jews in Poland during the Second World War shows that no particular common belief system dictated their actions. They were not uniformly religious or politically-aligned, and many had shown no pre-existing tendency to self-sacrifice or great humanitarianism; some were even demonstrably anti-Semitic, but still opposed what Germany was doing to the Jews. If anything, the only uniting factor among these rescuers was a certain non-conformity, a moral stubbornness, in refusing to adhere to the norms imposed upon them.[29] Is there really a governmental desire for us to do the moral equivalent of what Martin Luther King described as the duty of every just citizen: to disobey unjust law, to protest in ways outside the conventional and historically inadequate conduits of religion and conventional political organization? Tony Blair's contemptuous dismissal of 'anti-globalization' activism suggests not.

If my propositions thus far are accepted, what, it might be asked, is the point of HMD beyond a simple official recognition of something terrible, and perhaps a way of gaining the Labour government some moral capital? That is only a pertinent question if we take the title and stated aims of the day at face value. Yet if we argue that the day is much more about Britain than about the Holocaust, we may begin to understand why the conceptual problems hitherto identified have not been addressed.

IV

A project related to the HMD has featured on the European scene. An international 'task force', constituted of a not-dissimilar membership to the original working group for the HMD, but organized by the Foreign Office rather then the Home Office, is responsible, along with similar organizations from other 'enlightened' western states, for ensuring that the basic tenets of Holocaust history are recognized by former eastern-bloc states. This is a small part of the carrot-and-stick approach to ensuring that countries seeking EU membership fulfil socio-cultural as well as economic criteria for inclusion. On one level, it is all to the good: any national historiography that fails to observe the fundamentally racist, and particularly antisemitic, thrust of Nazi policy needs to be exposed. The more so if, as is frequently the case, that historical misrepresentation is a function of anti-Semitic agendas in the modern day.

Rightly, also, western historians, pressure groups and politicians long lambasted the former Soviet orthodoxy that Nazi genocide was an expression of capitalism in a terminal, crisis phase, rather than the action of a regime for which race was a more important cleavage than class. (Hence the prevailing depiction in Soviet historiography of the Nazis' victims as members of particular national groups rather than 'racial' categories.) Yet we would do well to remember that wartime myths die hard everywhere, and that no international political organization has thought to take France or various other western European countries to task for their nationalist historiographies that retrospectively minimize the extent of collaboration with Nazi Germany (including in the Holocaust) and maximize the scale of resistance.[30]

The universal politicization of history should be a salutary reminder to the HMD architects and the international task-force who, while promoting contemporary occidental values, have neglected to heed the post-modern lessons accompanying multi-culturalism that no political system, fascist, communist, liberal-democratic or otherwise, can claim ownership of absolute *interpretive* 'truth'. Here I am not talking about the obvious *factual* truth of the Holocaust, but the reasons for the invocation of the Holocaust at this precise moment in time and in this fashion, and the 'lessons' that are supposed to be drawn from it. The integrity of the historical record is not just harmed by Stalinist-style distortions; it is also affected by silences and de-contextualizations. In the case of HMD the problem is manifest on different levels: straightforward distortions of history stemming from *realpolitik* considerations; prevailing misconceptions or 'governing myths' of history; and present day socio-cultural agendas for which particular lessons from the past are deemed 'useful'. (Echoing Tony Kushner,[31] none of the following is to cast any doubt on the personal integrity of the Home Office or DfEE/DfES officials involved in HMD, each of whom are also constrained by government lines. About the motivations of the Labour government itself, I am inclined to be rather less charitable given its opportunism, populism and veneration of style over substance.)

The Armenian genocide will remain as a thorn in the flesh of the British government until it is recognized as such. Not as a particularly important thorn, because of the temporal, geographical and 'cultural' distance of its occurrence, and the diminutive weight of Armenian official representation in Britain. It is the very relative weakness of that pressure that enables the British government, like the American government, to continue to succumb to Turkish pressure to avoid the epithet 'genocide'.[32] For the purposes of this essay, the Armenian genocide is important because it has become *the* litmus test of the international politics of remembrance. 'Ethical foreign policy', and the unthinking mantra about the 'need to remember' are compromised by non-recognition. My emphasis here, however, is not specifically on the murder of approximately one million Armenians in the First World War.[33] Very few genocides are recognized or held up for public dissection; modern-day Germany's embrace of the history of the Holocaust is distinctly atypical. Besides, the cause for recognition of the Armenian case has received considerable reflected attention as a result of HMD, though this was certainly an inadvertent consequence.

We need not stray nearly so far chronologically from the murder of the Jews to see significant politicized distortions of the historical record. At the larger conference taking place alongside the meeting of the foreign ministers in Stockholm, at which the 'need to remember' was repeatedly affirmed, two of the largest victim groups of the Nazis, Soviet POWs and civilians, were not even included in the publicly-pronounced roster of the murdered. This all-too-common omission reflects the failure of the post-war world to come to terms with the massive losses inflicted on the Soviet Union, for reasons that surely pertain to the cold war, to opposition to the new 'totalitarian' power and in addition to the reluctance to recognize that Russian blood and resilience – if also American money – were the decisive factors in defeating Hitler, not the Battle of Britain and 'Dunkirk spirit'.

Conversely, certain groups, especially blacks, have been promoted as victims of Nazi persecution beyond all proportion to their relevance in the Nazi world-view. Thus in the 'background' comments to the commemorative programme for the second HMD, we read the following list of victims: 'the mentally and physically disabled, gays and lesbians, religiously independent, social outcasts, political rebels, Blacks, Gypsies as well as the Jews.' It continues: 'Forms of cultural expression which deviated from Nazi ideals – and these included most forms of modern art, literature and music which could be defined as

"Jewish" or "Black" – were proscribed as "degenerate".'[34] The absence from this breakdown of the mass vandalism of 'Slavic' cultural treasures is notable, but not nearly so notable as the absence of the fate of the 300,300 Soviet prisoners of war, victims of Nazi anti-Slav racism, either murdered in captivity or left quite deliberately to starve to death in open-air camps. I address the representation of the mass killing of Slavs in one sense because given its sheer scale the crime is such a significant absence from 'western memory'.

On a more conceptual level, which I shall simply touch upon here and then leave alone in the interests of space and continuity, the episode is indicative of a wider phenomenon of inter-ethnic massacre and 'cleansing' in central and eastern Europe during the Second World War. The war unleashed racist and nationalist forces across the continent, and the Nazis (and the Axis powers) were by no means the only perpetrators. This begs the question of the interconnectedness of the whole complex of war and genocide, and of the artificiality of selecting particular episodes for 'remembrance' while consigning others to oblivion.[35]

Only in the education pack for the first HMD do we read briefly that 'millions of Poles, Russians and others were killed by the German occupying forces in prisoner of war, labour and extermination camps. Their lives were seen as disposable.'[36] (Nothing more has been said about this colossal number of murdered human beings, either in the national ceremonies or in the educational material, despite the warning earlier in the education pack of the danger of dehumanizing genocide by simply quoting abstract numbers.)[37] Yet this comes lower in the pecking order than the un-numbered Senegalese of Alsace-Lorraine and the Africans from former German colonies who were subject to an unidentified 'persecution', and the 400 black children subjected to forced sterilization. Prefacing these summaries of victimhood is the statement that 'at the bottom of the [Nazi racial] scale were Jews, Roma and Black people … Such inferior "races" were seen as fit for extinction.'[38] The absence from this sentence of Slavs, of whom by pre-war Nazi estimates up to 30 million might have to die in order to provide space and sufficient food in the German *Lebensraum* when the eastern empire was established, is simply staggering.[39] Yet Slavs are left out of the list again on at least three separate occasions in that education pack, including in two school assembly plans.[40]

The number of 3.3 million dead Soviet POWs bears repeating,[41] and juxtaposition with some of the figures of the persecuted from the other victim classes. Let us select for the sake of argument the death toll of gay men, a toll which vastly exceeds that of blacks, the 'religiously independent', and lesbians. Of the presumably several millions dwelling under Nazi control, estimates suggest that between 5,000 and an absolute maximum of 15,000 gays perished in the concentration camps[42] (and these less from an orchestrated higher policy of total murder than of the arbitrary, homophobic-sadistic behaviour of individual guards),[43] thus somewhere between 0.15 and 0.45 per cent of the POW total. Had Germany been defeated at the end of 1941 the total of Soviet dead would have outnumbered the Jewish dead by a ratio of about 3:1. The POWs add up to approximately the same number as the combined total of Armenians, Cambodians and Rwandans killed in genocides in the twentieth century.

Likewise absent from most roll-calls of the dead, that of the second HMD included,[44] are the several uncounted millions of eastern European civilians who perished in Nazi scorched earth actions, indiscriminate shootings, starvations, bombardments and 'anti-partisan' actions,[45] including up to two million Poles and, for instance, the scores of thousands of Serbs who were either directly murdered by the Nazis or by the German client Ustasha regime – though Serbs as victims is not a particularly convenient image in the present day, just as Russians as victims were not useful during the cold war. Yet surely it is the job of an education day to correct historical misunderstandings, to fill in gaps, rather than to perpetuate a very partial picture of Nazi atrocity. The fact that most of the literature dealing with crimes against non-Jewish eastern Europeans is not in English is a very poor excuse. The back cover of the commemorative programme for the second HMD quotes Albert Camus to the effect that 'good intentions may do as much harm as malevolence if they lack understanding'. Relatives of those millions of dead Poles, Russians, Belorussians, Ukrainians, etc. etc. (some of whose countries are the recipients of the international Holocaust education 'task force's' attentions) would, I am sure, loudly concur, if only they were able to organize and press for 'representation' in the ranks of the HMD advisory groups.

Let me be clear here since I do not in any way intend to belittle the fate of those other groups that I have singled out. It is certainly no bad thing to flag up the fact that the Nazis were anti-black, and the fates of any who died from any group, for whatever reasons, are equally worthy of commemoration, as I have already contended. But the retrospective emphasis on the Nazi persecution of blacks, particularly in contrast to the treatment of the 'Slavs', suggests a latter-day agenda. The programme for the second HMD reads like a political wish-list for modern social inclusion as much as a historical record. Equally importantly, the focus on Nazi homophobia and anti-black racism distracts attention from the parallel prejudices in the rest of the 'civilized' world during the Nazi period. What each group suffered under Nazism fits much more easily into a continuum of occidental racist or homophobic intolerance than does the Holocaust into a continuum of occidental anti-Semitism.

It was remarkable indeed, given that Britain was a prime perpetrator of the much greater anti-black crime of slavery, and that many more descendants of slavery's victims reside in Britain than do victims of the Holocaust or descendants thereof, that the primary representation of blacks in the first HMD was as victims of Nazism, that anti-liberal 'other' against whom 'we' (and the USA) fought. Here we move towards some concluding considerations on the way in which the HMD functions *vis-à-vis* British identity. This seems the crux of the matter, and may well explain the very existence of HMD, as well as all its apparent internal inconsistencies.

V

The 'lessons of the Holocaust' and other synonymous expressions were repeated throughout the build-up to both HMDs as if they were truisms. Yet precisely what these lessons are has yet to be spelled out. The one concrete notion is what Anne Karpf called the 'Spielberg agenda of using the Holocaust to teach liberal values'.[46] To emphasize the positive values of Britain and of civilization [*sic*] and draw attention to the consequences of the 'alternative' is Dismore's touted version of this.[47] Another, a direct Blair quote: HMD 'provides an opportunity to re-assert the democratic and civil values which we share';[48] and a third claims that the day 'promotes a democratic and tolerant society'.[49] At the Stockholm conference, democracy was again placed squarely as the polar opposite of Nazism. In fact, as Bill Williams has assessed,[50] far from being a purely memorial event, this was explicitly and shamelessly political, even reflecting a post-cold war liberal triumphalism, which may be a vital ingredient in the notable resurgence of 'memory' in the 1990s.

Yet if we are to define the lessons of Nazism in terms of those many things to which Nazism was ideologically opposed, then beyond liberal democracy we might also have to examine communism as its nemesis. And how comfortable can we really be with this sort of negative definitionalism when it can be co-opted from any point on the political spectrum? 'If it wasn't for us you'd all be Germans', chanted bellicose, nationalist football 'fans' on the streets of Belgian Charleroi during the Euro 2000 tournament, echoing in an intensified form the failure of the

British to conquer a century of Germanophobia, or to recognize the achievements of a society which has done more than most to encourage popular democratic participation amongst its citizens, to confront its wartime record and to fight political extremism – in contrast, again, to other members of the EU.

Negative definition is not a novelty in British society. If we accept Linda Colley's analysis, we see that in the eighteenth and early nineteenth centuries a polity consisting of several different nationalities or ethnic groups opted to root its collective Protestant identity in direct distinction to Catholic France and to a lesser extent Orthodox Russia.[51] Arguably now, in an age of multiculturalism and with a government keen to make a sort of national 'mission statement' in recognition of that, in which HMD must be a keynote, negative definitionalism is almost inevitable. Positive tenets of identity, even those laid down with far greater sensitivity or appropriateness than by the Home Secretary David Blunkett in the last few years, will generally raise objections of exclusivity or over-prescriptivity from some quarter. The notable thing about the choice of the Holocaust/Nazism as identificational 'other' is how timid that choice seems; how easy it appears to define ourselves against events that are universally condemned and recognized, and in a past which is as a result increasingly 'safe' to examine, the recent rise of the European far right notwithstanding.

Colley also notes the significance of the Anglo-French wars in cementing the mutual identification of 'Britons' during her period.[52] This is a tradition into which fits Britain's oft-observed obsession with 'the war',[53] in a post-war period in which it has had no large scale conflicts to bind together its increasingly dissolutionist citizenry. Arguably since the rise of the 'Anglo-German antagonism' in the late nineteenth century, and particularly in the two world wars, Germany has supplanted France in this capacity in the British consciousness. Now, Germany, perpetrator of the most extreme of the crimes of the Europeans in the modern period, has come to bear all of the sins of the Europeans – a process to which the label of Holocaust 'uniqueness' has contributed significantly. 'Our' imperial record simply does not enter into the British collective memory as objectionable, and 'our' history of discriminations is seen as nowhere near as relevant as those visited by someone else.

Seen in this context, the Imperial War Museum looks like an ever more appropriate *lieu de memoire* for the new icon of universal negative definition, the Holocaust. While out of one side of the mouth we are warned about the dangers of resurgent racism, out of the other we are encouraged, in the words of Tony Blair, to value 'the courage and commitment of our fellow citizens who resisted such evil',[54] and to see the Holocaust as another war story, albeit with a significant twist. HMD actually allows us to tie in a new statement of multicultural intent with an old rallying cry. The pathos approach to the Holocaust adds emotional force to this old–new bonding exercise while preventing any of the meaningful, genuinely universal but potentially divisive questions about the role of the state or of individual perpetrators being addressed. Victims that are not politically relevant are ignored, no matter how numerous they may be, while those groups who may be gainfully addressed through the mirror of Nazi discrimination are accorded an inflated status.

A cause for slight optimism about a more self-critical use of history for today in Britain is the possibility of another memorial day addressing slavery. This is a more historically appropriate and politically relevant context for examining in Britain the persecutions of black history, and addressing some of the realities which continue to influence black-white relations. And whatever the groundswell of contemporary American opinion about the revival of anti-Semitism throughout Europe, in Britain, France and Germany at least, 'non-"whites"' are much the greater victims of discrimination and violence.

There is one word of warning, however, should a slavery memorial day materialize. If it is true that the written history of slavery in Britain is in fact more the history of anti-slavery, with Britain's complicity in the crime rather obscured by the role of a minority of Britons in bringing the crime to an end, then the temptation must be avoided to replicate this failing, to put a similar spin on those events as HMD has put on the Holocaust. As in HMD, the aspiration to draw positive lessons from the past is laudable, but 'positive' should not become a euphemism for 'easy', because easy lessons are not worth learning. We also need to think long and hard about who is 'teaching' these lessons and if they are qualified to do so, or whether they are saying the wrong things in the confusion between recognizing that the Holocaust is important and recognizing why it is important today.

NOTES

1. For various discussions see Alan S. Rosenbaum (ed.), *Is the Holocaust Unique? Perspectives on Comparative Genocide* (Boulder, CO, 1996). See also Alvin Rosenfeld, 'The Politics of Uniqueness: Reflections on the Recent Polemical Turn in Holocaust and Genocide Scholarship', *Holocaust and Genocide Studies,* Vol.13, No.1 (1999), pp.28–61.

2. Similar arguments to those raised in support of the Imperial War Museum Holocaust exhibition. See David Cesarani, 'Should Britain have a National Holocaust Memorial Museum', *Journal of Holocaust Education*, Vol. 7, No.3 (1998), pp.19–20.
3. Zygmunt Bauman, *Modernity and the Holocaust* (New York, 1992).
4. Hansard (Commons), col. 362 (Bill No.131), 30 June 1999.
5. For a list of these groups, see David Cesarani, 'Seizing the Day: Why Britain Will Benefit from Holocaust Memorial Day', *Patterns of Prejudice*, Vol.34, No.4 (2000), pp.61–6, here p. 64.
6. For the works which have sparked the key debates, see Peter Novick, *The Holocaust in American Life* (New York, 1999); and especially Norman Finkelstein, *The Holocaust Industry: Reflections on the Exploitation of Jewish Suffering* (London, 2000).
7. 'Government Proposal for a Holocaust Remembrance Day' (Home Office Communications Directorate, Oct. 1999), pp.2–3.
8. For example, Saul Friedländer, *Nazi Germany and the Jews: The Years of Persecution, 1933–1939* (New York, 1997).
9. Yehuda Bauer, 'The Place of the Holocaust in Contemporary History', *Studies in Contemporary Jewry*, Vol.1 (1984), pp.201–24, here p.202.
10. As reproduced, for instance, in Frank Chalk, 'Redefining Genocide', in George J. Andreopoulos (ed.), *Genocide: Conceptual and Historical Dimensions* (Philadelphia, PA, 1994), pp.47–63, here p.48.
11. Raul Hilberg, *The Destruction of the European Jews* (New York, 1961).
12. For example, Reuben Ainsztein, review, *Jewish Observer and Middle East Review*, 16 March 1962, pp.26–7.
13. Donald Bloxham, *Genocide on Trial: War Crimes Trials in the Formation of Holocaust History and Memory* (Oxford, 2001), p.222.
14. Hilberg, *Destruction*, p.v.
15. Personal communication.
16. 'Government Proposal', p.1.
17. The Imperial War Museum's exhibition also fails to adduce any perpetrators with whom the visitor can identify. I thank Thomas Lawson for suggesting this point. See also Donald Bloxham and Tony Kushner, 'Exhibiting Racism: Cultural Imperialism, Genocide and Representation', *Rethinking History*, Vol.2, No.3 (1998), pp.349–58.
18. Gitta Sereny, *Into that Darkness: From Mercy Killing to Mass Murder* (New York, 1974).
19. Christopher Browning, *The Final Solution and the German Foreign Office: a Study of Referat D III of Abteilung Deutschland 1940–1943* (New York, 1991).
20. Christopher Browning, *Ordinary Men: Reserve Police Batallion 101 and the Final Solution in Poland* (New York, 1992). This book alone of the three actually appears in the bibliography attached to the education pack, but is not referred to in any of the exercises of the pack and its presence in the bibliography was at the suggestion of this author.
21. The obvious counter-case is presented in Daniel Jonah Goldhagen's highly simplistic and flawed, *Hitler's Willing Executioners: Ordinary Germans and the Holocaust* (London, 1997). For pointers to a wider body of far more sophisticated scholarship – much of which is sadly only in German – see Ulrich Herbert (ed.), *National Socialist Extermination Policies* (Oxford, 1999).
22. 'The Effects of Holocaust Education on Students' Level of Anti-Semitism: Results of a Two Year Analysis', forthcoming in *Journal of Holocaust Education*.
23. This argument was repeated by Dan Stone in his 'Day of Remembrance or Day of Forgetting? Or, Why Britain Does Not Need a Holocaust Memorial Day', *Patterns of Prejudice*, Vol.34, No.4 (2000), pp.53–9, here pp.57–8.
24. See the examples cited in ibid., p.58.
25. See, among many works by Mark Levene on this subject, 'A Moving Target, the Usual Suspects and (Maybe) a Smoking Gun: The Problem of Pinning Blame in Modern Genocide', *Patterns of Prejudice*, Vol.33, No.4 (1999), pp.3–24.
26. Of which more shortly. Here, see for example pp.15–19, section 'bystanders and rescuers' of the education pack for the first HMD (2001), which may be downloaded

Britain's Holocaust Memorial Days   61

from the internet at the following address: <www.holocaustmemorialday.gov.uk/archive/2001/sections/4/Edupack/edupack.pdf>

27. 'Holocaust Memorial Day: Britain and the Holocaust: Commemorative Programme, Bridgewater Hall', 27 Jan. 2002, p.5.
28. 'Government proposal', p.2: HMD 'supports the Government's commitment that all citizens – without distinction – should participate freely and fully in the economic, social and public life of the nation'.
29. Nechama Tec, *When Light Pierced the Darkness: Christian Rescue of Jews in Nazi-Occupied Poland* (New York, 1986).
30. Henri Rousso, *The Vichy Syndrome: History and Memory in France since 1944* (Cambridge, MA, 1991).
31. Tony Kushner, 'Reflections on Britain's Holocaust Memorial Day', paper presented at 'After Eichmann' conference, University of Southampton, April 2002.
32. For a recent statement of the British government's position, see Hansard (Commons), 30 Nov. 2000, cols. 916/7W. On the politics of non-recognition more generally, Vigen Guroian, 'Post-Holocaust Political Morality: The Litmus of Bitburg and the Armenian Genocide Resolution', *Holocaust and Genocide Studies*, Vol. 3, No.3 (1988), pp.305–22.
33. That genocide is the subject of the author's ongoing research project.
34. 'Britain and the Holocaust: Commemorative Programme', p.4.
35. As a general introduction to these subjects, I would draw the reader's attention to the parts on the Second World War of Mark Mazower's *Dark Continent: Europe's Twentieth Century* (Harmondsworth, 1998).
36. HMD 2001 education pack, p.8.
37. Ibid., pp.6–7.
38. Ibid., p.7.
39. Götz Aly and Suzanne Heim, *Vordenker der Vernichtung: Auschwitz und die deutschen Pläne für eine neue europäische Ordnung* (Frankfurt am Main, 1993); Götz Aly, *'Final Solution': Nazi Population Policy and the Murder of the European Jews* (London, 1999); Christian Gerlach, *Krieg, Ernährung, Völkermord: Forschungen zur deutschen Vernichtungspolitik im zweiten Weltkrieg* (Hamburg, 1998).
40. HMD 2001 education pack, pp.11–12, 20, 28.
41. Christian Streit, *Keine Kamaraden: Die Wehrmacht und die sowjetischen Kriegsgefangenen 1941–1945* (Stuttgart, 1981), is the classic analysis of the fate of the POWs. See also Gerlach, *Krieg, Ernährung, Völkermord* and Reinhard Otto, *Wehrmacht, Gestapo und sowjetische Kriegsgefangene im deutschen Reichsgebiete 1941/42* (Munich, 1998) for additional information and more recent references.
42. Richard Plant, *The Pink Triangle: the Nazi War against Homosexuals* (New York, 1986), p.154; see Donald Niewyk and Francis Nicosia (eds.), *The Columbia Guide to the Holocaust* (New York, 2000), p.50.
43. Rüdiger Lautmann, 'The Pink Triangle: Homosexuals as "Enemies of the State"', in Michael Berenbaum and Abraham Peck (eds.), *The Holocaust and History: the Known, the Unknown, the Disputed and the Reexamined* (Bloomington, IN, 1998), pp.345–57, which contrasts the persecution of homosexuals with the extermination of the Jews. It is this absence of exterminatory intent *vis-à-vis* homosexuals that undermines potential arguments for excluding the Slavs from the focus of the day. For while it may be that not every single Slav was slated for murder, and that different Slavic groups were treated differently, the Soviet populations and the Poles were to be subject to massive attrition, and beyond those who were murdered outright, the deaths of the remainder – aside from those slated for use as slave labour – was a matter of supreme indifference to the German leadership. This mindset was clearly racist.
44. 'Britain and the Holocaust: Commemorative Programme', p.4.
45. For some of these colossal estimates, see Niewyk and Nicosia, *The Columbia Guide to the Holocaust*, pp.49–50.
46. *The Guardian*, 26 Jan. 2000.
47. Hansard (Commons), col. 362, 30 June 1999.

48. 'Britain and the Holocaust: Commemorative Programme', p.1.
49. 'Government Proposal', p.2.
50. Personal communication.
51. Linda Colley, *Britons: Forging the Nation 1707—1837* (London, 1996).
52. Ibid.
53. This is an obsession which David Cesarani interprets as a sign that 'the British are very good at remembering', without considering that it may be indicative of a specific public need rather than a peculiarly British facility to recall the past in general. See Cesarani, 'Seizing the Day', pp.62–3.
54. 'Britain and the Holocaust: Commemorative Programme', p.1.

Holocaust Refugees in Great Britain and the Research Centre for German and Austrian Exile Studies in London

J.M. RITCHIE

By the time the war started in 1939 there were some 70,000 or 80,000 refugees from Germany, Austria and Czechoslovakia in Great Britain, and many thousands more had passed through on their way to exile in other countries. Yet despite the inevitable impact of such massive immigration Exile Studies were slow to start in this country. It will be the intention of the present study to show the steps which led to the establishment of a national Centre for German and Austrian Exile Studies in London and to give a description of the work of the Centre to date and of its plans for the future.

In J.M. Ritchie's article 'Willy Sternfeld and Exile Studies in Great Britain'[1] a brief indication was given of the slow start to Exile Studies in this country. Yet the fact that the academic study of the fates of refugees from National Socialism seeking asylum in this country was slow to develop does not mean that the increasing waves of refugees from 1933 onwards went unnoticed. Their impact was recorded in such studies as Norman Bentwich's *They Found Refuge*, Bernard Wasserstein's *Britain and the Jews of Europe*, Marion Berghahn's *Continental Britons*; the London German Historical Institute's collection of essays *Exile in Great Britain* and the Leo Baeck Institute's *Second Chance*.[2] But still Germanists in British universities were for a long while reluctant to take notice of such studies: certainly there was nothing in this country to compare with *German Literature in Exile after 1933* (Munich, 1976–94),[3] the existing parts of the planned eleven volume set of reference works on the German-speaking emigration to the United States of America put together over a long period by John Spalek and his teams of experts. So far four volumes of essays and four bibliographies in this series have been completed and published.

Yet it is perhaps not surprising that immigration into the United States, covering particularly literary and artistic immigration, should attract so much attention. There is a general awareness of the extent of German-speaking immigration into America in the nineteenth as well as the twentieth century, but a corresponding lack of awareness that – even though perhaps to a lesser degree – the same was true of German-speaking immigration into the British Isles. Britain in fact had enjoyed a fine liberal tradition as regards the granting of asylum in the nineteenth century, though this generous policy was modified shortly before and immediately after the First World War. In the nineteenth century Great Britain had experienced a flood of Jewish refugees escaping from the pogroms in Russia and elsewhere. In addition Germany had also been a source of many immigrants to Britain; indeed by the beginning of the twentieth century it was estimated that some 60,000 persons of German origin were living in London alone. Outside London there were similar but smaller German settlements. Bradford had its Little Germany and, as Neville David Ballin has shown in his study *For King or Kaiser?*,[4] even an industrial city such as Sheffield had seen an influx of German citizens.

All this changed, regrettably, following the First World War. The Aliens Restriction Act of 1919 and the Aliens Order of 1920 made it extremely difficult for any immigrants to gain entry to the United Kingdom without a work permit or a guarantee that they would not be a burden on the public purse. By the 1930s immigration had become even more difficult, and British treatment of refugees from Germany in particular had become part of the prevailing 'appeasement policy', characterized by a reluctance to intrude upon 'internal' German interests. Nevertheless, the British authorities did become aware of what the political implications of the coming to power of Adolf Hitler really were. Whereas in the early 1930s no emergency measures had been necessary, because those seeking asylum from Nazi Germany were few in number, by the end of the decade the numbers had greatly increased. British policy had been to regard the United Kingdom as a transit country for refugees, permitting entry in the expectation that those admitted would continue their emigration to another country, such as the United States of America. By May and June 1940, and faced with some 70,000 refugees who could not make their way elsewhere, a harsh programme of internment and/or deportation was introduced. All this was recorded at the time by two remarkable women, Yvonne Kapp and Margaret Mynatt. Unfortunately their book was not published then, though accepted by a leading publisher. While negotiations were still in progress Penguin published François Lafitte's

The Internment of Aliens[5] and it was thought that there was no need for a further book on the refugee problem. The manuscript then remained untouched and unread until nearly 30 years later. Since then, as Charmian Brinson records in the foreword to her edition of Kapp and Mynatt's *British Policy and the Refugees, 1933–1941*,[6] there has been a spate of books on the internment of aliens.

Some work was undertaken in the 1980s and 1990s in the area of Exile Studies in Britain, despite its slow start. Professor J.M. Ritchie had brought out his book *German Literature under National Socialism*,[7] which was in itself something of a departure since this was an area, like Exile Studies, which Germanists generally avoided. This book not only dealt with real Nazi literature, after a section on '1933–1945 – Inside Germany', it continued with a section entitled '1933–1945 – Outside Germany', covering German anti-fascists fighting in the Spanish Civil War and the fate and literary production of exiles world-wide. This left little space for a consideration of literary and other exiles in Great Britain, but still the significance of exile had been recognized. When in 1988 Ritchie moved from Sheffield University to return to his alma mater, King's College, Old Aberdeen, he was able to make good the failure to focus on exile in Great Britain by setting up a Research Centre for Germans and Austrians in Exile with this purpose in mind. In Aberdeen a group of postgraduates gathered to work on British exile problems. All of them completed their doctorates. Some indication of the work of this group can be found in the J.M. Ritchie Special Issue of *German Life and Letters* of 1992, which contains the following articles on exile:

'Caveat Editor: World War II, Exiles and Ha'p'orths of Tar', by G.P.G. Butler (University of Bath);
'In the Dark: Erich Fried's Portrayal of Austria' by Steven W. Lawrie;
'"Zur Begleitmusik von Hitlers Bombern": The German-language newspaper *Die Zeitung* in War-time London (1941–1945)', by Donal McLaughlin (Heriot Watt University);
'A Hard Life: Martina Wied in Exile', by Audrey Milne (University of Aberdeen);
'The French Exile of René Schickele and Ernst Erich Noth', by Eric Robertson (University of London);
'Oskar Kokoschka's Attitude to his Host Country During his Exile in Great Britain', by Margaret Stone (University of Aberdeen);
'Exil oder zweite Heimat? Peter de Mendelssohn in London (1936–1970)', by Waltraud Strickhausen;
'Tenochtitlan, Time, Transit: Anna Seghers's Novel of Exile', by J.K.A. Thomaneck (University of Aberdeen).[8]

Steven Lawrie, whose dissertation was published as *Erich Fried: A Writer Without a Country*[9] in the American exile series 'Austrian Culture', remained in Aberdeen as recently as 2002 as a lecturer in the University of Aberdeen's German Department and continued with his exile researches. Donal McLaughlin, the post-doctoral research fellow in the Aberdeen Research Centre, moved to Heriot-Watt University, where he continued his work on the Austrian poet Stella Rotenberg, who still lives in exile in Leeds.

In September 1990, McLaughlin organized a conference which brought together some 50 scholars from around the world to Aberdeen. This exile symposium was successful because of the co-operation of a group of exile researchers from London, and also because of the presence and support of Siglinde Bolbecher and Konstantin Kaiser from the Theodor Kramer Gesellschaft in Vienna. This society bears the name of the Austrian poet, Theodor Kramer (1879–1958), who was in exile in London for 18 years. It publishes the quarterly *Mit der Ziehharmonika. Zeitschrift für Literatur des Exils und des Widerstands* (now re-named *Zwischenwelt*) and a series of yearbooks dedicated to exile and anti-fascist issues world-wide. After some time, during which further information and background material was being gathered, the Theodor Kramer Gesellschaft published *Literatur und Kultur des Exils in Großbritannien*,[10] recording in extended form the papers presented at the Aberdeen symposium. In many respects these papers reflected not only many of the past difficulties of exile research in Great Britain, but also many of the new directions Exile Studies were to take in the future, namely close co-operation between the Aberdeen Research Centre and the London Exile Group formally created after the Aberdeen symposium; the link with the Leo Baeck Institute, through the presence of its Director, Arnold Paucker, who gave a key-note address on 'History in Exile: Writing the Story of German Jewry'; and the recognition of the particular importance of Austrian immigration into Great Britain.

Shortly thereafter the importance of immigration from Austria into Great Britain in the 1930s and 1940s was further underlined by the decision of Professor Edward Timms (Director of the Centre for German-Jewish Studies at the University of Sussex) and Professor Ritchie Robertson (of St John's College, Oxford) to devote a complete number of their *Austrian Studies* series to this topic. The volume edited by them appeared as *Austrian Exodus: The Creative Achievements of Refugees from National Socialism*.[11] The fact that Exile Studies was beginning to arouse interest in traditional Germanistic circles was further indicated by the fact that the editors of the long-established journal of German studies, *German Life and Letters*, decided to devote a special issue to this topic. This special number, which appeared in April 1998, was subsequently published as a book: *The Legacy of Exile: Lives, Letters, Literature*, edited by Deborah Vietor-Engländer.[12]

Deborah, herself the child of refugee parents from Prague who settled in Britain, put together an impressive collection of essays which included contributions by four outstanding German-American scholars, Guy Stern (Wayne State University, Detroit), Alexander Stephan (University of Florida), Jost Hermand (University of Wisconsin, Madison) and Dagmar Lorenz (Ohio State University). Guy Stern's essay, 'The Americanisation of Günther', reveals how he escaped from Nazi Germany, while his family did not. Stern went on to become a distinguished professor and exile researcher in the USA. The volume also contains contributions by Inge Jens (Tübingen) on Thomas Mann's exile diary, and Helmut Müssener (University of Stockholm) on German-language exiles in Scandinavia. Professor Ritchie contributed an essay on Kurt Hiller, the most famous polemicist of the Weimar Republic, who was in exile in London from 1934 until 1945; Charmian Brinson an essay on 'German-speaking Women in Exile in Britain, 1933–1945', while Anthony Grenville wrote on 'The Earliest Reception of the Holocaust: Ernst Sommer's *Revolte der Heiligen*'.

While the academic discipline of Exile Studies was starting up in Scotland, a similar development had been taking place in England and, as already indicated, by 1990 a London Research Group for German Exile Studies had been founded. This group brought out the volume *Between Two Languages: German-speaking Exiles in Great Britain 1933–45*, edited by Charmian Brinson, Marian Malet, Jennifer Taylor and Richard Dove.[13] The three sections in this volume – 'Alerting the English', 'Crossing the Language Barrier', and 'German for Germans' – give a clear indication of the ground covered, namely contemporary attempts to make the British public aware of the Nazi threat; and, on the one hand the problem of language change whereby immigrant intellectuals and writers had to face up to the need to communicate with the British public in English rather than in German; on the other hand the demand for up-to-date reading material in German in Britain for the exiled German-speaking immigrants.

To meet this need newspapers were established, such as the British-government sponsored paper *Die Zeitung*, the Austrian *Zeitspiegel* and the Czech/German paper *Einheit*. The contributions in *Between Two Languages* by Charmian Brinson and Marian Malet on *Die Zeitung* and by Jennifer Taylor on *Einheit* show the value of such newspapers in wartime Britain as source material for exile research. Detailed study of the Austrian *Zeitspiegel* is at present being undertaken by Jennifer Taylor for the current Austrian Centre Project on this topic. Also of particular value in Brinson's edited volume was the essay by W. Abbey, the Librarian of the Institute of Germanic Studies in London on 'The German PEN Group and the English Centre 1933–45', not only because of the subject itself – the position of PEN in relation to the German-language writers in exile from National Socialism – but also because of the author's position as Librarian of the Institute of Germanic Studies, the future home of the national Research Centre for German and Austrian Exile Studies. This library was also to become the home of the Ritchie Collection of exile books.

At about this time, in the mid-1990s, Exile Studies gained a new ally in Professor Ian Wallace of the University of Bath. Through a long-standing association with Rodopi, the Dutch publishers, Wallace was able to put together and publish another volume of exile essays, *Aliens: Uneingebürgerte: German and Austrian Writers in Exile*.[14] In his preface Professor Wallace sums up his intentions as follows:

> The exiling of so many German and Austrian writers after the Fascist take-over of power in 1933 may be seen as a vitally important part of 'the greatest collection of transplanted intellect, talent, and scholarship the world has ever seen' (Peter Gay). Hardly surprisingly, it is a subject which intrigues and horrifies in turn as scholars continue the process of improving our knowledge and understanding of a literature which achieved a precarious survival despite being torn from its cultural roots. The aim of the present volume is to make a contribution to this process.

As Wallace goes on to explain, some of the writers selected for study – for instance, Anna Seghers, Arnold Zweig, Johannes R. Becher, Gustav Regler, Lion Feuchtwanger, Ernst Glaeser and F.T. Csokor – while significant literary figures in their own right, have little or no connection with the experience of exile in Great Britain. Gustav Regler, for example, is remembered primarily for his novel *The Great Crusade* about the Spanish Civil War, while the name of Lion Feuchtwanger, one of the most successful of all German writers of this period, immediately conjures up associations with his earlier novel *Jew Süß* and the ensuing film versions of it, one British and philo-Semitic and the other Nazi and viciously anti-Semitic. However, the final chapters of this volume *are* concerned with writers who spent their exile years in Great Britain, an indication, as Professor Wallace puts it, of the growing interest in exile literature among British scholars. Not surprisingly the

Austrian poet Theodor Kramer, living in exile in England, figures again in Wallace's collection in an essay by Axel Goodbody of the University of Bath, as do German-language exile newspapers in an essay by Donal McLaughlin entitled 'Women Only? The Feuilleton of *Die Zeitung*'.

The spirit of co-operation established at the Aberdeen symposium reached its fruition on 8 November 1995. On this date, a meeting of the board of the Institute of Germanic Studies at the University of London approved a proposal to set up and locate a national Research Centre for German and Austrian Exile Studies at the Institute, bringing together the London Research Group for Exile Studies founded in 1990 and the Research Centre for Germans and Austrians in Exile in Great Britain at the University of Aberdeen. Professor Ritchie had retired from Aberdeen and that university's German Department had decided not to continue with the Exile Centre. From the beginning, the aims of the new national centre were formulated very clearly, namely to focus on the history of those German-speaking émigrés who had found refuge in Great Britain, on their personal recollections and experiences, their reception in British society, and their enrichment of the life of their new country of residence in such varied spheres as the professions, industry and commerce, literature, art and culture, politics, publishing, the media and the world of entertainment and leisure. The concept of German-speaking exiles was taken to extend to those who came from the then Czechoslovakia, Hungary, Poland and other European countries, as well as from Germany and Austria. Clearly the main focus of the centre would be on those émigrés who came to Britain in the 1930s and 1940s, but the centre also declared its intention to embrace the important group of émigrés who had arrived in the nineteenth century and earlier. Karl Marx was by no means alone in London in the second half of the nineteenth century.

Following its foundation in November 1995, when the new research centre was given its base in the Institute, the year 1996–97 was one of both achievement and consolidation. The Committee of the Centre was established, consisting of Professor J.M. Ritchie as Chairman; the Director and Deputy Director of the Institute of Germanic Studies; Dr M. Malet, Dr J. Taylor, Dr R. Dove, Dr C. Brinson; and Dr A. Grenville as Honorary Secretary. Professor Ian Wallace was also welcomed as a committee member. The Centre was also very fortunate in the appointment, funded through the Institute, of a Development Officer, Mrs Bridget Knapper, who started work in January 1997 and who began developing a strategic plan for raising funds for the Centre, for raising its public profile and for widening its range of contacts and potential supporters. A number of colleagues working in the field of exile studies, principally younger scholars, were invited to become Associate Members, again through the Institute.

In September 1996 a three-day conference was held at the Institute under the title '"Hitler's Gift to Britain": German and Austrian Exiles in Great Britain 1933–1945'. This was very well attended, and participants enjoyed a reception at the Austrian Cultural Centre as well as the academic papers read. The proceedings of the conference enjoyed the generous support of the Institute of Germanic Studies, the Goethe Institute and of the Leo Baeck Institute, whose director Arnold Paucker gave one of the opening addresses. The proceedings were published as *'England? Aber wo liegt es?': deutsche und österreichische Emigranten in Großbritannien 1933–1945*, edited by Charmian Brinson, Richard Dove, Marian Malet and Jennifer Taylor.[15] Apart from contributions on exile writers in Britain such as Anna Gmeyner, Franz Baermann Steiner, Stefan Zweig, Robert Neumann, Bert Brecht and Richard Friedenthal, the volume contains papers on the German evangelical parishes in Britain and their treatment of 'non-aryan' refugees; the psychiatrist Wilhelm Stekel; the British Academic Community and university refugees from Germany; German pacifists in exile; Otto Lehmann-Rußbueldt; and much more. Work in Progress seminars held in 1996 and 1997 included one given by Dr Karola Decker of the Wellcome Foundation, Oxford, entitled, 'Refugee Doctors in Great Britain'; and one by Dr Anthony Grenville on 'The Wartime Reception of the Holocaust in Works by Ernst Sommer and Anna Seghers'.

At about this time members of the Centre began co-operating on an Oral History Project, involving interviews with 34 former refugees, and writing a book based on the interviews. Planning and preliminary work also started shortly thereafter for the next collaborative project involving members, namely a study of the Austrian Centre, probably the largest organization set up for German-speaking refugees in London in the wartime years. The Ritchie Collection of books on Exile Studies, which had earlier been deposited in the Institute, was now being shelved separately on the third floor of the Institute; it was being professionally catalogued and additions were being made to it. The Research Centre's second year was one of consolidation and of continuation of the activities begun in the first year. The book based on the Centre's Oral History interviews with former refugees from Hitler in Great Britain, entitled *Home from Home?*, was now substantially complete, while Charmian Brinson published her book *The Strange Case of Dora Fabian and Mathilde Wurm: A Study of German Political Exiles during the 1930's*.[16]

Work in Progress seminars held during 1997 and 1998 included a paper by Professor Lucio Sponza (University of Westminster) on Italian internees in Britain in the Second World War; one by Joanna Labon (Birkbeck) entitled 'At Home Among Exiles: The Novelist Storm Jameson and Her Presidency of the PEN Club (1938–1945)'; another by Marion Hamm (Tübingen) called 'Spaces of Memory: Collective Memory Around German-speaking Jewish Refugees from German Fascism in Contemporary London'. The work of the Centre was crowned in 1997 by the award of one of the British Academy's Larger Research Grants to carry out its study of the Austrian Centre in London, 1939–47. In the *Institute of Germanic Studies Newsletter* for 2000, Richard Dove has given a brief picture of the significance of the London-based Austrian Centre and of what this first full-length study of it aims to do:

> Founded in March 1939, when the stream of Austrian refugees arriving in Britain was reaching its peak, it was wound up in January 1947, as many of its activists were returning to Austria, while others had chosen to settle and assimilate into British society. Set up to represent the interests of Austrian refugees in Britain, the Centre focused primarily on relief work and quickly developed into a comprehensive social, cultural and political organisation. In 1940 it campaigned against the internment of 'enemy aliens'. With the entry of the Soviet Union into the war in June 1941, the Centre was able to pursue a more overtly political agenda, playing an influential role in moves to establish the Free Austrian Movement (FAM) which campaigned for the post-war restoration of a democratic and independent Austrian state. By this time the Austrian Centre had three bases in London, one in Glasgow, as well as several provincial branches. The Centre at Westbourne Terrace comprised a restaurant and a library/reading room, and promoted a wide range of cultural activities, both directly and through its affiliated youth organisations. It produced the weekly newspaper *Zeitspiegel* with a circulation of some 3,000, and also published a wide range of books and pamphlets under several imprints ('Free Austrian Books', 'Jugend voran', etc.). The premises at 69 Eton Avenue housed the 'Laterndl' theatre, which from June 1941 to June 1945 produced a regular programme of plays and revues, featuring well-known actors and directors. The Centre also sponsored a regular musical programme of concerts and choral performances, the aim of these activities being not only to satisfy the cultural aspirations of Austrian refugees, but also to establish a specific Austrian cultural identity: a conscious correlative to the political agenda pursued more overtly through other organisations.

The project's objective is to investigate the interaction of politics and culture in the situation of exile in Britain. Some early results are contained in the article 'Free Austrian Books' published in the first issue of the Centre's Yearbook.[17]

The last two years of the century saw a significant raising of the Research Centre's profile, when from 19 to 21 March 1999 the Research Centre collaborated with the Austrian Cultural Institute in London and the German *Gesellschaft für Exilforschung* in hosting this Society's annual general meeting. The conference, entitled 'Die sichere Insel? Soziale und kulturelle Integration der Emigranten aus Mitteleuropa in Großbritannien', was held under the auspices of the University of London's School of Advanced Study at Senate House. During the conference, participants had the opportunity to visit both the Wiener Library and the Austrian Cultural Institute where an exhibition 'Fluchtpunkt England' had been arranged by Dr Reinhard Müller of the University of Graz.

For the conference Professor Ritchie prepared a booklet based on the catalogue edited and designed by Dr Müller for the exhibition of the same material in the Graz University Library.[18] The objects on display in the exhibition at the London Austrian Cultural Institute came from the holdings of the Archive for the History of Sociology in Austria and from the libraries and estates of Hans Winterberg and Friedrich Otto Hertz. These holdings can be studied in the Archive for the History of Sociology in Austria in the Institut für Soziologie, Karl Franzens-Universität in Graz, which also has a complete list of the library of Hans Winterberg. The exhibition was dedicated to the memory of David Herzog (1869–1946), Professor of Semitic Languages at the University of Graz, who found refuge in Great Britain in 1938 and died there in exile. Papers given at the conference covered a wide range of exile experience. The German-American scholar, Professor Alexander Stephan, long recognized as one of the leading researchers in Exile on the strength of works like *Die deutsche Exilliteratur 1933–1945* and *Anna Seghers im Exil. Essays, Texte, Dokumente* (Bonn, 1993),[19] gave a paper devoted to the influence of the German Foreign Office in wartime on its representatives in London and their attitude to Germans in exile in Britain.

There were further papers on the Fight for Freedom Publishing Company; internment camp newspapers; the Free Austrian Movement; the pioneering work of German photographers in Britain; the Capitol Film Corporation and also Alfred Kerr's London exile. Papers followed on the Catholic social philosopher Johannes Messner;

on Esther Simpson and the Society for the Protection of Science and Learning; on Austrian economic and social historians in English exile; on the Viennese lawyer Friedrich Schnek; on Magda Kelber; on Michael Hamburger's work for the BBC; and on Silvia Rodgers' *Red Saint, Pink Daughter*. Tony Grenville, the secretary of the Centre, gave a paper on the development of community identity as conveyed in the early issues of the *Association of Jewish Refugees Information, 1946–50*. It was agreed that a range of these papers be published in Exile Yearbook Three.[20] Work in Progress seminars held during the year included a paper by Monica Lowenberg (University of Sussex) entitled '"The Last of My Line": Life History Work with a Holocaust Survivor'; and another by Richard Dove (University of Greenwich): '"Die Zeit gibt die Bilder": Representation and Misrepresentation in Stefan Zweig's *Die Welt von Gestern*'.

The proceedings of the conference 'Hitler's Gift to Britain', held at the Institute in September 1996, were published as *Keine Klage über England? Deutsche und österreichische Exilerfahrungen in Großbritannien 1933–1945*.[21] The title of the published volume came from the words of the Austrian writer, Hilde Spiel, who had 'no complaints about England', an opinion not shared by all refugees. Likewise, the conference title 'Hitler's Gift to Britain' caused some controversy. The original intention had been to show what the contributions of these immigrants had been to British society in all the various spheres of science and technology, architecture, economics, the creative arts of design, theatre, film literature and so on. Instead, in some quarters, the title 'Hitler's Gift to Britain' gave offence – some refugees felt it implied that they, as worthy citizens of Germany and Austria who were forced into exile, had somehow been worthless people Hitler was glad to be rid of. Thus a decision was taken to change the wording for the title of the book. It was also the intention of the conference to focus on the importance of women's experience in exile, which certainly comes through in the published volume of conference proceedings.

The highlight of the session 1999/2000 for the Centre was Ian Wallace's edited volume *German-Speaking Exiles in Great Britain*, the first issue of the Yearbook of the Research Centre for German and Austrian Exile Studies.[22] The Yearbook is the first academic journal devoted to the subject of German-speaking exiles in Great Britain, and it aims to establish itself as the leading publication in its field. Volume 2 of the Yearbook, edited by Anthony Grenville, came out in 2000. Volume 3 will make available the proceedings of the conference of the *Gesellschaft für Exilforschung*, held at Senate House, University of London in March 1999. Work on the Oral History Project is completed, and a book based on it was published as *Changing Countries: The Experience and Achievement of German-Speaking Exiles from Hitler in Britain, from 1933 to Today*, edited by M. Malet and A. Grenville.[23] Based on 34 extensive interviews with ex-refugees from Germany, Austria and Czechoslovakia, it analyses their pre-emigration backgrounds; their move to Britain; everyday life in Great Britain after arrival and in the war; internment and life as 'enemy aliens'; religious issues; relations with the Heimat; and settling down in the post-war period.

Work in Progress seminars held during 1999–2000 included Dr Jennifer Taylor (London) speaking on '"Nation Shall Speak Peace unto Nation" or "Drop the Dead Donkey"? Some Thoughts on BBC Radio Propaganda During the Second World War'; and Dr Marian Malet (London) on 'Artists and the Austrian Centre'. These seminars continued in 2001 with Elizabeth Welt Trahan (the author of *Walking with Ghosts: A Jewish Childhood in Wartime Vienna*) speaking on 'Evidence, Memory, Perspective – Reflections of a Holocaust Survivor'; and Dr Ursula Hudson-Wiedenmann's paper 'From Hael (Berlin) to Greta Pottery (Stoke-on-Trent): A "New Woman's" Exile in Great Britain'.

Jennifer Taylor's paper on the BBC and radio propaganda led into one aspect of future developments for the Research Centre, as it planned a major international conference to mark the end of 60 years of the BBC World Service's German-language broadcasts in March 1999. The German-language broadcasts were an essential part of the BBC's contribution to the war effort against Nazi Germany; they also involved many notable figures from British political and literary life and from the BBC itself, as well as drawing on the German-speaking refugees from Germany, Austria and Czechoslovakia who had found refuge in Britain. After the war, the influence of the BBC on the broadcasting organizations in Germany was great, in terms both of personal connections and of institutional values and structures. Over the decades, the BBC's German-language service remained a respected voice for its dedicated band of listeners, often reaching opinion-formers out of proportion to its numbers. 'Stimme der Wahrheit': A Conference on the German-language Broadcasting of the BBC World Service was held at the Centre in September 2002.

While members of the Research Centre for Exile Studies had been much involved in collaborative research such as the Oral History Project and the Austrian Centre Project, individual work also went ahead. J.M. Ritchie published his *German Exiles/British Perspectives* as volume six of the interdisciplinary series of Exile Studies edited by Alexander Stephan, and the 'Exil in Großbritannien' section in the vast

Handbuch des Exiltheaters 1933–45.[24] Professor Dove followed up his extremely successful Ernst Toller studies *I was a German* and its German edition *Ein Leben in Deutschland*, with his *Journey of No Return: Five German-Speaking Literary Exiles in Britain 1933–1945*.[25] Anthony Grenville, the secretary of the Research Centre, has principal research interests in the literature and history of the Weimar Republic, as shown by his *Cockpit of Ideologies: The Literature and Political History of the Weimar Republic*, and, more recently has devoted his attention to German-speaking refugees from Hitler in Great Britain and German-Jewish culture in exile. This is reflected, for example, in Grenville's essay, 'The Integration of Aliens: The Early Years of *The Association of Jewish Refugees Information*, 1946–50', *Yearbook of the Research Centre for German and Austrian Exile Studies*.[26]

Since the publication of her major study, *The Strange Case of Dora Fabian and Mathilde Wurm*, Charmian Brinson has produced a whole series of publications on exile topics, and then focused on researching the many thousands of German-speaking women in exile in Britain, 1933–45, their life and work, including the wartime internment of some 4,000. Marian Malet has done considerable research on Irmgard and Hans Litten. The former's exile in Britain was very much devoted to publicising the treatment meted out to political prisoners as exemplified by the fate of her son Hans in Nazi prisons and concentration camps. Dr Malet has also researched Austrian artists in wartime Britain. Jennifer Taylor, who had previously demonstrated her interest in immigration from Czechoslovakia in her article 'Stimmen aus Böhmen. Die deutschsprachige literarische Emigration aus der Tschechoslowakei in Großbritannien nach 1938: Rudolf Fuchs, Ernst Sommer und Ludwig Winder' in *Drehscheibe Prag. Zur deutschen Emigration in der Tschechoslowakei 1933–1939*; edited by Peter Becher and Peter Houmos, also published 'Hans Vogel, the Flight of the Exiled German Social Democrats from France, 1940–41, and the British Labour Party' in the *Yearbook of the Research Centre for German and Austrian Exile Studies*;[27] a study of the work of the Prague-born editor and author Grete Fischer in exile in Great Britain in *Keine Klage über England?*, and has been working on Grete Fischer and Bruno Adler's propaganda work for the BBC.

In conclusion, altogether it can be seen that after a slow start for Exile Studies in Great Britain a great deal of catching up has been accomplished, some good work is in the pipeline and some very valuable research projects are near completion. The future looks brighter than the past.

NOTES

1. J.M. Ritchie, 'Willy Sternfeld and Exile Studies in Great Britain', *Immigrants & Minorities*, Vol.15, No.2 (1996), pp.120–34.
2. Norman Bentwich, *They Found Refuge: An Account of British Jewry's Work for Victims of the Nazis* (London, 1956); Bernard Wasserstein, *Britain and the Jews of Europe* (Oxford, 1979); Marion Berghahn, *Continental Britons: German-Jewish Refugees in England* (Oxford, 1984); the London German Historical Institute's collection of essays *Exile in Great Britain: Refugees from Hitler's Germany* (London, 1984) and the Leo Baeck Institute's *Second Chance: Two Centuries of German-speaking Jews in the United Kingdom* (Tübingen, 1991).
3. John Spalek, *et al.* (eds.), *German Literature in Exile after 1933* (Munich, 1976–94).
4. David Ballin, *For King or Kaiser? The Life of Sir Joseph Jonas, Lord Mayor of Sheffield* (Sheffield, 1998).
5. François Lafitte, *The Internment of Aliens* (Harmondsworth, 1940).
6. Kapp and Mynatt, *British Policy and the Refugees, 1933-1941* (London, 1997).
7. J.M. Ritchie, *German Literature under National Socialism* (Beckenham, 1983).
8. G.P.G. Butler, 'Caveat Editor: World War II, Exiles and Ha'p'orths of Tar', pp.226–9; Steven W. Lawrie, 'In the Dark: Erich Fried's Portrayal of Austria', pp.230–33; Donal McLaughlin, '"Zur Begleitmusik von Hitlers Bombern": The German-Language Newspaper *Die Zeitung* in Wartime London (1941–1945)', pp.234–8; Audrey Milne, 'A Hard Life: Martina Wied in Exile', pp.239–43; Eric Robertson, 'The French Exile of René Schickele and Ernst Erich Noth', pp.244–8; Margaret Stone, 'Oskar Kokoschka's Attitude to his Host Country During His Exile in Great Britain', pp.249–53; Waltraud Strickhausen, 'Exil oder zweite Heimat? Peter de Mendelssohn in London (1936–1970)', pp.254–60; J.K.A. Thomaneck, 'Tenochtitlan, Time, Transit: Anna Seghers's Novel of Exile', pp.261–7, all in *German Life and Letters*, Vol.XLV, No.3 (1992).
9. Steven Lawrie, *Erich Fried: A Writer Without a Country* (New York, 1996).
10. Siglinde Bolbecher, Konstantin Kaiser, Donal McLaughlin, J.M. Ritchie (eds.), *Literatur und Kultur des Exils in Großbritannien* (Vienna, 1995).
11. Ritchie Robertson and Edward Timms (eds.), *Austrian Exodus: The Creative Achievements of Refugees from National Socialism* (Edinburgh, 1995).
12. Deborah Vietor-Engländer (ed.), *The Legacy of Exile: Lives, Letters, Literature* (Oxford, 1998).
13. Charmian Brinson, Marian Malet, Jennifer Taylor and Richard Dove (eds.), *Between Two Languages: German-Speaking Exiles in Great Britain 1933–45* (Stuttgart, 1995).
14. Ian Wallace (ed.), *Aliens: Uneingebürgerte: German and Austrian Writers in Exile* (Amsterdam, 1994).
15. Charmian Brinson, Richard Dove, Marian Malet and Jennifer Taylor (eds.), *'England? Aber wo liegt es?': deutsche und österreichische Emigranten in Großbritannien 1933–1945* (Munich, 1996) (Publications of the Institute of Germanic Studies, Vol.64).
16. Charmian Brinson, *The Strange Case of Dora Fabian and Mathilde Wurm: A Study of German Political Exiles during the 1930's* (Publications of the Institute of Germanic Studies Vol.67) (Berne, 1997)
17. Richard Dove, *Institute of Germanic Studies Newsletter*, 2000.
18. J.M. Ritchie, *Destination England. Austrian Exile in Great Britain 1938–1945* (London, 1999).
19. Alexander Stephan, *Die deutsche Exilliteratur 1933–1945* (Munich, 1979); *Anna Seghers im Exil: Essays, Texte, Dokumente* (Bonn, 1993).
20. J.M. Ritchie (ed.), *Yearbook of the Research Centre for German and Austrian Exile Studies*, Vol.3 (Amsterdam and New York, 2001).
21. Charmian Brinson, Richard Dove, Anthony Grenville, Marian Malet and Jennifer Taylor (eds.), *'Keine Klage über England? Deutsche und österreichische Exilerfahrungen in Großbritannien 1933–1945* (London and Munich, 1998).
22. Ian Wallace (ed.), *German-Speaking Exiles in Great Britain*, Yearbook of the Research Centre for German and Austrian Exile Studies Vol.1 (Amsterdam, 1999).

23. Marian Malet and Anthony Grenville (eds.), *Changing Countries: The Experience and Achievement of German-Speaking Exiles from Hitler in Britain, from 1933 to Today* (London, 2002).
24. J.M. Ritchie, *German Exiles/British Perspectives*, Exile Studies, Vol.VI (New York, 1997); 'Exil in Großbritannien' in Frithjof Trapp et al. (eds.), *Handbuch des Exiltheaters 1933–45* (Munich, 1999).
25. Richard Dove, *I Was a German* (London, 1990); *Ein Leben in Deutschland* (Göttingen, 1993); *Journey of No Return: Five German-Speaking Literary Exiles in Britain 1933–1945* (London, 2000).
26. Anthony Grenville, *Cockpit of Ideologies: The Literature and Political History of the Weimar Republic* (British and Irish Studies in German Language and Literature, Vol.11) (Berne, 1995); 'The Integration of Aliens: The Early Years of *The Association of Jewish Refugees Information, 1946–50'*, *Yearbook of the Research Centre for German and Austrian Exile Studies*, Vol.1 (Amsterdam, 1999), pp.1–23.
27. Jennifer Taylor, 'Stimmen aus Böhmen. Die deutschsprachige literarische Emigration aus der Tschechoslowakei in Großbritannien nach 1938: Rudolf Fuchs, Ernst Sommer und Ludwig Winder', in Peter Becher and Peter Houmos (eds.), *Drehscheibe Prag: Zur deutschen Emigration in der Tschechoslowakei 1933–1939* (Munich, 1992), pp.165–80; 'Hans Vogel, the Flight of the Exiled German Social Democrats from France, 1940–41, and the British Labour Party', *Yearbook of the Research Centre for German and Austrian Exile Studies*, Vol.2 (2000), pp.123–42.

Film

4

Fiction of the Real: Shoah *and Documentary*

BRYAN BURNS

Claude Lanzmann undertook his Holocaust film, *Shoah*, which appeared after ten years of preparation, in 1985, with a well-developed sense of the difficulties of the enterprise. He had seen fictional films on the subject, as well as the American teledrama of 1978 which attempts to present the Holocaust using the techniques of Hollywood, and which he despised. He also knew the work of Modernist documentarists such as Frederick Wiseman and treatments of the Holocaust like Alain Resnais' *Night and Fog* (*Nuit et Brouillard*), a brief, historically eclectic film of 1955 in which the director, making considerable use of stills and also of some contemporary footage, dramatically sets images of the extermination camps in the past, shot in black and white, against shots of the same locations today, shot in colour.

But the cinematic possibilities offered by neither fiction nor documentary quite suited Lanzmann. He was not trained in the making of fiction films, and was suspicious of their manipulative freedom and of the fact that they could be so little restrained by historical truth. Lanzmann's background was in works of witness, where found materials are shaped so as to produce meaning and the aim is for the finished film to contribute, with other documents, to debates within society. *Shoah* is certainly a work of witness, and certainly intervenes in controversies (especially in Poland). But if it is a documentary film of the Holocaust, it is a rather strange one.

It is set entirely in the present, not in the past; it consists principally of scenes in which survivors of the Holocaust simply tell their stories to Lanzmann, often via an interpreter; it is largely devoid of the expected, almost the necessary, images and tropes of the Holocaust film, though we *are* shown the familiar rail-entrance to Auschwitz through which so many Jews and others went to their deaths; it mentions hardly one well-known name – indeed, Lanzmann himself, and the historian Raul

Hilberg whom he interviews, may be the most famous figures in the whole work; it focuses on tiny details – the words that the Nazis assigned to describe the bodies of dead Jews, the exact procedures involved in the disinterring, burning and disposal of these bodies – rather than on grand statements, and privileges individual rather than collective responses; and it is always, it seems narrowly, concerned with *how* rather than *why* the Holocaust occurred.

In addition, it is a demanding nine-and-a-half hours long, whereas many documentaries, such as Resnais', are short. Even more than this, though, Lanzmann admits that his materials are not all found: he arranged for the Polish train-driver, Gawkowski, to drive a rented train along a specially re-opened track to Treblinka, thus mimicking the work he had done during the war; and in Tel Aviv he persuaded Abraham Bomba out of retirement and filmed the aggressive but moving scene with him in a specially rented barber's shop. *Shoah* seems, therefore, to have documentary elements, though not exactly those we might anticipate, and also fictional elements, though these are unannounced and often subtle. It mingles genres and disturbs conventions perhaps more than any other Holocaust film, and does this from its first moments and throughout.

Shoah begins by recording Lanzmann's thanks to his collaborators and then passes to a long, carefully circumstanced and entirely verbal introduction to the materials of the film, paying attention to facts rather than opinions, showing an acute eye for details which are not usually the stuff of history, and relayed in austere white on black and in complete silence. Thus are we acclimatized from the start to *Shoah*'s unique slowness and deliberation and its recognition that only words, not images, now remain of its primary subject. In fact, the procedure of the film is regularly to set words relating to the past against images relating to the present, and to encourage us to derive meaning from this conjunction. Appropriately, we acquire a sense not of the general sweep of the Holocaust, but of the extraordinariness of the escape of particular figures such as Simon Srebnik and Mordechai Podchlebnik, Lanzmann's splendidly chosen first survivors, from seemingly inevitable annihilation.

The film's first, slow, dramatized act, which gives an impression of the difficulty or pain of what is being attempted, is to present Srebnik, an uneasy, hesitant man of 47, boating on the river at Chelmno and singing a Polish song as he did in his childhood for members of the SS. The scene is quiet and unassuming, but resonant: the boat passes tree-

Fiction of the Real: Shoah and Documentary

trunks which stand like portals into another world, that of the past; the song is about remembering, and prepares us, as music often does in the cinema, for a movement into the realm of memory; and the river is that of life in general, but also relates to Srebnik's individual life. An unidentified Polish speaker authenticates Srebnik's past, the words given weight and rendered in full, as they constantly are in this film, rather than being conveniently elided into French or English. Srebnik himself continues apart, tracked on the river in a way which implies his centrality and continuance as against the rapid rushing by of the landscape of the past in which he now again surprisingly finds himself. He seems to float magically across the water, as if uninvolved in this tranquil but once terrible setting. Later, however, as with the other survivors whom he studies, Lanzmann will contrive to break Srebnik's impassivity and recall to him in the present the horror of his earlier life.

This process begins with a sudden, oneiric cut to Srebnik walking in a featureless wooded landscape, tracked again as he looks questioningly from side to side while avoiding direct engagement with the eye of the camera. Srebnik takes a well-defined path, as before he followed a river, in each case giving the lie to his apparent new unfetteredness. The movement of the camera is halting and uncertain, to suggest the anguish of the voyage it records. When Srebnik stops and begins to speak it is in a clearing in the woods almost ironically devoid of evident significance: just grass, a few straight lines of masonry and pine-trees in the distance. Yet, as he says, this is the place where thousands of people were burned. A very slow pan around the empty scene gives us time to try to reinterpret it in the light of the words we have just heard, to arouse our imaginations sufficiently to recreate 'das Platz' as it once was. As if in recognition of the extreme difficulty of this task, the camera constantly returns to Srebnik, the only tangible link that now exists between the present and the past.

So far, this introductory section of *Shoah* has demonstrated the themes and procedures of the film, and indicated how extremely problematic (in fact, how *impossible*) Lanzmann's enterprise will be. Absence and inference are central to *Shoah*, and contribute to the difficulty we (like his characters) will have in putting together and assimilating the materials presented to us. Now the camera tracks Srebnik from behind as he admits, 'No one can describe it', thus confirming the artistic rationale of a work which cannot honestly offer description or recreation, but instead must content itself with putative evocation. Then from afar we see Srebnik following yet another foreordained path, that of the foundation-stones leading off into the distance, and hear his comment that during his adolescence it was peaceful in that spot just as it is in his maturity. The exposition ends with another sudden cut returning us to the river, where we see Srebnik on a boat once more, but in long-shot rather than close-up, singing in German rather than Polish and moving from left to right across the frame rather than from right to left. This seems fitting. The materials are the same, only rearranged; their management assures us of the repeated nature of the terrible memories that inhabit this place and of the fact that neither Srebnik nor ourselves will ever be able to escape from them (whatever he or we may once have thought).

The materials in this episode are astonishingly reduced. It consists largely of faces and words, and so does the rest of the film. What we find repeatedly in *Shoah* are relentless close-ups of the faces of certain survivors of the Holocaust, who recount the horrors of their past under Lanzmann's insistent probing and against backgrounds which are unemphatic or blank. The camera peers at these faces, fills the frame with them and does not move aside even when they begin to splutter and cry, and when the survivors say that they cannot go on. (This is one of the things Lanzmann is after: the moment at which even words become insufficient.) The faces provide the foreground of the film, its human mooring, and compensate for the barrenness that might have resulted from Lanzmann's enforced decision to give us only stories about events rather than the events themselves. Thus, if we do not see momentous things happening in this film, we do at least see the people to whom momentous things once happened.

The figures whom Lanzmann interviews, too, may be unknown, but that does not mean that they are ordinary: they have a compelling watchability which comes not just from the remarkable tales they tell, but also also from the moral and psychological strengths they seem to embody. Like Simon Srebnik, most of them are powerful, healthy, good-looking, as one might expect survivors to be, and they speak in an individual way and respond forcefully to the camera. Lanzmann makes the most of their presence and personality. (He chose them with the care of a casting-director, and coolly rejected the testimony of those who were, in his words, 'unable to become "characters" in the story, with whom [he] could establish no relationship, or whose tone could not be accommodated').[1]

The stories of characters like Srebnik take the place in *Shoah* that would normally be occupied in a fiction film by a narrative of imagined events or in a documentary by the extant objects, persons, actions or places that the director wished to present and interpret. These stories are therefore of crucial importance to Lanzmann. They do not seem to add up, and it is hard to believe at first that one necessarily follows on from the other in a progression. *Shoah* is a cumulative, repeating, circular film, in which stories like Srebnik's, but taking place at different times, in different locales and to different people, are placed abruptly one after the other, and sometimes mingled together, in an initially disorienting and apparently haphazard way. Only, as we may see after the film has ended, it has after all had some shape, and has moved from the amateur exterminations by gas van at Chelmno, through systematic improvements to the mechanized, large-scale slaughter of the extermination camps (proudly described by Franz Suchomel, a member of the SS at Treblinka) to the need for works of witness such as *Shoah* itself.

The tales, told in a variety of languages, are often presented like Srebnik's in their original setting, so that we have the curious situation of a present-day world of cheerful villages and beautiful woods apparently devoid of menace being overcast by stories of the terrible things which happened there in the past. This is one of Lanzmann's key techniques, the superimposition of unlikely or even contradictory materials one upon the other, and of one, two or three languages (for us, seeing a subtitled version of the film) used serially or simultaneously. It means, although the director privileges his stories' emotional effect, that we cannot quite assimilate them as they proceed: their circumstances are disunified, somehow incomplete, perhaps under- or over-determined.

There is one other feature of the film which adds to this impression of unfinishedness or obstruction. This is the curious situation of the characters, who have ourselves as an audience, of course, but also at least two other audiences to contend with. The first is themselves, for their words are first spoken and then immediately translated, while they sit or stand by, halted in their tracks and seeming to dwell on or in some way to be registering the words they have just uttered. The second is composed of Lanzmann himself accompanied by his translator, whom we obtrusively see and hear setting up each scene, maintaining its momentum and making certain that all necessary questions are asked and answered. Often this situation appears wasteful but, even more, strangely distancing and disruptive of our attention – and it would have been perfectly easy to tidy up, so as to create the smooth flow of narrative that characterizes the 'talking heads' documentaries we often see in the cinema and on television.

The mise-en-scène of the film is similarly fractured. The camera often looks at what appears to be nothing, at clearings in the forest now devoid of evident interest, almost always with the unsteady, impromptu air which we associate with a documentary. The range of shots is restricted, with the close-up privileged above all other possibilities, and the pan and track employed more than any other camera movements. None of the images is obviously beautiful – some seem even awkward – and there is no sense at all of the search for aesthetic pleasure which we find, say, in *Night and Fog*. The editing, too, is as far as possible from the Hollywood ideal of polished inconspicuousness. There are precipitate cuts from scene to scene, sudden movements within scenes and, in general, little smoothness to any aspect of the film's development. From the point of view of its management of its materials and cinematography, then, *Shoah* may seem, as the historian Tony Judt has complained, 'anything but "art" in the conventional sense'.[2] But the important word in his comment is the word 'conventional'.

So far, I have commented on the subject matter and techniques of *Shoah*, and have pointed to what seem to be its reducedness, the eccentricity of its handling of the interview framework and the brusqueness of its presentation. A few critics have found in the film nothing more than this, and have written it off as self-indulgent, odd or amateur. But a more usual experience of *Shoah* is that it is an extremely powerful work, and not a film in which one is aware of a lack of art, or a failure of art. The problem with *Shoah*, is the problem of its format, not fiction, not just oral history, as historians such as Judt have said, and not documentary, as Lanzmann has several times protested, but instead an original attempt to promote historical recreation which the director has called a 'fiction du réel'.[3]

The images in this film are remarkably uncluttered: in most of them, as I have said, we see a face, or a pine-grove, or two or three people walking in the grass. But when these bare images are slowly recorded by Lanzmann's deliberate, meditative camera, we are encouraged to dwell on them and to think that there must be more in them that at first appears: every object acquires significance and presence, and we are sensitized to the interpretative role that each may play in the drama of the scene in which it appears. So, for example, at the end of Srebnik's account of the horrors of his early life in Chelmno, the spire of a church, shown above and apparently commanding the landscape, may provoke us to think of the role of Polish Catholicism in colluding with, or in some way even overseeing, the Holocaust. Throughout the film, in fact, carefully placed shots of churches and crucifixes make it

Fiction of the Real: Shoah and Documentary

impossible to forget that the Christian religion, and the Polish people, were inextricably involved in the murder of the Jews.

This keying of viewers to make the most of what they see carries over into other aspects of the film; it encourages us to be alert, to take on a more active interpretative role than we are used to either in the simpler sort of descriptive documentary or in the fast-paced popular fiction films of the moment. The understatedness of Lanzmann's overall scheme for *Shoah*, the fact that so many episodes seem like versions of other episodes, the languorous movement of the whole work and the deliberate lack of 'effective' transitions between or even within scenes means that we are forced to work hard in this film. Some information is given us, as at the beginning, and the survivors tell their stories with vigour and point, but on the whole we are not easy in *Shoah* and are constantly trying to correlate materials and to see how and where the whole work is going. In other words, the slowness, absence and awkwardness in the film are not clumsy; they are means to the end of preparing viewers to act and to read differently, and in a more aroused and participatory way.

But why is this necessary, and why does Lanzmann take things so far? After all, 30 years before him, Resnais needed only half an hour of film time, some stock footage, colour shots of the camps in the present day and a poetically charged commentary by Jean Cayrol. But what happened between 1955 and 1985 was that the repertoire of contemporary film material directly relating to the Holocaust (which, thanks to Nazi thoroughness, was never very large) became exhausted and could no longer produce an appropriate emotional effect. So Lanzmann, having rejected outright fiction as a suitable mode for a work on the Holocaust, and influenced by the vogue for 'witness' in the films of the New Documentarists, chooses instead to rethink what a film about past events might be. This is partly perforce, since sufficient and fresh materials do not exist to act otherwise. And even if immediate, contemporary materials existed in abundance, they might be too terrible for him to use or us to bear.

All films of the Holocaust face difficulties, and the director himself says, 'I precisely started with the impossibility to tell this story. I put this impossibility at the very beginning.'[4] The archetypally Modernist task he sets himself is exactly registered in the episode described earlier, when Lanzmann takes Srebnik back to the now deserted site where the bodies of the Jews of Chelmno were burnt and records his response: 'It was terrible ... No one can recreate what happened here ... And no one can understand it.' But to do that which cannot be done is the aim of *Shoah*. Lanzmann recognizes that he will have to change our existing expectations of the Holocaust film if he is to succeed in this aim.

He jettisons the (in his terms) *falsity* of fiction, but also the recitals of established information and the recyclings of established images of many documentaries. What he chooses instead is to opt for a series of people who are alive and in the present talking about people who are generally dead and in the past. But merely to record the survivors and their stories, interesting though they are, would not go far enough. Indeed, Lanzmann treats his material so that we are disturbed and encouraged to hope that its discontinuties will become continuous and its historicity will become actual. This lies at the root of the disorienting techniques Lanzmann uses, and of his teasing placing of stories of long ago in the mouths of contemporary figures and in locales which once suited them but do so no longer.

The conundrum of *Shoah* is, how can its elements be unified and thus grasped, how can the past and present be brought together? In other words, in this self-conscious work, which puts so many difficulties in the way of our straightforwardly managing its materials, what is the mode of representation which will be sufficient for the refractory subject which Lanzmann has chosen? The director's solution is remarkable. For it seems to me that *Shoah* in fact consists of two films. The one that we see is suggestively uncompleted, but provides the materials from which we may be prompted to create a second film, one where the survivors' stories are fully realized within us and the empty foreground of now is peopled by the extraordinary events of then. This is the way in which the film overcomes, or at least seeks to overcome, the 'impossible' task that it sets itself. It allows for the practical difficulties of showing the Holocaust in action; it usefully details the testimony of the survivors as to the ghastly work they were forced to do by the Nazis, as well as minute but telling particulars of their individual sufferings; and it stimulates the imagination of its audiences, so that they may be able definitively to recreate the murder of the Jews as the film itself admits it cannot do. Thus, Lanzmann hopes, *Shoah* will combine the documentary and the fictional, as well as producing the *newest* treatment of the Holocaust in the cinema.

NOTES

1. Jonathan Davis, 'Introduction to *Shoah*', in Jonathan Davis (ed.), *Film, History and the Jewish Experience* (London, 1986), pp.50–51.
2. Tony Judt, 'Moving Pictures', *Radical History Review*, Vol.41 (1988), p.130.
3. Claude Lanzmann, 'Le lieu et la parole', *Cahiers du cinéma*, Vol.374 (1985), p.21.
4. Quoted in André Colombat, 'Claude Lanzmann's *Shoah*', in *The Holocaust in French Film* (Metuchen, NJ, 1993), p.305.

5

Public Memory and Active Recall in Two Holocaust Films: Partisans of Vilna *(1986) and* Come and See *(1985)*

BEN SMITH

This essay will reflect on issues of memorialisation in relation to two central films: Josh Waletzky's *Partisans of Vilna* (1986) and Elem Klimov's *Come and See* (1985). I will also discuss Alain Resnais' *Night and Fog* (1995) and Steven Spielberg's *Schindler's List* (1993) as contrasts. By the term 'public memory' I am referring to a range of practices centring on cultural or ethnic narratives and official state commemoration (monuments, days of remembrance and other institutional forms). 'Active recall' is considerably less easy to pin down. It is unreliable, certainly from a historian's perspective, and frequently eludes the safety-net of public memory. The term refers to the *process* of memory. It is an act rather than a fixed event, and one that is associated inevitably with distortion, elision, communication problems and, in this context, trauma. Active recall's nearest cinematic analogue is Claude Lanzmann's *Shoah* (1985). Lanzmann's film suggests to us that the struggle to retell is as important as the substance of what is retold and that the clearest communication possible is that of allowing the viewer to witness the breakdown in that communication. This paradigm presents the past as an ongoing process rather than a finished event.

Cinema, by virtue of an inherent sensory power, can override conventional historiography's tendency to codify the past within blocks of impersonal data. As the film critic Vivian Sobchack remarks, '[a] film presents and represents acts of seeing, hearing and moving as both the *original structures of existential being* and the *mediating structures of language*'[1] and that it 'makes itself sensuously and sensibly manifest as the expression of experience by experience'.[2] This sensuousness is a resource that *Shoah* refuses to draw on, but that is not to say that the majority of films that do must necessarily reject the problematical in favour of an unexamined emotional rush.

Partisans of Vilna and *Come and See* are both firmly located within the range of pre-existing cinema forms so firmly rejected by *Shoah*. *Partisans of Vilna* (hereafter shortened to *Vilna*) uses conventional documentary techniques (old footage, illustrative maps, voice-over) very subtly. It runs shy of stifling the testimony of its witnesses with an overuse of these techniques and, following the initial set-up of the situation for the Jewish population of the Vilna region both before and immediately after the German invasion, there is an almost tangible sense of extraneous formal clutter being cleared away so that the survivors' voices may be heard.

By contrast, *Come and See* is a fictionalised account of the Nazi and Soviet partisan activity that took place in Belarus during 1943 over a 48-hour period, culminating in the Nazi destruction of a village (here named Perekhody), and seen through the eyes of an adolescent partisan called Florian. The film's narrative traces a brief and brutal rite-of-passage. Florian is first represented as a child whose initial contact with the resistance seems little more than an extension of the war games he is playing in the opening scene. When the camp of the group he has joined is bombed while the fighters are away, he and a girl, Glasha, return to Florian's home where they find his family dead. He then sets out with some other fighters (all of whom are eventually killed) before being finally reunited with his partisan group – after two days, already a veteran of war.

Come and See does not deal specifically with the genocide of the Jews but rather inhabits the indeterminate zone where the war, as the western Allies might have recognised it, and the Holocaust cross over. Quite unlike *Vilna*, *Come and See* rejects restraint and works its way into a sensory overload not dissimilar at times to such a film as Francis Ford Coppola's *Apocalypse Now* (1979). Its cumulative effect is of an overpowering visual and aural symphony of static close-ups interrupting expansive camera movements, screams, artillery fire, engine drones and silence.

Despite these huge differences, the two films are not merely linked by the similarity of their subject matter. On a basic level, both films express a need to unpick the privately experienced past from the public, collective past – thus attempting to resolve the problem expressed by Geoffrey H. Hartman of whether 'public memory' can 'still be called memory when it is increasingly alienated by personal and active recall?'.[3] At a deeper level, the films examine the process whereby the circumstances that made Hartman's question so necessary came about. Whereas *Shoah*'s indeterminacy of form leaves us with a profound feeling of disorientation, both *Vilna* and *Come and See* use more determinate film forms, not to create closure but to act as correlatives for the sense of an atrocity's cessation that is created in public memory.

Saul Friedländer has written that 'the memory of the Shoah will be essentially ritualised for some and historicised for the great majority'.[4] While querying Friedländer's clear separation of history and ritual (what is collective, cultural history if not ultimately ritualised?), his distinction between those directly affected and those who come after is a valid one, and it is the narrative that the 'great majority' will have access to which is at stake in these films. While the partisan struggle of *Come and See* would eventually form the basis of post-war Eastern bloc national ideologies, the equivalent struggle depicted in *Vilna* would be lost amid the creation of these ideologies.

PARTISANS OF VILNA

Partisans of Vilna is about armed Jewish resistance within the Vilna ghetto. The key issue for the ghetto inhabitants was whether a form of controlled 'collaboration' (via the 'Judenrat' or Jewish Council) was a better course of action for the population than the risky business of open resistance, and the film (rightly, I think) does not take up an obvious position on this. After failing to prevent the liquidation of the ghetto by local SS units and Estonian Auxiliaries, the partisans headed for the forests where they attempted to forge alliances with other, predominantly non-Jewish resistance groups.

Vilna's defining markers are what Eric Hobsbawm has described as 'the past as a generalised record' and 'the past as part of, or background to, one's own life'.[5] The film has to negotiate a tricky route that does not lead to the inflating of Jewish resistance into a new Holocaust 'myth' culled from personal memories, but which also does not allow memory to be swamped by historiography. Waletzky has remarked in relation to his film that '[d]eath and destruction are more important in the overall scheme [of the Holocaust]. Resistance becomes significant only after basic facts are known and assimilated into the culture as a whole'.[6] As Waletzky's comments indicate, *Vilna* cleaves its view of the past away from the collective view that the post-Holocaust audience would share, rather than seeking to replace that view; its power is based on a dialectic enacted between the events depicted and the audience's implicit set of collective images and narratives. It follows a path that, superficially, resembles but, in reality, reverses processes enacted within *Shoah* and *Schindler's List*. Like *Shoah*, *Vilna* privileges the survivor over any obviously imposed historiographical narrative, and like *Schindler's List* it apparently restores the survivors' narratives to some collective resolution. However, neither of these two films could be described in any conventional sense as dialectical in form.

If *Schindler's List* offers us an undialectical view – ultimately affirming fixed structures over processes – then *Shoah* offers an *anti-dialectical* view. It is set in a dialectical form but its self-interrogatory imperative has nothing to interrogate except its mode of re-presenting experiences it rejects the power to represent in the first place. With *Shoah* the audience is invited to go through the motions of negotiating some kind of relationship to the Holocaust as actually experienced rather than mediated, but in the full knowledge that, whatever means it chooses to do so, it can only fail. The film locates the Holocaust as a continuing process but does not allow the audience to integrate itself comfortably within this: we remain excluded, albeit in a self-aware fashion.

In *Schindler's List*, on the other hand, a more familiar Holocaust context – largely expressed by allusions to other films including, at various points, *Night and Fog*, Nazi footage of ghettos and *Shoah* itself – is confirmed as an environment within which to enact an untypical Holocaust story, but is negated by the film's narrative form, so as to create the illusion that its account embodies a defining aspect of the Holocaust. Despite our wider knowledge of certain facts and despite Spielberg's acknowledgement of these in the written text that closes the film, *Schindler's List* leaves us with the sense of emotional uplift that *Vilna* ultimately denies us.

The documentary form is not used in *Vilna* to fit survivors' accounts within a pre-existing historiographical framework; instead it is created *by* them and the means of representation are put at their disposal. Most of the documentary tropes – the voice-over, the use of maps – are deployed early on and thereafter recur only intermittently. One reason for this is that such devices serve to destroy the uniqueness of individual experiences (something that has unfortunate parallels with Nazi efforts to reduce mass-murder to bureaucratic data). The close shots of documents being typed are tied in explicitly with the mass shootings at Ponar by the amplification of the sound of keys being hit. The final use of this device ends as the resetting of the printer is rhymed with jerky camera movements over an artist's impression of the newly created ghetto (Figure 1).

The scene has been set and from now on the Nazis remain off-stage and the survivors occupy the film's centre. The film becomes a

FIGURE 1

community of voices and potential folk memories. This concept of community bonds the fragmentary voices across space (in the linking together of different accounts) and time (in the linking together of accounts with artefacts from the past), as well as in the ultimate creation of a cultural community. Where *Shoah*'s testimonies were often linked together in the most oblique of ways, *Vilna* creates a montage of accounts that corroborate one another in a form of near dialogue. Very early on, for example, accounts from Abba Kovner and Nisan Reznick on the creation of the FPO (Fareynikte Partizaner Organizatyse, the United Partisan Organization in the ghetto) are intercut, while an account of Baruch Goldstein's near-fatal attempt to smuggle weapons into the ghetto is started by Kovner and continued to and fro between Kovner and Goldstein.

Although Waletzky displays no interest in highlighting any contradictions or ellipses in any of the testimonies, he is not simply concerned with factual 'authentication'. He is making sure that voices are not heard in isolation: the people and their interaction may have been defined by events but, in this film, they are not absorbed by them. The time element adds a third dimension. Individuals are frequently identified by old photographs. For instance, Reznick's first account is introduced by an old picture of himself, and when Chajka Grossman relates the problem of obtaining appropriate ID papers for the 'Aryan' side we see those papers, again with a photograph of her (Figures 2 and

FIGURE 2

FIGURE 3

3). This technique is at its most powerful when combined with the spatial montage. In the Goldstein–Kovner exchange mentioned before, the story continues as a friend distracts the German guards, allowing Goldstein to slip back into the ghetto. This friend is shown only in an old photograph and one presumes that he is dead, but Waletzky's scheme does not accentuate his absence so much as his continuing presence within the evolving community matrix. Later on the process is reversed as the recollection of Alexander Tamir as a six year old playing the piano at a youth club concert leads in to an interview with the adult Tamir playing the same piece. Similarly, Yechiel Burgin remembers singing at a ghetto concert and, like Tamir, re-enacts the moment. The overall effect is of a dialogue both with the past, as embodied in evidence, and the past as continually lived out. The past in *Vilna* is never finished; it is a space in which the survivors are restored, both to their actions and to each other.

Here a comparison might be made with *Schindler's List*. Spielberg's film freezes the process of creating collective memory through active recall. By failing to locate its particular narrative in relation to the wider Holocaust environment, it is consequently able to maintain the illusion that its version of events is broadly representative of the Holocaust as a whole. For example, during commandant Amon Goeth's 'today is history' speech, where he addresses his men prior to the liquidation of the Kraków ghetto, Miriam Bratu Hansen maintains that because all the characters we see in the documentary-style shots accompanying the speech ultimately survive, the sequence 'give[s] the lie to Goeth's project'.[7]

Within the context of *Schindler's List* alone this is undoubtedly so but in a wider context it is untrue; Goeth's project, in fact, succeeded perfectly. As the film moves towards its conclusion at Schindler's Brinnlitz factory, where the Jews he has saved from extermination are officially 'put to work' for the Reich, both narrative complexity and personal ambiguity in the Schindler-figure are condensed and brought into synchronisation by the removal of Goeth's potentially problematic function. If allowed to remain, Goeth could morally compromise the film's narrative of the strong male by introducing troubling analogies between himself and Schindler.

The film's implicit master-narrative jettisons those to whom narrative strength is occasionally subcontracted (Goeth, and some of the more identifiable Jews like Itzak Stern) and centres entirely on Schindler who is given iconic status as object of the film's gaze. When Schindler returns along the railway track with the women from Auschwitz, for instance, it is an echo of the photographs of Schindler with women at the beginning of the film – in the night-club and with his secretaries – but 'sanctified' and stripped of any erotic implications. Schindler has taken on the function of a memorial-fetish and, in his Christ-like aura, causes the film to enact processes roughly analogous to those which, as Hartman has observed, afflict a great many actual monuments: '[they] produce a deceptive sense of totality, throwing into the shadows, even into oblivion, stories, details and unexpected points of view that keep the intellect active and the memory digging'.[8] This entirely undercuts efforts in the film's final scenes to pass narrative control to the Jewish survivors. As Schindler's car draws away, we see a repeat of his gaze from the film's earliest sequences, with the faces of the survivors reflected in the window gradually moving into focus as his face fades away. Henry Greenspan quotes a survivor saying of his experiences, '"It is *not* a story. It has to be *made* a story"'.[9] Spielberg's efforts to render the Holocaust as a coherent narrative make this final transference impossible without codifying the collective experience as public memory. As will be seen in the final moments of *Come and See*, *Schindler's List* seeks closure by making the Holocaust the spur for some future state of being which it then explicitly states by moving 'outside' the film's parameters, as the survivors approach Israel to a song ('Jerusalem of Gold') which had come to symbolise victory in the Six Day War. Schindler's continuing presence 'outside' the film is reconfigured as a literal monument (a grave) serving as a focal point for our view of the survivors. This apparent adoption of a Zionist agenda is, in turn, a narrative device that ties together the collective (survivors) and the single (Schindler) into a totality that is able to respect Hollywood's need for a hero figure, the epic form's need for collective group affirmation and the audience's (perceived) need for catharsis and closure. Yosefa Loshitzky has seen the film as expressing 'a deep anxiety nurtured by the gradual disappearance of Holocaust survivors' and the final procession past Schindler's grave appears to bear this out.[10] In fact the film is about forgetting. It seeks to remove the cracks inherent in the act of memory and replace them with a fixed image held together by an implied but never examined state of communion with the post-Holocaust world.

Does *Vilna* then engage in a similar process of retrospective memorialisation? As Lawrence Langer has written on attempts to organise survivor accounts into coherent narratives, '[o]nly through the invention of a mythic narrative "afterward" can we reconstruct an idiom to change their death from a "forgettable" (because unbearable) occasion into a memorable one'.[11] After all, there are few Holocaust documentaries where a survivor such as Gabriel Sedlis might offer as an explanation for not executing a captured German soldier, 'we [his partisan group] were fighting for a new world'. We could therefore view certain key moments as an attempt to reorient the Holocaust away from mass-murder and towards cultural resistance. Kovner's memories of the intellectual activity around the Strashun library, the early shots of healthy happy Jewish youth (Figure 4), the stirring songs played throughout, could be seen as offering a more fitting view of the

FIGURE 4

Every step has its sound

past than the dismal epitaph of a centuries-old European culture contained in more familiar documents, testimonies and images. However, this is deceptive. *Vilna* offers up this potential cultural myth but subverts it. Although it occasionally uses documentary devices to illustrate the resistance rather than the Nazi side of the story (such as FPO documents replacing Nazi ones in the film's early stages, and the map used to trace Celia Rosenberg-Amit's journey to contact other partisan groups), *Vilna*'s narrative is structured solely around verbal accounts and photographs that tie in directly with these accounts. Despite the overall sense of coherence, the form within which the accounts are placed is fragmentary and no survivor is ever shown with another (a more 'Spielbergian' strategy might have been to stage some form of reunion).[12]

In essence, the pull of the 'other' Holocaust – of 'death and destruction'- is far too strong and the sense of a tangible communal myth is not built on safe ground because, in Hartman's words, the Holocaust is 'integrated not by distinctive communal forms but by politically motivated analogies',[13] and the Jews who survived lacked the institutional and, by extension, mass psychological framework to construct such analogies. In this respect *Vilna*'s conclusion is bleakly ironic. As the resistance finally triumphs, we are shown Soviet newsreel footage speaking of the Lithuanians' 'undefeatable nation' and its 'heroic deeds', which 'will be written in the annals of battle'. There is no word, however, of the Jewish groups who, only minutes before, we learn, suffered harassment and sometimes violence from the groups being celebrated. Here we see the politicisation of Holocaust memories discussed by the historian Tim Cole actually enacted within the event itself, and with rather more disturbing implications than Cole's notion of bastardised history.[14]

As an audience we want a fixed vision of the past, but the dialectic between the remarkable story of resistance portrayed in *Vilna* and our own knowledge of the extent of the genocide – as embodied in the film by survivor Musia Lipman's simple statement, 'Vilna without Jews is simply not Vilna'- does not resolve itself into the unproblematic image of heroism we desire. Accounts of individual death in *Vilna* are sparse in comparison to other Holocaust films. What we are actually seeing is the death of an entire culture and the ultimate destruction of the fragile communal memory, asserted throughout the film, by the 'new world' that Sedlis and his colleagues were fighting for.

COME AND SEE

Come and See deals with similar events to *Partisans of Vilna* but from the opposite direction. Rather than reconstruct a past narrative from fragments of memory, it enters the field of destruction itself, creates spaces, on a formal level analogous to those of the process of recollection, and then places the viewer within them. A number of writers have commented on the special nature of trauma-defined memory. Langer has remarked that, in these circumstances, memory 'leaps out of chronology, establishing its own momentum, or fixation',[15] and Karl A. Plank argues that such memory consists of 'broken continuities whose rupture has made us strangers in familiar lands'.[16] This relocation of the 'strange' within the 'familiar' shapes the film's formal strategies. They allow the viewer to perceive Florian's odyssey in such a way that the past events and present fixations inherent in recollection are grafted together.

In keeping with Plank's 'broken continuities', many sequences are elliptical and entirely disrupt classical spatial and temporal continuities. In the opening sequence, a temporal ellipse occurs when the shot of a boy talking to Florian (but directly into the camera) is cut to the two boys running away from the camera. The following scene, featuring Florian and his mother, is full of spatial ellipses. For example, when she hits Florian with a rope, the camera remains on Florian, only returning to the mother when she is running out of the hut. Such a scheme reduces our sense of spatial interaction between characters and consequently makes the dimensions of their immediate environment ambiguous.

As Francesco Casetti points out, the direct gaze into the camera, so prevalent in this film, creates, 'an offscreen space that can never become an onscreen space':[17] Klimov is not creating an unreflexive 'realist' environment but a psychological environment. To this end the soundtrack is particularly well developed. In certain instances, such as the loud buzzing fly leading up to the discovery of Florian's dead family, sound is used to indicate heightened senses, but the soundtrack is at its most effective when creating a feel of disorientation in tandem with the images. The lengthy forest sequence is particularly effective in conveying the feel of sensory 'disorder' intrinsic to memory. The initial conversation between Florian and Glasha is conducted as ever without reverse-field camera exchanges and, in each case, directly to camera – thus continuing the film's refusal to create stabilising eye-line matches.[18] The bombing of the partisan camp is mostly filmed without the sounds of explosions but with a high-pitched tone and the distorted, amplified sound of breathing. More noises return, as Florian and Glasha run, but these never correspond directly to the visuals and the soundtrack becomes a kind of expressionist patchwork of low electronic chords, breathing, drones and – just audibly – snatches of German song. The entire sequence is crystallised into vivid episodes such as Glasha dancing on a box, the shaking of trees and the heavily stylised fall of rain (Figures 5 and 6). At no point does one feel that the bombing is anything more than just one component in this stream of charged sensuousness.

FIGURE 5

FIGURE 6

At certain key points, *Come and See* references photography. The credit sequence takes place over a sepia-tinted shot of a bleak sandy landscape (Figure 7) and both the Soviet partisans and the Nazis take photographs of themselves. This is also implicitly referenced in the film's recurring motif of having characters directly facing, and talking into, the camera. Such a device – especially when people are interacting with one another- means that the gestures and interpolations inherent in communication, are frozen and isolated into 'poses'.

In *Schindler's List*, the photograph is an indicator that the actions are

FIGURE 7

safely consigned to the past while the literal use of such devices in non-fiction films frequently indicates a false stability in the relationship between historiographical discourse and its referent; it is deployed in an evidentiary manner implying an untroubled 'collaboration' between image and verbally rendered memory. In *Come and See*, it signifies both the means of recollection and the process itself, within which it places the viewer in order to exhibit a present-past continuum and expose it to reinterpretation. Communication in this film first draws attention to, then bounces off, the camera eye, which acts as an extra, absent but prevailing, character. Initially we assume that the injunction of the film's title is Florian's but he does not have sufficient foresight into, or control over, what happens for him to have such a mandate. The viewer could assume that he is perhaps 'directing' events as memory from some future point but there is nothing in the film to bear this out – especially as, during the bombing of the camp, he is shown with his back to the explosions (Figure 8).

As with *Night and Fog*, the role of the camera – the ultimate point-of-view – remains ambiguous and hard to locate, especially in its freedom to create exhilaration out of destruction. This is *Come and See*'s true theme: not the recreation of the past but an interrogation of the political origins of the means by which such a recreation can be

FIGURE 8

achieved. In Resnais' film we are offered a dual perspective. From an early stage there exists the implicit possibility that victim (spoken text) and visitor (camera) have entirely different motives for being at the extermination site. The early intervention of Nazi footage from Leni Riefenstahl's *Triumph of the Will* (1934) seems to join with Resnais' contemporary colour footage, acting as a kind of reverse negative – different but inextricably related. It indicates potential complicity and the possibility that the post-Holocaust 'bystander' might 'liberate' him/herself from his/her experiential ignorance in the shadow of the survivor by recourse to a quasi-Nazi aesthetic of power.

The pivotal moment is when Resnais' camera enters the watchtower. This is the one part of the camp that the survivor can speak of with no more authority than the observer (s/he could never have had access to it) but which has an empowering function for the observer. Here the post-Holocaust eye achieves the metaphorical status of a guard: both detached and omniscient. The camera is effectively 'loaded' and, as such, places the observer in the same symbolic space as the bureaucrat, the transport administrator, the architect: an individual performing a task commonplace in itself but charged with lethal consequences in the right environment. From this point on, the images operate on a different level from the text. In the gas chambers, for instance, the camera sweeps upwards to catch sight of the scratch marks left by the struggling victims referred to haltingly in the commentary, but the camera-movements' new-found confidence is less that of depiction in service of the victim as of impassive loitering in the service of the voyeur. The film leaves us finally with an unresolvable dialectic between the Holocaust as a real, experienced event, and the modes of representation, which are less a function of that event itself than of the agendas and cultural sub-texts of those who choose to approach it.

In *Come and See*, it is as if Klimov's eye – which is also the post-Holocaust world's eye – can only represent the Holocaust in such a way as to realize, in Adorno's words, 'the potentiality of wringing pleasure from it'.[19] Like Resnais, Klimov is aware that such problems can only be resolved by drawing attention to them, then implicating both filmmaker and audience. The lengthy sequence in which an SS division destroys Perekhody is among the most perversely euphoric ever to occur in a film about war. However, the sense of exhilaration is tied in with the formal strategies used throughout the film and, unlike the comparable ghetto liquidation sequence in *Schindler's List*, the exact nature of the film's master-narrative has yet to be established. The Perekhody sequence has a precise role in turning the audience's gaze away from the representation itself and towards its source. Here the camera effectively joins with the Nazis rather than retaining detachment and turns these strategies into direct correlatives of the Nazis' own 'aesthetic' of destruction.

Throughout this sequence the formal strategies are unpicked and given functions and origins in the immediate environment. The vast camera sweeps are now at the service of the swerving motorcycles and juddering armoured divisions; the soldiers stare and laugh into the camera (Figures 9, 10 and 11) – showing little effort to interact with each other – as though fully aware of its presence and its recording function and not trapped by its gaze like Florian and his compatriots. The screams of the burning villagers have been anticipated by the cacophonous sounds used earlier, and the German songs that form a constituent part of the film's soundtrack are sourced here in the enormous PA system rigged up to accompany the massacre. As the sequence reaches its climax with grenades being tossed into the village hall, the soldiers burst into a round of applause (Figure 12) – this is Klimov's grotesque parody of himself and us. We are made to feel that our sense of aesthetic satisfaction at this extraordinary piece of film-making is complicit with the Nazi actions.

FIGURE 9

The last segments of *Come and See* introduce a yet greater 'editorial' role – that of the partisans whose victory will ultimately wrest control of the representation of the Soviet past. On the surface, Klimov avoids the kind of triumphalism that characterized the newsreel footage at the end of *Partisans of Vilna*. The use of concentration camp footage, along

104   *Representing the Holocaust*

FIGURE 10

FIGURE 11

FIGURE 12

with some written text stating that 628 villages were destroyed in Belarus by the Nazis, introduces documentary tropes that reverse-zoom away from the events, implying a future that would have greater access to what occurred. As with *Schindler's List*, the citation of documentary signifies authority but because it is introduced so late - and because on a narrative level it is so disruptive – it is 'charged' with the ideological struggle that made its ascendancy possible as an authorial intrusion. It also lacks the sense of inevitability implicit in Spielberg's stylistic usage because the film's previous two-and-a-half hours have already indicated how easily post-Holocaust representations could have been – and could still become – 'Nazi-fied'.

As with *Vilna*, *Come and See* remains unresolved at this point, and the triumph, in the context of what would subsequently become known, is rendered empty. However, the final moments renege on this. Florian's imaginary shooting of Hitler back to infancy, via backwards footage showing Hitler's rise to power in reverse, suggests that defeating the Nazis simply means wresting control of the media by which the past would be re-ordered. The film's final shot – of a sky devoid, for the first time, of German planes dropping propaganda leaflets – with its accompanying 'Amen' from Mozart's *Requiem*, can only be read as the false resolution that comes with accepting state versions of history (the past is Hell but the future, as ever, is Heaven). This is a false touch but it comes too late to alter radically the film's questioning of ideological representation. It nonetheless provides an intriguing parallel with *Schindler's List* in the similar need for big budget films – irrespective of cultural origin – ultimately to settle on some sense of narrative triumphalism with which to define the rituals of their cultural environments.

Vilna's conclusion carries greater conviction as a portrayal of the past because its representation remains at one remove from any political ideology. For it to be entirely unmediated by political ideology would be impossible but it allows that ideology to be *visibly* side-stepped.[20] In this, it shows great restraint. Friedlander writes that, 'the catastrophe of European Jewry has not been incorporated into any compelling framework of meaning in public consciousness',[21] and the temptation to try to assemble such a framework must have been great. There is little sense of the discontinuity of perception and the rupturing of consciousness remarked upon by such survivors as Jean Améry[22] because the survivors in *Vilna* were able to *act* according to the ideological axioms they adhered to both before and after the Holocaust. For those who resisted because of their Zionist, socialist or communist beliefs – or simply due to a sense of cultural solidarity – there appears to be no incompatibility between their survival and their experiences: Shamai Davidson's remark that 'through guilt, survivors re-establish continuity with *non*-Holocaust memories'[23] does not apply here because, through the partisan struggle, these survivors established a symbolic community with groups across occupied Europe. However, as *Vilna* indicates, that symbolic community would prove to be false and the past relegated to the memory of a heritage lost except in the minds of the few survivors who were able to reject victimhood. The sudden affirmation of ideological analogies in *Come and See*'s conclusion should not distract us from the crucial insights the film has to offer. As with *Partisans of Vilna* we are offered, until the very closing moments, a representation of a past unfinished – suspended forever and not restored to any sense of collective cohesion.

NOTES

1. Vivian Sobchack, *The Address of the Eye: A Phenomenology of Film Experience* (Princeton, NJ, 1992) p.11.
2. Ibid., p.3
3. Geoffrey H. Hartman, *The Longest Shadow* (Bloomington, IN, 1996), p.99.
4. Saul Friedländer, *Memory, History and the Extermination of the Jews of Europe* (Bloomington, IN, 1993), p.48.
5. Ibid., p.vii.
6. Annette Insdorf, *Indelible Shadows: Film and the Holocaust*, Second Edition (Cambridge, 1989), p.166.
7. Miriam Bratu Hansen, '*Schindler's List* is Not *Shoah*: Second Commandment, Popular Modernism and Public Memory', in Yosefa Loshitzky (ed.), *Spielberg's Holocaust: Critical Perspectives On* Schindler's List (Bloomington, IN, 1997), p.93.
8. Hartman, 'The Book of the Destruction', in Saul Friedländer (ed.), *Probing the Limits of Representation* (Cambridge, MA, 1992), p.319.
9. Henry Greenspan, *On Listening to Holocaust Survivors: Recounting and Life History* (Westport, CT, 1998), p.xvi.
10. Yosefa Loshitzky, 'Introduction' to *Spielberg's Holocaust*, p.3.
11. Lawrence L. Langer, *Admitting the Holocaust* (Oxford; New York, 1995), p.20.
12. The one exception to this is the brief interview with Yechiel Burstein. The lighting screens out the surrounding people, none of whom makes any contribution, and there appears to be no significance in this aberration. The effort Waletzky clearly made to isolate Burstein within the shot suggests expediency as an explanation.
13. Hartman, 'Introduction: Darkness Visible', in *Holocaust Remembrance: The Shapes of Memory* (Oxford, 1994), p.14.
14. Tim Cole, *Images of the Holocaust: The Myth of the 'Shoah Business'* (London, 1999), pp.23–47, 146–71 (the 'Americanisation' of the Holocaust through Anne Frank and the Holocaust Memorial Museum, Washington DC respectively); pp.121–46 (Israeli self-images as embodied at Yad Vashem).
15. Langer, *Admitting the Holocaust*, p.15.
16. Karl A. Plank, 'A Survivor's Return: Reflections On Memory and Place', in Alice L. Eckardt (ed.), *Burning Memory: Times of Testing and Reckoning* (Oxford, 1993), p.186.
17. Francesco Casetti, *Inside the Gaze: The Fiction Film and Its Spectator* (trans. Nell Andrew and Charles O'Brien) (Bloomington, IN, 1998), p.17.
18. Here I am referring to the classical shot system. In mainstream narrative cinema it is

Public Memory and Active Recall in Two Films

customary to cut between two people having a conversation by maintaining eye contact between the two so as to ensure that the physical proximity of each figure, both to each other and to their overall environment, is always clear. Needless to say this 'rule' is frequently broken in number of perfectly conventional films but rarely with such obstinacy as in *Come and See*.

19. Langer, *The Holocaust and the Literary Imagination* (New Haven, CT and London, 1975), p.1.
20. It is notable that none of the interviewees in *Partisans of Vilna* make explicit comments on Israel (or, at least, none are retained in the film). Israel's power is alluded to in footage of Eichmann's trial, but the film pointedly refuses to identify Israel as a potential site for the creation of a future Jewish identity.
21. Friedländer, *Memory, History*, p.43; by 'compelling framework' I assume that Friedländer means the conversion of the Jewish genocide into self-contained redemptive narratives as only through a form of redemption can narratives of destruction be made to have a 'compelling' ('heroic', tragic, folkloric) dynamic. *Schindler's List* does not really fit into this framework because the redemption is achieved by its non-Jewish hero, whilst survivor narratives contained in Elie Wiesel's *Night* (1960) or the poetry of Paul Celan are in part about the failure of traditional forms to render the experiences recounted. Zionist narratives (such as that at the conclusion of *Schindler's List*) also fail to convince because they re-read the European Jewish experience as weak and intrinsically doomed rather than having formed a strong set of cultural identities.
22. Jean Améry, *At the Mind's Limits* (trans. Sidney and Stella Rosenfield) (London, 1999) pp.1–21.
23. Greenspan, *On Listening to Holocaust Survivors*, p.32.

Cultural Approaches

6

Ghetto Journals: The Case of Kovno

BRYAN BURNS

The experience of living in the ghetto, the deliberately mock-mediaeval situation into which the Nazis forced many of the Jews of Eastern Europe from about 1941 onwards, has always been fascinating to both fictional and non-fictional writers. Life in the ghetto, cut off from the outside world except for the few, usually antagonistic local Gentiles allowed dealings with its inhabitants, and the even fewer members of the SS who directed policy, and life and death, within its walls, offers a distillation of the nature of the Jewish tragedy to which there is perhaps no other parallel. The ghetto is a unique microcosm: in Lodz, in Warsaw, in Vilna (now Vilnius) and Kovno (now Kaunas; both the latter in Lithuania) Gentiles walked the streets often only yards away from Jewish compatriots whose existence was almost completely separated from theirs and almost completely different.

Both at the time, and later, many of those who endured the hardships of the ghettoes (all eventually, in the specialized phrase, 'liquidated') realized that they were living through an extraordinary situation to which it was their duty to bear witness. The forms of this bearing witness are very varied: sometimes poetry or stories, sometimes paintings or drawings, sometimes, remarkably (given the risks and the technical difficulties), even photographs. But the most popular, the apparently 'natural' form seems to have been that of reminiscence. So we have the records of the Warsaw Ghetto carefully collected and preserved by Emanuel Ringelblum and his 'Joy of Shabbath' circle; the substantial chronicles of the Łódź Ghetto, the work of fifteen archivists specially directed to their task by the egotistical and deluded leader of the Jews in that city, Chaim Rumkowski; a large body of material from Bialystok, and smaller quantities from Minsk and Vilnius, as well as from several small towns now mostly *Judenfrei*, renamed and transferred to Ukraine or Belarus. We know that in a number of other cities, above all in Lvov, records that were meticulously kept by the inmates of the ghetto were meticulously destroyed by the Nazis as they covered their tracks and withdrew towards Germany.

It is these collections of documents which interest me and which I would like to discuss now. They seem to me to be most unusual and probably unique. They are the conscious attempt of a people and civilization which knew that their extinction was certain both to bear witness to iniquity, as they were enjoined to do in Torah and Talmud, and also to leave behind some enduring trace of themselves, some validation of their lives. These are grand aims and they were taken seriously. Often, the Council of Jews in a particular city would direct that a compilation of the happenings of the ghetto and the regulations imposed upon it should be undertaken, in the case of Łódź very elaborately, and in other places as the responsibility of a single, carefully selected individual. Those entrusted with these complilations were (as far as I have been able to discover) never writers and had no association with literature: what was wanted was forensic skill and meticulousness in the assembling of evidence, so that scientists and figures from the worlds of medicine and law were preferred to those from the arts.

In Kaunas, the brilliant young lawyer and Zionist, Avraham Golub, who later changed his name to Tory and was at the centre of ghetto affairs from its inception in 1941 until its liquidation in July, 1944, began on 22 June 1941 ('a sunny Sunday morning', he says) to put together documents issued by the Nazi and Lithuanian authorities. To these Tory added brief reports of events (as 'Israel Berlin, fifty-two, committed suicide by hanging himself. Lately he had been apathetic to his surroundings', 19 July 1942), notices issued by the Jewish Council under the respected *Oberjude*, the physician Dr Elkhanan Elkes and, most interestingly, longer entries in which he describes the deliberations of the Council, their assessment of quality of information available to them, the terrible choices they were daily forced to make, the hopes which sustained them and the fear which also drove them on. At first, this was done surreptitiously, but soon Dr Elkes was told and gave approval and assistance to the enterprise. Tory's work, originally written in Yiddish, miraculously survived the war (at least, about two-thirds of it did), and was published in English in 1990 as *Surviving the Holocaust: The Kovno Ghetto Diary*.[1]

I would like now to try to describe this form, mostly by reference to Tory's book, but also by comparisons with two other works. The first is *Łódź Ghetto: Inside a Community Under Seige*, the source for the documentary film of the same name, compiled and edited by Alan

Adelson and Robert Lapides.[2] The interest of this book lies in the extreme variety of witnesses upon whom it calls and the sense of a communal response to tragedy which it offers; the difficulty in its use comes from the fact that it is a selection made in the present day, with a particular, ultimately commercial purpose in mind. The second is by the engineer William W. Mishell (originally Mishelski), a survivor of the Kaunas ghetto who published his own long-considered memoir, *Kaddish for Kovno: Life and Death in a Lithuanian Ghetto, 1941–1945*, in English in 1988.[3] The interest of this book comes from the fact that it covers exactly the same ground as *Surviving the Holocaust*, but with a more evident personal content, talking for example of fears for the writer's family, meetings with attractive girls which sometimes lead to love affairs and sometimes do not, and surprising joys like the discovery of a functioning piano, in a way that Tory does not. Mishell's work is fascinating, and gives us an alternative to the emotional restraint of Tory, but it is written in a blunt and unnuanced (if correct) American that can be very hard to take.

What I would like to do is to say something now about nomenclature. I have described Mishell's book as a memoir, and that seems to me to be appropriate: its centre is an individual, albeit an individual in extraordinary circumstances, and its aim is, from the standpoint and with the knowledge of the present, to record the doings and feelings of that individual in the past; it of course reflects upon the outside world, but its focus is above all on Mishell, his family and friends (Tory, for example, figures in the book, but glancingly and unnamed). The first title I gave to this talk was 'The Ghetto Diary: The Case of Kovno', but that now seems to me to be misleading. A diary is specifically *of* a person: the diary of Anne Frank, the valuable Warsaw Ghetto diary of Adam Czerniakow, the classic diaries of eighteenth-century English Literature; again, the focus is overwhelmingly upon the individual (who may well reflect illuminatingly upon events outside his or her small, private sphere), only this time the entries are generally simultaneous with the situations they evoke.

Given this definition, and in spite of my original title and its own self-description, it does not now seem to me that we can really call *Surviving the Holocaust* a diary, for although it was put together and substantially written by Tory, it is not evidently about *him* as a person at all. Very occasionally, he ends one of his accounts with a cry as, most strikingly, at the end of December 1942, 'REVENGE! NEVER FORGET! NEVER FORGIVE!' But it is almost always the case that his affective as opposed to his practical response to events has to be inferred from the material he supplies: he is one of the most discreet and self-effacing narrators I have ever encountered. This extends even further. Mishell gives one passionate, sustained account of his relationships with his mother, his siblings and their husbands and wives, his nephews and nieces, his many friends, his work-mates; really, this is the substance of his book. But Tory mentions his three sisters and their husbands only at the beginning of *Surviving the Holocaust*, and one of them again at the end; it is only in the Epilogue, evidently written well after the end of the war, that he reveals that he eventually married Pnina Sheinzon, previously presented merely as his helper, and that they have a daughter, Alina. Given these features, it seems to me that 'journal' (defined by the *Oxford English Dictionary* as 'A daily record of events or occurrences kept by anyone for his own use. Now usually implying something more elaborate than a *diary*' and 'A record of public events or transactions noted down as they occur ... ') rather than 'diary', is therefore the most suitable category within which to place Tory's book.

I would like now to describe the features, and what I see as the successes of the ghetto-journal as exemplified in *Surviving the Holocaust*. In his *Holocaust Testimonies*, Lawrence Langer comments that the oral records which he is principally studying 'do not function in time like other narratives'.[4] But one of the great virtues of the ghetto-journal is precisely its immediacy; it gives us snapshots, sometimes brief, sometimes longer, but generally taken as it were on the day, at the moment, without the need or the possibility for a veil of reflection or interpretation. Certainly, many of the events recorded by Tory seem untouched by memory and devoid of the softening or heightening, or the literary exacerbation, which we often find in narratives which (like Mishell's) have been extensively thought over and carefully worked up. Literally, many of the accounts were produced late at night, after desperate difficulties, and some dictated to Sheinzon when Tory himself was too exhausted to write. So, throughout *Surviving the Holocaust* there is an air of the moment, of the mere eye of the camera registering what passes before it. The work is a kind of time-capsule, containing not the emotional traumas which beset Mishell and other memoirists, but shards, distinct and tangible like the report of the suicide of Israel Berlin which I have already quoted. More than in any other work known to me, therefore, in *Surviving the Holocaust* we seem to be in the presence of the events themselves, and not distanced or manipulated as we often are in fiction, for example. (As I shall show later, however, Tory is capable of powerful but subdued artistic effects.)

In addition, in Tory's hands, the ghetto-journal form proves itself remarkably both public and private. On the one hand, Tory always privileges coolness and the displaying of evidence: he gives times, dates, persons present at meetings, numbers of Jews killed, quantities of (often inedible) meat delivered, sums of Reichsmarks pocketed by corrupt officials – every available detail which might flesh out the life of the ghetto is meticulously recorded, as if by a scientist or a mere bureaucrat. As I have said, although he himself evidently suffered during the ghetto period, and members of his family and friends suffered and were murdered, he never descends to special pleading or melodrama. In fact, the tone of his writing is conspicuously measured, he directs his mind sharply and efficiently towards the business in hand: one has the sense of a job of work (an important job of work) which he accomplishes with an almost artisanal craftsmanship and adequacy. (He even goes out of his way to indicate the cravenness of some Jews and the decency of some Nazis.) But this is only the public, formal, historical dimension of Tory's writing.

Implicit within it too is something which runs counter to the evil represented by the Nazis and their Lithuanian henchmen. In part, this is dramatized by vocabulary, with the terrible evasions of the Final Solution (the actions, the liquidations), and the arid proclamations of the authorities (forbidding women in the ghetto any longer from bearing children, upon pain of death, for example) set against the richer world of thought and feeling and the marvellous resilience and entrepreneurship which Tory presents from the side of the Jews.

It is also that he cannot from time to time prevent himself (increasingly as the book progresses) from thinking of redemption and believing that it will come. So, extraordinarily, as late as 4 May 1943, Tory can write, 'The sun fills the world with warmth and brightness. It also sends its light and warmth to us in the ghetto.' But it is perhaps most that, although this is only latent, and is never inflated, love and care, especially between members of the same family, are so abundant in the ghetto and so terrifyingly absent outside it. The point is never made, but the message is plain: despite everything, the Jews have maintained humanity and civilized standards. They have the antidote to Nazism. In this respect, *Surviving the Holocaust* entirely escapes the criticism made by Langer in *Holocaust Testimonies* (p.163) that commentators on the Holocaust recast their materials stereotypically using what he calls 'the grammar of heroism and maryrdom'. In Tory's book there are some villains, but no heroes and no martyrs; just Jewish people leading their lives.

The ghetto-journal in Tory's hands is capable of a wide variety of effects; even wider, and better managed than in the much longer Łódź Ghetto journal. He has an eye for telling details and for striking moments. He manages sharp, condensed reports, as well as longer accounts revealing to the full the extreme care with which the Jewish Council dealt with every detail of ghetto life, and above all its concern to be completely fair in administering the privileges to which it had access. But his work is full of action, too, and there are vigorous and well-paced renderings of individual events such as the account of the murder of 5,000 Jews from Riga at the killing fields of Ponar in 1943. In addition, towards the end of the work, whether because the original story was so well told, or because it is so inspiriting, Tory gives a description of the escape of the Russian Jew, Captain Vassilenko, and his companions, from the murderous Ninth Fort, which is a masterpiece of suspense writing.

I would like to say something now about the tact of *Surviving the Holocaust*. It deals with a situation in which good and evil could hardly be plainer, and where one group of people is constantly, unjustly tormented by another. But the work is not ostentatiously judgemental, and does not seek to impose a single viewpoint. It does not offer a sustained argument against the Nazis, but is interim; it presents the materials from which such an argument (or arguments) might be made. This is a final strength of the work. It trusts to us, using the facts that it provides, to be able to gather a fuller picture of the life in the Kovno Ghetto than was possible for those living through it.

NOTES

1. Abraham Tory, *Surviving theHolocaust: The Kovno Ghetto Diary* (trans. Jerzy Michaelowicz) (Cambridge, MA and London, 1990).
2. Alan Adelson and Robert Lapides (eds.), *Łódź Ghetto: Inside a Community Under Siege* (trans. Stanley Bergman *et al.*) (Harmondsworth and New York, 1989).
3. William W. Mishell, *Life and death in a Lithuanian Ghetto, 1941–1945* (Chicago, IL, 1999).
4. Lawrence L. Langer, *Holocaust Testimonies: The Ruins of Memory* (New Haven, CT and London, 1991), p.xi. All further page references in the text.

Identification and the Genre of Testimony

ROBERT EAGLESTONE

INTRODUCTION

Elie Wiesel has argued that, if 'the Greeks invented tragedy, the Romans the Epistle, the renaissance the Sonnet, our generation invented a new literature, that of testimony'.[1] While this claim may be debatable in terms of literary history, it certainly points to the development of a new genre of writing, the Holocaust testimony (and it may be that this genre is the forerunner for a way of understanding a whole range of 'traumatic' literature). While there has been much discussion of the significant issues about testimonies – about their relationship to, or role as, historical texts, about the importance of authorship and so on – there has been very little that considers them as a literary genre. Indeed, as one of the major books on the subject points out, 'the more we look closely at texts, the more they show us that, unwittingly, we do not even know what testimony is and that, in any case, it is not simply what we thought we knew it was'.[2] The aim of this contribution is to outline a taxonomy of the genre of Holocaust testimony.

But this, of course, presents the first problem. One can taxonomize a genre in many different ways: by date ('the eighteenth century novel'), by gender ('women's writing'), by location and language ('English poetry') and so on. However, one of the most important characteristics of the genre of testimony stems from the reader's experience of identification. 'Identification' is 'an embarrassingly ordinary process' that often takes place in reading or watching a text: it is the 'human interest' in the news story, the character in the novel with whom the reader feels most 'at home'.[3] It is so common and taken for granted that critics often neglect to examine it, like the reading spectacles forgotten at the end of one's nose. As Diana Fuss writes, identifications 'are the origin of some of our most powerful, enduring and deeply felt pleasures ... the source of considerable emotional turmoil, capable of unsettling or unmooring the precarious groundings of our everyday identities ... Identifications are erotic, intellectual and emotional. They delight, fascinate, confuse, unnerve, and sometimes terrify.'[4]

However, one of the fascinating things about the process of identification is that no one knows how it works. Fuss finds that

> the psychoanalytic literature on identification is littered with taxonomic qualifiers that seek to identify, with greater and greater precision, modes and types of identifications: primary and secondary, feminine and masculine, imaginary and symbolic, maternal and paternal, idiopathic and heteropathic, partial and total, centrifugal and centripetal, narcissistic and regressive, hysterical and melancholic, multiple and terminal, positive and negative ... [This] often incongruous proliferation of kinds of identification points to a theoretical difficulty psychoanalysis must routinely confront in laying hold of its object, a difficulty, that is, in identifying identification.[5]

Moreover, this is not to say that current descriptions of identity formation are not accurate: for example, one of the most powerful contemporary accounts of identity formation come from the gender theorist Judith Butler, who uses a basically Hegelian paradigm. However, her account, which argues that identity is constructed through the parody of texts – literary or living – does not explain *why* or *how* it happens. These sorts of accounts do not explain how identification works, how it gets from text to subject, or how it has such power.

In the case of Holocaust testimonies, identification, which underlies a range of important issues, raises a further and perhaps more significant problem. Fiction, of course, encourages (and often relies on) identification, and testimonies, in as much as they echo the form of fiction, do too. Indeed, as Andrea Reiter argues, survivors 'take their bearings from the realistic style of the nineteenth century, in the belief that this is best suited to what they have to communicate', and even those, like Charlotte Delbo's and Jorge Semprun's that are not realist in form, seem at first to encourage identification.[6] However, testimony aims to prohibit identification on epistemological grounds (a reader really cannnot become, or become identified, with the narrator of a testimony: any such identification is a illusion) and on ethical grounds (a reader should not become identified with narrator of a testimony, as it reduces and 'normalizes' or consumes the otherness of a narrator's experience and the illusion that such an identification creates is possibly pernicious). Testimony, then, is a genre which displays a paradoxical 'doubleness': the form leads to identification while the content and surrounding material lead away from it. I suggest that this conflict between centrifugal and centripetal forces is played out, but not resolved, in the texts of testimonies, and it is this, importantly, that actually characterizes the genre of testimony.

This contribution, then, looks at those tropes and textual strategies in testimony that make identification problematic, under six headings: the textual use of historical evidence and style, the narrative framing, a focus on key moments of horror, the way the texts interrupt or disrupt their own flow, moments of excessive over-identification and the lack of closure in testimony. These headings are not meant to be final or conclusive, or a complete taxonomy, but rather, only to point out some textual signs of this 'doubleness' that characterizes the genre of testimony.[7]

USING HISTORY

The genre of testimony clearly has a relationship with the discipline of history. Much work has been done on the ways in which historians draw on, use and judge testimonies (although testimonies are not simply works of history, or resources for historians). In turn, many testimonies use history. While most testimony narratives follow an autobiographical chronology, several have moments where the flow of narrative stops and the text, in its style or content, becomes 'historical', offering descriptive history or reportage. Several use historical documents or sourced evidence.

(a) Moments of Historical Style and Evidence

David Rousset's very early Marxist-influenced testimony *L'Univers Concentrationnaire* (1946) is a realist (and not surrealist, as is sometimes claimed) 'report' on the 'depths of the camps': something between a historical overview, in style, mixed with personal observations. For example Chapter 5 (ironically titled 'In my father's house there are many mansions') offers a breakdown of the camp system from a Marxist point of view: 'Buchenwald was a chaotic city ... by virtue of its proletariat ... and by reason of its swarming officials, its capitalists, its underworld.'[8] The next chapter offers an analysis of the different nationalities in the camps. Neftali Frankel's *I Survived Hell: The Testimony of a Survivor of the Nazi Extermination Camps (Prisoner Number 161040)*, an account of his life in Tarnow before the war, his imprisonment Auschwitz and then his survival of a death march to

Bergen Belsen, is all written in a dry and impersonal 'historical' style.[9] Kitty Hart interrupts the chronology of her second testimony *Return to Auschwitz* with a chapter called 'The Final Solution' which outlines the history and development of the persecution of the Jews and of the Auschwitz camp from the 1920s to the Holocaust.[10] This book, like many others, not only has personal photos of her family, but also documentary photos of Auschwitz itself. Olga Lengyel also has a documentary section, complete with a table of those 'liquidated'.[11] These moments serve to foreground the historical in the testimonies.

(b) Using Historical Documents

Other testimonies insert different sorts of texts into their narratives. After a reflective epilogue, Rudolph Vrba's testimony *I Cannot Forgive* has two appendices. The first of these is the sworn affidavit, placed and dated, that he submitted to the Eichmann trial. The widely available UK edition of Primo Levi's *If This is a Man* ends with letters from German readers to him. The final pages of Judith Magyar Isaacson's *Seed of Sarah: Memoirs of a Survivor* describe Isaacson's visits to Hessen, the site work camp she had been taken to after Auschwitz, and her thoughts about forgiveness. It ends with some letters to her family and finally with a collection of sources. These 'historical' sections, inserted to make the text more tied into wider accounts of the past, also prevent or disrupt simple identification by interrupting the narrative flow and by making clear to the reader that this particular story is part of a huge historical event.

(c) At the Level of Grammar

However, these sorts of interruptions do not just occur to offer a broad historical sweep. They also occur at much smaller levels and (in English) are often shown by a shift in tense from the perfect to the pluperfect, or from a particular event to a general or repeated event. Primo Levi is perhaps the most famous exponent of this common strategy. His testimony carries not only the narrative of his time in Auschwitz but also various excurses which describe events not in the narrative sequence but instead general instances that illustrate his time in Auschwitz. One of these – 'The Drowned and the Saved' – became a book in its own right. Because these disrupt the normal 'narrative timeline' one expects from a realist novel, they remind the reader that what they are reading is but one part of a much wider atrocity; they also work to disrupt the process of identification.

(d) Using History in Reverse

But these strategies based on using historical evidence, which aim to depersonalize a testimony and stress that it is not simply 'an adventure story', also have an opposite effect on which many testimonies rely. In most realist fiction, the readers echo the characters in not knowing what is going to happen: the reader and the character experience the events at the same time (in this way, most fiction is, in part an 'allegory of reading', in Paul de Man's phrase). In Holocaust testimonies, of course, the reader knows the events – at least in broad outline – and knows also that the narrator survives them. This leads in many cases to heavy and horrible irony. Olga Lenygel describes the following scene:

> We tramped past a charming forest on the outskirts of which stood a red brick building. Great flames belched from the chimney, and the strange sickening sweetish odour which had greeted us upon arrival, attacked us even more powerfully now ... We asked one of the guides, an old inmate, about this structure. 'It is a camp bakery', she replied. We absorbed that without the slightest suspicion. Had she revealed the truth we would not have believed her.[12]

And Kitty Hart writes, 'there was a sickly, fatty cloying smell. Mother and I glanced at each other, baffled. Who could be roasting meat, great quantities of it, at this hour of the morning?'.[13] This irony is often heightened in those testimonies that do not begin at the point of arrival in the camps but with the pre-war world. In occupied Warsaw, the father of Morris Wyszogrod believed that 'in the worst case, we would get ration cards and have to do forced labour'.[14] In these cases, the gap between what the narrator and audience knows, and what the 'characters' know, serves to make identification harder. This means that while the reader is distanced from the 'character' – there is no pleasure of anticipation, for example, and limited involvement – they are drawn to the narrator, their guide: the difficulty is, of course that the 'narrator' and the 'character' are the same. Thus, again, we see the 'doubleness' of testimony, which both repels and attracts identification.

NARRATIVE FRAMES

Another strategy that serves to distance the reader from the text and prevent or problematize identification is the choice of narrative frame. Many (often ghost written) testimonies begin with short 'in media res' vignettes which plunge the reader into the narrative: Fania Fénelon singing at her liberation at Bergen Belsen, Roman Frister with an account of losing both his father and his bread, Edith Hahn Beer with an account of being disguised as a nurse in a German hospital.[15] This tactic, of course, grabs the attention and draws the reader into the work. However, in contrast to this, some testimonies help preserve distance by framing the narrative in different ways. In most fiction, narrators efface themselves from the text to make it seem more 'immediate' and so easier to identify with. In contrast, these texts precisely stress what Michel Foucault called the 'author-function' to stress precisely the mediation between the events and the testimony that recounts them. In these texts, the mediation is foregrounded, often through narrative frames.

(a) Described Frames

Judith Magyar Isaacson frames her account, *Seed of Sarah*, with a story about a lecture. This ends with an issue of identification: towards the end of a question and answer session, Isaacson is asked by a woman student:

> 'How old were you in Auschwitz?'
> 'Nineteen – in 1944' ...
> Swinging back her braids with a shake of her head she shuddered as she said:
> 'Nineteen, like me ... Dean Isaacson, were you raped in the camps?'
> 'Raped?' I blanched, reliving the panic: 'Raped you said? I'll tell you how I escaped it ... '.[16]

These openings and the meta-textual sources and letters discussed earlier serve to frame Isaacson's testimony *as* Isaacson's testimony, a specific document from a specific time by a specific person. The reader is not free, in this case, to identify with and so 'take over', as it were, from Isaacson: despite the novelistic form (in the citation above, for example, suspense about the escape), it is clearly not a novel but a mediated, retold testimony.

(b) Formal Frames

Instead of full narratives, some testimonies – the later texts of Levi and Jean Améry, for example – use the essay, a form which by its nature (an *essai*, a try) already admits the incompleteness of its range and the fallibility of its author. Améry, for example, in *At the Mind's Limits* begins the first essay with a discussion about how he is going to mix the account with a meditation on them: he says, 'I do not want ... to give a documentary report' but rather that he will cover the 'theme of the confrontation of Auschwitz and the intellect': 'however', he writes, 'I cannot bypass what one calls the horrors'.[17] Here we see another instance of 'doubleness'. This contrast underlies all his essays, which are a mixture of reflection with personal narrative. The text moves constantly between the essayistic and reflective 'we' to the narrative or introspective 'I', from the general to the particular and back again. Again, this choice of form works to fix the location of the author/witness as separate from the reader: it impresses a sense of difference and otherness, and prevents Améry's narrative from being 'comfortably' assimilated.

(c) Inserted Tags

Beer achieves a similar result but in a more 'folksy' way. The text of her narrative is full of tropes and shifts of register aiming to give the impression that this is a story orally told, as it might be a to a family sitting around her chair: for example, 'You must understand ... '; 'Hold that in your mind as I tell you this story'; 'So, you see, ... '; 'I tell you ... '; 'Like lightning. Poof. A flame. Poof. Gone. Werner'.[18] In addition, the text specifically locates its contemporary audience in space and time: for example, Beer writes that the Jews in the Third Reich 'were not bold free Americans – remember that. And there were no Israelis then, no soldiers in the desert'.[19] The effect of this is rhetorically to frame the narrator as a mediator between the events and the text – and so not somebody whose experiences can be assimilated to one's own.

(d) Frames of Seeing and Knowing

Narrative frames are central to Charlotte Delbo's testimony, to how it works as testimony. Lawrence Langer, in the introduction to her *Auschwitz and After*, and Rosette Lamont, in the translator's preface, both stress Delbo's maxim 'Il faut donner à voir' (Langer translates this as 'they must be made to see' and suggests that her work 'invites us to "see" the unthinkable as a basis for all that follows').[20] Indeed, seeing and knowing, experiencing and remembering dominate Delbo's work. But throughout, and especially in the first volume *None of Us Will Return*, seeing and knowing are posed with each other in different combinations, in which seeing comes before knowing. Those *who haven't seen and don't know* are those arriving at Auschwitz: they 'do not know there is no arriving in this station', the intellectuals who 'made use of their imagination to write books, yet nothing they imagined ever came close to what they see now', the mother who hits her child 'and we who know cannot forgive her for it'.[21] Delbo continues, 'only those who enter the camp find out what happened to the others'.[22] These become those *who know and have seen*, the witnesses, Delbo herself and her 'camp sisters'. However, they are, at the same time, paradoxically trying not to see, although they know. The section called 'The Dummies' begins '"Look. Look"' as the women look at a huge piles of dead and dying in the yard. It ends,

> 'Don't stare! Why are you staring?' Yvonne P. pleads, her eyes wide open, riveted to a living corpse.
> 'Eat your soup' says Cecile. These women no longer need anything.
> I look too. I look at this corpse that moves but does not move me.
> I'm a big girl now. I can look at naked dummies without being afraid.[23]

Delbo has taught herself that she can know and see and yet not see: not seeing is vital to survive. In the next section, 'The Men', the camp sisters throw bread from women too sick to eat to a column of men with 'wolves' eyes': they 'did not even turn their heads in our direction' because they too have learnt to know and not to see.[24] Later again, in 'The Orchestra', Delbo writes repeatedly 'Do not look, do not listen' to the orchestra whose members play on stolen instruments while 'naked men' are reduced to skeletons.[25] Those who know and can see should try not to: 'I no longer look.'[26] And later: 'Do not look. Do not look at this dummy being dragged on the ground. Do not look at yourself.'[27] In contrast, those who *know and have not seen* should try to see. For example, Delbo writes,

> O you who know
> did you know that hunger makes the eyes sparkle that thirst dims them
> O you who know
> did you know that you can see your mother dead and not shed a tear[28]

and later gives three short images, and ends each one 'Try to look. Just try to see.'[29] This seems as much a challenge to do the impossible, and so presupposing the impossible, than an exhortation. Indeed, between Auschwitz and the world is an 'abyss'.[30]

(d) Allegories of Failed Understanding

That it is impossible to 'know and have not seen' is made clear later in

Delbo's *The Measure of Our Days* when the narrator meets Pierre, the supportive husband of her friend Marie-Louise. Pierre has an interest in experiences of his wife: he has read her notebooks, and read widely about the 'deportations'. His wife says that 'my memories have become his own. So much so I have the distinct impression he was there with me.' Pierre returns with 'Ah, Charlotte! I'm so happy to see you at last. I didn't say "make your acquaintance"; I've know you quite a long time.' Pierre lived in France during the war, sent parcels to his wife with messages hidden on them. He did not suspect that she might have died as 'at the time we didn't know anything about the camps'. After the war Pierre and Marie-Louise visited Birkenau. From his wife's descriptions, he recognizes it all, takes photographs, refines his wife's memory ('She no longer knew whether she was on the right or left side [of the block]'). Pierre says to Charlotte, the narrator, 'I saw more than you did when you were there: the crematoria, the gas chambers, the wall below against which the men were shot.'

As these sections are almost all in dialogue, it is only possible to gauge the narrator's feeling by her actions. Instead of staying overnight, she leaves – 'I can't stay. Forgive me.' Pierre wishes her well: 'Charlotte, you know that this is your home, here with us, with your comrades'. She writes that, 'I felt them there standing on the threshold of their pretty house at the end of a cool, shady walk lined with pine trees'.[31] It is clear here that – however supportive and well-intentioned Pierre was – he has colonized and assimilated memories that are not his, and assumed a role, through reading, talking and imagination, that does not reflect his experience, not what he actually saw. He is not, except in imagination, Charlotte's friend or comrade, though he may be friendly. Although he may have seen the crematoria and the gas chambers, this is not to have seen more of the camp, except in a banal sense. Indeed, their pretty house with its cool, shady walk of pine seems to be, somehow, a domestication or normalization of the events in Auschwitz – another house with pines and cold, dark walks. For Delbo, as Sara Horowitz argues, the 'problem lies not only in the survivor's inability to speak the unspeakable; it lies also in our inability – as non-participants – to imagine the unimaginable'.[32]

Delbo sets up Pierre as an allegory for those who read about the Holocaust and think that they have seen it: he thinks himself to be a 'witness though the imagination' and Delbo has nothing but scorn – and perhaps a feeling of disgust – for him. This account is an allegory of failed understanding. There is an identification taking place here: the reader (the reader who is not a survivor) is being identified with Pierre and is being shown, in the text, how ridiculous or pernicious they (we?) look if they claim to understand what Jorge Semprun calls 'the essential part of the experience'.[33] This serves to make identification with the survivor impossible precisely because there is a position for the reader to occupy: who 'knows and has not seen', and any claims made by a Pierre, as it were, are shown – with a chastening shock, perhaps – to be wrong, absurd or harmful.

But the discussion of Pierre has another implication, too. It seems to suggest that his wife, Marie-Louise, can no longer see what she has seen. She has identified herself with those who know but did not see. As Delbo writes in *Days and Memory*, the 'skin enfolding the memory of Auschwitz is tough. Even so, it gives way at times, revealing all it contains'.[34] And this leads us to uncover an ambiguity in her use of seeing and knowing as a motif. In the prose poem, cited earlier, 'O You Who Know', the knowers become not only those who know about and have not seen (experienced) the camp, but those who, like Marie-Louise (and others, in Delbo's account of 'after' Auschwitz), who have denied it, or 'domesticated' the experience. In this complex way, Delbo makes it clear that it is hard, even for a survivor, to access or to inhabit what Langer calls 'deep memory'. For Delbo (who began writing in 1946 and 1947, and publishing between 1965 and 1985), it seems as if those who have learnt not to see, sometimes need to be made to see.

(e) Memory of the Dead

Many testimonies end with specific acts of remembering individuals who were murdered. The main body of Rudolf Vrba's account ends with his participation in a partisan attack: 'tears of happiness were coursing down my cheeks. I was running forwards not backwards.'[35] However, there is an epilogue to *I Cannot Forgive*, and two appendices. The second deals with a transport from Vrba's region of Slovakia: the final words are 'In this way did young Mrs Tomasov, old Isaac Rabinowic and Mrs Polanska and all the others on that transport from Slovakia die'.[36] Similarly, Ezra BenGershôm's 'U-boat' narrative *David: Testimony of a Holocaust Survivor* ends with an account of the sufferings and deaths of his family and friends:

> My sister Toni, posing as an 'ethnic German' domestic help, had lived through the German occupation to the bitter end – only to experience the horrors of the Russian conquest. Toni survived the war. Leon and Lore, I learned, had fallen into the hands of the Hungarian police in July 1944. Soon afterwards they found themselves in a goods wagon, bound for Auschwitz.[37]

These turn the testimony into, in part, a personal memorial, not open to an easy assimilation.

It is possible to find such moments in Holocaust testimony precisely because the act of witnessing is always mediated, and because all such moments show that 'in addition to time and place' the writer's 'very language, traditions and world view played crucial roles in the making of their literary witness ... As raw as they may have been at the moment, the ghetto and camp experiences were immediately refined and organised by witnesses within in terms of their Weltanschauung'.[38]

EPIPHANIES

Another factor – hardly a strategy – that prevents identification is simply that the events of the texts are hardly bearable. This is especially clear at the moments that occur in many testimonies which, in other genres, might be called epiphanies. An epiphany, a term drawn from modernist writing and criticism, is a moment of 'showing forth' or 'revealing' something: the unveiling of a truth. The novels of James Joyce and Virginia Woolf are often discussed in terms of their central epiphanic moments. In testimonies, this trope serves to focus the horror in a specific, revealing, incident. In Elie Wiesel's *Night*, the murder of the babies is this moment of horror: 'Never shall I forget the little faces of the children, whose bodies I saw turned into wreaths of smoke beneath a silent blue sky.'[39] In Isabella Leitner's *Fragments of Isabella* there is a similar moment, entitled 'My Potyo, My Sister', when the narrator meditates on the murder of her baby sister. A matching emblematic moment occurs in Levi's *If This is a Man*, again very early in his imprisonment:

> Driven by thirst, I eyed a fine icicle outside the window, within hand's reach. I opened the window and broke off the icicle but at once a large, heavy guard prowling around outside snatched it way from me. 'Warum?' I asked him in my poor German. 'Hier ist kein warum'('there is no why here'), he replied, pushing me inside with a shove. The explanation is repugnant but simple: in this place everything is forbidden, not for hidden reasons, but because the camp has been created for that purpose.[40]

For the first two, the epiphany consists of the destruction of babies, as the hope and future of a community. The babies are more than a symbol of innocence, but innocence itself: for the other, the inversion of reason, the end of the possibility of understanding, the inverse of science.

In Semprun's *The Long Voyage* too, the 'day I saw the Jewish children die' – the murder of a group of Polish Jewish children by the SS and their dogs – is the central, structuring moment. The testimony builds up to this epiphanic event: the awful story 'has never been told ... [it has] lain buried in my memory like some mortal treasure preying on it with a sterile suffering'. Semprun tells this under protest by himself, uncertain if he can continue, if he wants to continue, certain he ought to continue:

> maybe I shall be able to tell about the death of the Jewish children ... perhaps it is out of pride that I have never told anyone the story ... as if I had the right, or even the possibility to keep it to myself any longer. It's true that I had decided to forget ... I had forgotten everything, from now on I can remember ... I feel compelled to tell it. I have to speak out in the name of things that happened.[41]

Retreating from the East, and emptying camps as they go, the SS discover about 15 Jewish children surviving in a boxcar. At first uncertain what to do, the SS return later with dogs and make a game of killing the children. The last two die, 'the older one's right hand clasping the smaller one's left hand'.[42] The episode has an 'epiphanic' and emblematic power for Semprun and sums up, metonymically, the horror of the Holocaust. These moments – it seems – are simply so awful that identifying with the narrators who describe them seems impossible. Indeed, even commenting on and quoting them, here, seems to be questionable.

INTERRUPTIONS

Testimony texts are also riven with interruptions that break up the flow of narrative. Very often these are to do with the chronology of events. Edith Hahn Beer's U-boat narrative regularly marks a distinction between the time of the narrative and the time of the narration (and so, the testimony tells its telling, as it were). Delbo, too, makes use of this trope quite frequently. After her description of 'living skeletons that dance' she writes, 'I am writing this story in a café – it is turning into a story': again disrupting the time of the telling from the time of the tale.[43] In his memoirs, Elie Wiesel writes that 'I reread what I have just written, and my hand trembles. I who rarely weep am in tears. I see the flames again, and the children, and yet again I tell myself that it is not enough to weep.'[44] Frister's testimony, *The Cap*, has an extremely complex time structure, mixing different periods together freely and easily. For example, one section moves from post-war Prague, to a radio interview 42 years later, to memories of his grandfather before the war and back to Prague in 1947 and then back to his family's attempt to flee Poland in the late 1930s.[45]

Semprun's work, too, is characterized by a complex time structure, involving leaps forward and backwards in the chronological narrative. His testimonies work in a similar way: taking a set period – a Sunday during his time at Buchenwald, for example – as a narrative frame, they weave an account of this with accounts of events before, during and after the war. Memories of one moment inevitably invoke other memories, and it is only through the whole contextual mesh of memories which make up a person that the events are approached. The style of the books aims to reflect this movement of memory and the problems of writing: they are shifting, uncertain. There are slips in the chronology – conversations in 1944 slide into conversations in the 1950s, for example – that serve to disrupt the text.

Other texts, more conventionally realist than Semprun's and Delbo's, organize their chronologies in different ways, telling the stories in different orders. These have different effects on the testimony. Fénelon begins her narrative with her liberation, singing – oddly in an echo of *Casablanca* – the 'Marseillaise', the 'Internationale' and 'God Save the King' into a microphone for the BBC, 'galvanised by joy'.[46] Despite the ominous English title – *Playing for Time* – it is clear that Fénelon survives victorious, able to sing, and this sets tone for the rest of the narrative. In his *I Cannot Forgive*, Vrba draws out the significance of Himmler's visit to Auschwitz as a leitmotif for the rest of his account: the evil, power and brutality of the Final Solution from the high (Himmler) to the low (the block Kapo who beats an incorrectly dressed prisoner to death before Himmler arrives). Hart, again, begins her *Return to Auschwitz* in 1946 with her arrival in England, allowing the camp to take up the centre of the testimony and to stress the need to tell an uninterested world.

Some prose texts do more than just disturb their narratives. They are, or consist in, interruption. In this they enact in prose – or in the case of Delbo, a mixture of prose and poetry – what Paul Celan and others enacted in poetry: the 'breakage of the verse enacts the breakage of the world'.[47] *Fragments of Isabella* is exactly that, consisting of short, broken fragments, picking up on moments of her experience of the camp, the death march, her escape from the death march, migration to the US. Although there is a narrative it is made up of gaps and 'snapshots'; it becomes impossible to identify with Isabella herself as there is little narrative with which to identify. Similarly, Delbo's work is made up of brief sections of text: some dialogues, some prose, some poetry. Although these make up a narrative, the fragmented form reflects the fragmentation that the experience has induced. The final page of the first volume has only one line, 'None of us was meant to return'.[48] The blankness of the rest of the page signifies all those who did not return: the emptiness remains empty, a reminder that, as Levi writes, 'each of us survivors is in more than one way an exception: something that we ourselves, to exorcise the past, tend to forget'.[49]

OVER-IDENTIFICATION

An exception to these particular strategies that serve to prevent identification and assimilation by creating distance is Simon Wiesenthal's *The Sunflower*. Although the book is a testimony, it can 'easily be seen as a moral fable invented to illustrate a universal dilemma'.[50] The sunflower of the title is a recurring motif: the column of slave workers in which Simon is marching passes a military cemetery and each grave has a sunflower on it. For Wiesenthal, the sunflowers are both memorials of and almost conduits to the dead: 'the dead were receiving light and messages ... I envied the dead soldiers. Each had a sunflower to connect him to the living world ... For me there would be no sunflower. I would be buried in a mass grave.'[51] The book, because of the way it is about relating to the dead, then becomes the sunflower of its own leitmotif, the sunflower by which we can talk to the dead. It specifically uses the way in which readers identify with narratives to pose a question about guilt and forgiveness. The narrative is straightforward. Simon Wiesenthal is a prisoner in the extermination camp system. From his column of slave labourers he is summoned, at random, by a nurse to tend to a young SS man, dying in great pain. The SS man, Karl, begs Wiesenthal to forgive him for the atrocities he has committed. Wiesenthal leaves without answering. The rest of the book is made up of the conversations he has with others about what he should have done.

The question is in part about the relationship between the perpetrators and the victims, but also about identification. Wiesenthal himself moves between identifying with Karl and feelings of hatred. On the one hand, he says, 'I admit I did feel some pity for the fellow'.[52] On the other, even thinking about forgiving the SS man leaves him feeling ashamed. Through an imagined conversation with a fellow inmate, Arthur, Wiesenthal accuses himself in Arthur's voice: 'you can't forget a dying SS man while countless Jews are tortured and killed every hour ... You are beginning to think the Germans are in some way superior, and that's why you are worrying about your dying SS man', and indeed, when Arthur does, in fact, call Karl 'your SS man' Wiesenthal is very hurt.[53] If Wiesenthal can identify with Karl, Karl can be forgiven: if he cannot, Karl will not be. To identify with Karl means admitting believing in exactly the sort of universal humanity that Karl, by his actions, has denied. And Wiesenthal the narrator ends by asking the reader, directly, what they would have done: by making the reader identify with the narrator, the book puts the reader in the position of deciding what she or he should do. Again, here there is a 'doubleness' – a demand that the reader assimilate and come to judgement of an aporia.

Each of the editions of *The Sunflower* published in 1969, 1976 and 1997 has a large meta-text, a 'symposium' in which, as the blurb states, 'fifty-three distinguished men and women give their response'. These include Holocaust survivors (Améry, Levi), religious leaders, experts in the field of Holocaust studies, survivors of other genocides and murderous regimes, and even Albert Speer. The answers are all considered. Primo Levi offers a gentle dismantling of the whole scenario. Langer, like many in the symposium, writes, 'I have no idea what I might have done'.[54] However, he goes on: 'nor do I believe the question is a legitimate one. Role-playing about the Holocaust trivializes the serious issues of judgement and forgiveness that *The Sunflower* raises.'[55] Clearly, Langer's position is not opposed to asking questions about the Holocaust in detail (for him the key issue is why people like Karl joined the SS in the first place): rather he is acutely aware of the way in which narrative accounts allow the Holocaust to become assimilated into everyday experience, and how readers identify ('role-play') with the victim narrators. For Langer, this assimilation leads to 'pre-empting the Holocaust', that is, 'using – and perhaps abusing – its grim details to fortify a prior commitment to an ideal of moral reality, community, responsibility, or religious belief that leaves us with space to retain faith in their pristine value in a post-Holocaust world'.[56] However, the 'over-identification' this seems to demand could be seen to overwhelm the normal processes of identification. The text asks: 'You, who have just read this sad and tragic episode in my life, can mentally change places with me and ask yourself the crucial question, "What would I have done?"'.[57] The answer seems often to be that the 'mentally changing place' just cannot really take place.

LACK OF CLOSURE

Primo Levi offers another sort of final disturbance in 'The Awakening', the last chapter of *The Truce*: he dreams he is in the 'Lager once more, and nothing is true outside the Lager ... a well-known voice resounds: a single word, not imperious, but brief and subdued. It is the dawn command of Auschwitz, a foreign word, feared and expected: get up, "Wstawàch".'[58] 'The Awakening' is not an awakening from a terrible 'dream' of the camps back into normal life, but the awakening into a tormented post-Holocaust existence in which the camps do not interrupt 'normal life' but, rather, 'normal life' interrupts the unceasing experience of the camps. The reason that these endings are disturbing and prevent identification is because, like the frequent practice of rewriting testimony, they reveal that the end is not the end: only a temporary respite.

Barbara Foley suggests that the 'great majority of Holocaust memoirists fall silent when they have completed their tales'.[59] In fact, I suggest that the opposite is true. Once they have told their tales, Holocaust memoirists tell them again: another characteristic of testimony writing is its lack of closure. In postmodern writing this is usually understood as a disavowal of, in Henry James's words, 'a distribution at the last of prizes, pensions, wives, babies, millions, appended paragraphs and cheerful remarks', in favour of an incomplete, unfinished ending. For testimony writing, the refusal of closure comes in other forms because many actual testimony texts about the Holocaust have a structure that ends with the war or with return or with settling after the war. Filip Müller, exhausted on a rafter, is awoken by shouts of 'We are free! Comrade, we are free!': he crawls out into a wood and falls asleep, to be awakened by a column of tanks; he writes: 'I realised that the hideous Nazi terror had ended at last.'[60] Neftali Frankel describes his emigration to America. This chronology offers a basic narrative structure. However, as I suggested earlier, this is often disturbed or disrupted by the inability to escape the events: Levi's terrible 'Wstawàch'.[61] Delbo, too, describes this return: the

> skin enfolding the memory of Auschwitz is tough. Even so, it gives way at times, revealing all it contains. Over dreams the conscious will has no power. And in these dreams I see myself, yes, my own self such as I know I was: hardly able to stand on my feet, my throat tight, my heart beating wildly, frozen to the marrow, filthy, skin and bones ... Luckily in my agony I cry out. My cry wakes me and I emerge from the nightmare, drained. It takes days from everything to get back to normal, for everything to get shoved back inside memory, for the skin of memory to mend again.[62]

But the lack of closure also occurs in – or more accurately, *as* – the oeuvre of a writer: survivors return again and again to write about the Holocaust. As Wiesel writes, the 'truth is I could spend the rest of my days recounting the weeks, months and eternities I lived in Auschwitz'.[63]

Talking with Carlos Fuentes about re-writing in Spanish *Le Grand Voyage* – in rather the same way Wiesel produced *Night* by translating and editing the Yiddish original *And the World Remained Silent*, with Jérôme Lindon – Semprun recounts Fuentes's joke: 'And so ... you will have realised every writer's dream: to spend your life writing a single book, endlessly renewed'.[64] For Fuentes this is a light-hearted remark: for Semprun – with the black humour of the inmate that Levi discussed – it is both a savage commentary and a reaffirmation that others cannot understand the experience. It is not a book that one would choose to rewrite endlessly but the only one possible (as Delbo writes, 'I was in despair at having lost the faculty of dreaming, of harbouring illusions; I was no longer open to imagination. This is the part of me that died in Auschwitz. This is what turned me into a ghost').[65]

Wiesel writes that, in all his stories, the 'teller of tales still lives in the shadow of the flames that once had illuminated and blinded him'.[66] Semprun's *Literature or Life*, in part a commentary on Levi and on the condition of survivor writing, knows of what closure on the text of this endless book consists: 'only a suicide could put a signature, a voluntary end to this unfinished – this unfinishable – process of mourning'.[67] And for Semprun, Levi's suicide was exactly this:

> Why, forty years later, had his recollections ceased to be a rich resource for him? Why had he lost the peace that writing seemed to have restored to him? What cataclysm had occurred in his memory that Saturday? Why did it suddenly become impossible for him to cope with the horrors of remembrance? One last time, with no help for it, anguish had quite simply overwhelmed him. Leaving no hope of any way out. The anguish he described in the last lines of *La tregua* [*The Truce*] ... Nothing was real outside the camp, that's all. The rest was only a brief pause, an illusion of the sense, an uncertain dream. And that's all there is to say.[68]

For others, they simply write and rewrite their testimony. Kitty Hart's *Return to Auschwitz* was preceded by *I am Alive*, published in 1961 and in a revised edition in 1974.[69] Levi's *The Drowned and the Saved* revisits and expands – if in a slightly different tone – parts of *If This is a Man*.[70]

The reasons for this consistent re-writing and consequent refusal of closure are not simple. Of course, and perhaps most importantly, it is a response to the events themselves. The impossibility of closure is simply a fact of life for the survivors. Wiesel goes a bit further: 'I have told the story before and will tell it again, will tell it forever, hoping to find in it some hidden truth, some vague hope of salvation.'[71] But there are other reasons. Writers such as Michael André Bernstein, Peter Novick and Tim Cole have shown how the reception of Holocaust history has developed since the war; approaches and interest have waned then waxed. Where once even Levi's work was turned down, now many publishers and filmmakers are interested in Holocaust testimonies. This has meant that the opportunity for rewriting, as well as the compulsion to rewrite, has emerged: Kitty Hart's *Return to Auschwitz* was developed in parallel with a Yorkshire TV documentary with the same name. In addition, Hart's second version picks up on issues passed over or ignored in the first, such as her cool reception in Britain, the lack of interest in or refusal to hear about her experiences in Auschwitz (her uncle, almost as soon as he meets her, says, 'there's one thing I must make quite clear. On no account are you to talk about any of the things that have happened to you. Not in my house, I don't want my girls upset. And I don't want to know').[72] Training to be a nurse in Birmingham was 'the nearest I ever came to total despair', she writes.[73] Much of the psychological and social aftermath of the Holocaust, its effect on, for example, her relationship with her mother, are all things that have only emerged in texts as time and with it the 'epistemological climate' has moved.[74]

Closure, then for these testimony writers, seems impossible: the compulsion to write, the 'bursting out' of the skin of their memories, and the changing relation of the contemporary world to the events of the Holocaust, mean that these texts are never finished. This, too, serves as an interruption to an identification as it disrupts the reader's expectations of closure and comprehension.

CONCLUSION

Here, then, is a taxonomy – partial, particular – of the ways in which testimony texts serve to disrupt identification. This essay has also outlined the generic markers of testimony that differentiate it from fiction and from autobiography. These texts sometimes utilize the style of writing more commonly associated with the discipline of history, and use documentary evidence. They set up (and sometimes explore) distinct narrative frames which prevent – or try to prevent – identification. They often use particular epiphanic moments to focus the horror. They are characterized by interruptions to their narrative and disruptions in their chronology. They can – in the case of *The Sunflower* – attempt to create an over-identification. And they lack closure, both as texts, and as part of each survivor's oeuvre.

The point of this taxonomy is not to be comprehensive, nor to do what Gérard Genette attempted in *Narrative Discourse* in essaying 'laws of narratology', but to bring to the fore illustrative textual characteristics of this genre. Not every testimony has to have each one, nor are these characteristics criteria for determining what is and is not a testimony: they mark only descriptive 'family resemblances', not prescriptions. (That such prescriptions are ineffective – a lesson leant from the Wilkomirski affair – is clear: prescriptions would also serve to delimit this still developing genre.) Moreover, each testimony changes and brings a different focus to the genre. All genres are shifting and developing: this one more than most. In part this is because, as Alvin Rosenfeld writes, Holocaust writing is

> a literature of fragments, or partial and provisional forms, no one of which by itself can suffice to express the Holocaust, but the totality of which begins to accomplish and register a powerful effect ... Holocaust writing is part of a composite literature, more impressive in the sum of its parts than a separate statements.[75]

No one testimony is 'the central testimony': testimony works most powerfully as a genre. Geoffrey Hartman, using a metaphor from Jean-François Lyotard, writes that the 'after-shocks are measurable; we are deep into the process of creating new instruments to record and express what happened'.[76] All this really serves to try to explain why reading testimony is not like reading a novel. These observations only to begin to offer a rhetorical and academic apparatus to explain this common feeling, as an attempt to begin to understand the genre of testimonies and how it differs from others.

Why do these texts share these characteristics or strategies? It is not simply academic 'pigeon-holing'. It is not, or is not usually, a consciously planned strategy taken by the author/survivor. While, of course, these texts are constructed and are not immediate – Levi writing furiously, Wiesel editing and editing his Yiddish version, Semprum writing and destroying his manuscripts, Beer persuaded to tell her story, and so on – they were not constructed as part of a movement, as (say) one postmodernist writer imitates another. Cathy Caruth writes that the figures of 'falling' or 'departure'

> engender stories that in fact emerge out of the rhetorical potential and literary resonance of these figures, a literary dimension that

cannot be reduced to the thematic content of the text or to what the theory encodes, and that, beyond what we can know or theorise about, stubbornly persists in bearing witness to some forgotten wound.[77]

I suggest that, similarly, the tropes and strategies I have looked at bear in relation to the context of western writing the 'rhetorical potential and literary resonance' to bear witness. That is, they are not a simple reflection in prose of the psychology of trauma. Rather, their tropes and strategies are empowered by their differences to other forms and genres of writing to offer – to be – testimony. This testimony is both personal (Primo Levi writes that one reason to write is to 'free oneself from anguish') and communal (in its bearing witness).[78] These texts draw on cultural resources (ideas about realism and modernism, say, and ideas about narrative time lines, the relation between fiction and history) and construct them in a new way. Indeed, it is the cultural resources that are the ground of possibility for these prose testimonies. As James Young writes:

> if modern responses to catastrophe have included the breakdown and repudiation of traditional forms and archetypes, then one postmodern response might be to recognize that even as we reject the absolute meanings and answers these 'archaic' forms provide, we are still unavoidably beholden to these same forms for both our expression and our understanding of the Holocaust.[79]

But this is not to say that this new or renewed genre is not innovative, but that its innovation consists in its reworking of the 'traditional forms', centrally, I have suggested, in such a way that identification – the staple of literature for two centuries – is thrown into question. After the Holocaust, reading has to be changed.

This also sheds light on the affinity between postmodern novels and testimony. Postmodern novels, too, mix genres, try to defy identification, lack closure and foreground their own textuality. Postmodern texts have found their way to similar textual strategies which have the 'rhetorical potential and literary resonance' which allow them perhaps to reflect a wider collective breakdown in the world, however this is to be understood (perhaps as a shift from cognitive questions to postcognitive questions, incredulity about metanarratives, the death of god, the cultural logic of late capitalism and so on). To say this is to suggest – following Wiesel's claim about testimony as a new genre which comes into being as a response to the Holocaust – that postmodern fiction shares or parallels the tropes of testimony. However, it is also the case that in testimony, signified by these tropes and strategies, something 'stubbornly persists', a link to a 'forgotten wound' or more accurately to a remembered event. It these textual signs that bear a trace: the trace, as Derrida makes clear in an interview, which marks 'the limits of the linguistic and the limits of the rhetorical'.[80] The trace is the grounds for that which refuses comprehension (here, through identification): it is the trace of incomprehensible other, the witness.

And it is this, the idea of the trace, which underlies the truth of testimony. There is much debate about the 'historical' truth of testimonies. Many historians, for example, find them very open to question as sources for historical truth.[81] As I will argue in detail in my forthcoming monograph, *The Holocaust and the Postmodern*, this sort of understanding assumes that there is only one way of understanding truth – as a positivist 'accurate record'. However, there is another way of understanding truth which is not contradictory but complementary: not as 'the agreement or correspondence of a judgement, an assertion or a proposition with its object', but as an existential uncovering or revelation, a way of showing 'who we are and how things are in the world'. This truth reveals something not quantitatively but qualitatively different from the historical record (yet it does not reveal the 'sublime', outside time). While it can be measured as a historical datum, a testimony is not only that. Breaking and remaking the codes of western literature – defying identification, mixing styles, and shifting narrative frames and so on – are not 'historical facts' but affective and revealing traits. Thus, Delbo's remark, 'Today, I am not sure that what I write is true. I am certain it is truthful',[82] can be taken to mean: 'what I write may not correspond to the "historical record"; it certainly reveals in a more profound way what happened in the camps'.

In his influential book *Zakhor*, Yosef Hayim Yerushalmi argues that literature has become the crucible of Jewish memory, not historiography. However, I would suggest that the crucible of Holocaust memory, Jewish or non-Jewish, is not literature understood as fiction, but the genre of testimony. Accounts are not just words that 'signify experiences, but ... become ... *traces* of [those] experiences'.[83] A testimony is an encounter with otherness: it constitutes such an encounter precisely because identification – a grasping or comprehension which reduces otherness to the same, events outside one's framework reduced to events inside one's framework – cannot (or should not) happen. Testimony is a witness to these events and should not be reduced simply to an historical account or a 'documentary novel' (these are both ways of reducing that otherness to the same): it is part of a genre of its own. And it is this genre – one that is strange not least because it denies the commonly accepted process of identification – that reveals the truth of the Holocaust.

NOTES

1. Elie Wiesel, 'The Holocaust as Literary Inspiration', in *Dimensions of the Holocaust* (Evanston, IL, 1990), p.7.
2. Shoshana Felman and Dori Laub, *Testimony: Crises of Witnessing in Literature, Psychoanalysis, and History* (London, 1992), p.7.
3. Diana Fuss, *Identification Papers* (London, 1995), p.1.
4. Ibid., p.2.
5. Ibid., p.4.
6. Andrea Reiter, *Narrating the Holocaust* (trans. Patrick Camiler) (London, 2000), p.193.
7. I discuss both the nature of literary identification and the 'doubleness' of testimony in more detail in *The Holocaust and the Postmodern*, forthcoming.
8. David Rousset, *A World Apart* (trans. Yvonne Mayse and Roger Senhouse) (London, 1951), pp.22–3.
9. Neftali Frankel with Roman Palazon Bertra, *I Survived Hell: The Testimony of a Survivor of the Nazi Extermination Camps (Prisoner Number 161040)* (New York, 1991).
10. Kitty Hart, *Return to Auschwitz* (London, 1983), pp.111–27.
11. Olga Lengyel, *Five Chimneys* (London, 1959), p.82
12. Lengyel, *Five Chimneys*, pp.33–4.
13. Hart, *Return*, p.79.
14. Morris Wyszogrod, *A Brush with Death: An Artist in the Death Camps* (Albany, NY, 1999), p.31.
15. Fania Fénelon with Marcelle Routier, *Playing for Time* (trans. Judith Landry) (New York, 1977); Roman Frister, *The Cap, or the Price of a Life* (trans. Hillel Halkin) (London, 1999); Edith Hahn Beer with Susan Dworkin, *The Nazi Officer's Wife* (London, 2000), p.26.
16. Judith Magyar Isaacson, *Seed of Sarah: Memoirs of a Survivor*, Second Edition (Chicago, IL, 1991), p.xi.
17. Jean Améry, *At the Mind's Limits* (trans. Sidney Rosenfeld and Stella P. Rosenfeld) (London, 1999), p.1.
18. Beer, *The Nazi Officer's Wife*, pp.26, 5, 26, 69, 187, 288.
19. Ibid., p.26.
20. Charlotte Delbo, *Auschwitz and After* (trans. Rosette C. Lamont) (London, 1995), pp.x, xvii.
21. Ibid., pp.4,6, 7.
22. Ibid., p.9.
23. Ibid., p.19.
24. Ibid., p.21.
25. Ibid., pp.106–7.
26. Ibid., p.52.
27. Ibid., p.89.
28. Ibid., p.11.
29. Ibid., pp.84, 85, 86.
30. Ibid., p.181.
31. Ibid., pp.280–88.
32. Sara Horowitz, 'Voices from the Killing Ground', in Geoffrey Hartman (ed.), *Holocaust Remembrance: The Shapes of Memory* (Oxford, 1994), pp.42–69, p.45.
33. Jorge Semprun, *Literature or Life*, trans. Linda Coverdale (London, 1997), pp.87–8.

Identification and the Genre of Testimony 139

34. Charlotte Delbo, *Days and Memory*, trans. Rosette Lamont (Marlboro, VT, 1990), p.3.
35. Rudolf Vrba and Alan Bestic, *I Cannot Forgive* (London, 1963), p.261.
36. Ibid., p.278.
37. Ezra BenGershôm, *David: Testimony of a Holocaust survivor* (trans. J. A. Underwood) (Oxford, 1988), p.283.
38. James Young, *Writing and Rewriting the Holocaust: Narrative and the Consequences of Interpretation* (Bloomington, IN, 1988), p.26.
39. Elie Wiesel, *Night* (trans Stella Rodway) (Harmondsworth, 1981), pp.43, 45.
40. Primo Levi, *If This is a Man* (trans. Stuart Woolf) (London, 1979), p.35.
41. Jorge Semprun, *The Long Voyage* (trans. Richard Seaver) (Harmondsworth, 1997), pp.162–3.
42. Ibid., p.166.
43. Delbo, *Auschwitz*, p.26.
44. Elie Wiesel, *All Rivers Run to the Sea* (London, 1996), p.78.
45. Frister, *The Cap*, pp.45–8.
46. Fania Fénelon, *Playing for Time*, p.9.
47. Felman and Laub, *Testimony*, p.25.
48. Delbo, *Auschwitz*, p.114.
49. Primo Levi, *The Drowned and the Saved* (trans. Raymond Rosenthal) (London, 1988), p.82.
50. Lawrence Langer, *Pre-empting the Holocaust* (London, 1998), p.166.
51. Simon Wiesenthal, *The Sunflower* (New York, 1997), p.14.
52. Ibid., p.83.
53. Ibid., pp.62, 69.
54. Langer in Wiesenthal, *The Sunflower*, p.186.
55. Ibid., p.186.
56. Langer, *Pre-empting the Holocaust*, p.1.
57. Wiesenthal, *The Sunflower*, p.98.
58. Levi, *If This is a Man* and *The Truce*, pp.380–81.
59. Barbara Foley, 'Fact, Fiction, Fascism: Testimony and Mimesis in Holocaust Narrative', *Comparative Literature*, Vol.34 (1982), pp.330–60, 339.
60. Müller, *Eyewitness Auschwitz*, p.171.
61. Levi, *If This is a Man* and *The Truce*, pp.380–81.
62. Delbo, *Days and Memory*, p.1.
63. Wiesel, *All Rivers Run to the Sea*, p.89.
64. Jorge Semprun, *Literature or Life* (trans. Linda Coverdale) (London, 1997), pp.275–6.
65. Delbo, *Days and Memory*, p.239.
66. Wiesel, *All Rivers*, p.89.
67. Semprun, *Literature or Life*, p.194.
68. Ibid., p.251.
69. Kitty Hart, *I am Alive* (London, 1961); Kitty Hart, *I am Alive*, Revised Edition (London, 1974).
70. Gillian Banner discusses these differences, illuminatingly, in *Holocaust Literature: Schulz, Levi, Spiegelman and the Memory of the Offence* (London, 2000), especially pp.117–20.
71. Wiesel, *All Rivers …*, p.67.
72. Hart, *Return to Auschwitz*, p.14.
73. Hart, *Return to Auschwitz*, p.17.
74. James Young, *Writing and Rewriting the Holocaust: Narrative and the Consequences of Interpretation* (Bloomington, IN, 1990), p.26.
75. Alvin Rosenfeld, *A Double Dying: Reflections on Holocaust Literature* (Bloomington, IN, 1988), pp.33, 34.
76. Geoffrey Hartman, *The Longest Shadow: In the Aftermath of the Holocaust* (Bloomington, IN, 1996), p.1.
77. Cathy Caruth, *Unclaimed Experience: Trauma, Narrative and History* (London, 1996), p.5.
78. Primo Levi, *Other People's Trades* (trans. Raymond Rosenthal) (London, 1989), p.65.

79. Young, *Writing and Rewriting the Holocaust*, p.192.
80. Jacques Derrida and Maurizio Ferraris, *A Taste for the Secret* (trans. Giacomo Donis; eds. Giacomo Donis and David Webb) (London, 2001), p.76.
81. Dan Stone summarises these well in 'Holocaust Testimony and the Challenge to the Philosophy of History', in Robert Fine and Charles Turner (eds.), *Social Theory after the Holocaust* (Liverpool, 2000), pp.219–34.
82. Delbo, *Auschwitz*, epigraph, n.p.
83. Young, *Writing and Rewriting the Holocaust*, p.26.

Biography

Breaking Free from 'A Scottish Shtetl': The Life, Times and Jewishness of C.P. Taylor

AVRAM TAYLOR

This study considers the life and work of the Glaswegian Jewish playwright C.P. Taylor (1929–81). It offers both a personal perspective (from his son) and an attempt to place him in the context of the community he came from (the Gorbals). Taylor's development as a playwright is considered, and all the strands of his work are discussed, although the main focus of the piece is on the themes of anti-Semitism and Jewish identity in his plays. These are used to explore the question of whether it is possible for an individual to separate religion and culture in their understanding of 'Jewishness'.

There is little to distinguish the Northumbrian village of Longhorsley from the other villages around it. It is not large, with a church, a pub, a butcher, a grocery store, and a post office. However, set in the fields just outside the village itself is a derelict and roofless church with a small cemetery. It is here that the dramatist C.P. Taylor is buried. I make an occasional, and emotional, pilgrimage to this spot, picking my way between the cowpats, in order to visit my father's grave. I am the oldest of his four children, all of whom were deeply shocked and grief-stricken by his untimely death, from a heart attack, at the age of 52. We all loved him very much, and still miss him tremendously. In addition, we are all fans of his work, and grew up reading, watching and talking about his plays, which are an integral

---

All dates of plays in the text refer to first performances.

The author would like to thank all the members of his family who gave so freely of their time and their memories for this piece, especially his mother. He could not have written it without her. He would also like to thank Susan Friesner for her help in preparing this study and acknowledges the contribution her own research has made. Finally, thanks are due to Colin Holmes for suggesting that he write this piece, and he would like to thank both him and Don MacRaild, at the University of Northumbria, for their comments on earlier drafts.

part of our lives. I was asked to write about his life and work for this collection because his background, as a Glaswegian Jew, makes him a particularly appropriate subject for inclusion.

Although there are many aspects to my father's work, the focus of the account will be on the community he came from, the Gorbals, and on his complex relationship to Judaism. As a consequence, I have chosen to focus on two of his plays in which this is the central theme: *Bread and Butter* (1966), and *Walter* (1977). This piece is intended to be both a discussion of my father's work and a contribution to British Jewish history. In terms of the latter, it forms part of the move away from a traditional – celebratory and apologetic – approach towards a reappraisal of the British Jewish experience 'incorporating the negative as well as the positive'.[1] As Lloyd P. Gartner points out,

> The newcomers, and some seasoned historians who encourage them, are especially interested in anti-Semitism, and in East European immigrants and their neighbourhoods, their labor movement, the socialization of their children to English ways, and their friction with the established Jewish community.[2]

This study presents some new challenges for myself. I am a historian and sociologist by training, and do not normally write about a subject as deeply personal as this. There are no rules for such an enterprise, and any claim for historical objectivity would not ring true. At the same time, though, I shall attempt to place my father in the context of his times, and come to as balanced an assessment of his life and work as possible. The approach I have adopted to this piece is to combine personal views, of both myself and others, with an evaluation of my father's work, and the written sources that are available.

My intention is to present a balanced picture of his life and work and the community he came from. In order to do this I asked members of my family to contribute a written memoir of their own. Some of us have been interviewed about my father before, others have never been offered a chance to talk about him, and I wanted to give them this opportunity to share their memories. My work as a historian has involved extensive use of oral history, and I see this project as an extension of that. I have also employed the device of referring to 'my father' when I am offering a personal memory, and to 'C.P. Taylor' when writing about him generally in order to help distinguish between the two. I shall begin with a brief summary of his life and work in order to introduce him to a readership which might know him in neither.

C.P. TAYLOR 1929-81

C.P. Taylor was born in Glasgow in 1929, of an Anglo-Jewish mother and an Eastern European Jewish father. He left Queen's Park Secondary School, Glasgow, at the age of 14, and took a succession of jobs including electrician and television engineer. He moved to Newcastle in early 1955 to work as a travelling salesman, and lived in the North East of England until his death in 1981. In 1956 he married Irene Diamond, my mother, with whom he had two children: myself and my sister Clare. He also had two children, David and Cathryn, with his second wife, Elizabeth Screen. His first professional production was the political drama *Aa Went Tae Blaydon Races*, which was chosen to open the new Flora Robson theatre in Newcastle in 1962.[3]

During the course of his career he wrote over 70 plays for stage, television and radio. Some of these appeared under notable imprints, including Hutchinson, Iron Press, Methuen and Penguin, among others. However, although he achieved a certain degree of recognition during his lifetime, and was well known within theatrical circles, he did not achieve the more general recognition of writers like Howard Brenton, or Harold Pinter, with whom he was roughly contemporary. This was despite having west end productions of two of his works, *The Plumber's Progress* and *And A Nightingale Sang*, and a further two plays performed by the RSC: *Bandits* and *Good*. It is the latter that he is most often remembered for. A recent *Guardian* piece on a revival of 'And A Nightingale Sang', is typical in stating that, '… the play is a reminder that Taylor was a writer of tremendous power who was only hitting his prime when he died, shortly after the premiere of his greatest play, *Good*.'[4]

The original production of *Good* transferred to Broadway in 1982. The play has subsequently been performed in Japan, Turkey, Israel and Croatia, and translated into nine different languages.[5] Since his death there have been several individual productions of his plays, and two festivals of his work. The first was in Newcastle in 1989, and the other was part of the 1992 Edinburgh International Festival. Despite these significant tributes, little has been written about him in academic circles, and a more general appreciation of his work is still lacking, as one of the few scholars to have studied his work, Susan Friesner, has noted.[6] It is hoped that this contribution will be a part of a more general re-evaluation of his work and reputation.

THE SINGING DRAMATIST: REMEMBERING MY FATHER

My father left two wives, four children, two houses, over 70 plays, a guitar, a piano, and his personal library. I inherited the guitar, which I still play, but not his piano, which was sold. Over the years, I acquired a large percentage of his personal library, through honest and dishonest means, and these books serve as a constant reminder of his life and work. They also serve as a good indicator of his intellectual life. To begin with, there are the predictable choices of a working-class autodidact of his generation, works by Marx, Engels, Lenin, George Orwell, Arthur Koestler, and a number of fading volumes published by the Left Book Club. The inclusion of Jack London and the Newcastle writer Jack Common, the son of a Newcastle railwayman and author of *Kiddar's Luck*, is not unexpected either.

However a further examination of his choice of fiction shows that his horizons were by no means narrow. Here are works by Honoré de Balzac, Anton Chekhov, Joseph Conrad, Feodor Dostoevsky, Gogol, E.M. Forster, Graham Greene, and Jaroslav Hasek. Turn to the non-fiction collection and the range of his interests becomes clearer: *The Origin of Life, The Biological Bases of Behaviour, History of Western Philosophy, Jewish Philosophy and Philosophers, Jung: Man and Myth, Goethe: His Life and Times, The Making of the English Working Class, Industry and Empire, The Rise and Fall of the Third Reich, Northumberland and Durham, A History of the Scottish People 1560–1830* and a biography of Fidel Castro.

One problem in writing about my father's intellectual interests is that, at times, they appear inseparable from my own. Looking along the bookshelves, I have to think twice about whether I discovered an author for myself, or whether it is a writer suggested by my father. His influence on my siblings and myself is undeniable. I like to think that, as time has passed, I have become more aware of where some of my views originally came from, and re-evaluated his legacy. For example, I have to confess to regurgitating his scepticism about Shakespeare's continued relevance in my English Literature 'O'-Level essay on *Macbeth*. I have no idea what the examiners made of this, but it certainly would not have helped improve my poor grade in that subject!

As the oldest child, and one who discussed most things with him at some time or another, his influence on me was probably the most pronounced. The other problem writing about my father is that certain aspects of his character seem so obvious to me that they are hardly worth stating. He approached life with a sense of humour, which only rarely deserted him, and this is apparent in his plays. He loved food, music, the countryside and, much to my bemusement, gardening. Thus I have to continually remind myself that I am writing for a readership that not only did not know him personally, but also may well not know his work either. He would rarely actually express anger, although he had various methods of conveying disapproval. One of the few occasions he seemed to be genuinely annoyed was when I disturbed him at the typewriter: something I can now sympathize with. In order to avoid distractions he worked in a wooden shed, the type you would normally store tools in, at the bottom of the garden. Hence the title of the 1989 television documentary on my father, 'The Man in the Hut'.

Music was a big part of his life, and if he came across a piano or a guitar, he would invariably play it, wherever he was. One of the main things I remember about being with him on a daily basis was that he sang, all the time! He would sing anything. He made up songs about goblins when I was small, which we would sing as we walked around the Northumbrian countryside. He made up songs about himself, 'I'm a major Northern Dramatist!' Or he would just make up a song for a journey or an occasion. He sang 'The Skye Boat Song' interminably when we took a family holiday there. If the weather was fine, he would take his guitar, sit outside and sing Northumbrian folk songs, Yiddish songs, comic Glaswegian songs that sounded like they had been picked up in the music hall, or sometimes blues numbers. Looking back, it almost seemed as if that was one of the ways he would learn to master an idiom. Singing songs in his native Glaswegian and Yiddish, which was spoken frequently where he grew up, may have helped him maintain some of those speech patterns. When he moved to the northeast of England he had to learn the native tongue, and learning the local songs was as good a way of doing this as any. In retrospect I feel as if being able to sing the songs from those cultures gave him a direct route into their modes of expression.

Some of the issues raised by this piece are also quite uncomfortable. There is the fact that, because my father's work is often deeply autobiographical, my mother, my grandparents, my step-mother, and myself all appear in the plays. My younger siblings escaped depiction on stage but, had he lived to see them mature, then they too would have appeared in his scripts. There I am trying to mediate between my warring parents in *Me*. There is my conflict with authority at school, symbolized by my refusal to wear the school tie, in *The Tie*. I recognize myself as the son of an unemployed father in *Bring Me Sunshine Bring Me Smiles*. The characters in these plays were often based on people he knew, particularly family members, but we often appeared in hybrid form with elements taken from others. My grandparents certainly appear a lot in the early plays, and the scene in *Good* in which Halder's mother struggles to find her way around her own home after she loses her sight, was one I witnessed take place between my father and his mother. However, apart from the various incarnations of my father, it is my mother who appears most often in the plays. As the two were estranged, her depiction is not usually particularly flattering.

It is strange to look through the material for this study. As well as referring to many figures from the theatre that I have known since I was a child, here and there I recognize a name that I would often hear when I was growing up, but never met. I would accompany my father to his sessions with Northumberland Experimental Youth Theatre, or follow him around, what was then, 'The University Theatre' listening to conversations I was usually too young to understand. As I grew older, so my interest in his work increased and I attended drama workshops, rehearsals, and many of the original performances of his plays. On a couple of occasions I also assisted him in his work with people with learning disabilities.

We shared a lot, and his work was just one of the things that would form the topic of our conversations, the most memorable occasion being when he announced that he was going to write 'a comedy about the Holocaust!' I thought he was mad. This play, *Good*, eventually turned out to be his most acclaimed work. So I must declare an interest, I am a strong supporter of his work. I have also attempted on occasion to promote his work. So far this has only resulted in the publication of a posthumous volume of his plays: *North: Six Plays by C.P. Taylor*, but I would like to see his work more widely read and performed. This is because, at their best, his plays combine both compassion and tolerance for humanity with directness and honesty about our shortcomings and weaknesses as human beings. We should now consider some critical views of my father.

'A SCALING DOWN OF AMBITION'? THE PLAYS OF C.P. TAYLOR

A survey of some of the general literature on post-war British theatre reveals a lot about the way Taylor was viewed by contemporaries. He does not appear at all in *Post-War British Theatre Criticism* (1981) by John Elsom, or Andrew Davies' work *Other Theatres: The Development of Alternative and Experimental Theatre in Britain* (1987).[7] He is, however, mentioned in John Elsom's *Theatre Outside London* (1971) in connection with the Traverse Theatre Club in Edinburgh and the Tyneside Theatre Company based at the newly-built University Theatre in Newcastle.[8] He had a long association with both places. Ronald Hayman's *British*

Theatre since 1955: A Reassessment (1979) also merely mentions his name in a long list of authors associated with the RSC's 1977–78 season.[9] A more thorough appraisal appears in John Elsom's *Post-War British Theatre* (1976), where Taylor is granted a favourable, paragraph-long summary of his work to date which begins by describing him as 'a committed socialist', brought up 'among the slums of the Gorbals district'.[10] Elsom comments that, 'Taylor's plays, at best, are social comedies of manners, very funny and telling, and often set within the left-wing environment in Glasgow which he knows so well.'[11]

Much of Taylor's work up to the time that Elsom was writing was produced in association with the Traverse Theatre in Edinburgh where he made his reputation as a playwright. In *The Traverse Theatre Story* (1988) Joyce McMillan describes Taylor as 'almost a resident Traverse playwright'.[12] The Traverse opened on 2 January 1963, and quickly established itself as a venue for new writing.[13] It offered a particularly unrestricted environment for a playwright to develop in. Joyce McMillan describes it as 'a focus for the avant-garde interests and bohemian impulses of a small but considerable swathe of the Edinburgh bourgeoisie', with 'a committed audience, questioning, combative, and absolutely engaged with its work'.[14]

On the 24 August 1965, the Traverse presented the first of many plays by Taylor, the Pinteresque *Happy Days Are Here Again*.[15] The plays that Taylor produced for the Traverse are often located in a Scottish left-wing milieu and are peopled with characters that are constantly attempting to come to terms with the gap between their political ideals and the reality of their lives. Several of these plays were subsequently published, and we shall be considering two of them in depth: *Bread and Butter*, 1966, but not performed at the Traverse until 1969, and *Walter* (1977).[16] The former is Taylor's most successful attempt to portray the Glasgow-Jewish community he came from, while the latter has been seen as the play 'in which the dramatist finally came to terms with his Jewish heritage'.[17]

There were various strands to the work that Taylor produced. In 1966 he became script editor for a series of television plays, and writer for BBC Educational Television, thus beginning his long involvement in writing for television, something he eventually came to resent. He became the Literary Advisor to Northumberland Youth Theatre Association in 1968, the first time a British youth theatre had attempted to establish such a close relationship with a professional playwright.[18] This relationship lasted for the next ten years, during which time Taylor wrote several original plays and adapted classic dramas specifically for the group. In 1971, he became literary adviser to the Tyneside Theatre

Trust, Newcastle and to the Everyman Theatre, Liverpool.[19] The Youth Theatre appointment marked the beginning of his involvement with groups that were not part of the traditional audience for drama in this country. This part of his work is usually described as 'community theatre', but this does not give a true impression of the extent of the work he was involved in, and also the innovative way in which he approached this area of his work.

As a Socialist dramatist, Taylor had begun with the intention of writing drama that would inspire an audience to political action. As he says of *Aa Went Tae Blaydon Races*, a historical drama about a miners' strike, 'I thought the audience that saw a play of mine on Tuesday night would rise up en masse on Wednesday morning and set up the workers' state.'[20] His aims subsequently became more realistic.

> A gradual scaling down of ambition is probably the best description of my development as a playwright. Starting with the aim of theatre as a potent instrument of the revolution, I have been beaten down to theatre as another of the communication arts. I used to write plays such as BLAYDON RACES, genuinely convinced they would move the workers, by the insights the plays gave into the great political truths of socialism, to revolution. I now write plays as a novelist writes novels or as a poet writes poetry – to communicate my narrow, odd vision of the world as I see it at the time of writing. Always in the hope that my hang-ups, flaws, insecurities, and fears will at times cross those of my audience and they might feel a bit less on their own in this big world, as I do when I read a real book or see a real play.[21]

Although he lost his belief in the power of the theatre to inspire revolution, Taylor did not abandon his mission to reach a wider audience. One thing that he did take away from the experience of staging *Blaydon Races*, which attracted 'pitmen, shipyard workers, engineers – people who'd never been in the theatre before', was the realization that, 'there were audiences for the theatre outside the small, faithful band of "theatre people"'.[22]

His political commitment was subsequently expressed in a less direct manner. He frequently expressed his belief to me that it was the duty of a successful artist to 'put something back' into the community in which he lived. Although he never became particularly wealthy through his writing, it seemed that as soon as he was able to make a decent living from it he immediately felt the need to do something for others. He worked with children, teenagers, people with learning disabilities, labelled 'the mentally handicapped' at that time, and even helped other struggling writers in the region. It is this area of his work that tends to lead people to see him as St Francis of Longhorsley, and while it is certainly true that he did engage in projects that most writers in his position would not have considered worthy of their talents, his motives for doing so were not entirely altruistic. He described it as 'enlightened self-interest', in that he was doing something for the community but he was also gaining something for himself. The rewards that he obtained from working in schools, or 'Northgate Hospital for the Severely Educational Subnormal', were not usually material. He sought a deeper understanding of people and lives that were different from his own, thus enriching his knowledge of what it was to be a human being, in all sorts of social situations.

While still working with Northumberland Experimental Youth Theatre, Taylor also began to find a way of writing challenging plays for children. This project began in the early 1970s when Taylor decided to take his role as Literary Manager of the Tyneside Theatre Company seriously, and write for that part of the company that was working in schools.[23] Although Taylor's first play for children was a total failure by his own admission, and he came close to abandoning the project altogether, he persisted and eventually realized his ambition of writing plays for children that could embody some of the qualities of good adult theatre.[24]

The fruits of his work with children are the four plays originally staged for local schools by the Tyneside touring company 'Live Theatre Co.' and published by Methuen/Iron Press in 1983.[25] These plays came out of lengthy, and often difficult, periods in various local schools in which Taylor employed different methods of interacting with the children, a process he called 'tuning into an audience'.[26] They successfully manage to deal with some of the children's own prejudices: racism, preconceptions about those with learning disabilities, and attitudes to poverty in the Third World, while not preaching or shrinking from the harsh realities of those issues. The most frequently performed of these plays, *Operation Elvis* (1978), was filmed by BBC North East in 1980, and *Time Out* described the last of them, *Happy Lies* (1981), as 'a powerful and fitting contribution to the Year of the Disabled'.[27]

Part of the reason for the success of the children's plays was that they came out of the relationship that Taylor had developed with the Newcastle-based Live Theatre Company, and their artistic director at the time, Teddy Kiendl. This was a highly productive relationship that resulted in some of Taylor's best plays, for both children and adults, and it is his work for Live Theatre that he is best remembered for in the North-East.

The Live Theatre Company was formed in 1973 by a group committed to providing 'theatre for working-class audiences on Tyneside about their own experiences and performed by working-class actors', in the words of one of its founders.[28] The group performed in schools, community centres and working men's clubs. Taylor's first play for Live Theatre was *The Killingworth Play* (1976).[29] He went on to write a string of successful plays for the company, all of them set on Tyneside, using characters talking in the local dialect. Taylor employed the technique he had developed in his work with children and young people, 'tuning in to an audience', to great effect.[30] Peter Mortimer, a close friend and associate of Taylor, and also North-East theatre critic for the *Guardian*, offers this assessment of the resultant plays:

> These are regional plays, firmly rooted in the area. You might call them superior soap operas (though lasting two hours not 10 years, and written by one man, not a team). They are often both hilarious and moving. Their popularity has spread far beyond Tyneside.[31]

Several of these plays have been published, but the most successful of them so far has been, *And A Nightingale Sang* (1977).[32] This was transferred to London's West End in 1979, where it had only a brief run which Taylor believed to be the result of negative reviews in the *Guardian* and the *Observer*.[33] However, many of the London critics liked the play, and the failure of the transfer was probably due to the general downturn in ticket sales that closed many shows in the capital at the time.[34] Ten years later, a television version of the play was made by Tyne Tees Television starring Phyllis Logan, Joan Plowright and Tom Watt, famous for his role as 'Lofty' in *EastEnders*.[35]

The final strand of Taylor's work for the theatre is represented by his two RSC plays: *Bandits* (1976) and *Good* (1981).[36] *Bandits* is uncharacteristic of Taylor in many ways, as it is based on a notorious murder case that occurred in Newcastle in 1967, which Taylor, and many others, believed to be 'unsolved' as the men convicted of the crime were innocent.[37] In the Foreword to the published edition of the play Howard Davies, the director of the RSC production, wrote that the company had chosen this work because it was 'a fine example of social realism', and it represented 'the best of the excellent work that is being carried out by community theatres ... '.[38] The critical response to the play was mixed, with some critics feeling confused by the cinematic structure of the play, and others outraged by its 'strong language.'[39]

However, the response was favourable enough to prompt Howard Davies and the RSC to produce Taylor's last play, *Good*, in 1981.

This is set in Germany during the period of the Nazi dictatorship. It depicts the remarkable moral journey of Halder, a Professor of Literature, an intelligent and cultured person, and a 'good' man, who, by the end of the play, has joined the SS. Halder is significant in that he is not the stereotypical sadistic Nazi that we have become accustomed to in portrayals of the period. He is a liberal with many of the qualities that are valued in 'civilized' society, yet he allows himself to be seduced into joining the National Socialists. *Good* had the longest gestation period of any play in Taylor's career, starting life as a version of *Faust* in the 1970s, which was never performed, eventually becoming a play about the Final Solution.[40]

As noted earlier, the play eventually attracted an international audience. Critical response, to both the original RSC production and the 1999 revival of the work in London's Donmar Warehouse, has also been highly favourable.[41] At the time of his death, Taylor was working on a play about Stalin. That, along with *Good*, and the aforementioned *Happy Lies*, set in both Jarrow and Madras, and dealing with different types of poverty, indicated that his work was taking a whole new direction. It indicated that, if Taylor had previously 'scaled down his ambition', it was about to be 'scaled up' again in an entirely new way. We can only speculate as to the exact form this would have taken.[42] Before exploring his complex relationship with Judaism, we should first consider the community he came from: the Gorbals, of Glasgow.

LIFE IN 'A SCOTTISH SHTETL'

Between 1880 and 1914, the size and character of the Jewish population in Britain underwent a transformation. As a result of the pogroms, and legal restrictions, which followed the assassination of Alexander II in 1881, there was an enormous exodus of Jews from Eastern Europe. It has been estimated that one million Jews left Eastern Europe for the west between 1881 and 1905. The majority of these came from Russia itself, and over 80 per cent went to America, with probably more than 100,000 coming to Britain.[43] Harold Pollins estimates that there were about 60,000 Jews in the British Isles in 1880 and by 1914 the number had grown to about 300,000.[44]

Although London became the city with the largest number of these East European Jewish migrants, after New York and Chicago, more Jews entered the country than remained. Britain had a special role as a staging post, for those en-route elsewhere often, though not always, to

America. Up to 40 per cent of the Jews of Leeds were said to be in transit in 1889 and not expected to settle.[45] Those who did stay in this country tended to congregate together in particular urban areas, with the East End of London containing nine-tenths of the Jewish population of late Victorian Britain. Large communities also developed in inner city areas like the Leylands in Leeds, Cheetham Hill in Manchester, and the Gorbals in Glasgow.[46] The distinctiveness in dress, habits and language of the new arrivals cemented their identification as the 'other' in the eyes of many British observers. G.R. Sims' *Living London* (1904) carries a description of the Whitechapel ghetto:

> Its beshawled women with their pinched faces, its long-coated men with two thousand years of persecution stamped in their manner, its chaffering and huckstering, its hunger, its humour, the very Yiddish jargon which is scrawled on its walls and shop windows, are part of the grand passion of the chosen people.
>
> But it is its utterly alien aspect which strikes you first and foremost. For the Ghetto is a fragment of Poland torn off from Central Europe and dropped haphazard into the heart of Britain – a re-banished Jewry weeping beside the waters of 'Modern Babylon'.[47]

If the 'alien' aspect of these 'fragments of Central Europe' alienated some British commentators, it was reassuring to new arrivals from the Continent. Chaim Bermant describes how it felt to move from the small Latvian village of Barovke to Glasgow in 1937:

> Our first address was the Gorbals where Father had lodgings with distant relatives and the Gorbals, somehow, was less intimidating than other parts of the town for it reminded me vaguely of Dvinsk. There were Yiddish posters on the hoardings, Hebrew lettering on the shops, Jewish names, Jewish faces, Jewish butchers, Jewish bakers with Jewish bread, and Jewish grocers with barrels of herring in the doorway. The herrings in particular brought a strong whiff of home. One heard Yiddish in the streets – more so, in fact, than English – and one encountered figures who would not have been out of place in Barovke.[48]

The Jewish population of Glasgow was considerably swollen by the influx from Eastern Europe in the late nineteenth century, most of whom settled in the Gorbals. There were about 4,000 Jews in Glasgow in 1897, and this went up to 6,500 in 1902 and 9,200 in 1919.[49] David Cesarani estimates that there were about 15,000 Jews in Glasgow during the inter-war years, which was considerably less than the number in Manchester and Leeds, the largest provincial communities during the same period.[50]

A significant characteristic of the Gorbals was the left-wing views of many of its residents. Geoffrey Alderman points out that, 'The immigrant Jews came from societies which were rich in political and industrial organization.'[51] In the Pale of Settlement Jewish factory owners preferred hiring non-Jewish workers because they were less militant than Jewish workers, and many of the Jewish trade unions were socialist-inspired.[52] Jewish socialism in the Pale of Settlement was split between those who sought freedom from Tsarist oppression through a socialist revolution in company with other social-democratic groups, and those whose conception of socialism required the formation of a Jewish homeland first.

The Bund was an anti-Zionist organization, while the Jewish Social Democratic Party (*Poale Zion*) was committed to the formation of a Jewish state in Palestine. Geoffrey Alderman argues that support for *Poale Zion* among Jews in Britain was very limited until the First World War, with the influence of mainstream socialism, and to a lesser extent, anarchism being more significant.[53] The Glasgow Socialist League was formed in 1934 to work for Jewish and Socialist aims within the Jewish community and the labour movement.[54] In the Gorbals itself, the Workers' Circle performed several functions, partly friendly society, partly socialist and trade union meeting place, and also a forum for discussion.[55] After the outbreak of the Spanish Civil War, in 1936, many residents of the Gorbals joined the International Brigade and went to fight for the Republican cause.[56]

REBEL WITHOUT A TIE: PLACING MY FATHER IN HIS COMMUNITY

Let us now return to John Elsom's description of my father as brought up 'among the slums of the Gorbals district'.[57] My father was born on 6 November 1929 in the Maryhill district of Glasgow.[58] He himself has said that, he grew up 'in the rough heart of Glasgow, full of knives and broken bottles'.[59] Susan Friesner has, with some justification, called this 'something of an exaggeration'.[60] The facts of his upbringing have caused some genuine confusion. Maryhill, the area he was born into, was a slum district, and would deserve to be described as a 'rough' area. This was also not a Jewish area, but a working-class district of Glasgow. Also, at some point between 1929 and 1939 my father's family moved to Forth Street in Pollokshields to live in a basement rented from my grandmother's cousin. This must have come as something of a relief because this was a quiet middle-class area. Then, in 1939, the family moved to 96 Bowman Street in Crosshill which, as Susan Friesner says, was by no means a slum, 'and could better be described as a respectable lower middle-class area, although most people who lived there at the time were short of money'.[61]

The Crosshill Synagogue was founded in 1932, and was known as 'the cut price *shul*' as subscriptions were not more than a shilling a week.[62] To put this in perspective, my mother, who was actually brought up in the Gorbals, saw Crosshill as two steps above the Gorbals.[63] This was where my father lived from ten years of age, and although this was a Jewish area, and was also very close to the Gorbals, it was a different district. My father's family lived in one of the traditional Glasgow tenement blocks, but there were only two flats on each of the landings, and the flats had indoor sanitation and running water.[64] While the family lived in Crosshill, the instability of their income meant that their standard of living was never much higher than those who lived in the Gorbals. Although my father did not grow up within the Gorbals itself, he had strong ties with the area. His family frequently visited relatives in the area, it was where they shopped, and my mother was also from there. So, in many ways, it was the community that formed him.

My father's parents were Max and Fay Taylor and my father was their only child. My grandfather was born on 20 March 1898 in Grodno, Grodno Gubernia, Russia. His original family name was Girschovitz, but he was known as Max Taylor after he arrived in England. He was naturalized as a British subject on 19 February 1920 in Glasgow. His occupation at that time is listed as picture frame maker, and a note in brackets next to it states that he 'served in his Majesty's Forces'.[65] It is not known exactly when he came to Britain, but my father's cousin, Issy Dentist, estimates it to have been about 1912.[66]

As the oldest grandchild, I have now become the best available source of information on my grandfather's origins. My grandfather talked to me about life in Russia. He talked about Cossacks spearing fruit in the village marketplace, and about the time that some soldiers tricked him into drinking a whole glass of vodka by telling him it was lemonade. What was the soldiers' motivation for such a prank? Just a bit of fun at the expense of a small boy? Or, was there some kind of anti-Semitism involved? I am not sure. I loved my grandfather's stories of the homeland, and I think he knew that, and probably edited out all the episodes of persecution for my consumption. I am also not entirely sure about the circumstances in which he left Russia, but he said that he did not have all the right papers, and he crawled through the snow between the border guard's legs. The guard, meanwhile, had been bribed to look the other way and was shooting into the air. I have no way of verifying this story, but it was what he told me.

My father's cousin wrote the following account of my grandfather, and how he met my grandmother (Fay Leventhal):

> Regarding your grandfather, Avram, I remember him as a very intelligent and knowledgeable man. He had very little schooling, and consequently was self-taught. He came from Russia as a young boy. He lost his father early on, and lived with a stepmother. I understand that she treated him shabbily. He had a very hard life. As he reached manhood he lived in various lodgings. In those days, in order to make ends meet, your great-grandmother, Clara, took in lodgers. They had a fair sized flat, situated near the city centre. Anyway Max obtained 'digs' at the Leventhal household. Then Fay, Ray, and Jack (all single) lived with their parents. Consequently Max and Fay were attracted to each other, and that was that. Romance blossomed.[67]

My grandmother's father (Wolf Leventhal) came to Britain from Riga in Lithuania some time after 1880 to stay with his brother in London. My father's cousin also supplied a description of him, which is consistent with what my father told me about my great-grandfather:

> Firstly Wolf Leventhal was a very pious man, deeply steeped in religion. I would describe him as a fundamentalist. As long as it was physically possible, he attended the services at Synagogue 'religiously' (pardon the pun). He revered the clergy with almost idolatry. I personally was walking with him on many occasions when we encountered a minister or a rabbi. Then he would bow, right down to his waist. Needless to say the house was scrupulously Kosher. All the religious festivals were observed meticulously. I recall particularly the Passover services, when the family would all be invited to the 'Seder'. This is the evening meal at the advent of Passover. Then all the ritual was performed, with the appropriate meal served ... Wolf glorified in directing every aspect of it. At this stage I would like to point out, that grandfather (Wolf) lived with aunt Fay at this time. This was at Bowman Street, where Cecil grew up.[68]

As to my grandfather's period as a picture frame-maker, I can only assume it was quite brief, because my father's cousin never knew him as that. He seemed to have tried various jobs, and then began selling rubber mats in the Highlands. After this he became what was known as a 'gold clapper', which meant that he used to buy and sell watches and jewellery both in Glasgow and in Western Scotland. This was what he did when I was a boy, and the wall cupboard in my grandparents' bedroom was always full of second-hand watches, which he would proudly show me, and sometimes I was allowed to select one of them for myself. One thing is certain, though, even if the family did not live in slum conditions, they never had very much money.

If he was never very rich materially, my grandfather had quite a rich intellectual life. He had a wide and varied library, and was a member of both *Poale Zion* and the Workers' Circle in the Gorbals. So he had strong views on politics and current affairs, and liked to air them publicly. He regularly wrote letters to the *Jewish Chronicle*, and other newspapers, and he also wrote stories. Obviously my grandfather's left-wing views, and literary aspirations influenced my father. My father's cousin also played a role in shaping my father's opinions, as he points out:

> I was then (and still am) an ardent left-winger. I used to buy all the provocative books on socialism. I was a member of a 'Left wing Book Club', and there was available a series of books under the heading of the 'Thinkers Library'. I had a very large collection of these books. As Cecil grew older, I would pass them on to him. As an enquiring teenager, he became very interested in the aforementioned subjects.[69]

Despite my father's intellectual ability, his formal education ended at the age of 14. He had passed the entrance examination for Queen's Park Secondary School at the age of 12, but left it as soon as he reached what was then the statutory school-leaving age. My mother maintains that he did not leave school because the family could no longer afford to keep him there, as Jewish families have a reverence for education. She says that he left because he was a rebel who could not adapt to school discipline.[70] My father's best friend from about the age of nine was his cousin Phil Dentist, and their close relationship was central to his early life in Glasgow. Phil also left school at the age of 14. He says that,

> We were both also interested in electrics and radios and set out to be radio mechanics, wrecking not only the equipment but also many friendships. We both wanted to leave school to train as radio engineers, but in your father's case it was unfortunate as he should have carried on his education and could have achieved even greater opportunities. But this is in hindsight.
>
> We both had many jobs after leaving school at 14, but at 16 we decided to go into business. We started in an electrical business

that was going into liquidation, and they allowed us to run it whilst they found a buyer. As soon as we did a repair and got paid, we closed the shop and went to play golf.[71]

Then, as television began to establish itself, my father branched out into television repairs.

Throughout his youth my father wrote short stories and poems, as Cordelia Oliver describes:

> Writing began with poetry in his late teens then 'descended' to short stories (since they were Jewish short stories they found a ready outlet in the local Jewish press). Finally, since 'the stories were nearly all dialogue anyway,' he thought of trying his hands at plays.[72]

Again, when he began to write plays, his first thought was that they should be perfomed within his own community, and this was his motivation for becoming involved with the local branch of the Jewish youth club, the Maccabi. This was how he met my mother, Irene Rebecca Diamond, in 1953. My mother was born into an Orthodox Jewish family in Glasgow on 30 April 1931, and her family moved to the Gorbals in 1932. Her own mother was born in 1896 in Berdychev in the Ukraine, and left Russia in 1912, journeying alone to Britain to join her uncle in Leeds. My mother's father was born in Leeds in 1891, the same year that his family migrated from Russia. He only narrowly missed being born on Russian soil, as my great-grandmother was carrying him when she left Riga.[73]

My mother had become interested in amateur dramatics, and started attending the Maccabi drama group. Initially my father joined the group as an actor, and he suggested to my mother that they should perform one of the Greek dramas. My father eventually wrote a short play, *Bontsha The Silent*, for the group based on a Yiddish short story. The group performed this play in 1953 or 1954 for the anniversary of Israel Independence Day. He also wrote another play for Maccabi, this time based on one of his own Yiddish stories, which was rehearsed but not performed.[74] His first full-length play was *Mr David*, which was about a young man, David, who turns out to be a messiah sent to bring peace and justice to the earth. Jewish tradition holds that, when the messiah appears, he will be called David. The play is obviously firmly rooted in the Jewish community, and the characters include two tailor's cutters and two rabbis.[75] *Mr David* won a prize from the World Jewish Congress in 1954, but was not produced for another 13 years.[76]

So, my father's first attempts at writing were largely based on

Jewish themes, and he initially sought recognition from his own community. He also still attended synagogue, even if this was only on the major holidays. In addition, he had become involved with, and then married to, a good Jewish girl, thus fulfilling both their families' expectations. The spectre of 'marrying out' was always present among the Jewish community, and both of my mother's older brothers actually did so, much to my grandmother's horror. It must have come as a great relief to my grandmother when my parents became engaged.

So, although my father was not a devout Jew by any stretch of the imagination, on the surface, at least, he was conforming to what his community expected of him. After all, only the very *froom*, as those who are scrupulously religiously observant are described, attended Synagogue every day, and even attendance every *Shabbas* was not always expected by every family. However, his feelings about religion, and his internal dialogue with himself at the time about the subject, told quite a different story. My stepmother, Liz, has offered the following assessments of my father's relationship to Judaism.

> Cecil was not a religious Jew at the time that we met. As far as I could remember he had not been one since his adolescence, and would tell me anecdotes of eating bacon sandwiches on Holy days with his cousin Phil as a mark of rebellion, but his Jewishness was utterly intrinsic to him, and informed his sensitivities and (obviously) his writing.[77]

> He wasn't a practising Jew in a religious sense, but he was Jewish racially, so I think ... His family were obviously. He'd been brought up within the Jewish community in Glasgow, he had feelings about the history of the Jews.[78]

My mother also said that by the time she met my father he was no longer religious, and he was only attending the Synagogue to please his parents. After my parents were married, contrary to my mother's expectations, he refused to attend the Synagogue at all.[79] My own memories support this assessment. The only time I can ever recall seeing him in a Synagogue was for my *Bar Mitzvah*, and that came as a total surprise to me. In fact, he sometimes expressed more than indifference to his religion at times. Whenever he was present during one of the religious festivals conducted by my mother, he would actively ridicule it, leaving my sister and myself in no doubt about his lack of faith. Is that the whole story though?

'Is "Jew" a religion or a race?' This is a question that my father would frequently raise with my mother during their courtship.[80] It is also a question that my father returned to again and again during the course of his life, often through his plays, and never actually resolved. As my brother David wrote, 'My Dad was a Jew turned something; but I was never too sure quite what. He loved his bacon, but never could bring himself to eat a cheeseburger ... .'[81] I, on the other hand, have eaten bacon and cheeseburgers, does that mean that I have totally abandoned my Jewishness? What does it mean to be a Jew? This is an incredibly complex question, which it is not possible to resolve here, but we can consider some aspects of it.

First, in response to my father's question, we could consider Jewishness as both a religion and a race, it does not necessarily have to be a case of either or. Neither is Jewish identity fixed or static, as even the most superficial consideration of the contemporary situation shows. Even if we consider Jewish identity in purely religious terms, it has historically been a contested space. There are obvious differences between Hassidic, Orthodox, and Reform Jews, for one thing, then there is the issue of the distinct identity of Israeli Jews. In terms of genetics, my parents' Jewish identity could not be questioned and, by extension, my own. But how important is 'racial purity' to Jewish identity? Perhaps many more liberal Jews today would like to play down this aspect, but it was certainly important in the past, and it was certainly important to my grandparents. We also have to account for converts to Judaism. Can a gentile ever be totally accepted by the Jewish community as a Jew?

The situation is further complicated by the fact that the majority of British Jews exist in a grey area between strict religious observance and total rejection of all religious beliefs and practices. Within the mainstream of British Jewry, in communities like that in Newcastle upon Tyne, for example, one would be regarded as a bit peculiar if one showed signs of being too *froom*. Obviously, completely different rules apply in ultra-Orthodox communities such as the one that exists on Gateshead in Tyneside, but then the Jews of Gateshead and Newcastle are separated by far more than the river Tyne.

The average British Jew regularly 'bends the rules', and this is hardly surprising in some ways, as there are so many of them to follow. So, for example, driving to the Synagogue on the Sabbath, forbidden by Jewish Law, is a common practice, as long as one does not park too near the Synagogue. Keeping a *kosher* home is obviously central to Orthodox Judaism, and the majority of British Jews probably follow Jewish dietary laws in their own home. However, once outside, there is often the feeling that it is somehow permissible to eat whatever you like as long as you do not contaminate the home with forbidden delicacies. So here is another problem in defining what is 'accepted' Jewish behaviour. In reality there is no generally accepted standard of religious observance. Thus my father's rather casual attitude towards Synagogue attendance when he was a youth would not necessarily be seen as anything particularly unusual in most British Jewish communities.

Some of his elders' attitudes muddied the waters of religious observance even further. Although, as we have seen, his grandfather, Wolf Leventhal, was a straightforward example of an individual with deep religious convictions who obeyed the laws of his fathers, there were other role models that were not so clear. In the course of researching this study, I was surprised to discover that some of my older relatives were not quite as pious as I had imagined. I had previously seen my grandfather, and my great uncle, Alec Dentist, as religious Jews who held to a 'normal' level of religious observance for the community they came from. I had been aware that my father's cousin Issy was, in fact, an agnostic, and that he went to the Synagogue out of some kind of sense of duty. However, when asking him about his father, Alec Dentist, and my grandfather, Max Taylor, he revealed that neither of them were really religious either. My father's cousin pointed out that he himself is a member of Queen's Park Synagogue in Glasgow, and still attends Synagogue regularly. He does this partly as a mark of respect for his father who had said, 'A Jew must belong to a Synagogue'.[82] I asked him why his father's generation had seen Synagogue attendance as so important if some of them were not actually religious? He replied that, 'It was religion that bound them together as an identifiable group.'[83]

However, some of my father's generation no longer felt totally comfortable being part of that group, as Ralph Glasser asserts:

> We longed to reject the world view that the preceding generation seemed to be passing on to us, attitudes of submission, of 'make do', of finding comfort in old saws and signs and portents, in thrift, prudence, automatic religious observance with little faith, in survival one day at a time.[84]

There was a strong current of agnosticism or doubt about religion running through the environment my father grew up in. However, his father's generation had kept that at bay through 'automatic religious observance', which was also the thing that gave the community its identity. So it was not that surprising that many in my father's generation began to question the values of their elders and consider rethinking everything that had been passed on to them. Rebellion was made even more inevitable by the restrictive social norms of the community that my father grew up in, as my father's cousin Phil explains:

> We were both non-conformists in the area we lived, mainly Jewish. We didn't wear ties as a rebellion, we mixed with non-Jewish friends, in today's life this seems tame, but 56 years ago it was something.[85]

> The Jewish population was a close-knit community and it was not common to mix with other religions, which we did. We also did a lot of cycling and would travel down to the coast and stay overnight at weekends, which was not for 'Jewish boys'.[86]

Although some of the older members of the community may have disapproved of these activities, my father and his cousin were not unique, as Ralph Glasser and his friends had also discovered the delights of the surrounding countryside, and often went to stay in the nearby 'Socialist Camp' at weekends.[87]

For my siblings and myself, Glasgow was a place that we visited occasionally to see our relatives. It also had a certain aura of mystique as a result of the fact that we heard so much about it second-hand. In *Coming Back Brockens* Mark Hudson describes similar feelings about returning to Horden, the Durham mining village where his parents and grandparents lived. He says that the name of the village '… reverberated through my childhood like a dull gong'.[88] Thus it was for us with places such as Queen's Park, Maryhill, and the Gorbals. As my sister, Cat, says, our father was '… always busy with plays and interviews and actors and directors and another family, and my mother'.[89] There were many demands on his time, and our childhood visits to Glasgow were also one of the few occasions when we were able to have our father's undivided attention for a protracted period, as she describes:

> My favourite time was when I had him to myself. We'd go to Glasgow and visit relatives. They pressed 50 pence pieces into the palm of my hand and told me my father had a very sweet tooth. He bought me *Vogue* magazine to shut me up as he conversed with them about their problems in their big gas-smelling flat. He'd tease my gran.
> 'Cathryn doesn't believe in Jesus, do you Cathryn?'
> 'No I don't.'
> 'Good girl', gran would say.

'And she doesn't believe in God either, do you Cathryn?'
'No I don't.'
'Oh Cathryn, why ever not?'
Then he'd take me round Glasgow and show me all the places he'd played as a child and what he used to get up to.[90]

This exchange is quite typical of my father, in many ways, as it shows the playful side of his attitude towards Judaism, and the way that he would have fun with, and make fun of, his past. There was also a deeper, and more serious element to this, and both are present in his plays.

COMING TO TERMS WITH THE PAST: JUDAISM IN MY FATHER'S PLAYS

The dedication at the front of the published version of *Good* reads, 'In memory of my father, Max George Taylor, a refugee from antisemitism in Czarist Russia'.[91] My father undoubtedly had a deep awareness of the troubled past of the Jewish people, and the themes of Jewish identity and anti-Semitism appear repeatedly in his plays. What varied was his level of discomfort with that identity. Two notable examples of this concern are *Oil and Water* (1967) and *Me* (1972). It is worth briefly considering these before moving on to look at the two plays I have chosen to focus on. *Oil and Water* is the story of David, a Glasgow-Jewish boy living with his parents and his Orthodox grandfather (Joe), who meets Joyce, a Catholic on a political demonstration, and the familial conflict that ensues. In the following discussion David's father (Max) begins by advocating a liberal position but changes his tone when he realizes the implications of his son's new relationship:

> MAX: Joseph. You're living in a museum! That's not Czarist Russia out there, Joseph!
> JOE: Listen ... I know better than you what's out there!
> MAX: The walls are down, Joseph. You just need to walk through ... they've knocked down the ghetto, Joseph!
> JOE: Yes! So we can all go and mix up with the Gentiles and finish being Jews ...That's what you want?
> DAVID: Maybe it's not worth it, Granda ... You know? And it would be better if we did?
> JOE: Davidel ... The intermarriages I've seen –
> MAX: (alarmed at this new note from DAVID) What's not worth it son? What do you mean?

DAVID: I don't know, Dad ... I mean ... All those Jews killed ... millions ... just to be Jews ...
JOE: Just to be Jews! That's nothing! She's turning you into a gentile, already ...
MAX: That's our culture, son ... That's who we are ... What kind of question is that, David ... You might as well say it is not worth it to survive just as David Kaplan ...? David ... That's part of what you are son. You're a Jew ... [92]

My father did not need reminding that he was a Jew, but his feelings about it were another thing. In a 1977 interview with Cordelia Oliver he conceded that he had initially bitterly resented his Jewishness, and had only gradually came to terms with it.[93]

My own childhood memories are mainly of his hostility to his religion. He conducted a sort of guerrilla warfare with my mother over my Jewish education. As I went to a state school my Hebrew education had to be conducted in special after-school classes in the evening, which I was never particularly fond of. My father would sometimes 'kidnap' me after school in order to avoid these, a misdemeanour I would gladly consent to regardless of the distress it caused my mother. The conflict between my parents is depicted verbatim in *Me*.

This play has no real plot as it was simply an account of my father's own life at the time of writing interspersed with fantasy sequences. In fact, in the original drafts of the play, such as the one quoted here, he did not even bother to change the names of his family members. I later appear as Yuri! The opening scene of this version of the play takes place not long after my father has left my mother to live with Liz, and is indicative of the type of 'conversations' that took place on his return to the family home. After a brief 'discussion' about my mother's general untidiness, my father turns to her continued maintenance of Jewish dietary laws:

C.P: And the bloody dishes and pots and pans you have. I mean ... You've got four sets of dishes ... and crockery and everything.
AVRAM: Yes. But she believes in it, Da.
IRENE: You want me to eat milk out of the same dishes as I eat meat? And have the same dishes for Passover I have all the year round. Like you.[94]

Me was one of his most controversial plays, and caused offence to many, including my father's parents. My mother seriously contemplated suing him for libel after reading it. The play was first staged in Glasgow in 1972, where its portrayal of Glasgow Jewish life did nothing to endear him to its Jewish community. The play goes between 'reportage' of my father's family life and imaginary sequences that portray conversations between him and various political figures of the day, and at one point God! In another scene he tells Golda Meir that the founding of the State of Israel was a mistake. While the play was a genuine attempt to present his internal and external life at the time of writing to an audience it was not a commercial or a critical success, and some Jews even felt it to be anti-Semitic.[95]

The play in which my father most directly depicts the community he grew up in is *Bread and Butter* (1966). *Bread and Butter* was critically acclaimed when it opened at the Jeannetta Cochrane Theatre in London on 7 July 1966, and the playwright and critic, Stanley Eveling, has described it as 'a perfect play'.[96] Although this is a play about the Jewish community in the Gorbals, and the Citizens' Theatre in Glasgow was the first venue that it was offered to, the theatre rejected the play. The reason seems to have been that the depiction of Glasgow-Jewish life in the play was not to the taste of influential members of the Jewish community there.[97]

This play depicts the lives of two Jewish couples: Alec and Miriam and Morris and Sharon from November 1931 to March 1965, and much of the play's poignancy comes from the way that we see the fortunes of its characters change over the passage of time. Alec is a presser in a clothing factory, and Miriam is a machinist, both characteristic occupations for members of their community. Morris is the son of the owner of the factory where Alec and Miriam work. However this is no obstacle to the close friendship between Alec and Morris, although Miriam alludes to it frequently. The play opens with Alec and Miriam, accompanied by Morris, inspecting a flat in the Gorbals, which they are considering moving into after they are married. Morris, used to better things, is critical of the accommodation:

> MORRIS: This is no use to you! It's like a prison!
> ALEC [*miserably*]: Only one room?
> MIRIAM: I told you it was only one room.
> MORRIS [*looking out the window*]: Give a look! Give a look out there!
> Prisoner's exercise yard, Duke Street Prison!
> MIRIAM: It's a tenement.
> ALEC: It's shut in all round. It's shut in.
> MORRIS: You wouldn't get me to live here.
> MIRIAM [sharply]: You don't need to.
> ALEC: That's right Morris. You're a capitalist.[98]

Morris does not like to be reminded of the fact that he is 'the boss's son', as he sees himself as a Communist with deeply-held convictions that cannot be corrupted by the possession of property. He even applies to join the Garment Workers' Union, and is baffled when he is refused.

> MORRIS: I said to him 'Bernstein, look here. I'm a Communist. I'm in the tailoring trade. All I'm asking is my rights. To join the Garment Workers' Union. I want to show solidarity.' ...
> MORRIS: You're the boss's son. The boss's son. That's all I got from him! I said: 'Listen Bernstein, I'll put it to you dialectically: I'm getting wages from my father, just like everybody else in the factory. I'm a wage earner. Tell me one sentence in the whole of Marx and Engels that says capitalism is a hereditary disease.'[99]

Morris's desperate attempts to prove his credibility as a member of the proletariat are comic, but Miriam is unrelenting in her criticism of him, and asks whether Morris will pay Alec twenty pounds a week when he takes over his father's business. Morris deflects the question by pointing out that by the time his father dies 'It could well be that the factory will have already been taken over by the dictatorship of the proletariat.'[100]

Many of the scenes in the play take place in Queen's Park, where the characters spend much of their time trying to escape their oppressive surroundings and the circumstances of their lives. They take comfort in the small pleasures life has to offer, picnicking in the park, watching the pigeons, and each other's company. Meanwhile, the events outside their own immediate environment become increasingly threatening. In one scene, set in May 1933, Morris demonstrates a misunderstanding of events in Germany that was quite common, even among members of the Jewish community at the time. By this time, Morris has become engaged to the rather conventional and unimaginative Sharon, whom he subsequently marries.

> MORRIS: ... Hitler is not against the Jews. I do not believe that for one minute!
> [SHARON *begins to feed the pigeons*]
> ALEC: Do it gently, Sharon ... like this ... slowly ... If you do it too sudden, it gives them a fright and they fly off.
> MORRIS: The way I see it is – what Hitler is against is capitalism. He's against the *rich* Jews. The same as we're against the rich Jews. Against all the rich ...

> MORRIS: Once Hitler settles down, and the new regime is consolidated, they'll forget all about anti-Jewish campaigns. It's just an election stunt – a show for the people.
> MIRIAM: What about them closing all the Jewish shops? …
> MORRIS: A few anti-semites broke out – windows were broken. A shirt torn off a Jew's back. But you know our people – the minute some gentile gives a Jew a dirty look, they're shouting already – Pogrom! Pogrom![101]

In the event, of course, the clothing factory is not taken over by the dictatorship of the proletariat. Instead Morris's father loses it as a result of trading on the black market during the war and Morris, by this time married, has to take as a job as a presser, and moves from Queen's Park to the Gorbals. After the war, the conversations in the park turn to dreams of a Jewish homeland:

> MORRIS: We have to turn to Palestine, Alec. Palestine is the key to our future role …
> MORRIS: What Palestine is going to need is leaders, Alec, with clear, Marxist outlook, a firm progressive sense of direction … Give me some tea, Alec.[102]

This is not, however, an idealized picture of life in the Jewish community. While Morris holds forth on his ideal of Palestine as a state for the Jewish workers of the world, Alec is more interested in finding out about Morris's regular visits to a local brothel.

In many ways, *Bread and Butter* is a play about disappointment and frustration, only some of which is sexual.

> MORRIS: I'm forty-five, Alec. I've got political ability. I have drive, ideas. When am I going to do something with my life? Am I just going to bury my talents at the pressing?[103]

Morris has various enthusiasms. During the war he draws up elaborate 'plans' for the defence of the Jewish population in the event of a German invasion, determined to be 'prepared.' Later, Alec defends his friends' lack of action to Miriam, 'It's not Morris's fault that Hitler didn't invade Britain … '.[104] Morris drafts Socialist manifestoes, and at one point begins to make a film, as he sees it as the only way to communicate his political vision to the masses. However, he is ultimately revealed as a selfish egotist. When Alec and Miriam come into some money, the ever-practical Miriam works out a scheme whereby the couple can spend six months of the year in the nearby seaside town of Dunoon. Instead of being delighted that his friend has partially liberated himself from wage-slavery, Morris laments the fact that he will be left in 'isolation'.

> MORRIS: And you're going away, for half a year every year, in the summer. You're going to leave me in bloody Glasgow. With nothing to look forward to in the evenings. To have to wander around the park on my own all summer.
> MIRIAM: Morris, you have Sharon and the children. You have even more than us!
> MORRIS: [*with passion*] It's not enough! It's not enough![105]

It is not, indeed, enough as Morris is not satisfied either physically or intellectually within his marriage. Morris is representative of those agnostic Jews that my father encountered in his own life who were still unable, or unwilling, to ditch the façade of conformity. His lack of faith is clear enough.

> MORRIS: The conclusion you come to is that God isn't interested in people – if he exists. If you're working out an objective picture of the world in other words, you can leave out God. To all intents and purposes, he doesn't exist. If he exists, he has nothing to do with the world. Marx and Engels have been proved absolutely right![106]

However, he gets engaged to the nice Jewish girl chosen for him by his uncle Sroka, who is also the local Rabbi and, although he continually asserts that he is going to make a grand gesture of rebellion, he never has the moral courage to carry it out. After Morris and Sharon become engaged he proclaims his refusal to accept the marriage ceremony, and 'grovel on the ground before superstition and mysticism'.[107]

> MORRIS: The temptation is going to be very strong. I'll probably never get another opportunity in my life again like this. To strike a powerful and telling blow for science and reason.
> ALEC: I don't follow you, Morris.
> MORRIS: I'm standing there, under the marriage canopy with Sharon. Sroka says: Do you take this woman … ?
> ALEC: He reads the marriage contract, Morris. The groom made the following declaration to his bride and so on …
> MORRIS: And I will stand up …

ALEC: You're already standing, Morris.
MORRIS: And stretch up to my height. And in a loud ringing voice I will proclaim ...
ALEC: What will you proclaim, Morris?
MORRIS: I'm just trying to phrase it in my mind ... I REPUDIATE THE RIGHT AND THE AUTHORITY OF RELIGION TO DIRECT THE AFFAIRS OF MAN AND WOMAN! Take Sharon's hand, and *stride* out of the synagogue!
SHARON: I could never look at my father and mother again! I'd have to run away from the country![108]

Of course, Sharon does not have to flee the country in shame, as Morris acquiesces in the wedding ceremony; he also says Kaddish (the Jewish prayer for the dead) for his father and, after more protests, consents to his son's Bar Mitzvah. As he eventually admits, 'On religion, it's just one miserable rout! From my wedding onwards!'[109] In many ways Morris represents the person my father could have been had he not made the decisive break from tradition and religion that he eventually did. *Bread and Butter* depicts the restrictions of the community that my father came from, and the many personal compromises that result from a person, such as my father was, remaining within it. It is also, as Susan Friesner says, 'an easy play to underestimate'.[110]

The reason for this is that the characters gradually grow in complexity, and that the expectations aroused by the first act of the play are exceeded by the developments in the second. Given the setting of the play, and the apparently mundane lives of the characters, we feel that, after some trials and tribulations, there will be a 'cosy' resolution of the conflict, but this never comes. Both male characters are left unsatisfied at the end of the play. Even though Alec is more accepting of what life throws at him than Morris, he begins to question whether he even likes Miriam after more than twenty years of marriage. After Miriam dies, Alec goes to London with the intention of sleeping with a prostitute, but is unable to go through with it, and instead makes do with pornography.

The play ends with the two men having one of their frequent conversations in the park, during which Morris makes a last desperate attempt at a gesture of defiance.

ALEC: Here's Sroka coming back with Epstein.
MORRIS: Alec, when he comes near us, let's make some gesture, throw off this respectability for five minutes, Alec. Let's show them.

ALEC: What do you want to do, Morris?
MORRIS: Something that'll turn them white, shatter them. Something outrageous, so that they won't bow to us and give us their good afternoons like brothers in the conspiracy.
ALEC: If you want, Morris. If it'll give you any satisfaction.
MORRIS: What can it be? Something like: Down with God – the Marriage Contract and the United Synagogue Council! Israel! Kosher Meat! Jewish Culture!
ALEC: If you want, Morris. I've nothing to lose, only…your position, Morris – the family …
MORRIS: They're coming up now. Climb up on the seat.
ALEC: Standing'll be enough, Morris.
MORRIS [*climbing on to the seat*]: No. Get up, we've got to look conspicuous, outrageous.
[ALEC *climbs up beside him.*]
Are you ready? One … two … three …
ALEC: They're looking at us.
MORRIS: Yes. Look as if you're putting a bird back on that branch. Is that plausible?
ALEC: It's better than nothing.
MORRIS [*explaining to* SROKA]: Bird fell off the tree. It's all right, now.
ALEC: I've just put it back.
[*They climb down.*][111]

If *Bread and Butter* demonstrates the consequences for the individual when they are unable to break the bonds of tradition, and escape the restrictions of the Jewish community, *Walter* is partly an expression of regret at leaving behind the support and comfort that the community provided. *Walter* was first performed on the 19 July 1977 at the Traverse Theatre in Edinburgh.[112] The play is in two parts: 'Getting By' and 'Going Home', originally performed over two evenings, and cut to a single play, 'Walter' for the 1992 Edinburgh Festival revival.[113] It is loosely based on the life of the Scottish music-hall performer, Walter Jackson, whom Taylor knew, and interviewed for the play. Walter Jackson was born in 1916, the son of Jewish immigrants living in the Gorbals, and made his debut in Glasgow in 1932.[114] So Jackson comes from a similar background to Taylor, and the protagonist in the play, Walter Isaacs, contains more elements of the author than Jackson.

For dramatic reasons, the stage character in C.P. Taylor's play is a fictionalised portrait. The real Walter was never regarded as an outspoken or abrasive man. Friends remember him as kind-hearted and generous who would always lend a hand to anyone. Although he graduated from the Empress to the Glasgow Empire he never assumed he was a star and seemed content to remain second or third on the bill.[115]

The arts editor for the *Scotsman*, Allen Wright, is thus justified in calling the play 'Taylor's autobiographical masterpiece'.[116]

Taylor's Walter is content with little in his life. The play opens with Walter's fatal heart attack, and then ranges freely across the events of the protagonist's life, as he tries to make sense of his past. Walter is a highly complex figure, who has long ago rejected Judaism, and is also disenchanted with the left-wing politics of his youth, and currently espouses a position of moral relativism. Taylor described it as follows in an interview with Cordelia Oliver:

> Walter ... realises quite well the limitations of straight-line logic, is full of kinks, that far more is unknown than known, but even so he can't help trying to analyse the situation. And he tries to evolve a philosophy. He tells the old Jewish story about the man whose blanket is too short (when he pulls it up to keep his chest warm his feet get cold and vice versa) and presents it as an image to fit the human condition. In all the planning, no matter how well meant, somebody's feet are going to freeze.[117]

It is interesting to read these sentiments attributed to Walter knowing that they are thoughts my father frequently expressed himself. Walter, and my father, put it more succinctly as, 'Man plans and God laughs'.[118]

Walter, by now 69, at the end of his career and in poor health, is living in comparative luxury beside Loch Lomond with his housekeeper/lover Joyce, and his old music-hall partner, Rickie. His career as a music-hall entertainer was brought to an abrupt end by the advent of television.

> WALTER: That time television hit us. All the Halls closing down. One by one. Empress, Metropole, Empire – God I bloody died that time! I mean. Spend all my bloody life learning to work the Halls, and the bastards close down practically overnight.[119]

He was reduced to performing for old-age pensioners, where he was spotted by a representative of STV who were on the point of making 'Glasgow's answer to Coronation Street'.[120] Walter was offered a role in the series, which the entire Scottish press agree is 'a major breakthrough in rock bottom telly', but was also incredibly popular, and makes his fortune.[121] Although now attempting to cut himself off from the world, and his past, both beat a path to his door, beginning with an ex-lover from almost 40 years ago, Doris. Her arrival coincides with an improvement in Walter's health, thus leading Walter to wonder if her presence has a mystical healing power. Then Walter's nephew, Ian, visits him to tell him that his wife, whom he has not seen for 40 years, is still alive and wants to see him, thus bringing back a whole host of associations.

> WALTER: ... One afternoon ... this winged messenger in a Volvo turns up from the Jews. My nephew. Nobody's in the house. Rickie's up in the hills, trying to organise me a path up this buzzard's nest he found. Joyce is doing her Open University Sociology course. He just walks in in his hand-made ninety pound suit. He comes out with an incredible piece of information ... I mean to me. I'd forgotten all about my bloody wife's existence. But he comes to me, Ian, and tells us ... Beckie is alive, and half blind, crippled with varicose veins, and living in Langside, in Glasgow. In a Board of Guardian's home.[122]

In *Walter*, as in many of Taylor's mature plays, the central character continually addresses the audience directly, and much of the play is taken up with long monologues in which Walter reflects on his past. Here he describes his music-hall beginnings:

> WALTER: The whole problem was books ... I couldn't keep from reading books. Time I was fourteen I'd read every bloody book in the Gorbals library ... including the Yiddish section. Time I started on the Halls ... I was light years ahead of the audience I was performing to ... I got this dummy ... as moral support. Did a dance routine at the end of the act with him ... I mean. The whole spiel was leading to me singing the number to bring the house down with.[123]

Given the similarities between the two figures, it is not easy to distinguish between the autobiographical elements in the play, and those parts taken from Walter Jackson's life. Bearing in mind Taylor's beginnings writing for the local Jewish community, it is difficult to see the following passage, where he describes his first meeting with his wife, as anything but self-description.

> WALTER: First time I saw her. I was what you call a Jewish romantic. Reading all these Jewish books. Very small she was,

Beckie. Pale. Dark under her eyes. Real Jewish girl. Sitting beside her at the supper ... They'd invited us all to her uncle's for supper. To meet her ... I fancied her ... I'd just been reading a Jewish play. At that time I hadn't made up my mind if I should be a singer, an actor, a comedian ... or the greatest Jewish writer in history ... The Dybbuk ... Quite a nice play. I kept seeing Beckie as the girl in the play.[124]

Walter plays various roles during the course of the play, re-enacting his old music-hall routines, donning a prayer shawl and playing the 'old Jew', acting the part of John Maclean in a television drama, and posing as the self-made philosopher. When he is talking to others it becomes hard to tell when he is performing and when he is 'being himself', and this imparts an air of intimacy to his monologues.

> WALTER: (*to audience*) Tell you the truth ... sometimes I'm not interested in anybody but myself. Most times I'm not interested in anybody but myself. That's not a very good situation to be in, is it? I mean people should be interested in other people ... [125]

Although intellectually Walter has rejected both politics and religion he is still moved by the rhetoric of both. Throughout the play he makes speeches as John Maclean, in character as the Scottish revolutionary, for the programme he is in the process of making:

> WALTER: (*as* MACLEAN) ... I was born in King Street, Pollockshaws, on August 14th 1879. My father came from Mull, like the Irish, he said. After the potato crop had blighted two years running and folk all round him were dying of hunger. Time I was born, he was working at Lockhart's pottery ... keeping his family that wee bit above starvation. Nine years later, he was dead, 43 years old. An average age for a wage slave to die in those days. He lasted longer than if he'd stayed in Mull mind! (*to audience*) It wasn't the man ... The man wasn't getting me at all. It was that bloody song. And the kind of myths that he stirred up to get anybody to write a song like that ...
> Hey, Man did you see him,
> As he came down by Georgie,
> Awa up the Lammerlaw
> And North up te the Tay ...
> The whole town is turning oot...
> Great John Maclean's coming down to the Clyde.[126]

The Life, Times and Jewishness of C.P. Taylor

As the play goes on it emerges that Walter is highly critical of Maclean's uncompromising and 'impractical' political strategy, and refers to him as 'an idiot', but is still drawn to his idealism.[127] At one point the director of the television programme Walter is working on asks him to put on his *Tallith* (praying shawl) and say a prayer:

> WALTER: Boruch atah adonia elowheinu melech ho Oolom. Ager keedeshonu Bemeetzvowsov vetzeeyonu al Meetzvat Tzeetzees Behold me, Lord enwrapping my body with the fringes of my commandment. In a like manner do thou enwrap my soul and my body too even all its members and sinews, in the spiritual light diffused by the holy precept of the fringes. (*to audience*). How about that for a wee bit of Jewish rhetoric and symbolism? But it has a good ring to it, hasn't it? (*to* ERIC) I've got to sit down again, Eric.[128]

Walter's internal struggle to reconcile his Jewish heritage with his current beliefs and circumstances manifests itself in a literal way when his ex-wife sends him the praying shawl mentioned above from her deathbed. His partner, Joyce, a gentile, has difficulty accepting Walter's cultural background, and resists the idea of him attending his ex-wife's funeral.

> JOYCE: I'll tell you what it is, Ian, I can't stand about Jews.
> IAN: Yes. I think you should come out with what you've got against us, Joyce. Openly...that's the best way.
> WALTER: She is, man. That's what she's doing.
> JOYCE: The way they make a meal out of everything that happens to them, Ian. Deaths ... births ... marriages. Go bloody hysterical.
> WALTER: Joyce, you're right. That's a penetrating comment. Everything happens to us, is the greatest event of the century. Sometimes it is, but isn't it?[129]

Walter, wishing to avoid a confrontation with Joyce, hides the praying shawl from her. When he dons the praying shawl he is careful to do so when Joyce is out of the house. After he attends his ex-wife's funeral he retrieves two further remnants of his past she had kept for him, his Left Book Club library, and his great grandfather's *Sepher Torah* (scroll of the law) carried 'all the way from Russia ... through a hail of frontier guards' bullets'.[130] The scroll is the physical manifestation of Walter's heritage, preserved at the cost of so much human suffering that it has to be treated with respect. In fact the *Sepher Torah* is treated with such reverence that one is not actually allowed to touch it, and it must be read with a pointer to keep the place. At first Walter intends to open the scroll and show it to Joyce so that the 'Whole ghost of her thing about Jews' is 'laid in one fell swoop…along with mine'.[131] However, he loses his nerve at the last minute, and hurriedly hides the scroll from Joyce. Eventually he shows it to Joyce and they have a conversation during which Walter tries to play down the significance of the scroll.

> WALTER: All it is is the first five books of the Bible.
> JOYCE: Not what you'd call a pocket edition, is it?
> WALTER: That's exactly the right attitude, Joyce … absolutely.
> JOYCE: What were you hiding it from me for then, if it means nothing to you?
> WALTER: Honestly … I'll swear on that Scroll it means nothing to me …
> JOYCE: What did you bring it back here for…then? If it means nothing to you.[132]

What does the Scroll mean to Walter? He is the grandson of a Rabbi, and has a high level of Jewish education. Walter can read the Hebrew in the scroll, which is written without any vowels, while his nephew cannot. However, despite his deeply Orthodox background, Walter has long ago cast off religious belief as 'superstition and mysticism'.[133] However he wants the scroll to be with him in the house, and rejects Rickie's suggestion of hiding it from Joyce in the shed. He talks about his attendance at his ex-wife's funeral as an 'exorcism', in which he has laid the ghosts of his past to rest.[134] Then he wonders if he is turning into 'a mystical old Jew in old age'.[135] What is Walter's attitude to Jewishness? The funeral is a key moment in his reappraisal of this question. After it he comments that, 'The Jews are definitely a workable proposition', but then goes on to say that anything is a workable proposition as long as people believe in it.[136] At another point he wonders whether the Jews 'are a kind of Master Race'.[137]

> WALTER: What about the Jewish geniuses? That bothers me. That's the one element Joyce is always leaving out. There's obviously something about a culture that produces Einsteins and Karl Marxes and me …
> RICKIE: You bloody believe that, too, don't you? You and Karl Marx.
> WALTER: (*to audience*) I did. It wasn't vanity. It seemed just an unavoidable fact.[138]

There is obviously a great deal of ambivalence in Walter's attitudes. In the space of a few lines he goes from saying that the Jews, 'have that wee extra touch of civilisation. Even the way they drink,' to the complaint that, 'Sometimes of course they go too far with their refinements. All the apparatus they need to talk to God ... Phylacteries ... Fringes ... Yamulkes ... Praying Shawls.'[139] Then there is his obvious enjoyment of the potato latkes (potato cakes) that he asks his nephew Ian to make for him on his first visit, prompting Walter to reflect that 'I haven't had a latke for more than twenty years'.[140]

These observations return us to the question my father addressed to my mother, 'Is "Jew" a religion or a race?' Walter does not seem able to separate the two. His feelings for his culture are partly based on nostalgia, partly a consequence of general intellectual disenchantment, and also a consequence of the link between religious beliefs and belief in the family, so strong in Judaism. This is derived from the authority of one's father, and, by extension, of one's ancestors in general.[141]

Walter continually quotes his grandfather, as did my father. Walter has cut all links between both himself and his religion, but this has also left him with no contact with his culture. Walter is an illustration of the difficulty of separating religion from culture. He is unable to distinguish between the significance of the potato latkes and the *Sepher Torah*. Ultimately, it is impossible to say to what extent Walter's views accord with those of my father at the time he wrote the play. Even though this is something I raised with my family, we reached no real agreement on the issue. It is, however, worth noting that, of all the characters my father created, apart from the age difference, Walter is the one that seems most like him. As I have indicated, Walter is continually repeating sentiments that I heard my father express. So it is difficult not to conclude that Walter represents the fullest expression of my father's feelings about his Jewishness. However, given the ambivalence of Walter's feelings, Allen Wright's judgement that this was the play 'in which the dramatist finally came to terms with his Jewish heritage', seems to be an over-simplification.[142]

Of course, there is always more than one source of identity for any individual from an immigrant community, and Walter is no exception. It is clear from Ralph Glasser's autobiography that he and his friends converse in Glaswegian dialect and are just as much Scottish as they are Jewish. Walter makes frequent references to his identity as a Scot. In one of his conversations with his doctor he asserts, 'I was born in Glasgow. I'm as native born a Scot as you!' Then an immediate retraction, 'No ... you're quite right, Michael I'm not.'[143] Walter expresses similar feelings of ambivalence about visiting his birthplace:

WALTER: (*to audience*) We got through Clydebank and into Glasgow. High rises on either side of us. Rickie said something about being back in the old town. I couldn't stand the bloody place, for God's sake. But coming back to it ... There was a definite lift. Recognising places you'd been when you were a kid. Even though they'd knocked down most of the old landmarks.[144]

Walter found that it was easier to gain acceptance as an entertainer if he suppressed his Jewish identity. He was discovered performing at a wedding by the manager of the Metropole, who was impressed by his ability, 'But he wasn't sure of the Jewish angle ... So I showed him I could do the Glesga comic as well.'[145] The character he played in the television soap opera that makes his fortune is also clearly Glaswegian, and has no connection with his Jewishness.

This brings us to the thin line between immigrants' desire for acceptance by the host community, and the fear of provoking hostility through over expressions of 'difference'. Zygmunt Bauman feels that cultural outsiders become caught up in a game they can never win:

> Frequently they go out of their way to get rid of and to suppress everything which makes them distinct from the rightful members of the native community – and hope that a devoted emulation of native ways will render them indistinguishable from the hosts, and by the same token guarantee their classification as insiders, entitled to the same treatment the friends routinely receive. The harder they try, however, the faster the finishing-line seems to be receding. When, at last, it seems to be within their grasp, a dagger of racism is flung from beneath the liberal cloak. The rules of the game are changed with little warning.[146]

Such an analysis is particularly applicable to British Jewry's attempts at assimilation, as Tony Kushner points out.[147] The widespread phenomenon of the alteration of family names is a good example of such a phenomenon. As we saw earlier, my original family name is not 'Taylor', it was 'Girschovitz'. Similarly, my mother's family name was not originally 'Diamond', it was 'Pearlman'.[148] The reasons for individuals changing their names are often quite complex, but they come down to a desire for acceptance, if not an overt fear of anti-Semitism. In the case of my mother's family it was apparently the result of a genuine misunderstanding on the part of an English landlord. Walter's nephew 'Ian' is, it turns out, actually 'Izzie',

> RICKIE: What's he keep calling you Izzie one minute and Ian the next for?

IAN: When in Rome do as the Romans do. Know what I mean, Rickie? Purely for business reasons. Nothing to do with being ashamed of my religion, God forbid ...

IAN (*to* RICKIE): Got to face facts haven't you, Rickie? I mean, nobody's mad on Jewish people in this country. I'm not saying they're Nazis or anything. God forbid. Same time, if you go into a shop and hand in your card ... Izzie Black ... [149]

Ian's wife, Rhoda, draws the curtains on Friday nights before lighting the Sabbath candles because 'She doesn't want the Gentiles to know her business'.[150] The motivation behind these small efforts to 'blend in' with one's surroundings is not straightforward, but it is a fundamental part of the experience of British Jewry.

CONCLUSION

It is not easy to draw neat conclusions from a discussion of such diverse issues, many of which are difficult to resolve. As indicated at the outset of the discussion, the 'new wave' of British Jewish history has raised many issues, some of which this article has sought to address. We have seen that 'Jewishness' is not a singular or unitary identity. The majority of British Jews exist in a grey area between strict religious observance and total rejection of all religious beliefs and practices. Individuals may also participate in the religious life of their community without any real faith. In terms of my father's work we saw that the themes of Jewish identity and anti-Semitism appear repeatedly in his plays. However, this was not an exclusive focus, as much of his work is concerned with issues that do not directly relate to these themes. As my sister, Clare, puts it,

> My father's work reflects his many self-images. His plays with Live Theatre drew on his experiences as an adopted Geordie, his earlier plays reflected the way of life in his native Glasgow, however, the Jewish experience was present, if not in every play then as a recurring theme throughout his working life.[151]

We saw that my father rebelled against the constraints of the community he grew up in, and this rejection of traditional values eventually led him to pursue quite a separate path, particularly after he left my mother. However, it is doubtful whether he ever 'resolved' his relationship with his past. In my sister's reflections on her, and our father's, feeling about Jewishness, she refers to 'people like us who are culturally but not religiously Jewish' and maintains that Jewish racial identity 'is quite separate from any spiritual belief'.[152] However, is it possible to make such a clear distinction between culture and religion as Jewish culture stems from religion? How easy is it to separate the potato latkes from the *Sepher Torah*? The conclusion one reaches from a consideration of my father's plays is, that he never satisfactorily answered the question he addressed to my mother all those years ago, 'Is "Jew" a religion or a race?' This is because the relationship between race, culture and religion in Jewish identity is a conundrum that is almost impossible to solve. My father, at least, dealt with it in an honest and revealing manner, capturing much of the essence of the experience of his community.

NOTES

1. Anne J. Kershen, 'From Celebrationists to Confrontationists: Some Thoughts on British Jewish Historiography in the Twentieth Century', *Immigrants & Minorities*, Vol.19, No.2 (2000), p.102.
2. Lloyd P. Gartner, 'A Recent Look at Anglo-Jewish History: A Review Essay', *American Jewish History*, Vol.80, No.4 (1991), p.566.
3. Susan Friesner, 'Travails of a Naked Typist: The Plays of C.P. Taylor', *New Theatre Quarterly*, Vol.IX, No.33 (1993), p.46.
4. Lyn Gardner,'The Guide', *The Guardian*, 26 Feb. 2000.
5. Letter to the author from Alan Brodie Representation Ltd., 17 April 2002. *Good* has been translated into: Japanese, Hebrew, Croatian, Catalan, Castilian, Spanish, Polish, French and Dutch.
6. Friesner, 'Travails of a Naked Typist', p.44.
7. John Elsom, *Post-War British Theatre Criticism* (London, 1981); Andrew Davies, *Other Theatres: The Development of Alternative and Experimental Theatre in Britain* (Basingstoke, 1987).
8. John Elsom, *Theatre Outside London* (London, 1971), pp.192 and 210.
9. Ronald Hayman, *British Theatre since 1955: A Reassessment* (Oxford, 1979), p.133.
10. Elsom, *Post-War British Theatre*, p.184.
11. Ibid., pp.184–5.
12. Joyce McMillan, *The Traverse Theatre Story 1963–1988* (London, 1988), p.24.
13. Ibid., p.9.
14. Ibid., p.10.
15. Ibid., p.111.
16. Jim Haynes (ed.), *Traverse Plays* (Harmondsworth, 1966); C.P. Taylor et al., *Penguin Plays: New English Dramatists 10* (Harmondsworth, 1967); C.P. Taylor et al., *Penguin Plays: New English Dramatists 12* (Harmondsworth, 1968); C.P. Taylor et al., *A Decade's Drama* (Todmorden, 1980); C.P. Taylor, *North: Six Plays by C.P. Taylor* (London/Newcastle, 1987).
17. Allen Wright, 'C.P. Taylor Remembered', in 'C.P. Taylor: A Life in the Theatre', *Scotland on Sunday*, 19 April 1992.
18. 'C.P. Taylor: The Life and Times', in 'C.P. Taylor: A Life in the Theatre'; Helen Lovat Fraser quoted in the Edinburgh International Festival 1992 Programme for 'The Ballachulish Beat'.
19. 'C.P. Taylor: The Life and Times'.
20. Friesner, 'Travails of a Naked Typist', p.47.
21. C.P. Taylor quoted on back cover of C.P. Taylor, *Bandits* (Newcastle, 1977).
22. Friesner , 'Travails of a Naked Typist', p.47.

23. C.P. Taylor, *Live Theatre: Three Plays by C.P. Taylor* (Newcastle, 1981), p.1. (Although Taylor says that this project began in 1972, the rehearsal script for the resultant play is dated December 1971.)
24. Ibid., pp.1–7.
25. C.P. Taylor, *Live Theatre: Four Plays for Young People by C.P. Taylor* (London/Newcastle, 1983). (These are the same plays that appeared in the 1981 volume cited in note 23 above, but with the addition of a fourth play *Happy Lies*.)
26. Ibid., p.4.
27. Ibid., back cover; *Radio Times*, 24–30 Jan. 1981.
28. Susan Friesner 'The Plays of C.P. Taylor' (unpublished M.A. thesis, City University, London, 1990), p.135.
29. C.P. Taylor et al., *3 North East Plays* (Newcastle, 1976).
30. C.P. Taylor, 'A Silent Nightingale', *The Guardian*, 8 Sept. 1979.
31. Peter Mortimer, 'Northern Light', in 'C.P. Taylor: A Life in the Theatre'.
32. C.P. Taylor, *And A Nightingale Sang* ... (London, 1979); C.P. Taylor, *Good* and *And A Nightingale Sang* ... (London, 1990).
33. Taylor, 'A Silent Nightingale'.
34. Friesner, 'The Plays of C.P. Taylor', pp.145–7. Favourable reviews for the West End production appear in Taylor, *And A Nightingale Sang* ... .
35. *TV Times*, 15–21 April 1989.
36. Taylor, *Bandits*; C.P. Taylor, *Good* (London, 1982).
37. Friesner, 'Travails of a Naked Typist, p.52.
38. Taylor, *Bandits*, p.5.
39. Friesner, 'The Plays of C.P. Taylor', pp.162–4.
40. Ibid, p.174-8.
41. Favourable reviews for the original version of the play are quoted in Taylor, *Good*. Favourable reviews for the 1999 revival of the play are quoted on: http://www.albemarle-london.com/good.html, 15 April 2002. There have also been several British performances of *Good* outside the capital; for example, it was performed during the 'C.P. Taylor Festival' in Newcastle in 1989, and during the 1992 Edinburgh International Festival.
42. This suggestion was made by Peter Mortimer in 'C.P. Taylor: An Appreciation of his Work and Life', *Drama* (1982), pp.16–17.
43. Colin Holmes, *Anti-Semitism in British Society 1876–1939* (London, 1979), p.3.
44. Harold Pollins, *Economic History of the Jews in England* (London/Toronto, 1982), p.130.
45. Ibid., p.131; Harold Pollins 'Immigration into Britain: The Jews', *History Today*, Vol.34 (1985), p.9.
46. David Englander (ed.), *A Documentary History of Jewish Immigrants In Britain 1840–1920* (London, 1994), p.63.
47. Pollins, 'Immigration into Britain', p.11.
48. Chaim Bermant, *Coming Home* (London, 1976), pp.52–3.
49. Henry Maitles, 'Jewish Trade Unionists in Glasgow', *Immigrants & Minorities*, Vol.10, No.3 (1991), p.51.
50. David Cesarani, 'The Transformation of Communal Authority in Anglo-Jewry 1914–1940', in David Cesarani (ed.), *The Making of Modern Anglo-Jewry* (Oxford, 1990), p.118.
51. Geoffrey Alderman, *Modern British Jewry* (Oxford, 1992), p.174.
52. Ibid.
53. Ibid., p.175.
54. Kenneth Collins (ed.), *Aspects of Scottish Jewry* (Glasgow, 1987), p.2.
55. Maitles, 'Jewish Trade Unionists in Glasgow', p.58.
56. Ralph Glasser, *Growing Up in the Gorbals* (London, 1987), p.58. Interview conducted by the author with Issy Dentist, 24 April 2002.
57. Elsom, *Post-War British Theatre* (London, 1976), p.184.
58. 'C.P. Taylor: The Life and Times'.
59. Friesner, 'Travails of a Naked Typist', pp.44–5.

60. Ibid., p.45
61. Ibid.
62. Collins, *Aspects of Scottish Jewry*, p.26.
63. Interview conducted by the author with his mother (Irene Taylor), 26 April 2002.
64. Friesner, 'The Plays of C.P. Taylor', p.4.
65. Max Girschovitz/Taylor, 'Certificate of Naturalization', 19 Feb. 1920.
66. Interview conducted by the author with Issy Dentist, 24 April 2002.
67. Letter to the author from Issy Dentist, 11 April 2002.
68. Ibid.
69. Ibid.
70. Friesner, 'The Plays of C.P. Taylor', p.6.
71. Letter to the author from Phil Dentist, 14 March 2002.
72. The *Guardian*, 2 Aug. 1977.
73. Interview conducted by the author with his mother (Irene Taylor), 9 April 2002.
74. Ibid.
75. Friesner, 'The Plays of C.P. Taylor', p.10.
76. 'C.P. Taylor: The Life and Times'.
77. Letter to the author from Liz Taylor, 28 March 2002.
78. Liz Taylor interviewed on the Tyne-Tees Television programme, *The Man in the Hut*, Dec. 1989.
79. Interview conducted by the author with his mother (Irene Taylor), 9 April 2002.
80. Ibid.
81. Letter to the author from David Taylor, 10 April 2002.
82. Interview conducted by the author with Issy Dentist, 24 April 2002.
83. Ibid.
84. Glasser, *Growing Up in the Gorbals*, p.47.
85. Letter to the author from Phil Dentist, 14 March 2002.
86. Letter to the author from Phil Dentist, 7 April 2002.
87. Glasser, Growing Up in the Gorbals, pp.87–96.
88. Mark Hudson, *Coming Back Brockens: A Year in a Mining Village* (London, 1995), p.1.
89. Letter to the author from Cat Taylor, 22 April 2002.
90. Ibid.
91. Taylor, *Good*, p.iii.
92. Taylor, *Oil and Water*, p.20.
93. The *Guardian*, 2 Aug. 1977.
94. C.P. Taylor, 'Me' (unpublished original draft), p.5.
95. Friesner 'The Plays of C.P. Taylor', p.35.
96. Taylor et al., *Penguin Plays: New English Dramatists 10*, p.158; Stanley Eveling, 'C.P. Taylor: The Life in the Theatre'in 'C.P. Taylor: A Life in the Theatre'; 'C.P. Taylor: The Life and Times', in 'C.P. Taylor: The Life in the Theatre'.
97. Ibid.; Friesner 'The Plays of C.P. Taylor', p.33.
98. Taylor et al., *Penguin Plays: New English Dramatists 10*, p.159.
99. Ibid., p.161.
100. Ibid., p.164.
101. Ibid., pp.168–9.
102. Ibid., p.183.
103. Ibid., p.184.
104. Ibid., p.186.
105. Ibid., p.190.
106. Ibid., p.182.
107. Ibid., p.171.
108. Ibid., p.172.
109. Ibid., p.199.
110. Friesner 'The Plays of C.P. Taylor', p.52.
111. Taylor et al., *Penguin Plays: New English Dramatists 10*, pp.220–21.
112. Taylor et al., *A Decade's Drama* (Todmorden, 1980), p.254.

113. Cordelia Oliver, 'Home and Away', in 'C.P. Taylor: A Life in the Theatre'. The shortened version of the play appears in C.P. Taylor, *The Plays of C.P. Taylor as Performed at the Edinburgh International Festival 1992* (Edinburgh, 1992).
114. Vivien Devlin, quoted in the Edinburgh International Festival 1992 Programme for *Walter*.
115. Ibid.
116. Wright, 'C.P. Taylor Remembered'.
117. *The Guardian*, 2 Aug. 1977.
118. Taylor et al., *A Decade's Drama*, p.270.
119. Ibid., p.295.
120. Ibid., p.296.
121. Ibid., p.302.
122. Ibid., p.265.
123. Ibid., p.257.
124. Ibid., p.267.
125. Ibid., p.291.
126. Ibid., p.264.
127. Ibid., pp.303, 326.
128. Ibid., p.319.
129. Ibid., p.279.
130. Ibid., p.290.
131. Ibid., p.291.
132. Ibid., p.299.
133. Ibid., p 319.
134. Ibid., p.299.
135. Ibid., p.318.
136. Ibid., p.317.
137. Ibid., p.284.
138. Ibid.
139. Ibid., p.315.
140. Ibid., p.270.
141. Chaim Bermant, *The Jews* (London, 1977), pp.13–14.
142. Wright, 'C.P. Taylor '.
143. Taylor et al., *A Decade's Drama*, p.262.
144. Ibid., p.315.
145. Ibid., p.265.
146. Zygmunt Bauman, 'Allosemitism: Premodern, Modern, Postmodern', in Bryan Cheyette and Laura Marcus (eds.), *Modernity, Culture and 'the Jew'* (Cambridge/Oxford, 1998), p.227.
147. Tony Kushner, 'Remembering to Forget: Racism and Anti-Racism in Post-war Britain', in ibid., p. 238.
148. Interview conducted by the author with his mother (Irene Taylor), 9 April 2002.
149. Taylor et al., *A Decade's Drama*, p.268.
150. Ibid., p.322.
151. Letter to the author from Clare Taylor, 24 April 2002.
152. Ibid.

Sidney Pollard: The Refugee Historian

DAVID RENTON

In his academic interests, Sidney Pollard (1925–98) was among the most wide-ranging of post-war British historians. An historical economist by training, he contributed to several key debates in that field. His books discussed the nature of underdevelopment and the means to achieve relative growth,[1] the role played by investment in the industrial revolution,[2] the early history of management,[3] the part played by monetary policy in the inter-war period,[4] the reasons for Britain's economic decline after 1945,[5] and the economic history of European integration.[6] In addition, Pollard was a labour historian.[7] His postdoctoral research examining the history of labour in Sheffield was one of the first British studies to anticipate history from below. He contributed to the foundation of the Society for the Study of Labour History, and later edited its bulletin, today's *Labour History Review*. The medium in which Pollard's labour history was expressed was the history of the region. His last book, *Marginal Europe*, is a study of development across state boundaries, which treats the history of regions in much the same way as Karl Marx had previously discussed the history of social classes, or Raúl Prebisch the story of developed and developing nations,[8] as self-conscious, organic entities engaged in a system of economic rivalry in which even marginal or dispossessed groups could flourish.[9]

The focus of the essay here, however, is on one specific aspect of Pollard's life and work, his experience of exile. In 1938, Pollard left his

---

Many thanks to colleagues in the Department of History at Sunderland University for supporting a one-year research fellowship, during which time the author was able to study the papers of Sidney Pollard, and also to the library staff at Sunderland University library for granting him access to the Pollard collection. Regards should also be given to a number of colleagues whose ideas have contributed to this study. They include Peter Wilson, Peter Waldron, Tony Hepburn, Matt Perry and John Burnett at Sunderland University, as well as Sidney Pollard's surviving relatives, his wife Helen, and his children, Brian, David and Veronica. Thanks especially to Colin Holmes.

native Vienna to travel as a child refugee to Britain. The decision to leave was not taken lightly. His parents were unable to accompany him into exile, and the months that followed were the most difficult of Pollard's life. Part of this discussion is biographical. It tells briefly Pollard's story, and concentrates especially on this key incident. It is argued that the traumas he underwent in 1938 and afterwards remained with Pollard to shape his later choices, including his decision to become an academic and also the nature of the books that he wrote. The focus then shifts towards Pollard's books and articles. The suggestion is that we can find traces of this childhood memory embodied in them.

Some readers may find this point surprising, for unlike many of the Jewish refugee historians, Pollard did not write directly about inter-war Germany or the Holocaust, or at least not in any sustained way. He did not often comment on his early experiences.[10] Nor did he talk much with his friends and colleagues on the experience of exile. He was not invited to attend the reunions for those who had come to Britain on the Children's transports.[11] Yet following the argument of Peter Pulzer, another historian who escaped from that Nazis, it can be advanced that 'Most historical writing – at any rate writing on modern history is also autobiography.' Pulzer went on to suggest that history could be autobiographical even when the links between the two were opaque:

> Often this works indirectly. The writing may be entirely impersonal and dryly objective, with no connection to the author's life story. The details may be derived from archives, newspapers or interiors, and therefore not part of the author's own experience. But what about the choice of subject itself? The agenda? The questions to be addressed and the conclusions to be formulated? Are they chosen at random? Or do they come from inside the scholar, because something that once happened to him goes on growing inside, because the world as he has experienced it has features that cry out for explanation?[12]

The implication of Pulzer's argument is that although the biographer may sometimes be obliged to proceed in a roundabout way, when searching for links between memoir and publication that are not always obvious, they can do so fruitfully. It is suggested here that one major theme of Pollard's published work was his continued engagement with the experiences of 1938. This task compels us to look beyond Pollard's main books and consider his articles, his correspondence, and the memories of family and friends.

LIFE AND LEARNING

Sidney Pollard was born Siegfried Pollak in April 1925. His father Moses was a commercial traveller and his mother Leontine Katz a teacher. Both parents had lived in Stryy[13] near Lvov in Galicia before settling in Vienna, where Siegfried was born. The young Pollak was born in a house overlooking a chocolate factory, and could later recall the smell of the works. He received his education at the Chajes Realgymnasium, a Jewish school, where he excelled at mathematics and music.[14] Yet for all his evident success, these were not happy times. Austrian society already exhibited signs of anti-Semitic feeling, and the children of the Realgymnasium were undoubtedly affected by these developments. The majority of students, including Pollak, were *Ostjuden*, the children of recent immigrants from the *shtetl*. Unlike the more established Jewish families, they had not yet been integrated into liberal Viennese society. Many *Ostjuden* were orthodox in their religion; they were visible and at risk.

Following the German annexation of Austria in 1938, the Pollaks were forced to leave their family flat, and Moses Pollak was removed from his job. Elderly Jews were forced to scrub the streets. Pollard later wrote that racism in Austria had possessed a 'unique populist bite', which had been missing even in Germany.[15] The *Kristallnacht* pogrom of 9-10 November 1938 indicated that there would be no relaxation of state-directed antis-Semitism in the greater Germany. In such circumstances, Pollak's parents discussed a range of plans to achieve their own escape, or at least their younger son's. A cousin John Katz lived in London; could he help? Various plans failed; but in December 1938, Siegfried's parents were able to send him to Britain on the children's transports. A local committee in Edinburgh raised the necessary funds.

Having arrived in Britain, Pollak was sent to Whittingehame Farm School, a camp for refugee children situated on grounds near Edinburgh. The organizers had designed it as a preparation for future life in Israel, and encouraged the students to take part in manual work, such as cleaning, cooking, and work in the fields. We do not have any trace of Siegfried's letters to his parents. Yet we do know that he must have written, for we can detect traces of his correspondence in the letters that Siegfried's parents sent to him and which he kept. One communication was sent from Vienna in March 1939. Certain paragraphs read as if the young man had criticized conditions in the camp. Moses Pollak attempted to reassure his son, 'approach it without prejudice, but with love ... with a desire to work and a will'. Sigi was encouraged to tell himself, 'first, I'm doing this for myself, because everything I do to succeed helps me and us Jews, second, it is only temporary, and third, you should always have hope in your endeavours. The situation won't last for ever.' Despite these words of encouragement, the times were bleak.[16] The letters soon stopped. Moses and Leontine Pollak both disappeared in the Holocaust. Recently published records suggest that they were sent to the camp at Opole and died there in 1941.[17] Yet Siegfried never found out what happened to his parents. All he knew was that he did not see them again.

Young Siegfried was part of a large movement of people. Some 50,000 Jewish men and women arrived in Britain between 1933–39.[18] Although they were exiles from Nazi Germany, their time in Britain was not always happy as widespread suspicion was shown towards these foreigners. Indigenous racist traditions guaranteed that the refugees were often treated with contempt, by Britain's fascists certainly, but also more widely. In the wartime conditions that soon followed, the British government would intern all enemy aliens, known fascists and committed anti-Nazis alike.[19]

At Whittingehame, Pollak learned to speak English. His cousin Katz provided a German-English dictionary. Formal schooling was minimal, and the young refugee had to find alternative interests, which included editing the school magazine.[20] For several reasons, including perhaps a gradual disillusionment with Zionism, Siegfried Pollak's initial plan of emigrating from Britain to Palestine failed. When funds ran out to support the school at Whittingehame, in the winter of 1941–42, the world conflict was still at its height and the route East was closed. Instead of leaving Europe, Pollak found himself working as a market gardener, for a firm called Rideon's in Cambridge. 'I wanted to escape from my agricultural labourer's work, which I hated. But at the time I had no specific profession in mind.'[21]

To resolve his dilemma, Siegfried Pollak resumed his studies, with John Katz contributing the fees. Soon, Pollak had passed the London Matriculation, and could search for a university place. Although he enjoyed mathematics best, Pollak knew he could not study it to degree level. He had no knowledge of other natural sciences, and neither did he possess access to laboratories or specimens from which to learn.[22] 'It had to be a subject to be mastered from books only.' After mathematics, economics was the subject that came next. His choice made, Pollak won a place at the London School of Economics. He was also able to pass the first year of the London B.Sc. (Econ) Intermediate, on a correspondence basis. The course included options on economic history, at which Pollard excelled.

In 1943, Pollak joined the British Army Reconnaissance Corps in Belgium and Germany, serving as a radio operator.[23] It is at this point that Siegfried Pollak officially became Sidney Pollard. While other members of his generation living in Britain had to be conscripted, Pollard volunteered. He later described strong feelings of guilt 'at having survived when my family had perished'.[24] He left the army a corporal in the winter of 1946–47.

After the war, Sidney Pollard was able to resume his place at the London School of Economics. Some of his energy was devoted to left-wing causes, and he was briefly a member of the Communist Party of Great Britain. Yet Pollard spent only six months inside the party. 'I was not a political animal ... moreover, I had the nagging feeling that as a foreigner ... I ought not to engage directly in political action in my host country.'[25] He stayed with a working-class couple, the Ransomes, who impressed him with their kindness and patient commitment to the Labour movement. Through them, Pollard came into contact with the Holiday Fellowship, where he met his first wife Eileen Andrews. They married in 1949.

Sidney Pollard eventually graduated with a first, the only one in his year. Colin Holmes suggests that Pollard's academic activity may have concealed other areas of sadness in the young man's life. 'During the war his possessions had fitted into one suitcase, a symbol of his loneliness, and there was no family home to which he could return on leave from the armed forces.'[26] T.S. Ashton, a senior academic in the School, persuaded Pollard to continue his studies.[27] Because Sidney had been released from the army late, he had been able to complete the second part of his degree in just five terms. Yet the LSE course had a two-year residential requirement, so Pollard was obliged to remain in London. Following Ashton's advice, Pollard went on to complete a doctorate on the subject of the British shipbuilding industry between 1870 and 1914.[28] Despite the emotional support that Ashton offered to his student, Pollard's supervisor was an intellectual ally of F.A. von Hayek and contributed to an early cold war text *Capitalism and the Historians*.[29]

Although he began work as a part-time lecturer for the London Services committee and at Westminster College, Oxford, Pollard had difficulty in securing a full academic appointment. He was able to secure only short-term, part-time teaching work. Other young left-wing scholars experienced similar difficulties. Eric Hobsbawm thought himself fortunate to find a place 'under the wire' at Birkbeck 1947.[30] The difficulties were intensified after the Labour government began a purge of Communists in the civil service. In addition to people directly employed by the ministries, there were also sackings among post office workers, shop stewards in nationalized industries, schoolteachers, and university lecturers.[31] As for Pollard, he assumed that anti-Semitism was a major cause of his difficulties. Another colleague eventually explained that T.S. Ashton was writing hostile references 'because of my dangerous political beliefs'.[32] Finally, in 1950 Pollard was able to take a research fellowship at the University of Sheffield. This was a research post with no teaching attached, and Ashton saw less need to write the sort of letter that would have blocked any appointment. Surprisingly, Pollard continued to use Ashton as a referee for some years afterwards.[33]

At Sheffield, Sidney Pollard concentrated on labour history. In 1952, the department created an assistant lectureship in Economic History, which was renewed in 1955. By 1960, he was a senior lecturer. Slowly, Pollard was able to surmount his early difficulties and rise to the top of the department. Soon publications appeared, including histories of the local firms Marsh Brothers and Shirley, Aldred and Company.[34] Pollard's interest in the history of British industry was also expressed in *The Development of the British Economy*, which told the story of Britain's industrial economy up to the 1950s.[35] Three further editions of *The Development* appeared in his lifetime. Another book, *The Genesis of Modern Management* described the rise of a managerial class from the eighteenth century onwards, composed of men whose complex job was to control the execution of the total labour process.[36]

From the early 1960s, the story of Sidney Pollard's life was expressed largely in three fields. The first was the study of history. This aspect of his life resulted in many books and journal articles, which were to reach a total of some 200 items by the time of his death. Then there was Pollard the colleague, a Professor and head of economic history at Sheffield. In 1980, Pollard left this department to take up a new post at the University of Bielefeld in West Germany, and took retirement there in 1990. There was also Pollard the family man. Three children were born in the 1950s, Brian, David and Veronica. After the children reached adulthood, he and Eileen divorced. Sidney Pollard then married his second wife Helen Trippett in 1982. Each of these themes was important to Pollard, but to do any justice to them would take us far beyond the narrow scope of this article. Fortunately, his former colleague Colin Holmes has already told these aspects of his story elsewhere, and they also appear in a short memoir that was written in the late 1990s by Pollard himself.[37]

Through the 1960s and 1970s, Pollard received increasing public recognition for his work. He was perceived as one of Britain's leading labour historians,[38] and also an expert in several linked fields of economic history. Altogether he was successful in carving out a niche for himself. For example, when Michael Postan was looking for a historian to contribute an article on labour in Britain before and after the industrial revolution, for the seventh volume of *The Cambridge Economic History of Europe*, Pollard was his obvious choice for a demanding brief: 'We want labour to be studied as a factor of production, e.g. partly in the terms in which Marx and the Marxists have discussed the formation of the industrial proletariat, and partly in the terms in which the subject now features in economic literature, i.e. changes in the flow of labour supplies, including transfers of labour between sectors and industries in the utilization of labour.'[39] Few of Pollard's contemporaries could have played this dual role.

In Pollard's private life there were undoubtedly many happy times. All three of his children record an enormous sense of gratitude they feel towards their father. In the holidays, they would be driven across Europe on fully-fledged adventures; an experience of Europe was made open to them, which was closed to most of their contemporaries.[40] Yet there were also darker moments ahead. In 1970, Pollard worked briefly as a visiting Professor of History at Berkeley in California. The following year, he was offered and accepted a permanent post there. The family followed Sidney. According to Veronica, 'We love[d] everything we saw, including the sun, the blue sea, the fresh orange juice, avocados and pizza, the hippy market stalls in Berkeley and what remained at Haight Ashbury in San Francisco.'[41] The Pollards sold their Sheffield home and prepared to move. This position should have been the fitting culmination of a successful academic career. Yet the American authorities would not give their backing to Pollard's application. John Saville describes the incident: 'The US immigration service was only prepared to issue him with a temporary work permit. Among the reasons cited for this decision were Pollard's six-month student membership of the Communist Party and two visits to the GDR, where he was on friendly terms with Jürgen Kuczynski, one of East Germany's leading intellectuals.'[42]

Following this crisis, Sidney Pollard managed to secure his reappointment at Sheffield. He was obliged to rely on the goodwill of university authorities from whom he already felt estranged. Pollard was fortunate, however, to receive the support of senior colleagues, who helped to persuade the University. More junior members of staff believed that their friend and mentor had experienced a second tragedy, to sit alongside his experience of the 1930s. Searching for the right words to describe the extent of Pollard's unhappiness at this time,

Colin Holmes and Alan Booth quote an old Yiddish phrase, *'Schwer und bitter ist dos leben.'*[43]

The Berkeley affair undoubtedly left its own scars. The impression is that Pollard was dissatisfied with Sheffield and eager to leave. Certainly the Sheffield of his public memories was a surprisingly complex place, a city that offered frustration as well as joy. 'Sheffield has no hinterlands', Pollard wrote, 'and it fits into no category':

> Northern by ancient county boundary (and Electricity Board's order), it is Midlands by access (and the Gas Board). Its speech is equally mixed – or should one say, its accents, for finely tuned ears can distinguish between the valleys, and between the major surrounding territories. It is not the capital of anything, and that is perhaps why it is consistently forgotten by the BBC – and by British rail, who give it the worst rail service of any half-million anywhere and then wonder that no one uses the trains. It all helps to create a beleaguered feeling of togetherness that would be absent were the city any larger or more metropolitan.[44]

The passage was written to convey affection, but there are parts of it that are deliberately obscure. We can note the impersonality of the final sentence. Who possessed the feeling of togetherness, and with whom was it shared? There is more than a hint that Pollard saw himself standing on the outside of the South Yorkshire solidarity he describes.

Pollard resigned his post at Sheffield University in 1980 and took up work at Bielefeld University in West Germany, alongside such scholars as Jürgen Kocka and Hans-Ulrich Wehler. Holmes describes Pollard's subsequent isolation from events in Britain; 'he was generally a fortnight behind with the news ... He remained still the intensely private person he had been in Sheffield where few of his contacts had known in any detail of his early life, little more about his interest in the cinema and nothing of his skills as a violinist.'[45] Following his retirement, Sidney Pollard returned with Helen to England in 1990. Another old friend, Peter Mathias of Downing College, provides a vivid image of the mature historian. 'Pollard was a striking figure – a benign, bearded, tousle-haired patriarch in his latter years; reticent, gentle and soft-spoken but with an inner determination, sustained throughout his life, which belied his personal modesty.'[46] This latter virtue was unusual in one so productive.

Roughly one-third of Sidney Pollard's books and articles were published in the last eight years of his life. His last book *Marginal Europe* may have been intended as a 'magnum opus', to use the words which he wrote on the side of one of his box files.[47] Pollard himself described the book as combining a study of 'much which has moved me in the past: the unity of European developments, the significance of regions, the sources of economic development and the fate of the underdog'.[48] Its author continued to write, even up to the last week of his life. Nothing was again attempted, though, on such a scale. Following a short illness, Pollard died in Sheffield on 22 November 1998. He was not quite 74 years old.

ENGAGING WITH EXILE

We have already seen that Pollard generally refrained from looking back on his childhood. While his history was autobiographical, this process tended to work at one remove. He did not engage directly with his own experience, until the publication of a short, autobiographical memoir, towards the very end of his life. Yet there were a small number of private, family occasions during which he must have reflected on the experience of the 1930s. His children remember that Pollard began to revisit his own childhood experience as they grew up. He took them on holidays to Vienna and Whittingehame, showing them the places where he had lived. He also expressed to them the distance that he felt between his adult and his younger self. Part of the gap concerned religion. According to his youngest child, Veronica, 'my father was not a believer in any religion. He took my brothers to Shul but only to give them the choice of having a religion. For their part, their response was: why should they believe if he didn't? The fact that he requested cremation in his will goes totally against the Jewish religion. He said that he lost his faith because of what happened to him.'[49] Brian Pollard confirms the important parts of this account. He recalled attending a Bar-Mitzvah preparation course between 1958 and 1961. After that, however, his father 'came to dislike the whole idea of religion ... neither my brother nor my sister were involved in any of this'.[50]

Following his second marriage, Sidney Pollard involved his new wife Helen in a similar process of reawakening memory. As with his children, he was understated. Yet 'there was sadness there', as Helen recalls, 'I have known a lot of people who came over as refugees. No-one had it tougher, but he never complained.' The most painful memories concerned his isolation on arrival in England. Helen Pollard takes up the story that she was told:

> On arrival, Sidney was with a lot of Jewish children. They were sent to a disused Butlin's holiday camp in East Anglia. It was December, some time like that. He suffered from a bad attack of

the measles. The camp was equipped for summer, not winter. He only had one pair of socks. One day he got them wet, by the next morning they were full of ice. It was so cold ... Every morning families used to come and claim the children, but he was never claimed. Each morning the names were called out.

Sidney had relatives in England. His uncle Jack, his mother's cousin, was married to Aunt Winnie. She was a Catholic; he was a philosopher at St. Paul's School, London. Sidney's mother wrote to say that she would like her son to be brought up in a Jewish way. But Winnie was a headmistress and an LCC councillor. She felt she couldn't take Sidney on. The first time Uncle Jack took Sidney out was after he had gone to Whittingehame. He hadn't had a haircut in all the time since he'd arrived. When Jack saw him, he had hair halfway down his back.[51]

All children fear abandonment, and Pollard suffered this reality at its worst. We can understand the pain that he must have felt as his fellow refugees were taken one by one from the first camp to safety, while he remained. We also know that Pollard was not unique in his experience. Other refugee children have complained of the petty cruelties, which they suffered, including being teased on account of their accents, or of the way they dressed or looked, all of which intensified the sense of isolation they felt living in their new homes.[52]

In his adult life, Pollard's experiences remained typical of his generation. We can view Pollard as one number of Central European intellectuals, who were both socialists and Jews. His Marxism gradually tended to lose its edge, as it did for many of his contemporaries, but a strong commitment to the values of pre-Marxist socialism remained. His choice of labour history reflected his identification with the industrial working class. 'It was natural for me to determine to write the history of the workers themselves, to sketch their lives from their own point of view.'[53] Sidney Pollard contributed to histories of the Sheffield Trades Council,[54] and corresponded with Labour MPs.[55] He also identified with the co-operative movement. Pollard spoke at co-operators' rallies and offered his own thoughts as to how the campaign should develop.[56] He was able to explain his sympathy for this cause in terms of its consensual approach. It was 'of the few movements who have no real enemies'.[57] As Pollard wrote in his memoir, 'Co-operation, unlike trade unionism, is non-confrontational and combines practical achievement with an inspiring ideal.'[58]

Would it be correct, then, to assume that ethnicity became more important to him, in place of active left-wing politics? Pollard's memoir discounts this possibility, 'any feeling of Jewishness has long since dropped away – except when Jews are persecuted for their race'.[59] Indeed Pollard's correspondence rarely mentions Judaism, or the Jews as a people. There is however one passage in his correspondence with Yehuda Don, in which he reflects on Don's explanations for the different economic conduct of Jews and non-Jews. 'I am not too happy with much of the argumentation commonly used to explain Jewish difference, especially since there are always, as you note, huge and conspicuous exceptions.'[60] The argument may have been technical, but the underlying politics were clear. Yehuda Don was looking for factual evidence to establish claims of Jewish particularity. Pollard preferred to see Jewish people as belonging to something universal.

Pollard's version of socialism, particularly his sympathy with the underdog and his distance from ethnic interpretations of history, were both closely related to his own past experiences. Another point at which we can detect the relationship between biography and history is in Sidney Pollard's last book, *Marginal Europe*. The account here combined a narrative of European history, with a new theme, that of 'marginality'. Pollard's own explanation of his book started with the conditions of the Industrial Revolution in Britain, a process that had begun at the margins, not the centre of the eighteenth-century economy:

> Instead of developing out of the background of the richest and in many ways most advanced regions such as London and the Home Counties, Bristol or East Anglia ... the great spurt in technological, economic and social change which we term the Industrial Revolution ... had its origins, rather surprisingly, in the main in parts of the country which may be termed 'marginal'.[61]

We can see the choice of marginality as the rediscovery of an interest in history's losing side, the oppressed and downtrodden, which goes back to Pollard's earliest political beliefs. The narrative is one of dispossessed peoples reclaiming basic rights. Through a process of economic development, marginal lives could conquer the heart of the historical process.[62] His suggestion was that this process was relatively typical of economic development in history. This account of history can also be interpreted as Pollard's opinion of his own life.[63]

There were also a few moments at which Pollard engaged directly with the history of interwar Germany. One such came in a 1990 article looking back on the part played by the German unions in 1929–33. Generally, this was the sort of question that Pollard avoided. As well as his natural disinclination to revisit moments of personal grief, he also disliked that strain of German history, which reduced the story of Weimar and earlier times to a simple prelude, a story culminating in Hitler's victory.[64] There was a personal interest, however, in the question of whether the Left could have acted to prevent the catastrophe? The key moment was the 'Papen Putsch' of 20 July 1932, when the government removed the elected Social Democratic government in Prussia, the largest and most important German state. Millions expected the unions to protest, so why did they not do more?

> In part because the leaders had made enquiries and found that there was little stomach for a fight, in part because of the abysmal state of the labour market, and in part because the unions would have to act against a legal, if scarcely legitimate authority, with the police and the army doubtless ranged against them. It would have been a gesture, but they would certainly have failed, as did the Austrians in 1934.

The failure of the German socialists to act in 1932 weighed on people's minds long afterwards. Resistance in January or February 1933 would inevitably have resulted in bloody defeat. The moment had already been lost. In a similar vein, Sidney Pollard continued, 'The German trade unions were victims rather than actors. Whether, as part of a larger pattern, they bore a share of responsibility, under what conditions the catastrophe could have been averted, or whether these are considerations appropriate to the professional tasks of an historian, are different questions altogether.'[65] Pollard's argument here has profound implications for his life's story. The social forces to which he had contributed in Britain were those of the socialist Left, including the trade unions and the co-operatives. Even though he defended such causes against their critics, he was prepared to consider the possibility that they had failed to act when required, and that the Left was therefore almost complicit in the worst catastrophe of the century, the greatest tragedy of his life.

There was one further incident during which Pollard was required to confront the demons of his past. It occurred during his failed application to Berkeley in 1971. Previous accounts have tended to concentrate on the cold war aspects to the story. Pollard himself contributed to this reading in his memoir, where he wrote, 'I did obtain a visa, but it was of a temporary nature only because of communist association, and in spite of the assurance of the American colleagues that there would be no problem in prolong it, I felt too insecure to entrust myself and my family to an uncertain future abroad.'[66] We should say more about these feelings of insecurity, which he described.

Alongside this later account, we can also cite the letter that Pollard wrote at the time to Gene Brucker of UCLA, expressing his regret and explaining the decision not to come. 'I am very sorry to have to write this letter', he began, 'I never thought I would have to write a letter of this kind to anyone.' Pollard blamed his decision on an unsuccessful interview at the US Consulate in Liverpool.

> Last week I was asked to attend at the American Consulate about my temporary entry visa to the USA, and after a long discussion with a very sympathetic Vice-Consul I was assured that although I would get my temporary J-1 entry as before (in fact she has now sent off for it) my chances of ever getting a permanent move were 'very thin'. In fact, in her whole career, she had never known it happen in cases like mine.

The Vice-Consul was able to quote details of unsuccessful applications, including 'one professor' who failed to get an immigrant's visa, 'another' who survived by joining the World Bank, also 'a third, a Jamaican', who left his university on a short visit to Europe, 'and has not been allowed back since'. So the historian made clear – his decision was absolutely fixed:

> Of course, you may say that this may turn out to be wrong, and Berkeley can deliver the goods. You may also say that I can always get a job back in England if necessary. But you know that Chairs in England are hard to come by, and I do not look forward to another two years of uncertainty and uprooting my family in order to end up, perhaps, with a Chair in a poorer University, or with a Senior Lectureship or perhaps a Chair in Canada, as a second best.

At this point, the tone of Pollard's letter may seem odd. Would it really be so disastrous to accept 'a Chair in a poorer university', indeed what else was Sheffield (not to mention Canada), if not poor in comparison to Berkeley? There is a suggestion here of a certain dissatisfaction, as if Pollard needed to see the visible signs of status in order to feel that he had really proved himself to the world. If so, then Pollard was no different from other refugees of his generation, many of whom displayed similar feelings of insecurity long after their arrival in Britain. Perhaps recognising that he had allowed his argument to become weak, he proceeded to give the most important, personal justification for his decision:

Even so, I should not have considered this sufficient grounds to go back on my word; but my encounter has brought up, out of the forgotten traumas of the past, such horrors of queuing in offices, of being a second-class citizen, of fearing the decisions of capricious officialdom, as I never thought I still had in me, and I suffered an almost total collapse over it. I simply cannot envisage myself surviving in sanity the next two uncertain years on this basis, and I if the last few days are anything to go by, I would not be much good to anyone in that state.

There could be no reply to arguments of this character. No sympathetic person would expect their friend to revisit personal crises, including the pain of the present, as well as the horrors of his childhood past. 'In consequence', Pollard continued, 'I shall have to withdraw my acceptance of the chair at Berkeley, and as mine was about to be advertised, I had to act quickly to retain it, which I have now done, so that I shall continue in Sheffield.'[67]

BELONGING AND NOT BELONGING

Presented with the chance to write his own memoir, Pollard's account ended with a description of the isolation that he felt in England. 'The feeling of not wholly belonging anywhere remains.'[68] With the destruction of liberal Vienna, Pollard was forced to flee. The experience of exile remained with him, shaping the rest of his days. Colin Holmes recalls that, 'On returning to Vienna after the war he was handed a tablecloth, embroidered by his mother, which a neighbour had kept through the war, hoping that the exiled son would return to collect it. That item remained of profound significance to him.'[69] The Berkeley affair appears in this narrative as an echo of the earlier tragedy. We can detect the anguish that Pollard expressed in his letter to Gene Brucker and in the fears, which he mentions, of reawakening the horror of his escape from Austria. We can take at face value Sidney Pollard's account of the fears he felt of revisiting what he called 'the forgotten traumas of the past'.[70]

Yet there are other ways in which to read Sidney Pollard's life. Alongside the periods of great crisis, there were other moments when Pollard was able to face and even transcend adversity. Pollard's choice of exile in Britain brought him into contact with the sources of future happiness, including career and family. The decision to stay in Sheffield in 1971 also proved ultimately positive. Remaining in South Yorkshire, Sidney Pollard was able to concentrate on publication, and he could therefore build up his European reputation. 'Any feeling of Jewishness has long since dropped away', Pollard wrote, 'but it is the consciousness of the continental heritage which obtrudes itself, possibly more with advancing age than before.'[71] Colin Holmes and Alan Booth conclude their account of Pollard's life by suggesting that the Jewish refugees to Britain could transcend the problems associated with their exile. 'In Britain generally, and Sheffield specifically, we need also to recover the contributions of those who came to Britain as child refugees. Their attempts at adjustment often proved difficult; in general they found it harder to carve out a satisfying life in exile ... However, some of these young people survived to succeed.'[72] The story of Sidney Pollard's life was expressed in a combination of frequent personal sadness with ultimate professional success.

NOTES

1. S. Pollard and C.H. Feinstein (eds.), *Studies in Capital Formation in the UK 1750–1920* (Oxford, 1988); S. Pollard (ed.), *Region und Industralisierung: Studien zur Rolle der Region in der Wirtschaftsgeschichte der letzen zwei Jahrhunderte* (Göttingen, 1980).
2. S. Pollard and J.P.P. Higgins (eds.), *Aspects of Capital Investment in Great Britain 1750–1850: A Preliminary Survey* (London, 1971).
3. S. Pollard, *The Genesis of Modern Management: A Study of the Industrial Revolution in Britain* (London and Cambridge, MA, 1965).
4. S. Pollard (ed.), *The Gold Standard and Employment Policies Between the Wars* (London, 1970).
5. S. Pollard, *Britain's Prime and Britain's Decline: The British Economy from 1870 to 1914* (London, 1989).
6. S. Pollard and C. Holmes, *Documents of European Economic History*, Vol.I: *The Process of Industrialisation, 1750–1870* (London, 1968); Vol.II: *Industrial Power and National Rivalry, 1870–1914* (London, 1972); Vol.III: *The End of the Old Europe 1914–1939* (London, 1973); S. Pollard, *European Economic Integration, 1815–1970* (London, 1974); S. Pollard, *Europa im Zeitalter der Industrialisierung. Eine Wirtschaftsgeschichte Europas 1750–1980* (Göttingen, 1990).
7. S. Pollard, *A History of Labour in Sheffield* (Liverpool, 1959); S. Pollard, *The Sheffield Outrages* (Bath, 1971); S. Pollard and C. Holmes (eds.), *Essays in the Economic and Social History of South Yorkshire* (Barnsley, 1977).
8. 'Manifesto of the Communist Party', in K. Marx and F. Engels, *Collected Works: Volume 6* (London, 1976), pp.477–519; R. Prebisch, *Theoretical and Practical Problems of Economic Growth* (Lake Success, NY, 1950).
9. S. Pollard, *Marginal Europe: The Contribution of Marginal Lands since the Middle Ages* (Oxford, 1997).
10. We can observe this point by comparing Pollard's autobiography to the other accounts that appear in P. Alter (ed.), *Out of the Third Reich: Refugee Historians in Post-war Britain* (London, 1998).
11. Pollard's second wife discusses this incident in the following terms, 'He would have liked to have gone. "They didn't invite me", he said. I replied, "but how would anybody know?"' Interview with Helen Pollard, 25 June 2002.
12. P. Pulzer, 'From Danube to Isis: A Career in Two Cultures', in Alter, *Out of the Third Reich*, pp.221–36, 221.
13. Stryy is sometimes also spelled Sttryj or even Strij in English.

14. S. Pollard, 'In Search of a Social Purpose', in Alter, *Out of the Third Reich*, pp.195–217, here p.199.
15. Pollard, 'In Search', pp.197–8.
16. Moses Pollak to Siegfried Pollak, 6 March 1939, 'Korrespondenz', Pollard papers. I am grateful to Peter Wilson for providing a translation of this passage.
17. See 'Namentliche Erfassung der Österreichen Holocauststopfer', http://www.doew.at/cgi-bin/shoah/shoah.pl.
18. C. Holmes, *John Bull's Island: Immigration and British Society 1871–1971* (Basingstoke, 1988), pp.118–19.
19. There is a already wide literature on this subject: see N. Stammers, *Civil Liberties in Britain during the Second World War* (London, 1983); F. Lafitte, *The Internment of Aliens* (Harmondsworth, 1940); P. and L. Gillman, *Collar the Lot: How Britain Interned and Expelled its Wartime Refugees* (London, 1980); R. Stent, 'The Internment of His Majesty's Loyal Enemy Aliens', *Oral History*, Vol.9, No.1 (1981), pp.35–40; and A.L. Goldmann, 'Defence Regulation 18B: Emergency Internment of Enemy Aliens and Political Dissenters in Great Britain during World War Two', *Journal of British Studies*, Vol.12, No.2 (1973), pp.120–36.
20. Charles Maxwell to Schmelzer *et al.*, 27 Aug. (1941?), 'Korrespondenz', Pollard papers.
21. Pollard, 'In Search', p.199.
22. Ibid.
23. Interview with David Pollard, 25 June 2002.
24. Pollard, 'In Search', p.200.
25. Ibid., pp.202–3.
26. C. Holmes, 'Sidney Pollard 1925–1998', *Proceedings of the British Academy*, Vol.105 (2000), pp.513–34, here p.517.
27. T.S. Ashton to Sidney Pollard, 25 July 1948, 'Korrespondenz', Pollard papers.
28. S. Pollard, 'The Economic History of British Shipbuilding, 1870–1914', Ph.D. thesis, University of London, 1951.
29. T.S. Ashton, 'The Treatment of Capitalism by Historians', in F.A. von Hayek (ed.), *Capitalism and the Historians* (London, 1954), pp.31–61.
30. T. Adams, 'The Lion of the Left', *The Observer*, 21 Jan. 2001.
31. T. Bunyan, *The History and Practice of the Political Police in Britain* (London, 1977), p.166; D. Renton, *Fascism, Anti-fascism and Britain in the 1940s* (London, 2000), pp.127–8.
32. Pollard, 'In Search', p.205.
33. A large part of Pollard's early correspondence relates to job applications. See 'Honours, offers', Pollard papers.
34. S. Pollard, *Three Centuries of Sheffield Steel: The Story of a Family Business* (Sheffield, 1954); S. Pollard, *Shirley Aldred and Co. Ltd. 1796–1958* (Worksop, 1958).
35. S. Pollard, *The Development of the British Economy 1914–1950* (London, 1962).
36. Pollard, *The Genesis of Modern Management*.
37. Holmes, 'Pollard'; Pollard, 'In Search'.
38. D. Martin, 'Sidney Pollard', *Labour History Review*, Vol.64 (1999), pp.139–42.
39. Michael Postan to Sidney Pollard, 19 May 1967, 'Honours, Offers', Pollard papers.
40. Letter from Brian Pollard to the author, 3 July 2002; letter from Veronica Pollard to the author, 27 Aug. 2002; interview with David Pollard, 25 June 2002.
41. Letter from Veronica Pollard to the author, 27 Aug. 2002.
42. Saville, 'Labour and Learning', p.18.
43. Holmes and Booth, *Economy and Society*, p.xvi.
44. S. Pollard, 'Farewell to Sheffield', *Quality*, Nov.–Dec. 1980, p.19.
45. Holmes, 'Pollard', p.527.
46. P. Mathias, 'Introduction', in S. Pollard, *Essays on the Industrial Revolution in Britain* (edited by Colin Holmes) (Aldershot, 2000), pp.vii–x, vii.
47. 'Region (inc. Trier) Magn. Opus', Pollard papers.
48. Pollard, 'In Search', p.215.
49. Letter from Veronica Pollard to the author, 27 Aug. 2002.
50. Letter from Brian Pollard to the author, 3 July 2002.

51. Interview with Helen Pollard, 25 June 2002.
52. D. Snowman, *The Hitler Emigrés* (London, 2002).
53. Pollard, 'In Search', pp.207–8.
54. S. Pollard et al., *Sheffield Trades Council 1858–1958* (Sheffield, 1958).
55. Sidney Pollard to Ann Taylor, 25 Nov. 1990; John Smith to Sidney Pollard, 20 Dec. 1991, Sidney Pollard to John Smith, 1 March 1993, all 'General Correspondence', Pollard papers; Sidney Pollard to John Prescott, 8 Dec. 1994, 'Bairoch – Festschr.', Pollard papers.
56. S. Pollard, 'Dr. William King: A Co-operative Pioneer', *Co-operative College Papers*, Vol.6 (April 1959), pp.17–33; S. Pollard, *The Co-operatives at the Crossroads* (London, 1965).
57. Sidney Pollard to Colin Holmes, 19 April 1990, 'Honours, offers', Pollard papers.
58. Pollard, 'In Search', p.208.
59. Ibid., p.215.
60. Sidney Pollard to Yehuda Don, 2 October 1990, 'Korrespondenz', Pollard papers.
61. Pollard, *Marginal Europe*, p.1.
62. Ibid., pp.193–4, 198, 208, 221, 268
63. This point is argued sympathetically in Holmes, 'Sidney Pollard'.
64. S. Pollard, 'Current German Economic and Social History: Attitudes to Hermeneutics and Objectivity', *South African Historical Journal*, Vol.16 (1984), pp.6–25.
65. S. Pollard, 'German Trade Union Policy 1929–1933 in the Light of the British Experience', in J. Baron von Krüdener (ed.), *Economic Crisis and Political Collapse: The Weimar Republic 1924–1933* (New York, 1990), pp.21–44, here p.44.
66. Pollard, 'In Search', p.213.
67. Sidney Pollard to Gene Brucker, 30 June 1971, 'Gast Professor', Pollard papers.
68. Pollard, 'In Search', p.216.
69. Ibid., p.197; Holmes, 'Pollard', p.532. Apart from the tablecloth he was handed over other items, including a prayer shawl. Interview with Helen Pollard, 25 June 2002.
70. Sidney Pollard to Gene Brucker, 30 June 1971, 'Gast Professor', Pollard papers.
71. Pollard, 'In Search', p.215.
72. Holmes and Booth, *Economy and Society*, p.xvii.

Literature

Selfhood in Descent:
Primo Levi's The Search for Roots and If This is a Man

RACHEL FALCONER

Readers of Primo Levi in English were privileged to gain access in 2001 to a seminal work, *La Ricerca delle Radici*, translated by Peter Forbes and published as *The Search for Roots: A Personal Anthology*.[1] Together with *The Voice of Memory* (a volume of recently translated interviews), *The Search* provides new light on a writer who might be regarded as the pre-eminent *katabasist* of modern times.[2] A *katabasist*, who writes about a descent into the underworld, characteristically employs the narrative structure of a journey to look inwards, downwards and back.[3] *The Search* is a late, self-reflective work by Levi, which is the culmination of many experimentations with autobiographical narrative. This 'personal anthology', which loosely comprises a 'history' of a lifetime's reading, provides fascinating insight into Levi's earlier writing, especially concerning Auschwitz. The extracts collected include works of fiction, poetry, history and science. Experienced through this new filter, the *katabatic* journey on which any reader of Levi embarks becomes a manifold experience, a testing of different routes simultaneously, rather than a quest for singular revelation.

From another writer, such heterogeneity of perspective, theme and genre would not necessarily unsettle us. But Levi is best known as a writer of Holocaust testimony, and of Holocaust writing (and writers?), there is still a demand for absolutes: for facticity, authenticity, stylistic minimalism and an unambiguous moral position. Nor would Primo Levi have been averse to some of these expectations. As a scientist, he values precision; many readers know how precise is his anatomization of evil, in discursive works such as *The Drowned and the Saved*. But Levi's *katabatic* narratives combine this truth-seeking drive with a wry instinct for ambivalence. *The Search for Roots* provides us with interconnections between Levi the truth-seeker and the equivocator, the humanist and the postmodernist.

In particular, I want to explore how, through a reading of *The Search*, we can begin to understand the Auschwitz of Levi's early work as a chronotope, rather than a spatially or temporally fixed point. Levi is a writer who 'strive[s] ... to pass from the darkness in to light'[4] (MM 127). He repeatedly emphasizes that retrospectively, he derived positive value from the experience of Auschwitz.[5] I would argue that certain premises inform all he has to say about Auschwitz: that meaning can be derived from nihilistic experience, that reason can help us to compass insanity, that language might fail to communicate the fullness of horror but nevertheless it should be used, because silence is self-internment and an expression of despair in other people. This is essentially the position of a *katabatic* writer, one for whom Hell is a journey and a process through which one 'arrives at' a more complex and rigorous understanding of the self.[6]

CHRONOTOPES OF *KATABATIC* NARRATION

Aligning Levi with the 'talkers' rather than the 'silent' survivors of a journey into Hell invites us to situate his writing somewhere in relation to the tradition of Dantean *katabasis*.[7] What I take to be fundamentally Dantean about Levi's narratives of descent is their extreme verticalization of experience, their attempt to map a historical, progressive journey of the self on to a reflective, evaluative and ahistorical plane. This vertical mapping of historical selfhood has been conceptualized by Mikhail Bakhtin as a productive tension between two chronotopes. Bakhtin observes that the diegetic 'reality' of Dante's Hell is visualized through a particular mix of chronotopic lenses, in which historical characters and events are perceived extra-temporally. Within the field of these intersecting chronotopes,

> everything must be perceived as being within *a single time*, that is, in the synchrony of a single moment; one must see this entire world as simultaneous ... To 'synchronize diachrony', to replace all temporal and historical divisions and linkages with purely interpretative, extratemporal and hierarchicized ones – such was Dante's form-generating impulse, which is defined by an image of the world structured according to a pure verticality.[8]

According to Bakhtin, *Inferno* contains two opposing energies, the historical and the evaluative (and the latter eventually wins out). These energies are registered, on the one hand, in the reader's engagement with the pilgrim's experience of the journey, and on the other, in our collusion with the construction of a coherent, immutable universal order. But in describing the *katabatic* chronotope as an *impulse* to synchronize, Bakhtin concedes that the opposing energies of Dante's poem are unresolved, for a good portion of the reading experience.

Looking beyond Dante, what Levi teaches us (and I think he is one of the first contemporary writers to do so) is that the journey through Hell can be multi-layered, discontinuous, revelatory, aporetic, but never finalized.[9] From Levi it becomes clear that no survivor achieves the position of outsideness which would transform observation into revelation. But, given this post-Dantean premise, what is interesting about Levi's *katabatic* writing is its demonstration of how, within the journey, the insider's perspective (for example, on the nature of human resilience) can be shifted, multiplied, and inter-illuminated with others.

In this sense, Levi's *katabatic* narratives are comparable to the distillation process described in *The Periodic Table*: 'a metamorphosis from liquid to vapour (invisible), and from this once again to liquid; but in this double journey, up and down, purity is attained, an ambiguous and fascinating condition'.[10] I will argue that the multiplication of perspectives in *If This is a Man* produces just such a *katabatic* distillation of experience, and that the layering of perspectives is one major way in which Auschwitz is transformed into an 'ambiguous and fascinating' chronotope. In *The Search*, we see the same phenomenon but more clearly, both because the text is less familiar, and because anthologies do not raise the same generic expectations as autobiography and Holocaust testimony.

The Search is, as it were, an anthology of autobiographies, rather than a narrative tracing a single, linear continuity of selfhood. One can easily trace at least five 'self-narratives', the first obviously being the order in which the 30 textual extracts appear. This order replicates the chronological history of Levi's reading, although Levi admits to interfering with the order 'to contrive contrasts'.[11] Against this temporally linear narrative of a developing taste and world-view, Levi contrastingly provides us with a spatial map of the work (the 'work' itself comprising a network of texts and the possible meanings created in the spaces between their contiguities). This map appears at the end of the Preface, and as Calvino writes, is probably the 'most important page of the book' (SR 222) (see Appendix).[12]

The map is spheroid in shape, and comprises four descending arrows, which are joined at top and bottom of the sphere. Levi suggests that the map traces 'four possible routes through the authors in view' (SR 8). We are invited, then, not to follow a single journey but, as we are reading, to tease out four different journeys, four contrasting sets of preoccupations, moods, intellectual positions. The four arrows are respectively labelled: salvation through laughter, man suffers unjustly, the stature of man, and salvation through knowledge. They are not ranked or numbered, but the two 'salvation' arrows form the outer axes of the sphere, while the two pertaining to 'man' run through its centre. Generically speaking, the texts named on each axis fall roughly into four types: comedy, tragedy, epic and science. The map can be read both vertically (on the tragic axis, for example, we find Eliot, Babel, Celan, Rigioni Stern) and horizontally (taking a cross-section of the four axes at their lowest – and darkest? – points, we find Aleichem, Stern, Saint Exupéry, Arthur C. Clarke). But the important point to remember, as we make these interconnections, is that the map is comprised of *arrows*. In other words, the business of forging connections is itself a temporal journey, not a privileged activity that happens outside the narrative of a developing self.

This type of autobiographical descent narrative contrasts markedly with Dante's *Inferno,* which produces a fairly constant set of tensions, between the poet's developing sense of self and the fixed perspectives of the damned, and between the poet's former and present selfhood. In *The Search,* retrospective evaluation of the journey turns out to be part of the chronological process; and chronological development involves a constant process of reflection, evaluation and comparison. The different insights gained along each axis are not hierarchized (it is difficult to visualize a tiered, immutable value system from this descent journey, as *Inferno* invites us to do). One kind of insight does not cancel out another. So, for example, Rabelais not wanting to accept human misery (SR 77) coexists with knowing that the Yiddish culture which produced Aleichem's Tevye has been entirely destroyed (SR 148).

BLACK HOLES AND THE BIBLICAL JOB

It remains to discuss where Levi situates Auschwitz in this multiply stranded autobiography. His year at the concentration camp was obviously not an experience in which much reading figured. But given the central importance of this event to any formulation of Levi's life trajectory, how is its influence felt on a personal history of reading? Is there a sense of a reading consciousness that alters from before to after? Or is the task of the reader–survivor to recuperate or reorient texts read before the event?

One novel does attach directly to the time Levi spent at Auschwitz. This is Roger Vercel's *Tug-Boat* which, as Levi explains, is 'important to me for my private reasons, symbolic and charged, because I read it on a day (18 January 1945) when I expected to die' (SR 6). With that exception, Levi admits that his 'experiences in the concentration camp ... weigh ... little' among the authors selected for *The Search* (SR 5).[13] We should perhaps begin, then, with the placement of Vercel in the linear order of texts, the most chronological of *The Search*'s narratives of the self. It appears almost at a mid-point in the sequence, thirteenth of 30 extracts. On either side, it is flanked by texts that either appear, or may be inferred to belong, on 'the stature of man' (epic) axis. Thomas Mann's *Tales of Jacob* precedes it; Melville's *Moby Dick*, Saint Exupéry and Marco Polo follow immediately after.

Note how easily questions of sequence become enmeshed in evaluation; we have moved from the order of texts to their *re*-ordering on the map of the Preface. But another, more surprising point deserves emphasis. If, for the moment, we take Vercel as a sign of Auschwitz, we find that this potentially 'caesural' experience does not attract to itself the darkest, most pessimistic texts of the anthology. On the contrary, it is flanked by, and is itself ranked as one of, those texts which illustrate how 'a man can remake himself'.[14] Even on the axis of 'the stature of man', Vercel does not appear as the lowest point on the map. So, while this extract is undoubtedly charged with negativity for Levi, there is also a certain buoyancy surrounding its placement in a narrative trajectory. This is our first indication of the complexity of Levi's chronotopic representation of Auschwitz.

A further layer of complexity is revealed when we ask ourselves where Auschwitz figures on the Preface's map of authors. As Calvino suggests, reference to Job (at the top of the sphere) reminds us that 'the journey of Primo Levi passed through Auschwitz' (SR 222) because Job is the archetypal 'just man oppressed by injustice' (SR 11). And as Calvino also notes, 'Black Holes' (at the bottom of the sphere) constitute a point 'no less charged with negativity' (SR 222). Introducing an article by the astrophysicist Kip Thorne, Levi reflects on the metaphorical significance of these dense, Charybdic pools of gravity in outer space: 'In the sky there are no Elysian Fields, only matter and light, distorted, compressed, dilated, and rarefied to degree that eludes our senses and our language ... ' (SR 214).

Like the Book of Job, Black Holes become tropes for an alien, hostile or indifferent universe. So on the map, Auschwitz figures (spatially) at top and bottom, and (temporally) at beginning and end, of all four axes of descent. Is this to imply that every autobiographical journey Levi makes must begin and end with Auschwitz? Excellent fodder for those critics who read despair into Levi's works, from the retrospective knowledge of his alleged suicide. But such an interpretation would crucially miss out on the counterbalancing energies of the anthology, the conceptual shifts from light to dark, and dark to light, that we are invited to make along vertical as well as lateral axes of development. It is preferable, I think, to view these two poles as initiating and attracting all movement and development of the self on its descent journey.[15]

In any case, as with the Vercel extract, we find that the 'negative poles' at top and base of the diagramme exert a powerful, positive charge. Turning to the headnotes of 'Job' and 'Black Holes', we'll discover Levi affirming human powers of resistance and endurance. The introduction to 'Black Holes' provides an excellent example of Levi's habit of mentally inverting 'darkness towards light'. Levi writes, 'certainly we are immeasurably small, weak and alone, but if the human mind has conceived Black Holes, and dares to speculate on what happened in the first moments of creation, why should it not know how to conquer fear, poverty and grief?' (SR 214–15). Our ability to conceptualize such phenomena as Black Holes also implies our ability to neutralize them. It is the scientist's ambivalent imagination that reaches beyond fear, to find pleasure in gained knowledge. This inverted perspective on Black Holes brings Levi's anthology to a close. The final words are given to Thorne: 'the future does not seem unpromising' (SR 220).

So Auschwitz figures at top and bottom, beginning and end of the descent journey, while also occupying a place somewhere in the middle. These points constitute negative centres but are also charged with positive energy. The way these positionings play against each other illustrates that Auschwitz cannot be said to occupy one fixed meaning or value in Levi's autobiographical narratives. Within *The Search*'s multiply stranded autobiography, Auschwitz is the interior chronotope which destabilizes the whole, which sends the self repeatedly on its *katabatic* journey.

A CONSTELLATION OF CHRONOTOPES

A similarly productive intersection of perspectives and temporalities seems to me to inform the structuration of selfhood in *If This is a Man*. Turning from *The Search*, I find it possible to distinguish at least five distinct 'pathways of descent' in Levi's earliest Holocaust narrative. These pathways more explicitly concern the journey of the self in Auschwitz than do those of *The Search*, although as we have seen, Auschwitz is centrally important even in the later text. But they are no less provisional and exploratory. Levi invites his readers to test out different lines of descent and, moreover, to seek out lateral connections and contrasts between these different journeys.

Recalling Bakhtin's observation that 'the image of man is always intrinsically chronotopic', we cannot understand Levi's conception of such a self, or selves, without at the same time understanding something about Levi's chronotopic representation of Auschwitz.[16] The world of the *lager* constantly assumes different shapes and connotes different meanings and values, indeed is best understood as a constellation of chronotopes, rather than a single, multifaceted one. The five chronotopic representations of Auschwitz which I wish to discuss may be labelled: threshold, education, visionary world, trial and sea voyage. All bear marked affinities with the four pathways of *The Search:* 'man suffers unjustly' with threshold and trial, the 'stature of man' with education and sea voyaging, 'salvation through understanding' with visionary world. Within each of these spatiotemporal categories, the 'self' experiences a different kind of journey, comes to know itself differently, and recognizes different capabilities and limits.

Too often there is a tendency amongst Levi's readers to extract general insights about 'human nature'. In my view, we should recognize a series of illuminations, from different vantage points within an interconnected set of experiences. Levi encourages us to think about his experiences evaluatively, but as in *The Search*, this evaluative process is understood to constitute a temporal journey in itself. Some chronotopic representations emphasize the evaluative over the experiential (vision, trial); others concentrate more on the process of journeying than arrival, reflection and assessment (education, sea voyage).

AUSCHWITZ AS THRESHOLD

The threshold chronotope provides the dominant spatiotemporal field of the first four chapters of *If This is a Man*, which describe Levi's deportation into the camp. This representation of Auschwitz offers us a series of absolute contrasts, between 'up here' and 'down there', between the rational and insane, human and infernal, historical and mythic. The threshold self is constrained by the particular spatio-temporality of the threshold.[17] Here there is no possibility for interior development, and little sense of time as *durée*. The condition of threshold existence is handled much more starkly than in Dante's *Inferno*, even though the narrative momentum of the medieval text is entirely dependent on threshold crossings. In *Inferno*, the radical changes in selfhood, which occur in the pilgrim's passage from one ring of Hell to the next, do accumulate into a sequential narrative.[18] But in Levi's text, there is no orchestration of crossings-over, no gradual crescendo towards a final, definitive break, because the first crossing is already final. We get to the bottom, 'Sul Fundo', in the second chapter. All thresholds crossed thereafter are experienced as absurd repetition.

No development, and little individuation, of the self are possible when the *lager* is conceptualized as threshold. Historical time appears to have ceased, and the prisoners 'cross over' into mythic time. In an unmistakable echo of Dante's *Inferno,* Levi registers the shift to mythic time at the moment of reading the sign over Auschwitz's gate: 'we saw a large door, and above it a sign, brightly illuminated (its memory still strikes me in my dreams): *Arbeit Macht Frei,* work gives freedom. We climb down, they make us enter an enormous empty room … ' (28). Like Dante, Levi omits any description of an actual crossing (Dante's pilgrim faints before the gate, and wakes up in Hell). Instead a new paragraph and shift of verbal tense indicate the alteration in metaphysical condition.

For a modern-day reader, the debilitating impression of *déja-lu* is particularly intense at this point. If we know anything of Auschwitz (or Dante), we are already familiar with the words over the gate. We thus participate in the uncanny as Freud defined it, an encounter with the unknown with which, fearfully, we already seem to be familiar.[19] This is the dominant mood of the threshold chronotope, a nightmarish sense that tells us Auschwitz occupies an eternal present, and has infinite capacity to haunt us. It is with this threshold perception of Auschwitz that Levi concludes *The Truce:* 'I am in the Lager once more, and nothing is true outside the Lager' (T 379). At this point, it might be observed that the self experiences threshold crossing as a sudden reversal of gravitational force, a shift from weight to a state of weightlessness.[20] We will return to this point later.

The chronotopic image that epitomizes the timescape of the threshold in Levi's writing is the goods train used to transport prisoners to the camps.[21] Note, for example, that in describing his own deportation, Levi represents the train as familiar:

> Here, then, before our very eyes, under our very feet, was one of those notorious transport trains, those which never return, and of which, shuddering and always a little incredulous, we had so often heard speak. Exactly like this, detail for detail: goods wagons closed from the outside, … for a journey towards nothingness, a journey down there, towards the bottom (IM 22).

The train is the vehicle by which the prisoners are metamorphosed from reality into myth. In *The Drowned and the Saved*, Levi writes that 'Almost always, at the beginning of the memory sequence, stands the train, which marked the departure towards the unknown not only for chronological reasons but also for the gratuitous cruelty ... ' (DS 85).[22] For Levi, Auschwitz as threshold has gates open, as it were, on both sides of the temporally localized event ('we are all in the ghetto ... close by the train is waiting' (DS 51)). As a chronotopic image, the freight train represents the instability of the ground on which the Holocaust survivor's sense of selfhood is based. Remembering that the gates of this threshold chronotope are still open to us, in our present, we are right to find this chronotopic representation of the *lager* unsettling. But as in *The Search*, it is only one of a number of possible representations explored by Levi.

AUSCHWITZ AS 'EDUCATION'

Besides experiencing Auschwitz as threshold, the reader of *If This is a Man* may also trace the pathway of a developing selfhood within the spatiotemporal horizons of an infernal *bildungsroman*. Here we hear a new note in Levi's intertextual dialogue with Dante's *Inferno*, a work which has been described as the 'first novel of the self'.[23] By positioning his former self at the start of an infernal journey involving duration and internal change, Levi sets that self on the pathway of Dante's pilgrim. But at the same time, Levi refuses to resurrect the *Inferno*'s play of subjectivities, the living pilgrim (subject-in-process) against the souls of the dead (fixed and finalized subjects). The story of his own 'education' is read alongside the experience of a collective crossing over. The central theme of *If This is a Man* is *not* the single self's survival, despite the title of the American edition, *Survival in Auschwitz*. Nevertheless, *one* of its trajectories describes the metamorphosis of this former self. Thus Levi writes, 'a friend of mine ... says that the camp was her university. I think I can say the same thing' (IM 398). This educative process is available retrospectively, and is activated by the gaze of the narrator on his former self.

The inter-illumination of one chronotope (that of the threshold) by another (education) is evident, for example, in the exchange between Levi and the Austrian sergeant Steinlaus (IM 47). The interview with Steinlaus prompts the beginning of a different way of conceptualizing 'damnation', one which involves awareness of a *journey* through darkness, not just a point of arrival *sul fundo*, at the absolute bottom. The fact that Levi is left asking questions after the interview reveals this change of consciousness; his questions are directed towards possible future behaviour ('would it not be better ... ').

When Auschwitz is conceptualized as an educative space, it becomes possible for a reader to trace the biographical development of the *häftling* from naïve newcomer, a 'high number', into a *vecchio,* or old-timer. In Chapters 1 to 4, the perspective of the 'high number' predominates; we witness a gradual shift in attitude: 'By now we are tired of being amazed. We seem to be watching some mad play, one of those in which the witches, the Holy Spirit and the devil appear' (IM 31).

From Chapters 4 to 9, the naïve spectator recedes from view and in his place emerges the *vecchio*, an alien, bleak, and toughly comic figure. The *vecchio* is no Dantean pilgrim travelling across the canvas of the underworld. He is now part of its fabric; he *belongs* to Hell. The character zone of *vecchio* Levi is not constituted as an individual consciousness or discourse; his idiolect is one strain of a monstrously hybrid language which is epitomized in the multilingual naming of the Carbide Tower (*Babelturm, Bobelturm* (IM 78–79)).

From Chapter 11 to the final chapter of *If This is a Man,* the doubled, reverse journey of the self, from *vecchio* to narrator also begins to take shape. From this point, two trajectories play off against each other. On the one hand, we watch *vecchio* Levi becoming mentally tougher and more resourceful. On the other hand, the narrator-to-be is increasingly ashamed of his *lager* identity; the latent theme of self-blame becomes most audible in the penultimate chapter, 'The Last One'.

It deserves emphasis that the educative chronotope we have been considering is developed *alongside* the representation of Auschwitz as threshold, rather than subsequently. In the book's opening paragraph, we are immediately made aware of the distance between different selves, between Levi as protagonist and as narrator of this autobiographical narrative:

> I was twenty-four, with little wisdom, no experience and a decided tendency – encouraged by the life of segregation forced on me for the previous four years by the racial laws – to live in an unrealistic world of my own, a world inhabited by civilized Cartesian phantoms, by sincere male and bloodless female friendships (19).

The gap between two selfhoods revealed in this opening paragraph raises generic expectations of a linear autobiographical narrative, which will shortly link together these two vastly different consciousnesses. At the same time, however, the chronotope of emergence and education is already destabilized by the nature of this type of autobiography

(Holocaust testimony), where the discontinuities of selfhood are almost expected to be unbridgeable. There are also elements of the threshold chronotope visible here, where former and present selves inhabit worlds on either side of the looking-glass. And disconcertingly, the pre-camp Levi, whose experience lies closest to the reader's, is the self who inhabits the dream world, the world of 'Cartesian phantoms'. The *vecchio* is the self who knows the world for what it is.

Furthermore, Levi's narrative begins by situating three points of selfhood, rather than the bi-partite, before-and-after selves of traditional autobiography.[24] Three first-person perspectives combine in the paragraph quoted above: the 24-year-old idealist, the 25-year-old *lager vecchio*, and the 27-year-old narrator. A remarkably short temporal span divides these three points of selfhood, but nevertheless each holds a radically different world view. But the transformation is not unidirectional. In fact, all three 'selves' are subject to ironic deflation or critique by each other. In the following sentence, for example, we find irony working in two directions: 'At that time I had not yet been taught the doctrine that I was later to learn so hurriedly in the Lager: that man is bound to pursue his own ends by all possible means, while he who errs but once pays dearly' (IM 19). The *vecchio* mocks the new inmate, implying that his punishment is 'justified' (IM 19); but the survivor-witness invites us to condemn the *vecchio*'s wisdom, insisting on a different system of values. The 'university' of Auschwitz thus precisely and delicately balances three different points of selfhood in an on-going dialogue between differing world-views.

VISIONARY INFERNAL WORLD

A third chronotopic representation surfaces in the second section of *If This is a Man* (Chapters 4 to 9); this chronotope represents the *lager* as a fully realized other world, existing in parallel (like Dante's three realms) to our actual, material one. In this respect, Levi's narrative demonstrates the chronotopic features of the genre of vision literature, though it must be added that for Levi, 'vision literature' encompasses Lucretius and Darwin, as much as it does Dante.[25] Here, we are approaching Auschwitz, as it were, along the fourth of *The Search*'s 'pathways', the axis of 'Salvation through understanding'.

It has often been noted that this section of *If This is a Man* is organized into the structure of a chemist's report, and that the narrator's tone in Chapter 9 is that of the a scientist presenting his data ('We would also like to consider that the Lager was pre-eminently a gigantic biological and social experiment ... ' (IM 93)). Like Dante in the eleventh circle of *Inferno*, Levi in his ninth chapter delivers a retrospective overview of the world he has travelled through. Like Dante, he not only describes but also delivers a moral assessment of this landscape. Of the two 'categories' of men he identifies, 'the drowned and the saved', the first derive their appellation from Dante's *sommersi*.[26] Just as Dante classifies the damned, Levi classifies the 'saved' (an ironic term) into three groups: 'organisator', 'kombinator' and 'prominent'.[27]

The shift from the pilgrim's experience of an infernal journey to the poet's assumption of divine knowledge about Hell is made possible in the *Inferno* by one non-negotiable premise: the damned are fixed in Hell forever, while Dante the pilgrim moves through it as a living, unfinalized being. In Levi's narrative, there are inconsistencies in the placement of the former self *vis-à-vis* the 'drowned', those who died at Auschwitz. In the first section of *If This is a Man*, as we have seen, Levi places his former self among those who arrive *sul fundo*.

In Chapter 9, however, where the narrator's voice addresses us directly, and the former self virtually disappears, Levi underlines the difference between his own experience and that of non-survivors. While his descent journey, and those of the 'saved' can be narrated, in Levi's view, the 'drowned' have 'the same story, or more exactly, have no story' (IM 96). Here only the 'drowned' may be said to have 'followed the slope to the bottom' to arrive *sul fundo* (IM 96). This is the closest Levi comes to adopting the position of the Dantean pilgrim, a living soul amongst the souls of the dead. In the following description, Levi places himself at an enormous distance from the experience of the 'drowned', almost as if he had passed through Hell as an invulnerable observer: 'They crowd my memory with their faceless presences, and if I could enclose all the evil of our time in one image, I would choose this image which is familiar to me; an emaciated man, with head dropped and shoulders curved, on whose face not a trace of a thought is to be seen' (IM 96).

Levi's writing has in fact contributed much to 'enclosing the evil of our time' into a single iconic image of the Holocaust victim. Looking back from the twenty-first century, we may question the usefulness of creating such icons, which obscure our attempts to know and understand the individual experiences of those Levi classes as 'drowned'. On the other hand, the fact that Levi, who was at Auschwitz, places himself at such great distance from the non-survivor, reminds readers of their own still greater distance from the survivor, let alone the non-survivor, of Auschwitz. Nor is this simply the commentary of a Dantean observer of Hell. Levi inserts the phrase 'which is familiar to me', a gentle hint to the reader that he did live and work among such 'icons'. In fact this image of the Holocaust victim, though constructed within the visionary chronotope, is shot through with the consciousness of the self on an infernal threshold. Such images 'crowd my memory', Levi tells us, indicating their infinite capacity to haunt him. This is Auschwitz as a mythic space, a threshold with gates opening onto the survivor's present.

Other distinctions need to be made between Dante's and Levi's construction of a visionary infernal world. Of particular importance is Levi's method of 'gradating' the 'crimes' committed in Auschwitz, as well as the degrees of the loss of selfhood. Whereas Dante ranks the damned according to their 'essential' sins, Levi observes only the material conditions leading to loss of individuality and humanity. Levi dismisses as fascistic the pronouncement on human *essence* ('that man is fundamentally brutal … ') and makes a series of highly conditional observations ('in the face of driving necessity … instincts are reduced to silence').

To illustrate the three classes of the 'saved', Levi narrates the *histories* of four men: Schepschel, Alfred L, Elias and Henri (IM 98f). Although one could argue that these characters are retrospectively finalized by Levi's tripartite classification, the use of present tense narration reduces the distance between observer and protagonist ('Schepschel has been living in the Lager for four years … ', IM 98). There is veiled judgment of these 'types' but Levi nevertheless offers due space to their opposing world views. This is particularly so in the case of Henri, whom Levi clearly dislikes, but refrains from judging: 'One seems to glimpse, behind his uncommon personality, a human soul, sorrowful and aware of itself' (IM 106). Of all four examples, Henri's is the one allowed to remain open-ended ('I would give much to know his life as a free man, but I do not want to see him again' (106)). This 'Henri', in actual life Paul Steinberg, survives to narrate his own story, in *Speak You Also*, a text we will consider in the next section.[28]

THE 'SELF' ON TRIAL

The *aporia* which the self encounters within the vision chronotope is that writing about the 'drowned' requires adopting an external position toward their histories, which ends up finalizing them. This *aporia* triggers another lateral shift in Levi's text, a fresh attempt to understand the self in Auschwitz through a new spatio-temporal configuration. Thus, after (or with) threshold, education, and visionary world, we arrive at Auschwitz as trial. In *The Drowned and the Saved*,

Levi says that Auschwitz constitutes 'a trial of planetary and epochal dimensions' (DS 121).[29] But the *lager* as trial must be understood somewhat differently in *If This is a Man*.

As with the educative chronotope (and that of the voyage, considered below), the trial brings *individual* selfhood (former and present) to the fore of Levi's narrative. The trial is the dominant chronotope of 'The Chemical Examination' (Chapter 10), 'October 1944' (Chapter 13) and 'The Last One' (Chapter 16). In contrast to the vision chronotope, in which the narrator addresses himself to God, or some abstract notion of justice or truth, the trial chronotope is dialogic in structure. The self on trial is oriented outwards, to another character in the work, to the text's narratee or to the actual reader. The work of defining a self becomes a negotiation between 'I' and 'you'. In *If This is a Man*, Levi's configuration of Auschwitz as a trial is further complicated by the interplay of different temporalities in the text. Since historically, labour-death-camps existed to execute sentence without trial or due process of law, the trial-scenes of *If This is a Man* are all glaringly inadequate. Reconstituted as trials in the narrative of the survivor, they become temporally asymmetric events, in which past events are judged by present non-participants.

This temporal asymmetry represents an absence at the heart of any constitution of Auschwitz as trial in *If This is a Man*. However hard the survivor works to make these scenes effect a kind of closure, closure is precisely what they can never achieve. This is the note of frustration I hear in Levi's apostrophe to the participants of Chapter 10, against whom he erupts in anger at the end of the chapter: 'he would be amazed, the poor brute Alex, if someone told him that today, on the basis of this action, I judge him and Pannwitz and the innumerable others like him, big and small, in Auschwitz and everywhere' (IM 114).

The declaration of judgment is also unusual in a narrative that, as Levi says elsewhere, deliberately refrains from explicit condemnation.[30] Levi's interjection here indicates something important about self-fashioning within the spatiotemporal dimensions of the trial. The distinctive feature here is that the self is always constructed retrospectively. Levi the narrator uses the present tense of narration to accuse his former enemies; in a similar way, Levi the protagonist invokes a former self, the scientist who attended Turin University, to succeed in the 'trial', the examination in chemistry, which takes place on the diegetic level of narrative. Both Levis invoke a past self in order to constitute a present one. In a later essay, Levi writes that 'living without one's actions being judged means renouncing a retrospective insight that is precious, thus exposing oneself and one's neighbours to serious risks' (MM 119). The trial is above all that temporal space in which past actions are brought to judgment; as such, it constitutes a mirror image of the spacetime of the threshold, in which all sense of connection to past or future time is lost.

This process of self-affirmation, through looking back, bears only superficial resemblance to the affirmation of pre-existent selfhood, which Bakhtin argues is characteristic of romance trials of the self.[31] In Levi's narrative, the 'affirmation' of a past self is reaccented by the present, and is fully dialogic. Although the 'I' may resist an alien 'you', the two subject-positions act as catalysts for internal change, each in the other. The central episode in *If This is a Man* which demonstrates this process is the examination Levi undergoes before the SS chemist, Pannwitz (chapter 10). Midway through the process of being 'tried' on his knowledge of chemistry, the *häftling* reconnects with a pre-*lager* identity. Under questioning, he recognizes, 'this sense of lucid elation, this excitement which I feel warm in my veins, I recognize it, it is the fever of examinations, *my* fever of *my* examinations, that spontaneous mobilization of all my logical faculties and all my knowledge, which my friends at university so envied me' (IM 112).

At first glance, this looks like a straightforward affirmation of pre-existent selfhood. But as the scene unfolds, I sense a more complex process working itself out. Levi at first rejects any possibility of kinship with his examiner, who looks at him, as if 'across the glass window of an aquarium between two beings who live in different worlds', the dehumanising gaze somehow expressive of all 'the great insanity of the third Germany' (IM 111–12).

But the 'fever' to which Levi succumbs is produced, as becomes clear, by a recognition of the shared body of knowledge between two men. Levi spots on Pannwitz's desk a copy of Gatterman's *A Practical Manual for Organic Chemists*, a textbook that, in *The Search for Roots*, Levi describes as 'the words of the father ... which awake you from your childhood and declare you an adult' (SR 74). This sign of a common patronage opens a communicative link even across the aquarium window. A connection is indicated, for example, in the hybridization of two languages that takes place in the prisoner's mind. Levi imagines how the doctor must view him, then describes how he views the doctor (both view points produce caricatures): 'And in my head, like seeds in an empty pumpkin: "Blue eyes and fair hair are essentially wicked ... I am a specialist in mine chemistry"' (IM 112). Levi's syntax has taken on a German inflection ('mine chemistry') characteristic of the speech of Pannwitz, but also of Levi's beloved Gatterman.

Levi writes that as he entered the doctor's office, he felt 'like

Oedipus in front of the Sphinx' (IM 111). The analogy is physically apt, since the Greek name means 'swollen footed' and Levi contrasts his hobbling, clogged gait with the leather-shod Alex, 'as light on his feet as the devils of Malebolge' (IM 113). But also, the answer to the riddle of the Sphinx is 'man', and what horrifies Levi about Pannwitz is the apparent inability of the doctor to see him as a man.[32] Particularly arresting is that Levi the protagonist feels he 'would leave a dirty stain [*una macchia sporca*] whatever I touched' in such a 'shining, clean and ordered' place (IM 111). This sense of being infected, of being potentially able to spread the disease, is not unconnected, I would argue, to the internal 'fever' Levi the protagonist is soon to experience, as the examination in chemistry gets underway. We will consider the nature of this 'fever' below.

First, the comparison Levi makes between Oedipus and his former self deserves closer attention, especially with regard to the 'dirty stain' which attaches to the *häftling* on trial. Steinberg alludes to a similar sense of having been polluted by his experience (as of course do other survivors). He describes slapping a fellow prisoner, an old Polish Jew: 'that incident, a banal event in the daily life of a death camp, has haunted me all my life ... the contagion had done its job, and I had not escaped corruption' (SYA 126–127). This sense of lingering contagion seems to be one of the forces driving Steinberg to relate his experience after a silence of 50 years: 'I'm purging myself as I write, and I have a vague feeling not of liberation, but of fulfilled obligation' (SYA 63). In the preface to *If This is a Man,* Levi indicates that the survivor's desire to narrate his story stems from the need for an inner purgation: 'The need to ... make "the rest" participate in it [our story], had taken on for us, before our liberation and after, the character of an immediate and violent impulse' (IM 15). This explanation for *writing* his testimony contrasts markedly with what he hopes will be the result of *reading* the book: 'it should be able to furnish documentation for a quiet study of certain aspects of the human mind' (IM 15).

One could, as some critics do, make a distinction between the narrative aims of *If This is a Man* and *The Truce,* arguing that the former is written impulsively, directly out of the experience of trauma, while the latter is more reflective, and more open to the processes of healing, for both narrator and reader. One could, in other words, separate the infernal from the purgatorial experience. But to do so would be to ignore that *If This is a Man* is structured discursively, designed to be read reflectively in 'quiet study' and conversely, that *The Truce* ends with a 'return of the repressed', a dream of waking in the *lager* and finding it to be the only truth. In fact, the narration of an infernal journey is *already* purgatorial, already a positive statement about the possibility of an exit from Hell through the 'gateway' of communication. And the narration of a purgatorial journey is already an admission of the continued presence of the 'demonic' within. Both texts, then, equally raise the question, in what sense is the protagonist 'stained' by entering this trial of the self? And are there possibilities of 'purgation' for Levi, as there seem to be for Steinberg in the passage quoted above?

The comparison Levi draws with Oedipus invites us to consider these questions within particular generic horizons. In Sophoclean and Aeschylean tragedy, one who has spilt the blood of his kindred is said to be *miaros*, blood-guilty, infectious.[33] While in Greek philosophy, *miasma* (corruption) only attaches itself to one who has *intentionally* committed a crime, it was common for Greek tragedians to represent any character involved in blood-crime as *miaros*, whether involved intentionally or not.[34] Thus, Sophocles' Oedipus may have been victim of the gods or fate (or in modern parlance, of unconscious drives), but he is still *miaros*, and responsible for the plague brought on Thebes by his presence.[35]

As opposed to the tragedians themselves, Aristotle seem to have thought that the *miaron* was an unfitting subject for tragedy, because such repugnant acts could not be 'purged' through pity and fear.[36] The classical context, to which Levi's text may or may not consciously refer, helps us to isolate two key questions for Holocaust autobiography: how can moral pollution attach itself to the consciousness of an innocent individual, one who has neither intended nor perpetrated any crime? And secondly, is such *miasma* 'purged' through the shared act of narrative communication, or (as Aristotle implies) does communicating it further spread the plague?

Addressing the first of these questions, we return to consider the *häftling*'s 'fever' experienced during the examination by Pannwitz. As argued above, Levi's 'recovery' of former selfhood is, at least in part, triggered by the presence of an other who is capable of recognizing and understanding that self. But in my view, this moment of recognition not only unites two minds in the narrative present of the interview. It also travels, like an electric shock, back to Levi's pre-*lager* selfhood, so that a Pannwitz insinuates itself into Levi's memories of being a student, of being examined and held to account; a genuine hybridization of perspectives takes place in at least one of the participants.[37]

For a chemical analogy, we might turn to the chapter, 'Zinc', in *The Periodic Table*, in which Levi celebrates the properties of the metal in its impure state. Impure, as opposed to pure, zinc acts as a catalyst for other chemical substances, inducing in them a radical metamorphosis. From the properties of pure and impure zinc, Levi suggests, one might derive two opposing principles: 'the praise of purity, which protects from evil like a coat of mail; the praise of impurity, which gives rise to changes, in other words to life' (PT 34). Levi's praise of impure zinc comes, in this later quasi-autobiography, at a point corresponding to his segregation from fellow students at university due to the introduction of Mussolini's racial laws. In those days, Levi came to feel that as a Jew, he was the catalyst for life-enhancing change in others: 'I am the impurity that makes the zinc react' (PT 35). So the *häftling* who might 'stain' anything he touched is also the 'fever' that might produce a living reaction from Pannwitz. But as a corollary, Levi himself is also catalyzed, metamorphosed by the encounter.

The meeting of minds that I am suggesting occurs here is only transitory. Pannwitz gives no indication that he recognizes Levi as a fellow human being, a fact underscored by the Kapo's humiliating treatment of the prisoner afterwards. And the prisoner, too, lapses into polarized, *lager* categories: 'the excitement which sustained me for the whole of the test suddenly gives way and, dull and flat, I stare at the fair skin of his hand writing down my fate' (IM 113). But the moment of recognition of self in other turns out to be far more destabilizing retrospectively, than the sense of deflation the protagonist experiences immediately after the event. The experience of 'fever' becomes a sign of the self's interiorization of the *lager*'s values (as Steinberg writes, remembering the slap, 'the contagion had done its job, and I had not escaped corruption').[38]

If the survivor recalls his 'feverish' participation as a corruption that stays with him, what are the effects of sharing this experience with an audience? Can such acts be 'purged'? Levi himself suggests that the 'poison of Auschwitz' which survivors bear is corrosive in its effects on listeners and readers. His collection of poems borrows its title, *Ad Ora Uncerta,* from these lines of Coleridge's *The Rime of the Ancient Mariner:* 'Since then, at an uncertain hour,/ That agony returns,/ And til my ghastly tale is told/ This heart within me burns.'[39] Like the mariner, Levi implies, the survivor is driven to narrate by an inner fever which may as easily transfer to a listener as allay his own symptoms.

But the idea of 'infection' can also be inverted to bear a positive charge; corrosion and infection can be reconstrued as positive metamorphosis. In *The Mirror Maker,* we find Levi making the characteristic mental shift; feeling collectively responsible for evil also allows us to take collective pride in human achievement:

Just as every person, even the most innocent, even the victim himself, feels some responsibility for Hiroshima, Dallas, and Vietnam, and is ashamed, so even the one least connected with the colossal labor of cosmic flights feels that a small particle of merit falls to the human species, and so also to himself, and because of this feels that he has greater value. For good or evil, we are a single people (MM 108).

SEA-VOYAGE ... SHIPWRECK

We come then to the fifth and final chronotope I wish to discuss in *If This is a Man*. The chronotopes of trial and voyage in *If This is a Man* are contiguous and complementary, in ways comparable to the contiguities linking *The Search*'s two inner pathways ('man suffers unjustly' and 'the stature of man').[40] In *If This is a Man*, the examination before Pannwitz, a trial of selfhood, is succeeded by the 'Canto of Ulysses' episode, in which the protagonist Levi 'voyages' with another inmate into friendship, Dante, and memories of the past.

Within what I am calling the 'voyage' chronotope, the protagonist discovers a model of selfhood to which he may, or may not, aspire; this is the Odysseus/Ulysses of Homer and Dante.[41] As Cicioni explains, the traditional (Italian) Romantic interpretation of Dante's Ulysses is of an 'individual whose "virtue" lies in his striving to push human "knowledge" further, and who maintains his sense of identity even in Hell'.[42] Levi's admiration for this traditional figure might be further particularized, however; in my estimation, Levi's Ulysses embodies the qualities of ingenuity, adaptability, cunning, intellectual curiosity, hunger for the unknown, love of collective endeavour, and desire to share and communicate knowledge, to narrate the self. In *If This is a Man*, two chapters present us with the protagonist as Ulyssean wanderer, within a chronotope of the *lager* conceptualized as a spiritual voyage ending in shipwreck: 'The Canto of Ulysses' and its inverted image, 'Kraus'.[43] My discussion will focus on the first of these.

In 'The Canto of Ulysses', the intellectual voyage of discovery on which *häftling* Levi embarks (that is, teaching his French guide, Jean Samuel, something of Italian and of Dante's *Commedia*) constitutes a trial of the self no less significant than the examination discussed above. Like that previous episode, the walk to the soup queue with Jean Samuel may be, and has been, interpreted as affirmation of a pre-existent self. In *The Drowned and the Saved*, Levi himself says that the incident 'made it possible for me to re-establish a link with the past, saving it from oblivion and reinforcing my identity' (DS 112).[44] But what exactly is meant by 'reinforcement'? Although Levi must have memorized the lines which he quotes to Jean, presumably while a schoolboy in Turin, the Dante he 'remembers' in the *lager* seems unfamiliar, unconnected to the past. Levi hears himself quoting Ulysses' speech, 'As if I also was hearing it for the first time'. Moreover, the immediate effect of hearing the speech is certainly not to 'reinforce his identity': 'For a moment I forget who I am and where I am' (IM 119). Self-'affirmation' in this chapter (as in the previous one) entails a prior *loss* of self.

Levi (the protagonist) then comes to identify closely with the Dantean Ulysses whom he quotes ('"Think of your breed; for brutish ignorance/ Your mettle was not made; you were men,/ To follow after knowledge and excellence"' (IM 119)). Critics have debated at length how to interpret this key passage in *If This is a Man*. Is the protagonist's identification with Ulysses validated by narrator and authorial voice, or not? Those who tend to read this passage ironically may point out that the protagonist's enthusiasm is soon undercut, and that Dante's Ulysses, a false counsellor, is not a character in whom one should place much trust. Those who read the passage 'straight' argue that this Ulysses articulates the humanistic values which Levi, as protagonist, was struggling to regain in the *lager*. These critics still have to ask themselves a further series of questions: even if we are to believe in Ulysses, are the values he represents valid in Auschwitz? Do they do the protagonist any good? And, finally, is the 'flash of intuition' experienced by a *lager* inmate in any way relevant to the text's addressees, outside the *lager* world?[45]

In Dante's *Inferno*, Ulysses is a narrator who, unlike Scheherezade, does not survive the telling of his tale. The Canto ends as the tale ends, and this is the last we hear or see of Ulysses. In *If This is a Man*, the end of the chapter seems doubly final, since Levi concludes with the last line of Dante's Canto, 'and over our heads the hollow seas closed up' (IM 121). Any intuition Levi (the protagonist) may have gained from his experience seems to drown with Ulysses here, to remain untransmissable to us. On the other hand, of course, Chapter 12 follows Chapter 11; the Ulyssean 'I' in Levi's narrative clearly escapes both this 'shipwreck' episode, and the journey through Hell generally.

In the shift from trial to voyage, the self's spatio-temporal horizons in Auschwitz also change, opening up certain possibilities and closing down others. As with the texts on the second, tragic pathway in *The Search*, the self on trial returns (compulsively?) to the scene of judgement. His orientation is predominantly toward the past, and any coherence of self he gains or retains involves a negotiation with the past. The self *en voyage*, by contrast, is oriented towards future time. The dangers (of spiritual shipwreck) lie before the voyaging self, rather than behind. Notably absent from the sense of self, configured along this chronotope, is any consciousness of bearing the past's *miasma*.

The Ulysses of Homer, Dante and Levi are mostly guilt-free. Unlike Coleridge's mariner and Kafka's Joseph K (another of Levi's self-projections, whom space constrains us from discussing here), Levi's Ulysses is undisturbed by the complexity of his motives in his pursuit of knowledge and adventure.[46] This heroic and single-minded orientation towards the future is something Levi clearly admires, and at times (like Ulysses himself) urges in others. In 'Hatching the Cobra', for example, he warns scientific researchers into nuclear energy not to pretend their work is neutral in its implications, but concludes nevertheless that 'basic research ... can and must continue: if we were to abandon it, we would betray our nature and our nobility as 'thinking reeds', and the human species would no longer have any reason to exist' (MM 214). This is Levi as Ulysses the 'thinking reed', counselling researchers to sail beyond 'brutish ignorance', despite the horrific risks involved in nuclear research of which he was himself acutely aware.

The voyage chronotope thus complements that of the trial by reorienting the self from past to future time. Interesting contiguities and contrasts also appear between self *en voyage* and on the threshold. As does the threshold, the voyage chronotope presents the self with a border that divides this and another state of being. The prisoner Levi glosses Dante's phrase in this way: '"I set forth" ... it is throwing oneself on the other side of a barrier, we know the impulse well' (IM 119). But this 'setting forth' across a 'barrier' contrasts with threshold crossing in a number of crucial ways. First, the crossing is willed, not enforced. Secondly, what lies on the other side of the barrier is the opposite of the Freudian uncanny; it is unknown and uncharted, not mythic and familiar territory. If threshold crossing leads the self into mythic time, that is, a time empty of all future, then the voluntary Ulyssean 'setting forth' precipitates the self into an arena of genuinely open-ended time. Thirdly, the self who crosses threshold and voyage barrier experiences, in each case, a sudden sense of gravitational release (Levi refers to Geryon as the monster who 'escapes weight' (MM 171)), but this crossed-over condition of 'weightlessness' bears different value within each chronotope.

The weightless 'exit via the chimney' is the ultimate horror for the self trapped in Auschwitz as threshold (between human and nonhuman, history and myth). But for the Ulyssean voyager, weightlessness is the condition of the survivor, one who adapts, improvises, thinks and moves lightly. This is the mood in which both Levi and Jean conduct their journey towards the soup queue, cunningly mapping a circuitous route so as to extend the burdenless outward leg of the journey. In 'The Man Who Flies', Levi argues that the ease with which astronauts adjust to the absence of gravity demonstrates the adaptability of the human species. Because we easily adjust to weightlessness in space, we have won ourselves 'vast and unforeseen margins of safety' (MM 172). As I pointed out above, the orientation of self within this chronotope is towards the future, its risks and its open possibilities.

But since the voyage of Ulysses described in Dante's Canto 26 ends in shipwreck, how can I describe such a journey (whose disastrous conclusion is foreknown) as in any real sense future-oriented, open-ended? The end of Chapter 11 (as we noted) presents us with a paradox: the Ulyssean 'I' shipwrecks and drowns, but the 'I' continues to speak. If we were to examine closely all the references Levi makes to shipwreck in his writing (and they are frequent), we would find that paradox writ large. Rather, we would discover an interesting slippage in the way he places himself with relation to any narrative of shipwreck. In some contexts, he is the man who *avoided* shipwreck (for example, in the Afterword to *If This is a Man*, p.398). In other contexts, he is the man who shipwrecks but survives the experience (for example, *The Mirror Maker*, p.4). In still others, he is grouped amongst those who went down (as we have seen, at the end of Chapter 11 of *If This is a Man*).

In terms of how a narrative of the self is being constructed, I think again we have an interesting contrast between voyage and trial chronotopes. Within the timespace of the trial, the temporal distance between former and present selves continually collapses, returning narrator and narratee, reader and writer, to the time of 'judgment'. Within the chronotope of the voyage, by contrast, the doubled journey of diegesis and narration splits and forks apart; a loophole opens up for the narrator/writer, while the former self in a spiritual sense shipwrecks and drowns. It is perhaps the fact that he has experienced drowning, at some level, that the self on this chronotope can feel accountable to the 'drowned' who do not live to narrate their stories.

Furthermore, in the shift of perspective from trial to voyage chronotope, there is, I feel, a positive readjustment in the relation between 'I' and 'you', between Levi and his narratees and readers. Unlike Coleridge's mariner, the Ulyssean narrator *assumes* his audience desires to hear his story.[47] In Chapter 11, both participants engage willingly and eagerly in conversation. Jean *encourages* Levi to speak of Dante, just as in the *Inferno,* Virgil with formal courtesy requests the Greek to speak. As noted above, Levi's Ulysses is a natural 'talker'; his desire is to name and narrate himself. This desire is unchecked even when his audience is a hostile one (a Cyclops!), as is illustrated by this extract from Homer's *Odyssey* in *The Search:*

> He [Odysseus] could have escaped in silence, but he prefers to take his revenge to the limit: he is proud of his name, which up till now he has kept quiet about, and proud of his courage and ingenuity. He is 'the man of no account', but he wants to make known to the tower of flesh just who is the mortal that has defeated him (SR 22).

Rather than sailing away in safe silence, Odysseus risks his life to make himself known to his enemy. In Chapter 10 of *If This is a Man,* Levi represses his resentments of Pannwitz and the Kapo, symbols of fascism's two aspects, brain and tower of flesh. In Chapter 11, by contrast, he 'names' himself, via Dante's Ulysses, in the presence of a sympathetic interlocutor.

INTERSECTING PATHWAYS

The self *en voyage* experiences a widening of horizons and possibilities not available to the self on the threshold or on trial. As I have argued before, however, Levi's text does not support the thesis that this voyaging self succeeds, or substitutes or predominates over other selves constituted within Auschwitz's chronotopes. Anxieties about audience reception are clearly recurrent, even after this Ulyssean chapter. The final pages of *If This is a Man* are directed, with painful diffidence and restraint, not towards us, but towards a fellow survivor (Charles). *The Truce* also concludes on a note of apprehension, as Levi relates the recurrent nightmare of return to a family who refuses to listen to his story. But near the end of *The Truce,* Levi describes his homeward crossing into Italy in terms that recall the multiplicity of pathways we have been exploring:

> As the train, more tired than us, climbed toward the Italian frontier it snapped in two like an overtaut cable ... we knew that on the thresholds of our homes, for good or ill, a trial awaited us, and we anticipated it with fear. We felt in our veins the poison of Auschwitz, flowing together with our thin blood ... We felt the weight of centuries on our shoulders, we felt oppressed by a year

of ferocious memories ... With these thoughts, which kept us from sleep, we passed our first night in Italy, as the train slowly descended the deserted, dark Adige Valley (T 378).

This paragraph contains the accents of all five chronotopes I have discussed above. There is the sense of threshold crossing, of a journey of education with its mid-line 'caesura' (the snapped cable), the sense of forever inhabiting an infernal, visionary world (Auschwitz 'in our veins'), and alternatively of being placed on trial, of embarking on a voyage that may end in the submersion of selfhood (the 'weight of centuries', oppression of memories, 'the poison ... flowing'). And finally all these chronotopes are gathered into the narrative trajectory of an unfinalized *katabatic* journey ('the train slowly descended').

Turning back to *The Search*, we might say that Levi is approaching the base point of his spherical map, that the self is about to encounter its 'black hole'. But if we have read *If This is a Man* through *The Search*, we will be more readily aware of the different pathways open to the journeying protagonist, narrator and reader. Reading this late anthology alongside Levi's first Auschwitz narrative encourages us to become canny and subtle travellers, able to make the lateral shifts necessary for survival, resistant to despair, curious about what metamorphoses lie ahead, excited by the prospect of an unfinalizable journey. *Katabasis* will have become a mental habit, a mode of existence, a timespace for discovering unlooked for connections, for making good the claim that 'we are a single people'.

NOTES

1. Primo Levi, *The Search for Roots: A Personal Anthology* (trans. Peter Forbes, afterword by Italo Calvino) (London, 2001). Hereafter referred to as SR.
2. *The Voice of Memory* was first published in Italian as *Primo Levi: Conversazioni e interviste 1963–87* (ed. Marco Belpoliti) (Turin, 1997).
3. Raymond Clark defines *katabasis* (literally, 'going down' in ancient Greek) as 'a Journey of the Dead made by a living person in the flesh who returns to our world to tell the tale' (p.32). For a survey of classical *katabatic* literature, see his *Catabasis: Vergil and the Wisdom-tradition* (Amsterdam, 1979). On the medieval tradition of descents into Hell, and ascents to Heaven (*anabasis*), see Carol Zaleski, *Otherworld Journeys: Accounts of Near-Death Experience in Medieval and Modern Times* (Oxford, 1987).
4. Primo Levi, *The Mirror Maker* (trans. Raymond Rosenthal) (London, 1997), p.127. Hereafter referred to as MM.
5. See Levi's *If This is a Man* and *The Truce* (trans. Stuart Woolf) (London, 1995), p.398 (hereafter referred to as IM and T, respectively); Ferdinando Camon's *Conversations with Primo Levi* (trans. John Shepley) (Marlboro, VT, 1989), pp.60–61, hereafter referred to as CL; and *The Drowned and the Saved* (trans. Raymond Rosenthal) (London, 1988), p.114.

Selfhood in Descent: Primo Levi

6. The 'chronotope' in Bakhtin's coinage, signifies the representation of 'time-space' in a text; more generally, it is a term which highlights 'the intrinsic connectedness of temporal and spatial relationships'. See Bakhtin, 'Forms of Time and of the Chronotope', *The Dialogic Imagination, Four Essays* (trans. Caryl Emerson and Michael Holquist) (Austin, 1984), p.86, hereafter referred to as FTC. I retain the terms 'self' and 'selfhood' in contexts where the term 'subject' would introduce too many tangential questions (subject to, or subject of?), see Paul Smith, *Discerning the Subject* (Minneapolis, 1988). When I use the term 'self' in relation to Levi's writing, I do not invoke its traditional essentialist associations. As my analysis should bear out, the self for Levi is constructed in dialogue with the other, and no essence precedes its social construction.
7. In *Conversations with Primo Levi*, Levi tells Camon that talking about the camps was a 'primary need', akin to food and drink (CL, p.42).
8. Bakhtin, FTC, p.157.
9. Two other outstanding *katabatic* works were published in 1947, the same year as *If This is a Man*: Thomas Mann's *Dr Faustus* and Malcolm Lowry's *Under the Volcano*. The contrasts in the three texts' representations of the self-in-descent are fascinating.
10. Primo Levi, *The Periodic Table* (trans. Raymond Rosenthal) (New York, 1984), p.58, hereafter referred to as PT.
11. 'I have followed approximately the succession in which I happened to discover and read them, but I have often succumbed to the temptation to contrive contrasts, as if I were staging a dialogue across the centuries: as if to see in this way how two neighbours can react to each other' (SR, p.8).
12. John Gross contrastingly writes that he finds 'this signposting too schematic, and not especially helpful'. See 'If this is a man's reading', *The Sunday Telegraph*, 24 June 2001.
13. Gross, ibid., argues that 'The experience of Auschwitz ... radiates out far beyond the passages which refer to it directly' and cites allusions in extracts from Sholem Aleichem, Stefano D'Arrigo, Arthur C. Clarke.
14. This quotation is from Levi's description of Joseph Conrad, a very important writer for illustrating 'man retaining stature' (SR, p.63).
15. See Calvino, writing in the Afterward: 'Between these two poles, ... Levi traces ... four lines of resistance to all forms of despair, four responses that define his stoicism' (SR, p.222).
16. Bakhtin, 'Forms of Time and of the Chronotope', p.85.
17. On the chronotope of the threshold (whose 'most fundamental instance is as the chronotope of *crisis* and *break* in a life'), see Bakhtin, FTC, p.248.
18. On the other hand, Dante knew that theologically speaking, there are only three classes of souls, the damned, the saved, and those who may yet be saved. Technically speaking, there is only one threshold crossing in *Inferno*, and that is the crossing into Hell. Theologically, the damned soul is *sul fundo* when he crosses the gate marked '*lasciate ogne speranza*', and Dante the pilgrim reaches that place very early on, in the third Canto of the poem.
19. 'The uncanny is that class of the frightening which leads back to what is known of old and long familiar', Sigmund Freud, 'The Uncanny' [1919], *The Complete Psychological Works of Sigmund Freud* Vol.XVII (London, 1955), p.220.
20. For classic inversions to weightlessness in earlier *katabatic* narratives, see Virgil's *Aeneid*, 6.411–414 and Milton's *Paradise Lost*, 4.1010-12. For an example contemporaneous with Levi's 1947 edition of *If This is a Man*, see the seventh chapter of Malcolm Lowry's *Under the Volcano*. Images of weightlessness are also very important in Liana Millu's *Smoke Over Birkenau* (trans. Lynne Sharon Schwartz) (New York, 1991), p.22, and *passim*.
21. In Bakhtinian terms, the train-journey might be described as a grotesque distortion of the chronotope of the road, see FTC, pp.243–5. The names of stations, spied through the slats, are negative versions of the road signs which would mark possible

digressions and subplots in a conventional adventure narrative. Instead these station names signify the towns and cities of Europe from which the deportees are now absolutely cut off. In the train's mythic time-space, *chance* and *digression* cease to be narrative possibilities.
22. It might be added that the freight-trains must figure as a dominant motif in Holocaust writing, because for those selected immediately to be gassed, this train-journey was all there was; the sum-total of their experience was this transportation out of historical time.
23. Freccero, *Poetics of Conversion* (Cambridge, 1986), p.58.
24. It is partly because of this element of foreclosure or 'entelechy' (fulfilling a pre-existent form) that Bakhtin viewed the genre of autobiography as lacking the potential to develop polyphony. See, for example, 'Forms of Time and of the Chronotope', p.141.
25. On the chronotope of the vision, see Bakhtin, FTC, pp.155–7. For Peter Forbes, 'It is Lucretius who provides the link between Levi's scientific, moral and aesthetic worldviews ... Lucretius's great achievement was to make a connection between the physical and the moral worlds; with superstition and irrational fears banished by scientific knowledge, men and women could lead a balanced life' (SR, pp.ix–x). In *The Mirror Maker*, Levi describes Dante as a 'poet scientist' with a systematizing imagination comparable to that of Lucretius (p.172).
26. These are the damned souls of soothsayers, see IM, p.93 and *Inferno*, 20.3. On Levi's borrowings from, and allusions to Dante, see Risa Sodi, *A Dante of Our Time (Primo Levi and Auschwitz)* (New York, 1990).
27. In *If This is a Man*, the three types of the 'saved' are not hierarchized in Dantean fashion, but they are in *The Drowned and the Saved* (the book which derives its title from this ninth chapter of *If This is a Man*).
28. Paul Steinberg, *Speak You Also: A Survivor's Reckoning* (London, 2000).
29. Levi thus addresses his German readers in *The Drowned and the Saved*: 'I am alive, and I would like to understand you in order to judge you' (p.143). In this later work, I can think of only one case, one issue, on which Levi suspends judgment completely: 'I ask that we meditate on the story of the 'crematorium ravens' with pity and rigour, but that a judgement of them be suspended' (p.43).
30. Levi says that he 'refrained from formulating judgements' of an explicit kind in *If This is a Man*, but he also emphasizes that the implicit judgments are there (CL,p.13).
31. Bakhtin argues that the trial of the hero in conventional romance narrative involves the hero affirming his identity against alien forces. The identity he affirms is *pre-existent* to the moment of trial itself; hence his heroism consists of the strength to *resist* change. The reaffirmed self of romance narrative is thus ahistorical, or more exactly, anti-historical. See FTC, pp.105–6.
32. 'That look was not one between two men' (*If This is a Man*, p.111).
33. Instances of the term in Greek tragedy include: Aeschylus, Se.682; Sophocles, *Oedipus at Colonnus*, 1374, *Antigone*, 172; Euripides, *Iphigenia in Taurus*, 1229, *Hippolytus*, 316–18.
34. I am grateful to Professor Glen Gould for these references, and for the distinction between Plato and Aristotle's use of the term *miaros* (by which they understood, someone who has *intentionally* committed a crime) and the tragedians' usage. For Aeschylus and Sophocles, the *miaros* is simply one who has committed a crime, whether intentionally so, or (like Oedipus) not.
35. In Sophocles, *Oedipus the King*, p.313, Oedipus orders Tiresias to help him find the '*miaros*' who is infecting Thebes; this criminal, of course, turns out to be himself. See *Sophocles I: Oedipus the King; Oedipus at Colonnus; Antigone* (trans. David Grene, Robert Fitzgerald and Elizabeth Wyckoff) (London, 1954). See *Oedipus at Colonnus*, 1374, where the word is consciously applied to Oedipus.
36. The 'repugnant' (*to miaron*) 'arouses neither fellow-feeling nor pity nor fear'.

Aristotle, *Poetics*, 13.35 (1453a) (trans. Stephen Halliwell) (London, 1995). On the well-known theory of *katharsis*, see *Poetics*, 6.28.
37. Levi learns from correspondence with another SS chemist, Dr Mueller, that Dr Pannwitz might not even have been responsible for Levi getting the job in the Auschwitz laboratory (which helped keep him alive in the winter of 1944). See PT, p.219ff.
38. Steinberg's testimony also places his former self on trial, but he is much more definite in his self-exoneration than Levi. Steinberg thus writes, 'Surely it's time to deliver a verdict. And the answer is yes: writing has helped me' (*Speak You Also*, p.163). In Dantean fashion, Steinberg turns the act of writing into a justification for survival: 'Perhaps I survived so that I might give an account, one of the last, that is both passionate and serene' (ibid., p.163).
39. The quotation is also used as an epigraph for other works by Levi: *Lilýt e altri racconti* (Turin, 1981) (*Lilit and Other Stories*), and *Moments of Reprieve* (trans. Ruth Feldman) (London, 1990).
40. An example of sea-voyage as trial in *The Search* is Melville's *Moby Dick*, about which Levi writes, 'the hunt [is] seen as both the judgment on, and justification of man, the dark well of humanity' (SR, p.118).
41. Losely, Jagendorf, and Sachs all interpret Levi's reading of the Ulysses Canto romantically, in which Ulysses is a noble character, unjustly condemned by Dante/God to Hell. According to this reading, Levi repeats Ulysses' speech to Jean without Dante's inflection of irony. By contrast, Risa Sodi is exceptionally strict in her medievalist approach to Dante (and Levi): 'It can be argued ... that Paolo and Francesca, ... Farinata, Bruno Latini, and Ulysses ... have less to do with Levi's victims and more to do with his oppressors. They, too, have readied a trap and were caught in it. They, too, suffer and it is just that they suffer' (*A Dante of Our Time*, p.62). According to Sodi, Ulysses should be classed among 'Levi's category of oppressors' because 'he would prefer to forget his past misdeeds' (p.66). I find this reading hardly credible, however, given the positive assessment Levi makes of Ulysses elsewhere. See Jay Loseley, 'From Savage Elements', *Journal of European Studies*, Vol.24, No.93 (1994), pp.1–21; Zvi Jagendorf, 'Primo Levi Goes For Soup and Remembers Dante', *Raritan*, Vol.12, No.4 (1993), pp.31–51; Dalya Sachs, 'The Language of Judgement: Primo Levi's *Se questo è un uomo*', *Modern Language Notes*, Vol.110, No.4 (1993), pp.757–84.
42. Cicioni, *Primo Levi: Bridges of Knowledge* (Oxford, 1995), p.34. Cicioni argues rightly, however, that in *If This is a Man*, this traditional interpretation is juxtaposed and held in tension with an image of 'human existence in Auschwitz' (ibid.).
43. But as Tony Judt points out, the presence of Ulysses, 'Levi's favorite literary figure and alter ego', is not confined to Chapter 11 of *If This is a Man*. Judt notes that Polyphemus appears as the *Blockälteste* in charge of the showers, and that numerous allusions to Ulysses's adventures appear in *The Truce* and *The Periodic Table*. See Tony Judt, 'The Courage of the Elementary', *Times Literary Supplement*, 20 May 1999, pp.31–8 (see p.32).
44. The passage in *The Drowned and the Saved* continues: 'They [Dante's lines] convinced me that my mind, though besieged by everyday necessities, had not ceased to function. They elevated me in my own eyes and those of my interlocutor. They granted me a respite ephemeral but not hebetudinous, in fact liberating and differentiating: in short, a way to find myself' (p.112) The emphasis has already moved well away from affirming a pre-existent self.
45. Jagendorf rightly questions whether the prisoner Levi experiences any revelation of an epiphanic nature, and even if he does, how significant this revelation is if it cannot be passed on. Jagendorf's reading emphasizes the lacuna [...] cloaking the nature of the prisoner's intuition. See note 41.
46. Levi's choice of Ulysses as a model of the voyaging subject contrasts, in this respect,

with the choice of Aeneas, by Louis Begley, in *Wartime Lies* (New York, 1991). Begley introduces his protagonist thus: 'He reveres the *Aeneid*. That is where he first found civil expression for his own shame at being alive, his skin intact and virgin of tattoo, when his kinsmen and almost all the others, so many surely more deserving than he, perished in the conflagration' (p.1).

47. See this passage from *The Drowned and the Saved*: 'we ... speak also because we are invited to do so [like] Ulysses, who immediately yields to the urgent need to tell his story... at the court of the king of the Phaeacians' (DS, p.121).

APPENDIX

FOUR POSSIBLE ROUTES THROUGH PRIMO LEVI'S LIFELONG READING

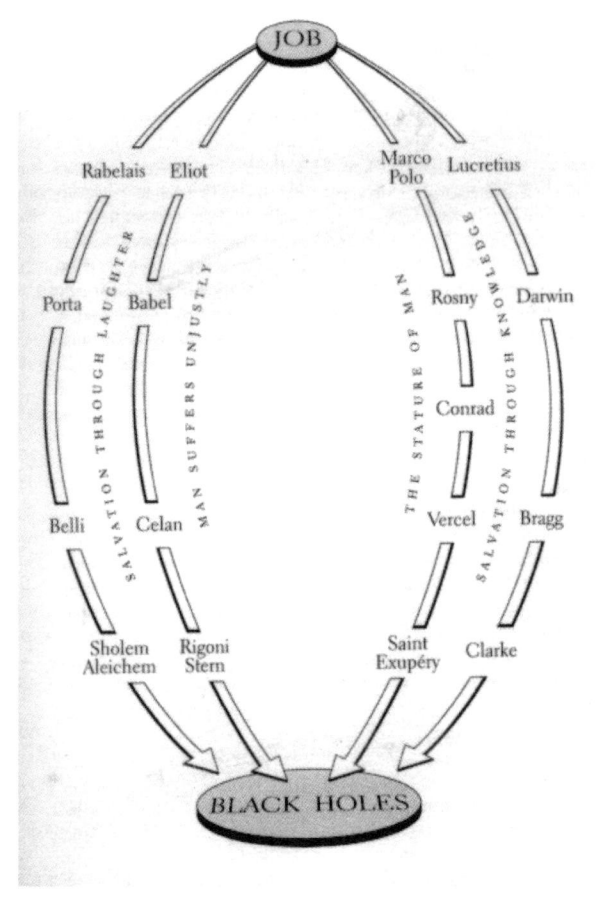

```
                        JOB
          Rabelais  Eliot        Marco  Lucretius
                                 Polo

      Porta   Babel                 Rosny    Darwin

                                    Conrad

      Belli   Celan                 Vercel   Bragg

       Sholem    Rigoni        Saint     Clarke
       Aleichem  Stern         Exupéry

                      BLACK HOLES
```

(Arcs labelled: SALVATION THROUGH LAUGHTER; MAN SUFFERS UNJUSTLY; THE STATURE OF MAN; SALVATION THROUGH KNOWLEDGE)

Source: Levi's map is taken from the Preface of *The Search for Roots: A Personal Anthology*, by Primo Levi (p.9). Translated and with an introduction by Peter Forbes, London: Allen Lane, The Penguin Press, 2001. Originally published in Italian as *La ricerca delle radici* by Giulio Einaudi Editore, 1981.

Sylvia Plath and Holocaust Poetry

GILLIAN BANNER

INTRODUCTION

'Take metaphor out of language and there is no memory, no history left.'
(Jacqueline Rose, *The Haunting of Sylvia Plath*)

When Sylvia Plath and the Holocaust are considered in tandem, a perplexing confluence of imperatives and denials comes into being. All of Plath's work attracts extremes of approval and censure, of allegiance and disaffection, constantly provoking questions of acceptability. This is especially apparent in discussions concerning her eligibility to write of the Holocaust and the disturbance about the forms that Holocaust writing takes. The criticism of Plath's 'Holocaust poems' is especially inclined to discover the unacceptable appropriation of a metaphor to which she had not established any rights. What follows is an attempt to show that the Holocaust metaphor was not used opportunistically or gratuitously as Plath approached the end of her life, but that her development of subject matter and metaphor, especially as they related to domesticity and patriarchy, became increasingly expressive of the coincident territory occupied by the private and the public.

This approach to the subject has been informed in particular by the work of two writers. Jacqueline Rose's insights provide feminist and psycho-analytical readings of Plath's work which are both helpful and appropriate, especially in Rose's discussion of issues of acceptability and Plath's refusal of boundaries. James Young's work on the relationship between writing and the Holocaust has been more generally useful in the construction of a matrix of ideas.[1] In addition, Young specifically discusses Plath's employment of the Holocaust as metaphor in a convincing examination of much of the negative criticism provoked by this aspect of her work. Together, Rose and Young have assisted the formation and development of my apprehensions of Plath and the Holocaust and it is their perceptions which have encouraged the particular 'way of seeing' adopted here.

This piece is an extract from a longer piece which gave close readings of 'The Thin People', 'Mushrooms', 'Tulips'; 'Little Fugue', 'The Bee Meeting', 'Daddy', and 'Lady Lazarus'. For the purpose of this discussion, only two poems, 'The Thin People' and 'Little Fugue',[2] will be considered in detail here.

JACQUELINE ROSE

The question of acceptability is central to the dilemmas which surround Plath and all of her work, not only that concerned with the Holocaust. Anne Stevenson makes this clear in her biography of Plath, *Bitter Fame*, as she describes the process Ted Hughes adopted when arranging *Ariel*. It is, she claims, necessary 'to make her extreme gift acceptable to readers'.[3] Rose also recognizes the disturbances which result from issues concerning creative permissibility:

> In my reading, Plath regularly unsettles certainties of language, identity and sexuality, troubling the forms of cohesion on which 'civilised' culture systematically and often oppressively relies [...] The question then arises – who is to decide the limits of the unacceptable? Who is to decide what it is acceptable for the unacceptable to be? (p.xiv).

This dilemma becomes more profound, inviting stronger criticism, when Plath's Holocaust poems are under discussion.

Plath wrote across the boundaries of inner and outer, of personal and political, of self and other. Her work evades unity and inscribes complexity and fragmentation, exemplifying the procedures and recommendations of analysts like Hélène Cixous, enacting the transgression reflected upon by Peter Stallybrass and Allon White, and articulating Kristevan notions of abjection.[4] Plath's refusal to recognize the limits elicits frustrated attempts from many critics, especially many of those who wrote immediately following her death, to discover and impose fixity and cohesion upon her work. This refusal to recognize boundaries coupled with the constant testing of limits and querying of the simple binaries, male:female, good:evil, mother:non-mother, inner:outer, is what brings Plath's work out from the area of the purely personal and into the widest engagement with history and politics. It is also what provokes the greatest criticism and discomfort. That there are no easy answers offered, no sides to take in her work, is a measure of Plath's accurate and disturbing analyses. In Plath's vision, according to Rose:

> psychic life in itself will not be relegated to the private, it will not stay in its proper place. It shows up on the side of the historical reality to which it is often opposed. Nowhere is this clearer than in Plath's own use of historical reference, where it is always the implication of the psyche in history, and history in the psyche, that is involved (p.7).

Rose sees this procedure especially clearly in Plath's use of the historical and factual in expressing and making available her inner self, recognizing too the accusations to which this exposes Plath. Rose's response is to offer a psycho-analytical rationale which considers the unavoidable repercussions momentous and terrible events like the Shoah have upon the perceptions and procedures of those who follow after. Rose makes clear the way in which 'fantasy operates inside historical process' (p.7). She argues that:

> In fascism, the realm of politics reveals itself as massively invested with the most private and intimate images of our fantasy life. Plath's writing presents us with those images at work, producing ... her own sexual iconography, as well as her own diagnosis, of one of the sub-texts of fascism. In doing so, she provides an extraordinary instance of *the inseparability of history and subjectivity* (p.7, my italics).

Rose's insistence that 'There is no history outside its subjective realisation ... just as there is no subjectivity uncoloured by the history to which it belongs' (p.8), does much to refute the compartmentalization of experience which allows, in extreme manifestations, one of fascism's most potent weapons. Anything which attacks and refuses the shared experience of a humane community of subjectivity, which offers the protection and solace of being able to discriminate – and in that discrimination to achieve a distance between the self and the despised, hence persecuted, Other, encouraging instead a denial of likeness with the Other – opens the route which leads, potentially, to the death camp.

Plath had an acute recognition, analogous to Kristeva's theories of abjection, of the way in which disgust, refusal, expulsion operate in the construction of identity. Jewishness, as represented by fascism, is seen as a threat to the 'clean and proper body' of culture; it takes over, like a fungus or a cancer upon the host body, debasing high art and its ideals, converting the pure, the clean, the elite into the impure, the debased, the popular. Masculinity, Nazism, cleanliness, purity, the permitted and high culture are opposed to femininity, Jewishness, popular culture, filth, impurity, the transgressive. In the light of this construction, to be a Jew, to adopt Jewishness as the speakers in Plath's poetry do, is to put aside any claims to be part of high art and to espouse the masses, the vulgar. Notions of degeneracy, not least sexual, are frequent elements of popular culture; degeneracy is also an accusation levelled at Jews by Nazis. The decay of civilization, the threat to culture which the Jews represented in Hitler's Germany, has echoes in the panic felt by proponents of high art faced with the 'flood' or 'tide' of low art popular culture.

It is the reader's, not Plath's, concept of Jewishness which might lead to criticism of her use of these images. If we figure the Holocaust Jew as only a passive sacrificial victim, we see Plath putting on a persona which may be inappropriate to the extent that the reader believes Plath could or should have escaped from her victimisation or madness, or that she was overstating the position in which she found herself. If, however, we see the Holocaust Jew as representing additional elements (and Nazi Germany has not been the only regime to fear the Jewish culture's difference), that is, the questioner, the resister of oppression, then the correlation with the threat which women pose to patriarchy, becomes clear. The Jew becomes available as an image of the subversive, a threat to the status quo, not merely a victim but also a challenger and a source of dissidence. So, Plath's 'I may be a bit of a Jew' in 'Daddy' becomes a threat, a call to arms, to resistance, rather than the passive whine of a victim. To place oneself alongside the derided object, to stand with whatever is construed as beyond the pale, and to claim kinship, renders the philosophical stance of the totalitarian state void. When most people and cultures define themselves in terms of not-being-the-Other, placing oneself on the Other side with the alien is an act of defiance, a refusal to recognize the boundaries which calls into question the validity of differentiation.

Rose also draws attention to the 'close link between fascist ideology and the fantasy of an abject femininity. They [recent writers] have argued that it is this feminine-connoted body of liquid, hollows and openings that fascism, at the level of unconscious fantasy, is struggling to control' (p.157). Plath's Holocaust poetry implicitly recognizes these other fantasy elements, so that it contains not only the adoption of the persona of 'Jew', standing in opposition to that of 'Nazi', but also expressions of femaleness/impurity set against maleness/purity. Plath frequently represents woman as the Thing or the Alien, which, by replicating the attributes of 'proper', male members of the population is able to pass for 'normal'. Plath recognizes that it is this ability to masquerade, to become frighteningly indistinguishable through the processes of assimilation, yet to remain female, or Jewish, which causes the most profound disturbance and hostility. This disgust is driven by a fear of self-pollution which is identified by Rose as 'opposition between masculine high culture and a culturally and sexually degraded female world' (p.191).

At the beginning of her relationship with Hughes, Plath was located, or located herself, alongside him, as superhuman, a Nietzschean *übermensch*. By the time she was writing 'Daddy' the reality of such an existence had intruded. Having been expelled from and no longer able to locate herself with her father Otto Plath and her husband Ted Hughes in the place of God (with the potential for Fascism such a position implies), Plath had to re-position her self as the Other, that is not-God, woman, Jew.

JAMES YOUNG, 'THE THIN PEOPLE' AND 'LITTLE FUGUE'

In addition to Rose's critique, there are other aspects to Plath's use of the Holocaust as a metaphor. Some of them arise out of Plath's recognition of the past as a modifier of the present. This acute consciousness of the insistence of the past, of the refusal of the dead to be put out of mind, forgotten or dispersed in the pragmatisms of the present, is frequently seen to be a state Plath inhabited which was close to pathology; an inability – or as some render it, refusal – to escape from or to manage her own past experience. This lays her work open to the criticism of an unacceptable readiness to wallow in self-indulgence and self-centredness. But this recognition of the past, of the existence of what Plath referred to as 'All the Dead Dears' permits a proper acknowledgement that, as T.S. Eliot expressed it, 'History is now'. In her story 'All the Dead Dears' four people chat over tea: 'calling up the names of the quick and the dead, reliving each past event as if it had no beginning and no end, but existed, vivid and irrevocable, from the beginning of time, and would continue to exist long after their own voices were stilled'.[5] This absence of differentiation, the slippage which occurs here between 'the quick and the dead', past and present, is exactly part of the procedure which enables Plath to 'slip' into the Holocaust, to adopt something like the persona of a Jew. Maybe memory plays a part in explaining Plath's urgent need to utilize another, much larger and more terrible project of memorial acting as an aid in her attempt to recoup and re-figure her smaller past.

In his essay 'Jewish Memory in Poland', James Young refers to the way in which shattered pieces of gravestones are pieced together to form new memorials, memorials which contain within their very being the recognition of absence, loss and fragmentation:

> Even as these remnants are gathered up and pieced together ... the fragments are not recuperated so much as reorganized around the theme of their own destruction.
> ... Rather than mending the words in a fissured epitaph, they preserve the break: in this way broken-tombstone monuments commemorate their own fragility, gather and exhibit the fragments as fragments, never as restored wholeness ... The fragments may still be broken, but finally they are pieced together into some order, if only that which signifies disorder (pp.215–16).

This description of the making of monuments out of and about destruction and dispersal offers a way of seeing Plath's perplexing poetry which itself frequently displays an 'order, if only that which signifies disorder'. Plath adopts a process which constantly recovers and focuses upon the fragments of her own life, pieces them together, possibly in an attempt to make wholeness, but always, 'preserve[s] the break'. Poetry and epitaph display many elements in common. Young again, writing of the objects made from the shattered headstones, refers to the way in which pieces fit side by side:

> Epitaphs are preserved in pieces, with chunks of the aleph-bet splintered in all directions; Polish script breaks into Hebrew, sentences are cut off mid-word, mid-letter ... When legible, the epitaphs read stammeringly, like this one from the wall in Kraków:
> Here lies our teach rab
> Benjamin Zeev Wolf the son of Ga
> of blessed mem
> Mind pours itself into the gaps between the fragments, like so much mortar, to bind the remnants together. We are reminded that memory is never seamless, but always a montage of collected fragments, recomposed by each person and generation (pp.218–19).

Something like this collage effect is evident throughout Plath's poetry, in which she juxtaposes odd details of her life alongside dreams, fictions, and history. Also evident, especially in her later poems, is an effect close to the 'stammering' which Young identifies in the epitaphs, where 'sentences are cut off mid-word' and German interrupts or is interrupted by English.

In 'The Holocaust becomes an Archetype' from his *Writing and Re-writing the Holocaust*, Young discusses the way in which unprecedented events inevitably attain the status of an archetype (it is apparent that the attacks upon the World Trade Centre on 11 September 2001 are already well on the way to attaining such a status):

> It is ironic that once an event is perceived to be without precedent, without adequate analogy, it would in itself become a kind of precedent for all that follows: a new figure against which subsequent experiences are measured and grasped ... The process is inevitable, for as new experiences are necessarily grasped and represented in the frame of remembered past experiences, 'incomparable' experiences like the Holocaust will always be made – at least rhetorically – comparable (p.99).

Young considers the way in which 'the figure of Holocaust Jew' comes to stand for 'the embattled victim, the sufferer and martyr', and offers examples as diverse as: 'suffering Russians in Yevgeny Yevtushenko's poetry; gulag prisoners for Andrei Sinyavsky; poets for Paul Celan' (p.99). He recognizes the way in which the Holocaust became, 'its own archetype' (p.100); even as events were still unfolding, writers were using earlier elements and experiences of the Holocaust to describe to themselves and their readers those events which occurred later. It seemed as though the figures of terror which were available were inadequate to describe this terror of terrors; only itself would serve to describe itself, resulting in the 'self-conscious displacement of past archetypes by contemporaneous figures' (p.100).

There are other aspects to this consideration of Plath's use of the Holocaust as metaphor. Those writers who survived the ghettos and the camps seem, of course, to have an inalienable and pre-eminent right to the use of these images, a sort of copyright bestowed by experience and paid for by virtue of their having witnessed the entrance of the unbelievable and incomparable, into time and history. But what of Plath, white, Anglo-Saxon, Protestant, safe? What right has such a person to appropriate those experiences? In the face of criticisms which suggest that it is only those who have direct cognisance of the Holocaust, what is to be made of Primo Levi's emphatic statement, 'We, the survivors, are not the true witnesses'? His argument, expressed most clearly in *The Drowned and the Saved*, is that the very fact of survival means that 'we are those who by their prevarications or abilities or good luck did not touch bottom':

> We who were favoured by fate tried, with more or less wisdom, to

recount not only our fate, but also that of the others, the submerged: but this was a discourse on 'behalf of third parties', the story of things seen from close by, not experienced personally ... We speak in their stead, by proxy.[6]

Even Levi, surely qualified to claim, if anyone is, 'I was there, this is my experience', speaks instead of not being 'the true witness', of speaking on behalf of others, of 'proxy'. His view is that this is not a matter of 'rights' or of 'ownership' but of a compulsion to tell, to refuse silence, which Levi emblematized by employing the figure of the Ancient Mariner.

Seeking to delineate the experience of psychic pain and elaborations of loss and fragmentation, Plath found that the Holocaust provided her with the only 'adequate images'. It might be argued that, rather than belittling the Event by using it to figure more ordinary, individual pain, by employing these metaphors to elaborate the sufferings of the individual, Plath makes it possible to *recognize* the individuality of those six million sufferings. In this context, Young cites Borowski's perceptions: 'Concentration camp existence ... had taught us that the whole world is really like the concentration camp; the weak work for the strong, and if they have no strength or will to work – then let them steal or let them die'[7] (Borowski, *This Way for the Gas*, p.168). Paradoxically, what Borowski takes pains to emphasize is the ordinariness and mundanity of camp existence and its relationship to life outside and after the Holocaust. Borowski conveys the hellishness of human existence during the Shoah but is determined to make the connection between what happened in the camps and what is daily happening outside.

Young gives much consideration to the way in which the new archetype of the Holocaust leads to a re-reading and re-figuring of ancient archetypes so that inevitably, the distant past is acted upon by the more recent past. This may also have been part of Plath's process: searching for ways to represent her analysis of relationships between men and women, master and slave, oppressor and victim, it became difficult to see past the figure of the Holocaust, the place where she discovers the only adequate representation of those relationships. Young points out that Plath was not attempting to describe the events of the Holocaust, she was not re-figuring or dramatizing the experiences of others which many writers on the Holocaust find impermissible. What she was doing, at the exact moment that the Holocaust was in the process of attaining its iconic and transcendently representative status, was to use that icon to represent the extremities of other pain and suffering.

Plath did not privilege certain kinds of history over others; unlike some writers her sense of history was not fixed in the distant past of a classical and educated consciousness, but was also composed of contemporaneous events revealed to her through the mass media. Young draws attention to the fact that Plath started using images of the Holocaust just as Adolf Eichmann was standing trial, suggesting that it was this new public attentiveness to the events of the Final Solution which drew Plath to the subject. Young links Plath's work closely with external events, contradicting the view, close to an orthodoxy, that Plath's concerns were only ever internal, egocentric; that she consumed external motifs voraciously as fodder for her interior, self-centred appetite. In 'The Holocaust becomes an Archetype', Young suggests a timetable linking the Eichmann trial with the progress of Plath's work in the last months of her life. In the period between April and December 1961, Eichmann was on trial in Jerusalem, fixing 'public and media attention on the ... neglected details of the Holocaust' (p.118) so that knowledge of and interest in the death camps became more widely available. At that time, Plath was in the process of moving to Devon with Hughes and writing *The Bell Jar*. Eichmann was convicted in December 1961 and executed in April 1962 which is the period when Plath was writing in Devon ('Little Fugue' was written 2 April 1962).

However, I would suggest that, while Holocaust images do become especially apparent in the months before her death, representations of entrapment, masquerade, alienation and victimisation, conflicts surrounding language and silence, and the figure of the Holocaust Jew are intrinsic to her earlier work, appearing in Plath's writing long before this period.

THE POEMS

Reading through Plath's *Collected Poems* chronologically, the sense of dislocation gathers force and momentum, appearing with increasing regularity and frequency, barely offset by positive life experiences. Negation too becomes an almost-constant state; there is a development of subject matter and metaphor which becomes increasingly expressive of the correlation between the private and the public. Plath represents a disjointed world full of a bizarre reality, a strange approach to meaning which recognizes the potential for non-meaning, a consciousness of the inadequacy of language and its corollary, the awesome power of silence. In this context, the use of metaphors which invoke the Holocaust is less evidently a gratuitously cynical use of extreme images to impart some weight or breadth to essentially personal, 'confessional' work, but rather the logical conclusion of many of her concerns. Given Plath's acute consciousness of the shiftiness of language and therefore of 'truth' and 'facts', it is hardly surprising that she should engage with the Holocaust, which provides an unequalled example of the unreliability of words, the power of euphemism, cliché and propaganda, and of, in Rose's phrase, 'the ease with which language can be turned against its intention' (p.67), to obfuscate rather than clarify. Rose draws our attention to the problems posed by language:

> Running through the various texts of Plath's writing – letters, journals, poetry – there is one line that appears as a refrain. It is the first line of a German song that Plath recalls from her childhood ... *'Ich weiss nicht was soll es bedeuten'* ... ['I do not know what it means']. It can be read twice over as the expression of an irreducible hesitancy in language – the foreignness of the German, the incomprehension voiced by the content of the words, the whole line appearing in Plath's writing as the relic of cultural memory which she endlessly fails to retrieve (p.112).

The phrase figures and dramatizes the collapse of meaning by describing and expressing the inability to understand the language, an inability so profound that even its expression cannot be understood. This 'refrain', with its emphasis upon the inaccessibility of understanding, relates unequivocally to the constant search after meaning, the desire to understand which suffuses the writing of Holocaust survivors. In *If This is a Man*, Primo Levi reports a typical exchange which exemplifies this struggle. Having broken off an icicle with which to slake his thirst, Levi has it snatched from his hand by a guard. '"*Warum?*" I asked him in my poor German. "*Hier ist kein warum*" (there is no why here), he replied'.[8] Clearly, in the shadow of the Chimney, Levi's experience of the no-why-ness of life is substantially different from Plath's but there is a correspondence here: both writers grapple with the terrible paradox, 'If we speak, they will not listen to us, and if they listen, they will not understand'.[9]

'The Thin People', written in 1957, might be read as the first appearance in Plath's poetry of a sustained engagement with and attempt to render an otherness which is of a Jewish 'type' along with the increasing effects of the Holocaust upon her own and the world's perceptions. Throughout the poem the speaker refers to a 'we', an 'our'. She is not yet the solitary speaker of the later 'Holocaust poems', but still belongs, she imagines, to a community which, though not directly experiencing the horrors of the war, has yet been in some way both profoundly moved and changed by the experience of the Jews. Like 'the poor', the thin people, 'Are always with us', a description which tends to locate their deprivations in Biblical times. Yet, and paradoxically in spite of their being ever-present, the speaker expresses the general lack of belief in their existence:

> ... They
> Are unreal, we say:
>
> It was only in a movie, it was only
> In a war making evil headlines when we
>
> Were small.

This is an acute recognition and expression of the self-protective means employed by onlookers of the Shoah when the knowledge of the death camps became widespread; it describes the putting-on of an attitude of non-involvement from which this speaker makes no attempt to exonerate or remove herself. There is an awareness too of the bizarre nature of self-excusing argument; the 'It was only', sits oddly next to 'In a war making evil headlines'. This poem also inscribes the way in which the Holocaust became icon and archetype, maintaining and expanding its metaphoric power until it entered into the unconscious of those who had not experienced it other than upon the movie screen in Pathé newsreels and in newspapers.

> They found their talent to persevere
> In thinness, to come, later,
>
> Into our bad dreams, their menace
> Not guns, not abuses,
>
> But a thin silence.

This is an ambiguous representation of the thin people: on the one hand they call up the deepest compassion and sympathy; on the other their presence, diminished and compromised though it is, provokes a sense of unease in those who are not the thin people which might be guilt, shame or anger at the continued reminder of their existence. It seems odd, too, that they may be construed as a menace when their only apparent weapon is silence. The perception of silence as having a significant destructive potential is a theme to which Plath constantly returns: it pre-figures the terrible silences and language failure, the 'Great silence of another order', of 'Little Fugue', and 'Daddy'.

The poem suggests that there is a wilfulness, a determined

obduracy, in the thin people's thinness, 'They ... would not round/ Out their stalky limbs again', but this might not be simple obstinacy; their 'thinness' might be acting for themselves and others as a memorial and a recognition that it is neither possible nor proper to put aside the past. The perseverance of the thin people in maintaining their 'thin' status, their silence and their ability to survive on nothing also connects with the dogged determination to survive expressed in Plath's poem 'Mushrooms'. This community of related metaphors appears with increasing frequency in the body of Plath's work: for this reason it is wrong to suppose that the Holocaust metaphors spring without precedent to appear only in her later poems.

In this poem the thin people are still a 'them': Plath has not taken that step which later leads her to identify the speakers in her poems so closely with the alienated and dispossessed. They exhibit many of the stereotypical attributes associated with Jewishness: their long-suffering ability to wait out adversity; their Job-ness ('empty of complaint'); their prophet status; the nobility of deprivation withstood; the 'insufferable nimbus' (though that 'insufferable' is ambiguous, implying also the self-righteousness of the religious prig); and their scapegoat status. Some of the potentially negative elements of these attributes are offset for a Christian culture by the thin people's correspondence with and likeness to Christ, which is expressed not only through the metaphor of the scapegoat but, more explicitly, their place upon the cross with Christ, signalled by their, 'forever/drinking vinegar from tin cups'.

Paradoxically again, it is their meagreness, their thinness, which propels them out of dreams and thoughts, so that they refuse to vanish with the dawn as sleep gives way to consciousness. Their very insubstantiality, their near-extinction, is what guarantees and confirms their present survival and enables the transition from the place of dreams, myth making and fairy tales into the everyday world of sunlight and wallpaper. Their entrance into the speaker's daylight reality brings a consequent dimming of the world and a diminution of that reality; the speaker becomes conscious that nothing in her life can mitigate or answer the challenge and implications of their presence. This consciousness is terrible: once the speaker has truly recognized and allowed the reality and existence of the thin people, to that extent her own life is diminished, marred and troubled; their movement out from their shadowy past has repercussions for her light-filled present. This poem, written five years before 'Daddy', is near-perfect in its strongly realized, closely argued logic which recognizes the impossibility of keeping the 'thin people' out of the 'real' world and the world-changing consequences of that acknowledgement. It is in this poem that Plath first begins to recognize the Holocaust, not as a personal metaphor, but as the Event that changed everything.

'Little Fugue' opens with an acutely distressing failure of communication which both mirrors the failure of language to describe the Holocaust and recalls the horrific misuse of language adopted by the Nazis:

> The yew's black fingers wag;
> Cold clouds go over.
> So the deaf and dumb
> Signal the blind, and are ignored.

The tree practises a kind of sign language: but, even if its signs could be interpreted, what 'language' would a yew tree use? The conjunction of deafness, dumbness and blindness is instantly recognizable as another re-working of the thin people's silence and the earless, eyeless, voiceless state of the mushrooms. There is a confusion of the proper skills and attributes of the senses leading to an inability to place trust in the form of reality that is revealed while communication is constantly frustrated. This utter confusion leads the speaker to objectify the senses so that touch and smell translocate: 'fingers had the noses of weasels'; she is able to 'see your voice/Black and leafy, as in my childhood', it becomes, 'A yew hedge of orders'; in each case there is a disconnection between the sense – touch, sight, hearing – and the messages it sends and receives.

The speaker cannot 'stop looking' at the blind man but here again communication is only one way: his blindness prevents him from knowing that she is looking at him. And, in this context, 'I couldn't stop looking', implies a kind of voyeurism: she is watching his inability to watch or see, she is conscious of and fixed upon his tragedy, able to indulge her scopophilia and fascination with the failure of sight at the expense of another. The thought of deafness, which is 'something else' and different in its menace from the sightlessness of the blind pianist, provokes in her the observation, 'Such a dark funnel, my father!'. Paradoxically, the speaker believes that the inability to hear makes one more vulnerable to the 'dark funnel' than the inability to see because it is silence and speech, language and its interpretations, which form the reality in which this speaker exists. The speaker's father is revealed as an ambiguous figure in her imagination: he is as much a place and a condition, like the Fatherland, as he is a person.

The confluence of 'father' with 'funnel' is troubling as it conjures disturbing images of a mechanistic process, an inevitable slipping into something: the funnel, perhaps, of the Fatherland's Final Solution. Like part of a huge silo, the 'funnel' conveys the idea of drowning, in grain or in liquid, being one insignificant part of a myriad of particles, of being not a person, but only a number. Thinking of the funnel reminds the speaker of her father's voice, 'A yew hedge of orders', therefore impenetrable and like the yew in the opening line, wagging 'black fingers' in an indecipherable, uninterpretable attempt at communication. Composed 'of orders', the 'yew hedge' is 'Gothic and barbarous, pure German', that is, something terrible and unloving, to the extent that 'Dead men cry from it.'

This line conveys different senses, none of which may be fixed. The dead men may literally 'cry from' the voice, in the sense that the 'yew hedge of orders' has caused them deep unhappiness, perhaps even their deaths. Or they may 'cry from' as in turn away, cry off, refuse, deny, even – if the voice can be seen, as has already been suggested – then to 'cry from' might be to look away from, to ignore the 'yew hedge of orders' and perhaps become implicated in their outcome. This turning away or deep sadness is entirely the fault of the father's voice; the speaker affirms that she is 'guilty of nothing'. Yet in the very act of denial, there is an implication of culpability or confession: the statement, 'I am guilty of nothing' can be read as an avowal of innocence; the refusal to see what is going on around her; or the acceptance that she is guilty of 'nothing', that is, of passivity, of the inaction which leads to tolerance or acceptance. So the speaker recognizes that it is acts of omission as much as acts of commission which make guilt, which make the worst happen. Evil for evil to exist – good men do nothing.

There seem to be at least two silences in operation in 'Little Fugue'. The first, 'There was a silence!' seems to lie between the child and her father and might take the form of an injunction laid upon the child. The second, the 'Great silence of another order' is in existence outside that dyad and is of a totally different 'order'. This might be the silence, the denial, the refusal to see or acknowledge the mechanism of the Final Solution; 'another order' might not only imply a silence of a different size but the 'order' might be the Third Reich and could include the orders imposed upon the Jews and the local populace. It might also refer to the order, that is, the organization of the Final Solution. Order is also numbers, tattooed on the arms of the camps' inhabitants; lines of people; the lists used in selections. And afterwards too, as Rose puts it, 'The silence figured in this poem thus mimics ... a more general postwar silence that was laid on the German tongue' (p.221). At the thought of that monumental silence, the speaker insists that she could not have spoken out: 'I was seven, I knew nothing', and so can not be held responsible for the war or the death camps.

In this context, 'The world occurred' is a phrase of absolute poignancy and painful accuracy to describe the loss of innocence and the advent of experience. The occurrence of 'the world' and its proximity to the seven-year-old child describes a sudden access to all that the world can reveal of terror, torture, death and chaos. The recollection of all that happened when, 'The world occurred' returns the speaker to thoughts of her father: 'You had one leg and a Prussian mind.' Prussian may be not only a description but also a metaphor for military pride, precision, or coldness so that whilst it contains images of gentlemanly virtues and the honour of an officer, it also conveys a sense of threat, as it alludes to the kind of precise capacity for decision-making and planning which were deployed in aspects of the Final Solution:

> Now similar clouds
> Are spreading their vacuous sheets.
> Do you say nothing?

The speaker seems to wonder at the fact that, in spite of the clearly identifiable approach of a similar disaster, her father says, 'nothing'. Whilst this silence is partly explained by his absence it is implied on the basis of previous experience that even if he could speak he might not, and again there is the sense of an untoward, sly silence. This dialogue of nothingness describes the two sides of silence, that is speechlessness and speech which says 'nothing' but takes refuge in banality, neither challenging nor querying what is happening, doing nothing to mitigate or prevent terrible events but instead colluding with or exonerating them.

What Rose calls the 'narrative of silence' (p.221) identified in 'Little Fugue' dramatizes denial and forgetfulness which are the necessary mechanisms of abuse whether perpetrated against an individual or against a community. Knowing nothing, committed, resolved or enjoined to silence, the narrator's recapitulation of memory is, literally, disabled; as the speaker's father faced life with one leg, so the speaker also 'knew nothing', and was 'lame in the memory'. This is dangerous and may allow the circumstances which gave rise to atrocity to occur again.

CONCLUSION

The speakers in Plath's poems occupy paradoxical and uncomfortable positions: they frequently attempt to refute suggestions of guilt, knowledge or complicity in the world's inhumanity – 'I had nothing to do with guilt or anything' ('Electra on Azalea Path'); 'I don't know a thing' ('Face Lift'); 'I am nobody, I have nothing to do with explosions' ('Tulips') while simultaneously recognizing and accepting that it is not possible to stand outside history, to ignore or refuse one's part in world events – 'Some things of this world are indigestible' ('The Zookeeper's Wife'); 'This is no time for the private point of view' ('Candles'). Given the oscillation of those speakers' viewpoints, it is not surprising that criticism of the poems is similarly oscillating.

Plath has frequently been criticized for not being historical enough, for including no social but only personal perspectives. She has been as frequently castigated for inscribing a history which, it is felt, belongs to others. It has been my intention to offer an analysis of the development of Plath's use of Holocaust imagery within her poetry which engages with both criticisms. I have tried to show that, while intensely personal, Plath's poetry was not only personal: that her engagement with the ramifications of domesticity and patriarchy in her own case informed and motivated her wider and painfully accurate social and political perspectives.

I have also been concerned to confront the difficulties of ownership and appropriation which arise in respect of the Holocaust metaphor. In my view the idea that a history may belong to only one constituency is in itself dangerous, suggestive of the terrible boast of SS militiamen which Levi cites in *The Drowned and the Saved*, 'We will be the ones to dictate the history of the Lagers'.[10] While I have argued that there is a case to be made for Plath's 'right' to use the Holocaust metaphor in her poetry, I have also experienced my own misgivings about that use, leading me to recognize the concerns of those who consider that Plath was possibly mistaken, perhaps even arrogant, in her appropriation. These concerns cannot be, nor should be, ignored or easily allayed.

There are at least two elements to take into consideration in this context. The 'material' which is being employed is deeply disturbing and, if the metaphor works, it is hardly surprising that it should provoke a range of – at the least – uncomfortable responses in its readers. It would be odd indeed to read Plath's poetry and to feel no concern about the issues of acceptability and appropriation which arise or to be immune to the realization that this metaphor, unlike the majority of others, carries with it a profound responsibility. And it might be felt by some, after due consideration, that the figures which Plath employed in an attempt to represent her pain metaphorically were really too powerful, too intense to be used in that way. It is completely appropriate that such wariness should be present in the reading of any work, especially that produced by non-Jews and non-survivors, which uses the Holocaust as metaphor.

However, Plath's poetry engages with issues surrounding language, its uses and abuses and the awful power of silence. These concerns, almost inevitably, led her to consider the unique engagement with and abuse of language which made the machinations of the Final Solution possible. The advocacy of silence as the only appropriate or permissible response to the Shoah, contains as many, though different dangers, as the vulgarisation of the Holocaust experience. And it was silence, not articulation of the Event, which was intrinsic to the success of the project of eradication and forgetfulness set in motion by the Nazis. In spite of my misgivings, it is this which forms the basis of my continuing defence of Plath's right to employ the Holocaust as metaphor. Whilst recognizing the degree of disturbance provoked by these issues, I believe, with Young, that the greater danger lies in censorship. Having entered the public domain as archetype, Young affirms in his 'The Holocaust becomes an Archetype' that the Holocaust must be available to all, even to those

> for whom the Holocaust was not 'authentic' experience. For in absorbing these experiences and making them its own, language might be said to remember experience long after all of its authentic witnesses are gone ... To remove the Holocaust from the realm of the imagination, however, to sanctify it and place it off-limits, is to risk excluding it altogether from public consciousness. And this seems to be too high a price to pay for saving it from those who would abuse its memory in inequitable metaphor. Better abused memory in this case, which might then be critically qualified, than no memory at all (p.133).

NOTES

1. Jacqueline Rose, *The Haunting of Sylvia Plath* (London, 1991); James E. Young, 'Jewish Memory in Poland', in Geoffrey H. Hartman (ed.), *Holocaust Remembrance: The Shapes of Memory* (Oxford, 1994); *Writing and Rewriting the Holocaust* (Bloomington, IN, 1988). All page references are in the text.
2. Gillian Banner, '"I began to talk like a Jew": The Holocaust Imagery of Sylvia Plath', (unpublished MA dissertation, University of Sheffield, 1994). All citations of Plath's poetry are from her *Collected Poems* (ed. Ted Hughes) (London, 1981).
3. Anne Stevenson, *Bitter Fame* (London, 1989), p.303.
4. See Hélène Cixous, 'Sorties', in Cixous and Catherine Clément, *The Newly Born Woman* (trans. Betsy Wing) (Manchester, 1987); Peter Stallybrass and Allon White, *The Politics and Poetics of Transgression* (Ithaca, NY, 1986); Julia Kristeva, *Powers of Horror: An Essay on Abjection* (trans. Léon S. Roudiez) (New York, 1982).
5. Sylvia Plath, *Johnny Panic and the Bible of Dreams* (London, 1977), p.178.
6. Primo Levi, *The Drowned and the Saved* (trans. Raymond Rosenthal) (London, 1988), pp.63–4.

7. Tadeusz Borowski, *This Way for the Gas, Ladies and Gentlemen* (trans. Rosemary Vedder) (Harmondsworth, 1979), p.168.
8. Levi, *The Drowned and the Saved*, p.35.
9. Ibid., p.33.
10. Ibid., p.1.

Binjamin Wilkomirski's Fragments and Holocaust Envy: 'Why Wasn't I There, Too?'[1]

SUE VICE

Binjamin Wilkomirski's *Fragments: Memories of a Childhood, 1939-1948* was published (in German in 1995 and in English translation in 1996) to great acclaim as a Holocaust memoir, but has since been shown to be fictional.[2] Wilkomirski claimed to have been born in Riga in 1939, interned in Majdanek and Auschwitz, taken via a Polish orphanage to Switzerland after the war, and urged by his adoptive Swiss parents to forget his experiences. However, it has emerged that the author's name is not really Binjamin Wilkomirski but Bruno Doessekker; Doessekker is a classical musician who was born in Switzerland in 1941, is not of Jewish origin, and was never interned in a camp in occupied Europe. The difference between Wilkomirski's[3] deception and that of other Holocaust writers whose works have turned out to be less autobiographical than they purported to be[4] is that Wilkomirski seems firmly to believe in his own myth of origin. His book is currently only available – as if it were a case history – in the form of an appendix to Stefan Maechler's *The Wilkomirski Affair*, which is a full account of the scandal and an investigation of the author and his text.[5]

In this essay I will argue that, as Binjamin Wilkomirski's *Fragments* is best viewed as the fictional portrait of a child preoccupied with Holocaust realities in the post-war world, it is an unwitting allegory of its own production. I will suggest that in this way *Fragments* is an extreme version of all post-Holocaust subjects' possession by these events – a fact which could partly explain the book's initial reverential reception. This approach seems to me more fruitful than, for instance, trying to locate the texts from which Wilkomirski 'borrowed' his material. An intertextual search of this kind would of course be a viable approach in its own terms, motivated partly by the knowledge that Wilkomirski must have gained his background knowledge from somewhere, and by the uncannily accurate psychological detail which constitutes the child survivor in *Fragments* – not to mention the apparently familiar specifics of certain kinds of incident and description, which I will also discuss.

It is possible to read Wilkomirski's *Fragments* as a novel, and various critics have, implicitly or explicitly, made this case.[6] However, it is difficult not to have an overdetermined view of this work. Certain details which at first seemed to endorse the text's authenticity can well be analysed from a literary standpoint now that we know it is fiction; and it is difficult not to continue to read such details as autobiographical in other ways. First, they may appear to be evidence of the creative process of transmuting and reconstructing historical details that Wilkomirski went through in order to write *Fragments*. Secondly, the text may indeed appear authentically to represent the childhood memory and trauma Wilkomirski claimed. However, it seems clear that while Wilkomirski's memories are not of death camps in Poland, they may be memories of unhappy early experiences in neutral Switzerland, reviewed in the light of later or even unconsciously-held knowledge of the Holocaust. It is true that Wilkomirski underwent the effects of illegitimacy, orphanages and adoption, and perhaps also the betrayal and capricious punishment, followed by exhortations to forget, suffered by his fictional counterpart Binjamin.

The way in which Wilkomirski infused his personal history with the 'external massive trauma' of Holocaust can be seen as an extension of Dori Laub and Nanette C. Auerhahn's argument that the Holocaust has become not only 'the cultural heritage of our times' but 'an unconscious organizing principle' which may affect any western, post-war subject's 'internal representation of reality'.[7] Indeed, Wilkomirski's unconscious tactic seems to have been to enact a reversal of a method widely used in psychological studies of child survivors. While psychologists describe the trauma undergone by children during the Holocaust years in terms of the usual developmental stages and known reactions to trauma, so Wilkomirski described his own history in terms of the Holocaust.[8] On the other hand, child psychologists also discuss the features of the Holocaust that differentiate this 'man-made disaster' from other experiences of trauma undergone by children; these include the targeting of a whole people for extermination.[9] It is precisely these 'unique' features of the Holocaust which Wilkomirski adopted and grafted on to his personal childhood trauma: while he may have felt that to be an illegitimate child in post-war Switzerland was the same as being a member of an ethnic group destined for extermination, this is only his fantasy.

A CHILD'S-EYE VIEW

Fragments describes three time-periods: the wartime experiences of the child Binjamin, who is aged around three when deported to Majdanek; the child's post-war experiences in orphanages and just after adoption; and brief observations from the present about the adult Binjamin's experiences. Inevitably in a text which narrates past events, there is a split between the narrator who tells the story and character who acts in it, even in a first-person novel like *Fragments*. Such a division is often emphasized in the effort to represent the Holocaust: although novels in which protagonist and narrator are united are uncommon due to the necessary temporal separation of action and writing,[10] the combined effect of representing the Holocaust and a child's-eye view tends to exacerbate this separation. Although it may seem as if *Fragments* represents the viewpoint of a child, it is in fact narrated by an adult in the present, using his younger self as a focalizer. Yet the way in which this split appears in *Fragments* is distinctive, and marks it off from the efforts made by other authors of Holocaust fiction – including Ida Fink and Louis Begley[11] – to reconcile the past and the present.

Despite initial appearances, the discourse of *Fragments* is almost always a mixture of the adult narrator's voice with that of the child protagonist, and not the latter by itself. As the critic Naomi Sokoloff points out, the direct citation of a child's language in fiction is rare[12] and when it does appear at once raises the spectre of aestheticisation, especially in quoted speech. This is partly because the author is almost invariably an adult and therefore must be inventing such language; and because of the temporal distance between narrator and character in first-person novels. In *Fragments* the child's voice in the text's first two time-periods is represented by a free indirect discourse which reads like a paraphrase using the present tense; for instance, about the death of Binjamin's father: 'I'm sad and very afraid because he turned away from me, but I feel that he didn't do it because he doesn't love me any more. His own upset must have been much too much for him, and he only turned away because something unknown was even stronger than he was' (p.7). Clearly these are not the words of a small child, but the words of the narrator attempting to represent the child's viewpoint. This is scarcely even irony,[13] as it is so clear to the reader that Binjamin's father has not 'turned away' but has been killed by an armoured vehicle (p.6). As well as representing a child's viewpoint, this method economically conveys information about the child: his inability to understand the moment of death is set against his sophistication in not interpreting the 'turning away' of death as emotional abandonment.

I would describe the technique of this passage as that of *pathetic irony*, in the sense of the irony of pathos. In this context, irony's usual gap between ostensible meaning and actual sense takes on a specific slant, that of a child's viewpoint set against adult understanding. The gap between the two here – Binjamin thinks his father has 'turned away', while the reader knows he has been violently killed – has pathos' effect of generating great sympathy and pity for the child. The older Binjamin narrates his younger self in such a way as to maximize the pathetic irony of many other episodes in *Fragments*. Each time Binjamin is tricked by an apparently friendly adult – the female soldier who takes him to Majdanek, the guard whose response to Binajmin's question is to strike him in the face with a whip, another guard who picks Binjamin up only to hurl him against a wall, and a third who appears to be playing football but kills another child – the reader knows from the start what the outcome will be. Moreover, the effect of each episode, which reveals Binjamin's initial innocent trust and is followed by a cruel disappointment, depends entirely upon such pathetic irony.

Wilkomirski's aesthetic choices in such passages have further implications now that we know the genesis of his writing. Like many passages from *Fragments* when quoted out of context, the father's death sounds like a description of the realm of the unconscious: the father has 'turned away' from his son, just as later the mother lying in the barracks, 'a body under gray covers' (p.49), may also represent an image of abandonment or death.[14] The child's failure to understand his parents' death is both plausible in the context of a Holocaust novel and provides a convenient alibi for the inventor of such a fiction: any generality and lack of historical detail arises from the child's viewpoint.

Further, we may be led by the episode of the father's death to speculate on the origins of Wilkomirski's impulse to write *Fragments*; the longing for an ideal father is recorded many times, in the figures of the brother Motti, the protector Jankl, and even the teacher Bercovici ('the kind of father I would have wished for myself', p.152), and also here, just before the first father-figure dies: 'In a shadowy corner, the outline of a man in hat and coat, his sweet face smiling at me' (p.5). Is this the 'shadowy corner' of a room in Riga, distant memory, the unconscious of a young boy – or the textual impulse of a troubled adult, staging the tragic death of a loving father?[15] Later, the fruit cellar and coal furnace at the house of Binjamin's adoptive parents act more clearly as an allegory of the author's state of mind: 'Wooden bunks for children, oven doors for children, it's all too much. As I thought this, I suddenly raced up the cellar stairs and into my room. ... The camp's still here. Everything's still here. ... The camp's still here, they just hid it' (p.125). Not only does the Holocaust world lurk beneath the surface of the everyday world, but 'they' deny its existence.

The representation of a child's viewpoint using the kind of paraphrase we saw in relation to the death of Binjamin's father characterizes the construction of the child throughout *Fragments*. For instance, 'There's a station in my memory. We have to go through a barrier, papers are shown and looked at – maybe false ones. Sighs of relief and we're standing on a station platform and it's sunny. I have the feeling that a danger has passed, but I don't know what danger' (p.8). In this extract, the narrator's interpretations are voiced – 'maybe false ones' – and more of a distance is maintained from the character despite the present tense; ignorance is described rather than a rendition given of the thoughts the child does have: 'I don't know what danger'. Again, for the reader such a statement may do double duty: as the representation of a child's-eye view, and as another alibi for the Holocaust novelist, or faker of testimonies. Because he is representing the world of a very young child, the novelist does not have to provide authenticating details here, just as later he does not name Auschwitz but allows it to be inferred that Binjamin has ended up there.

Such an omission leaves it up to the reader to work out that the protagonist is an Auschwitz survivor, while making an effort to represent the boy's memory accurately. This is a complex intertwining of a convincing representation with the mechanics of writing an imitation-testimony novel. The reader is left to fill in many details in both scenarios, most obviously on the many occasions when the young Binjamin says he cannot understand (pp.10, 76), notes that he has slept through a significant occasion (pp.14, 89, 107), or that he is always the last to know anything (p.107). Many statements in the text work both ways – as mimesis *and* as metafiction – ranging from the ambiguously imprecise, 'According to the logic of *the plan*, and the orderly rules *they* devised to carry it out, we should have been dead' (p.4, my italics), to the book's afterword, which is at once authenticatingly and underminingly general:

> I wrote these fragments of memory to explore both myself and my earliest childhood; it may also have been an attempt to set myself free. And I wrote them with the hope that perhaps other people in the same situation would find the necessary support and strength to cry out their own traumatic childhood memories, so that they too could learn that really are people today who will take them seriously, and who want to listen and to understand.
>
> They should know that they are not alone (p.155).

These final words were added at the suggestion of the book's German publishers Suhrkamp Verlag, who had been contacted by the journalist Hanno Helbling expressing doubts about Wilkomirski's past.[16] The afterword resounds with echoes of the recovered memory of child abuse: the reader may wonder exactly what the 'same situation' is that others may also be in.

THE IRONY OF PATHOS

Fragments is a highly patterned text and not at all the 'unadorned' and 'unselfconscious' work described in the blurb for the British edition. Such artistic structuring paradoxically increased the impression of authenticity given by this text before Wilkomirski's deception became known. What I have called the 'pathetic irony' of the scene in which Binjamin's father dies is a repeated feature from which the text draws its strength. In many scenes misunderstanding or innocence are shown rather than described, and this has an aesthetic as much as an ethical effect. The wartime betrayals Binjamin undergoes at the hands of camp guards who he thinks are friendly, but whose games turn out to be deadly (pp.17, 37), are matched by post-war instances of pathetic irony. In the orphanages Binjamin misinterprets the meaning of cheese-rinds left on a table (p.23), bread on plates (p.45), and even a bedroom (p.24). The post-war pathetic irony has just the same structure as the more brutal wartime episodes: Binjamin's inability to understand, his guilelessness and good faith betrayed, are revealed to the reader by ensuring that the latter knows more than Binjamin does. As readers, we are never left in confusion ourselves about the emotional meaning of an episode, due to these aesthetic strategies, however confused Binjamin himself may be.

Critics have mentioned the defamiliarizing effect in Holocaust writing of using a child's-eye viewpoint to represent events which the reader must decode,[17] and in *Fragments* defamiliarization is a twofold process. In the camp-time episodes, the genocidal world with which most readers are familiar is seen afresh by a child. Binjamin's most startling conclusion is that he need not have lived in hiding or behind the fence and that his suffering was pointless: 'Was it all about nothing?' (p.116). In this sense *Fragments* acts like other experimental works about the Holocaust in combating a sense of image-fatigue and over-familiarity with atrocity.[18] Secondly, in the post-war world of *Fragments* atrocity continues to be defamiliarized – but by linking it with the ordinary. This is the reverse of the usual pattern, where defamiliarization acts, according to the Russian Formalist critic Victor

Shklovsky, 'to make objects "unfamiliar"' in order that we should see them afresh; otherwise, 'habitualization devours works, clothes, furniture ... and the *fear of war*.'[19] Binjamin is shown the fruit-cellar by his adoptive Swiss mother but sees it as another camp barracks; at school, William Tell is not a Swiss national hero but an SS officer trying to shoot a child (pp.130–32); and, most strikingly, a ski-lift is a machine of death (p.142).

Yet again it is hard not to have a doubled view of the defamiliarizing process at work here. Seeing the everyday, myths, and even buildings as secretly infused with genocidal meaning may be exactly how Wilkomirski viewed the world in order to translate his experience of adoption in Switzerland into incarceration in Majdanek and Auschwitz. Survivors may react badly to words like 'transport' which have acquired extra historicized meaning,[20] but in Wilkomirski's case this seems to be the novelization of adult 'sado-masochistic identification'[21] with Holocaust victims into the response of young Binjamin (p.120). The structure of *Fragments* leads us to imagine that the child's incomprehension of whip-wielding guards was followed by an acclimatization into the camp world which meant he could later not understand the actions of cooking or eating an orange (p.121), even though the events are not always narrated in this order. We hear Jankl's name first in the context of the orphanage, where he seems to be an idealized protector for Binjamin, who cannot understand why the cheese rinds have been discarded: 'Never ever leave food unguarded, that's what Jankl always told me' (p.22). Only later do we encounter Jankl as a character in the camps (p.59).

This seems to be reversed chronology, as by the time Binjamin arrives in the orphanage Jankl has been dead for many months; but perhaps the disordered chronology is in fact the right way round, and the remembered/fantasied protector of whom we read first gives rise to the protector in the camp whom we encounter nearly 40 pages later, but at an earlier stage of the protagonist's life. This shows narratively what we know to be the case for Wilkomirski: rather than *preceding* the orphanage world, his knowledge of the death-camp world must have *followed* it. We are reading a work of reconstruction rather than one of memory, and only our assumptions about biographical and historical chronology lead us to make Wilkomirski's disordered story straight. In other words, the Holocaust must have reminded Wilkomirski of the orphanage and adoption, not the other way round. It is as if only a historical trauma like the Holocaust could give Wilkomirski's own experiences an adequate context.

This argument about reversed cause and effect involves speculation about the construction of *Fragments*, and the assumption that, as in the case of Georges Perec's novel *W or the Memory of Childhood*,[22] some of the fictional material is more obviously biographical than other parts. Wilkomirski describes learning about the Holocaust at school: he 'asked endless questions, followed up every suggestion to get hold of additional books, which [he] then secretly read' (p.146). Even if Wilkomirski had been a survivor rather than a novelist, such reading would have helped to shape his own memories; as it is, this reading must have actually *constituted* those memories. This is another case of Freud's belated memory, or *Nachträglichkeit*,[23] but a literary one in which one's own past may gain different meaning when considered with the hindsight of historical research.

TEXTUAL FRAGMENTS: *GUNS AND BARBED WIRE*

Although it is hard to say with any certainty what the schoolboy or adult Wilkomirski read about the Holocaust,[24] it seems likely that it is precisely fragments of other texts which make up the body of *Fragments*. Thomas Geve's *Guns and Barbed Wire: A Child Survives the Holocaust* is unusual in being the memoir of a child's survival in Auschwitz-Birkenau.[25] It is easy to imagine that Wilkomirski read it, as it is a classic work published as early as 1958.[26] Although Thomas Geve was brought up in Berlin and was older than Wilkomirski's invented Binjamin – Geve was born in 1929 and Thomas in *Guns and Barbed Wire* is able to recall a pre-war world – he too was from the Baltics and his text was published under a pseudonym. One of the most striking scenes in *Fragments* – which remains so even now that we know it is fiction – is Binjamin's visit to his mother in a death-camp barracks (pp.46–51). His inability to understand either the signifier or the signified of maternity combines defamiliarization with pathetic irony: 'And what did "mother" mean? I couldn't remember. ... One of the children had once said that if you have a mother, she belongs just to you! So this woman belonged to me, just me? I wondered' (pp.48–9).

This is a subjective defamiliarization. It does not ask us to look again at the concept of motherhood but rather, with the usual pathos, to imagine the mind of a child who cannot understand it. Indeed the text tends rather to uphold than question the notion of biological motherhood ('my mother's betrayer', the boy calls himself when made to address his adoptive parent as 'mother' (p.123)), as has Wilkomirski in his televised and published denunciations of his step-parents.

In *Guns and Barbed Wire* Geve also describes a fleeting moment spent with his mother, which is prefaced by Thomas receiving a letter and a similar, although briefer, consideration of the idea of 'a mother': 'News of my luck [in receiving a letter from mother] spread quickly and I was soon surrounded by dozens of roommates who, claiming to be my best friends, wanted to hear details – but above all to see the word 'mother'. ... Someone had found a mother, the being dearest to all of us' (p.70). Like Binjamin's, Thomas's mother 'wanted to give me some bread' (p.71), but, unlike Binjamin, Thomas refuses it. Thomas is 13 at this time, but a prototype closer in age to Binjamin is mentioned just a few pages after the mother incident: 'At the women's camp of Birkenau lived the only Jewish child, a boy of four' (p.77). Unlike Binjamin, this child is seen from the outside; he is 'popular with guards and prisoners alike', is tattooed and reacts with articulate aggression to Thomas's curiosity. However, it is possible to imagine Wilkomirski seeing in this small figure in Geve's text – the 'only' child in Birkenau – an image for his own suffering, and proceeding to invest it with subjectivity, just as he later claimed to recognize himself in a photograph of a Cracow orphanage.[27] Later on in *Guns and Barbed Wire*, when he has been deported to Buchenwald, Geve mentions another very young child who was hidden under the floorboards of a barrack: 'That', I was told, 'is the kid they keep hiding from the SS. ... Every time there is an inspection they gag the poor devil and tuck him away underneath the floorboards. What a life!' (p.178).[28] This could be what Wilkomirski remembers reading in portraying Binjamin's conditions at Auschwitz-Birkenau:

> For a time I wasn't allowed out of the barracks. I didn't know why. When it was time for roll call and everyone hurried outside, I was forbidden to go too. Each time someone grabbed hold of me and pushed me into a corner, or maybe it was a hole. A cover was put over me, and then a plank, and I wasn't supposed to move (p.99).

It seems that Binjamin is not allowed out because he is being hidden under the floorboards, although he experiences it as a punishment: 'I didn't want to be left alone. I was afraid and began to cry. A slap soon took care of that' (p.99). Geve notes that the four-year-old he encountered at Buchenwald was 'the saddest character I had ever come across, abnormal in his physique, behavior and speech. He staggered along like some weak, wounded animal and uttered cries in German–Polish–Yiddish gibberish'. These epithets sound like an observer's description of the child Wilkomirski represents from within: Binjamin too is 'the saddest', abnormal, weak and wounded. *Fragments* opens with a description of Binjamin's version of a mother-tongue, the same 'gibberish' spoken by the boy Geve mentions: 'My language has its roots in the Yiddish of my eldest brother, Mordechai, overlaid with the Babel-babble of an assortment of children's barracks in the Nazis' death camps in Europe ... it was no great loss that I more or less forgot this gibberish which lost its usefulness with the end of the war (p.3).

It is tempting to read even Geve's first impressions of Auschwitz – 'for miles ... only the empty field. Mist rising in the distance, to herald the dusk, hid whatever was lurking there' (p.35) – as the precursor to the young Binjamin's of a second camp which he does not name: 'Outside the big fence, there was nothing anymore, just flat fields and a pale wood, which was mostly covered in mist' (p.98). The narrator of *Fragments* certainly seems to expect the reader to be able to recognize Auschwitz from the minimal description of this new camp, set in surroundings as 'flat as a plate' (p.97).

However, the apparent congruence of detail between Geve's *Guns and Barbed Wire* and Wilkomirski's *Fragments* can work in at least two ways. It can suggest that Geve's memoir is one of Wilkomirski's intertexts; or simply that both texts portray Auschwitz, Geve's from memory and Wilkomirski's from reading. Norman Geras, in his article 'The True Wilkomirski', suggests that although we now know that the boy's experiences in *Fragments* did not actually happen, 'they are of a kind that happened, or at least that could have happened'. Geras goes on to argue that

> The philosophical distinction between 'types' and 'tokens' may be helpful here. If we take a particular case – [for instance], the boy's meeting with his mother – one can say that, had *Fragments* been a genuine memoir, the author would there have been describing an actual token of a type of event which occurred in the camps ... But if the book must instead be taken as a novel, then the same episode has to be read as describing only a fictional token of the relevant type.[29]

In other words, in *Guns and Barbed Wire* the meeting between son and mother is 'an actual token of a type of event which occurred in the camps', while the meeting in *Fragments* is 'only a fictional token of the relevant type'. The 'type' of event here might be described as, 'brief reunions between parents and children, or between family members, or simply between people well known to one another'.[30]

Indeed, the distinction between fictional and actual tokens can act as a critical alternative to trying to track down Wilkomirski's intertexts. For instance, the fact that there is a mentor to the protagonist named Yankel in Harold Gordon's childhood memoir *The Last Sunrise*[31] does not necessarily mean that this is the text from which Wilkomirski took the name for his character 'Jankl', but that both texts are using a name as a token: fictionally in Wilkomirski's case, actually in Gordon's.

Other such tokens include an incident related by Judith Hemmendinger in which young boys liberated from Buchenwald were reminded of the camps by the converted sanatorium they were taken to; Edgar Stern's Holocaust dreams, conveying the Wilkomirskian emotions of both guilt and envy at the fate of camp inmates: '"I could have been them!!" I screamed as I awoke, trying at the same time to shake a horrible feeling that I *wanted* to be them'; and, as if following the fictional Leon's great emphasis on the oranges which only exist in Palestine in Ilse Aichinger's novel *Herod's Children*, Wilkomirski undergoes an unhappy moment at his adoptive parents' when presented with an unrecognizable orange.[32] Once more, these instances – and reading either Holocaust literature or child psychologists' writings on survivors always produces many more – remain at the level of tokens, not intertextual moments.

Furthermore, even if they could be said to share the details mentioned above, the tone of Geve's memoir *Guns and Barbed Wire* could not be more different from Wilkomirski's in the fictional *Fragments*. In the former, Thomas associates youth not with incomprehension and betrayal but with hope and energy: 'It was only our youth we were aware of, the dynamic urge for progress that could never be wrong' (p.133); 'It was the present [we youngsters] were concerned with' (p.136). Unlike Binjamin, he is old enough to recall a 'lost world' and to experience the liberation of Buchenwald as just that (190). The post-war period is portrayed as an idyllic 'New World' whose future will be forged by youth (p.195). The narrator uses an irony which is more a matter of tone than that in *Fragments*: 'Even the hatefully big trousers had joined the conspiracy by slipping down towards its allies, the cold, splashing puddles' (p.38); 'Hardly having grasped the sardines' artful way of lying on one's side, straight with your head enclosed by both neighbors' feet (a must for bunk sleepers) ... ' (p.40). This is an irony of distance and control, in contrast to the pathetic irony of *Fragments*. Geve's text does not consist of Wilkomirski's tripartite, confused (and artful) narration, but is full of clear detail, reconstructed dialogue, footnotes giving historical detail, and even approving remarks on the behaviour of others: an Auschwitz block elder has an 'unconquerable sense of justice' (p.91), while suffering 'makes veterans respect each other' (p.104).

THREADS OF THE PAST

> 'I stare in horror at the picture, at this man called Tell, who's obviously a hero, and he's holding a strange weapon and aiming it, and he's aiming it at a child, and the child's just standing there, not knowing what's coming' (p.129).

The 'defamiliarization' in *Fragments* of the image of William Tell aiming at an apple on his son's head is not as simple as it seems. At first it appears that this is another example of Binjamin's inability to separate past from present, because no one has told him the war is over. In the quotation above Binjamin is asked to describe a picture of the Swiss hero at school, but he still associates the term 'hero' with the Nazis: 'Aren't heroes always the people who kill you?' (p.128).

One might take the defamiliarization of the image of this Swiss hero further, and argue that Binjamin is perceiving the mythic subtext of Tell's story, which reads like a version of Abraham's willingness to sacrifice his son Isaac. However, once again this is a subjective defamiliarization. It is not that Tell is to be seen in new terms; this 'familiar' image is just a pretext for an insight into the mind of an unhappy young child. Binjamin sees Tell as an SS man – 'The hero's shooting the children' (p.129) – but insists to the teacher, who he suddenly sees as the block warden from Majdanek, that something is 'not normal' as bullets would not usually be wasted on a child (p.130).

Perhaps this scene is an allegory of a misunderstood person trying to keep alive the memory of an atrocity Swiss society would sooner forget. (It appears that this atrocity is the Holocaust; however, there may also be buried traces in *Fragments* of what Frances Stonor Saunders calls 'The scandal of the Swiss slave-children', who were children from poor families sold into labour and often horribly mistreated; Saunders quotes a historian whose view on the cover-up is, '"It's just like the story of the Jews ... during the war"'.)[33] However, Binjamin's inability to recognize aesthetic representation is also striking in this episode. He sees not an image but a fact; the signifier is the signified:

> The warden ... explains that Tell isn't shooting children, he's shooting the apple on the child's head. I look at the child. The child's barefoot. No shoes, not even rags on his feet, he's so poor. ... His feet will freeze to the ground at rollcall. And look at his clothes: only a long shirt, tied around the middle, sleeveless, no trousers – he can't survive. And anyway – SS men don't shoot apples – that's just stupid. It's just another piece of cruelty: the child's hungry, and he's not allowed to eat the apple. A child

who's about to die doesn't need an apple. Tell will eat it once he's killed him (p.133).

This is not defamiliarization but fantasy. It represents a collapsing of different historical periods – Tell in the thirteenth century, the war, post-war – the fictional reason for which is that no one informed Binjamin the war was over. It also suggests that this is precisely what Wilkomirski has accomplished in his own fantasy: the elision of temporal differences, the substitution of the signifier for the signified, the re-attachment of particular emotions to different images, and a hallucination that the war did not take place between particular dates but is still waging. It is tempting once more to search for an intertextual origin for the William Tell episode. Carl Friedman's novel *Nightfather* was originally published in Dutch in 1991; in a scene highly reminiscent of that in *Fragments* the young daughter of a survivor draws a picture at school:

> 'A man flying through the air!' The teacher smiles, as she bends over my drawing.
> 'He isn't flying', I tell her, 'he's hanging. See, he's dead, his tongue is blue. And these prisoners have to look at him as a punishment. My father is there, too. Here, he's the one with the big ears'.
> 'That's nice', says the teacher.
> 'It's not', I say. 'They're starving and now they have to wait a long time for their soup'. But she's already moved on to the next desk.[34]

In *Nightfather* as in *Fragments*, a scene is transformed by a child preoccupied with the Holocaust into something horrifying and malign, although in the former the teacher remains oblivious to the child's violent imagery. It is significant that *Nightfather* is a novel about the second generation – that is, children who did not experience the Holocaust years themselves, but for whom the Holocaust has become a very strong 'unconscious organizing principle' through parental influence.

Wilkomirski's William Tell scene is like a depiction of the state of mind of someone similar to a second-generation survivor, but to whom society as a whole, rather than a parent, has transmitted what Auerhahn and Laub call a sense of 'post-Auschwitz reality'. They characterize this as 'a paradoxical and intensely charged mixture of life proceeding undisturbed in its natural rhythms alongside experiences of bleak terror and glimpses of life's disruption' (p.164).[35] The classroom scenes in both *Fragments* and *Nightfather* illustrate a 'glimpse' of such disruption. Stefan Maechler argues that 'a genuine former child camp-inmate' experiencing fear at the image of William Tell would precisely *not* know that the fear resulted from confusing Tell with the SS, as Binjamin does;[36] in this sense also the protagonist of *Fragments* resembles a second- rather than a first-generation survivor.

The notion of reversed temporal sequence in *Fragments* appears to be undermined but is actually upheld by the way in which the two different time-sequences – wartime and post-war – in the text are linked. These links appear to move from the present back to the past. For instance, Binjamin cries for the first time in years when travelling between orphanages, and this reminds him of 'the last time I'd really cried':[37]

> Frau Grosz was nowhere to be seen ... I felt helpless and alone. For the first time in a long time, I began to cry. It felt strangely warm as the tears ran down my face ... when was the last time I'd really cried because I was so sad? ...
>
> We were all sitting around the table in the main room, and for some reason I was crying. Motti, my eldest brother, stood up and bent over me. His face was full of love and concern, his broad back curved down over me like a great safe shield, and I listened to his comforting voice.
>
> A blissful moment – I had to cry all over again.
>
> But Motti had gone away a long time ago. So had my other brothers. In their place, a strange woman was suddenly bending over me. I looked up (pp.18–19).

Binjamin's memory is narrated in the present tense and the 'comforting' figure of Motti bent over the little boy is replaced by 'a strange woman', also narrated in the present tense, who is 'suddenly bending over me' (p.19). At first in this scene crying in the present at the loss of Frau Grosz recalls crying in the past; but then, more unusually, Motti's act of bending over in the past appears not to precede but to *foreshadow* or even conjure up the 'strange woman's' similar act in the present. Chronology is not presented in order here, which both offers authenticity and suggests a reconstruction.

If this episode bears any relation to Wilkomirski's own memories, then it seems to follow the temporal construction of a similar incident in Saul Friedländer's Holocaust memoir *When Memory Comes*. The adult narrator recalls a feverish dream from a period in his childhood when he was living in hiding, in which he imagined that his mother had been restored to him: 'I ran to her, threw myself into her arms sobbing, felt the coolness of her fingers on my face ... I opened my eyes: it was Madame Chancel stroking my face to comfort me'.[38]

Just as in the episode from *Fragments*, so in *When Memory Comes* it is the last detail to be recounted which is in fact the initiating one. Despite the way in which these episodes are told, Madame Chancel's stroking fingers conjured up the memory of Saul's mother, and the strange woman reminded Binjamin of Motti – not the other way round. In Saul's case, this effect was caused by a feverish hallucination, but in Binjamin's case the narrative's dream-logic supports the notion that Motti is a reconstruction who never existed. The same is true of the ski-lift death-machine, which Binjamin dreams about (pp.38–9) before he sees it: 'My nightmare was coming true' (p.141). Again it seems that the text's apparently disordered chronology is actually the right way round: seeing the ski-lift must have inspired the dreams.

Links between scenes, like the moment of crying and the bending figure mentioned above, are present throughout *Fragments*, despite the suggestion given by a form split between past and present that such links are missing. In fact, the past is not divided from but closely connected to the present. In Geve's *Guns and Barbed Wire* one result of the protagonist's youth, according to the narrator, is that he is constantly thinking of the future and looking forward to liberation; but in *Fragments* the future turns out to be almost as bad as the past. The narrator says of his younger self, 'No matter how hard I tried, I couldn't pull these two worlds together. I hunted in vain for some thread to hold onto' (p.68). But I have been tracing memories in *Fragments* hanging by just such 'threads'. Binjamin even checks his own scar, a physical link with the past, during an unpleasant moment at the orphanage to remind himself of an injury (p.55). The past appears only to be accessible through the matching affronts of the present, yet that past can also offer a means of escape from the present because it seems more real: 'I could only get away from this unbearable strange present by going back to the world and the images of my past. Yes, they were almost as unbearable, but they were familiar, at least I understood their rules' (p.68).

Once more, this is defamiliarization that is not what it seems. It is strange for the reader to imagine a person for whom the camp world was preferable to the post-war world; but the narrator's remark here could be a comment on the process of hallucinatory rather than historical memory, if we change a possessive pronoun: 'I could only get away from this unbearable strange present by going back to the world and the images of *the* past.' In the post-war world, ordinary events – shoes being put out to dry (p.128), central heating (p.125) – are infused with evil in just the way that, before, malevolence went unrecognized. I would suggest that this complementary pattern exists to maximize the effect of pathetic irony, and also to represent a temporal progress which is in fact psychic regression – there has been no day of liberation for Wilkomirski.

One such memorial 'thread' is inspired by Binjamin's awe at a 'big platter holding a mountain of bread' (p.45) at the orphanage which segues – through the bread's scent – backwards into the time 'before' and to the primal meeting with his mother, whose gift of bread taught him the meaning of the word (p.50). The unlikeliness that this was Binjamin's first encounter with bread is counterbalanced by the psychic truth in his knowledge of the importance of this gift. The bread may be what Freud would call a 'screen' or supplementary memory of having had something sweet-smelling and nourishing restored to him. In a psychotherapeutic investigation into the ego-organization of child survivors of the Holocaust, Yolanda Gampel notes that all her interviewees had 'held fast within himself' to something from home in order to endure – either literal objects like photographs, or memories, including those of tastes, smells and food from before the war.[39] For Binjamin this process is reversed. He only eats the bread his mother gives him during the war, and it is this food he recalls afterwards. The bread is not the '"symbol of normal everyday life"' one of Gampel's interviewees mentions, as Binjamin's extreme youth means he can recall no such prelude to dislocation, giving him fewer internal resources to call upon – as his apparent ignorance of bread suggests. And of course on another level we know that for Wilkomirski there was no 'normal everyday life' of this kind anyway.

These links between past and present produce different effects from those in other texts about Holocaust childhoods which also alternate past and present narration, for instance Perec's *W or the Memory of Childhood*, or Friedländer's non-fictional *When Memory Comes*. In *Fragments*, it seems that reversed chronology and the movement between traumatic moments during the war and afterwards reveal more about the text's production than about a child survivor. Our knowledge of Bruno Doessekker's masquerade as Binjamin Wilkomirski only supports what the text itself reveals: that the past and the present are not divided; everything in the present conceals, sometimes imperfectly, the reality of the Holocaust world; there has been no liberation; and everyone will doubt one's tale. Indeed, other children in the orphanage or at school mock Binjamin for trying to reenact moments from the camps, by wearing rags on his feet (p.56), fleeing from the ski-lift (p.144),[40] or begging in public (p.137).

In yet another paragraph which reads in hindsight like a confession of inauthenticity, the narrator of *Fragments* discusses his youthful researches into 'the Nazi system and the Second World War' (p.143):

> I hoped I would find answers for the pictures that came from my broken childhood memory some nights to stop me going to sleep or to give me terrifying nightmares. ... I wanted to subject [my own earliest memories] to intelligent reason, and arrange them in a pattern that made sense. But the longer I spent at it, the more I learned and absorbed empirically, the more elusive the answer – in the sense of what actually happened – became (p.147).

There is an opposition posed here between personal memory and historical fact, although the narrator expects the historical events of which he learns to tell him something about his 'earliest memories'. In other words, the history of the Holocaust can provide a pattern to explain incoherent memories, and to give a well-documented background for a childhood which otherwise has a purely random, personal meaning. Although the protagonist may wonder if his wartime experiences were 'all about nothing' (p.116), we know that such experiences certainly were not about 'nothing', even if they were also not about the historical event they purport to concern. Maybe this is the effect of the text's varieties of defamiliarization. They make the reader fill in what is missing – ranging from such details as the name of the second camp, to a Jewish background for Binjamin and the historical context of the Holocaust itself – and thus overlook the most strikingly absent fact: Binjamin Wilkomirski himself.

Fragments is not what it seems in several ways, starting of course with its author's imposture. The details which constitute its horrifying world often do double duty as both authenticating *and* deconstructing, so that at times *Fragments* reads like an indirect account of its own creation. The varieties of defamiliarization and pathetic irony that characterize the text support this effect. The world of a traumatized child it depicts is also extremely effective, as the book's original reception shows. This is not only because of the textual effects Wilkomirski deploys, but also because of the uncanny way that what he describes does often match up to readers' knowledge of the behaviour of young survivors or their offspring. I have mentioned some of these instances already; and Judith Hemmendinger cites another, in describing the reactions of a second-generation child to knowledge of her parents' experiences. In *Fragments*, this is also how Binjamin reacts in the post-war world, again like a second-generation child:

Recurring visions of terror haunted her. She imagined herself in a concentration camp where she would be killed. Her world consisted of hostility and danger and people who were bad and full of underlying aggression. The terrible blanket of silence that was spread over Auschwitz seemed to confirm her convictions.[41]

Auherhahn and Laub discuss the effect of Holocaust knowledge on later generations, and how individuals will take from this knowledge a 'sense of unsafety' and 'identification with the Holocaust survivor and his shattered world',[42] particularly if they have experienced anything at all analogous, such as the death of a loved one. The great initial success and continuing effect that *Fragments* has on its readers can be explained by its animation of such an identification – which for Wilkomirski shades into envy – and its combination of psychological accuracy with a Holocaust background. Wilkomirski's text is a perfect allegory of its own genesis and reception.

NOTES

1. Binjamin Wilkomirski, *Fragments: Memories of a Childhood, 1939–1948* (trans. Carol Brown Janeway) (London, 1996), p.151. All further page references are in the text.
2. See Philip Gourevitch,'The Memory Thief', *New Yorker*, 14 June 1999, pp.47–58; Elena Lappin, 'The Man with Two Heads', *Granta* Vol.66 (1999), pp.7–65.
3. I shall continue to refer to 'Wilkomirski' – the name is in effect a *nom de plume*.
4. See, for instance, the award-winning novel *The Hand that Signed the Paper*, originally published as the work of Helen Demidenko (Sydney, 1994), reissued in 1995 under the author's real name, Helen Darville. Darville pretended to be of Ukrainian origin, like the perpetrators in her novel (the affair is discussed in Sue Vice, *Holocaust Fiction* (London, 2000)).
5. Stefan Maechler, *The Wilkomirski Affair: A Study in Biographical Truth* (trans. John E. Woods) (New York, 2001). Maechler concludes unambiguously that Doessekker has written a work of fiction.
6. Andrea Reiter, 'The Holocaust as Seen Through the Eyes of Children', in A. Leak and G. Paizis (eds.), *The Holocaust and the Text: Speaking the Unspeakable* (Basingstoke, 2000), pp.84, 94, written before the unmasking; Mary Jacobus, 'Border Crossings: Traumatic Reading and Holocaust Memory', *Psychoanalysis and the Scene of Reading* (Oxford, 1999), written before but amended afterwards; and Sue Vice, '*Fragments* as Fiction', *Jewish Quarterly*, Vol.178 (2000), pp.51–4.
7. Dori Laub and Nanette C. Auerhahn, 'Reverberations of Genocide: Its Expression in the Conscious and Unconscious of Post-Holocaust Generations', in Steven A. Luel and Paul Marcus (eds.), *Psychoanalytic Reflections on the Holocaust: Selected Essays* (New York, 1984), p.153. Their concern is with children whose parents were not survivors but the contemporaries of survivors: Doessekker has gone one better in constructing *himself* and not just his parents as a survivor. See also Stefan Maechler, 'Wilkomirski the Victim: Individual Remembering as Social Interaction and Public Event', *History and Memory*, Vol.13, No.2 (2001), pp.59–95.
8. See, for instance, Hans Keilson, *Sequential Traumatization in Children: A Clinical and Statistical Follow-up of the Jewish War Orphans in the Netherlands*, with the collaboration of Herman R. Sarphatie (trans. Yvonne Bearne, Hilary Coleman, Deirdre Winter)

(Jerusalem, 1992), p.141.
9. Ibid., p.53.
10. Examples of fiction where the moment of action and writing appear to be united include Margaret Atwood's first-person novel *The Handmaid's Tale* (1984), narrated in the present tense; epistolary novels such as Samuel Richardson's *Clarissa* (1747–48) where the moment of action and narration are often one; and fictional diaries, such as Arnost Lustig's *The Unloved: From the Diary of Perla S.* (trans. Vera Kalina-Levine) (Evanston, IL, 1996).
11. Ida Fink, *The Journey* (trans. Joanna Wechsler and Francine Prose) (Harmondsworth, 1992); Louis Begley, *Wartime Lies* (London, 1992). Although both works are fiction, Fink and Begley are Holocaust survivors; the novels represent young protagonists whose adult selves have only unreliable memories and reconstructions for their narratives.
12. Naomi Sokoloff, *Imagining the Child in Modern Jewish Fiction* (Baltimore, MD, 1992), p.30.
13. Pace Sokoloff, *Imagining the Child in Modern Jewish Fiction*, p.16, and Reiter, 'The Holocaust as Seen Through the Eyes of Children', p.87.
14. Jacobus, 'Border Crossings', p.143.
15. Doessekker's biological father, very much alive, was interviewed in Christopher Olgiati's BBC 1 documentary *Child of the Death Camps: Truth and Lies*, first shown 3 Nov. 1999.
16. See Maechler, 'Wilkomirski the Victim', p.65.
17. Reiter, 'The Holocaust as Seen Through the Eyes of Children', p.87.
18. See, for instance, Martin Amis, *Time's Arrow* (Harmondsworth, 1991) and D.M. Thomas, *The White Hotel* (Harmondsworth, 1979).
19. Victor Shklovsky, 'Art as Technique', in *Russian Formalist Criticism: Four Essays* (trans. Lee T. Lemon and Marion J. Reis) (Lincoln, NE and London, 1965), p.13, my italics.
20. See Elie Wiesel, 'I cannot write the words "concentration", "night and fog", "selection" or "transport" without a feeling of sacrilege', *All Rivers Run to the Sea: Memoirs Volume One, 1928–1969* (London, 1996), p.321.
21. Michael André Bernstein, *Foregone Conclusions: Against Apocalyptic History* (Berkeley and London, 1994), p.58.
22. Georges Perec, *W or the Memory of Childhood* (trans. David Bellos) (London, 1996).
23. See Sigmund Freud's Case History of the Wolf Man, *The Standard Edition of the Complete Psychological Works of Sigmund Freud*, Vol.XVII (London, 1953).
24. See Maechler, 'Wilkomirski the Victim', p.80, for a summary.
25. Thomas Geve, *Guns and Barbed Wire: A Child Survives the Holocaust* (Chicago, 1987 [1958]); in the Preface, Geve writes, 'No one else has come forward to tell of those who grew up in concentration camps' (p.vii). All further page references in the text.
26. Geve's memoir was originally published in Jerusalem, in English, as *Youth in Chains*; the present title is taken from 'the concentration camp anthem' (*Guns and Barbed Wire*, p.164).
27. Lappin, 'The Man With Two Heads', p.64.
28. For further examples of this type, see Anita Lobel, *No Pretty Pictures: A Child of War* (New York, 1998): 'I could not really imagine that "mother" and "father" were anything but two more official words' (p.151); and Renée Fersen-Osten, *Don't They Know the World Stopped Breathing? Reminiscences of a French Child During the Holocaust Years* (New York, 1991): 'My voice could say the words: "Maman. Petite Mère. Maman". But I wasn't sure, anymore, exactly what they meant' (p.228).
29. Norman Geras, 'The True Wilkomirski', *Res Publica*, Vol.8 (2002), pp.111–22, 121.
30. Ibid. There are many instances in testimonies of true tokens of this type, mothers somehow meeting with or getting bread to their children in camps: see for instance Tola Friedman (née Grossman): 'When I opened the bag I found a piece of bread wrapped in a note: "Tola", it said, " tomorrow is your birthday. I love you. Mama"' (in Milton J. Nieuwsma (ed.), *Kinderlager: An Oral History of Young Holocaust Survivors* (New York, 1998), p.23).

31. Harold Gordon, *The Last Sunrise: A True Story* (Salinas, CA, 1992), p.140.
32. Judith Hemmendinger, *Survivors: Children of the Holocaust* (trans. unnamed) (Bethesda, MD, 1986), p.21; Edgar E. Stern, *The Peppermint Train: Journey to a German-Jewish Childhood* (Gainesville, 1992), p.216; Ilse Aichinger, *Herod's Children* (trans. Cornelia Schaeffer) (New York, 1963), p.52.
33. Frances Stonor Saunders, 'The Scandal of the Swiss Slave Children', *Areté*, Vol.1 (1999), pp.85–94: 89. Thanks to John Haffenden for this reference.
34. Carl Friedman, *Nightfather* (trans. Arnold and Erica Pomerans) (New York, 1994), p.5, quoted in Lawrence L. Langer, 'Damaged Childhood in Holocaust Fact and Fiction', in Michael A. Signer (ed.), *Humanity at the Limit: The Impact of the Holocaust Experience on Jews and Christians* (Bloomington, IN and London, 2000).
35. Auerhahn and Laub, 'Reverberations of Genocide', p.164.
36. Maechler, 'Wilkomirski the Victim', p.81.
37. See Yolanda Gampel, 'I Was a Shoah Child' (*British Journal of Psychotherapy*, Vol.8, No.4, 1992, pp.391–400) on children surviving the Holocaust without the 'comfort of tears' (p.391); and see Jacobus, *Psychoanalysis and the Scene of Reading*, p.156.
38. Saul Friedländer, *When Memory Comes* (trans. Helen R. Lane) (New York, 1979), p.102.
39. Gampel, 'I Was a Shoah Child', p.397.
40. Ironically, several contemporaries testify to Bruno Doessekker's proficiency as a skiier.
41. Hemmendinger, *Survivors*, p.145.
42. Auerhahn and Laub, 'Reverberations of Genocide', p.165.

Curriculum Vitae
March 2000

SURNAME: BURNS   First Names: Bryan Peter

DATE OF BIRTH: 18 June 1945

DEPARTMENT: English Literature

EDUCATION AFTER SCHOOL:

University College, University of Durham, 1963–66
Graduate Society, University of Durham, 1966–67
University of Bristol, 1967-8
King's College, University of London, 1972–74

QUALIFICATIONS:

- BA, Honours in English Language and Literature (IIi), University of Durham, 1966
- Dip.Ed., University of Bristol, 1968
- MA, University of Durham, 1970
  Thesis: 'The Revisions of Wordsworth's *Yarrow Revisited* Volume of 1835 and the Form of Wordworth's Later Poetry'
- PhD, King's College, University of London, 1980
  Thesis: 'Moods and Themes in the Writings of Thomas Love Peacock'

LANGUAGES:

French, German, Spanish, Italian, Latin, Serbo-Croatian, Farsi. I have a reading knowledge of Portuguese, Dutch and Hungarian

CURRENT APPOINTMENT IN THE UNIVERSITY OF SHEFFIELD:

Lecturer in English Literature since 1974; Senior Lecturer since 1998

OTHER APPOINTMENTS:

- Lecturer in English, University of Teheran, 1970–71
- Lecturer in English, University of Zagreb, 1971–72

- Visiting Professor of English, University of Southern California, Los Angeles, 1980–81

CURRENT ANNUAL TEACHING:

Semester One
Seminars and lectures for the *Restoration and Eighteenth-Century* course
Seminars for the *Jewish Writing* Approved Module
Seminars for the *Hollywood and the Cinema* course
Postgraduate supervision of six students (on Jane Austen and civilization; adaptations of Shakespeare in film and opera; testimony and the Holocaust; Holocaust documentary film; the presentation of time in Modernist novels and films derived from them; time and space in eighteenth-century fiction).

Semester Two
Seminars and lectures for the *Romanticism* course
Seminars for the *Memory and the Cinema* Approved Module
Seminars for the *Jewish Writing: Prelude to the Holocaust* MA module: 1½ hours per week
Postgraduate supervision of six students

My work involves the supervision of research students on a wide variety of topics
I play a substantial role in teaching and administering the Department's successful, expanding and innovatory Film and Holocaust courses for undergraduates, and its interdisciplinary MA course in Holocaust Studies. I will be a major contributor to the proposed new interdisciplinary MA in International Cinema.

CURRENT OR PAST PROFESSIONAL DUTIES OR ACTIVITIES:

External Examining:
External Examiner in English for the BEd degree in English, Sedgefield and De La Salle Colleges, Manchester, 1975–79
External Examiner in English for the BA (Hons.) degree in English, De La Salle College, 1982 to 1986
Member of Validating Board for the new degree in Film Studies, Bolton Institute, 1995
External Examiner for the BA degree in Film Studies, Bolton Institute, 1995 onwards

Visiting Lectureships:
I have frequently been invited to foreign universities to give lectures and classes on a variety of subjects
Visiting Lecturer, University of Łódź, 1983, 1987, 1993, 1994 (for a period of two weeks each time; lecturing on Romantic poetry and fiction, on British Counter-cultures and on the literature and film of the Holocaust)
Visiting Lecturer, University of Oviedo, 1984 (for a period of one week; discussing research in Modern literature with members of staff)
Visiting Lecturer, University of Malaga, 1985 (for a period of two weeks; lecturing on Romantic and Modern poetry and fiction)
Visiting Lecturer, Universities of Sofia and Veliko Tornovo, 1991 (for a period of two weeks; lecturing on British culture and on Romantic fiction).
Visiting Lecturer, University of Szeged, 2000 (for a period of one week; teaching a course on Shakespeare on Screen)

Conferences and Lectures:
Invited lecture on *Gryll Grange* given at the Thomas Love Peacock Conference, Wales, 1984
Invited lecture on the later novels of Jane Austen given at University of Neuchatel, 1991
Paper on *Shoah* and Documentary given at the Film and the Holocaust Conference, Sheffield, 1995
Paper on the Kovno Ghetto Journal given at the CCUE Conference, Loughborough, 1996

I largely organized a conference on Film and the Holocaust which took place in Sheffield on 19 December 1995 and involved a range of participants from Britain and abroad
I was one of the organizers of a conference on Romanticism and Violence which took place in Sheffield early in 1997

Research Visits and Awards:
Work on films of Miklós Jancsó, Budapest Film Archives, 1985
Work on modern Hungarian cinema, Budapest Film Archives, 1989, 1991, 1995
These research fieldwork visits, which offered unusual access for a foreigner to the riches of the Hungarian cinema, and were highly regarded by my hosts, were sponsored by the Hungarian Ministry of Culture and the British Council; in each case, the award to me was of the order of £1,000.

Other Activities:
Courses taught and lectures given for the Extra-Mural Department, including study days on the German and Japanese Film
Reviewer of critical books on fiction of the Romantic period for *Romanticism*, 1995 onwards
Reader of manuscripts on the Holocaust for Routledge

RESEARCH SUPERVISION:

I have successfully supervised the MPhil theses of:
- Angela Marritt (on the novels of Charles Maturin)
- Belinda Barber (on the influence of Greek drama on Victorian Literature)
- Patricia Newman (on female sexuality in the novels of Patrick White; with Distinction; now being considered for publication by the Sheffield Academic Press)
- John Saunders (on Conrad and Existentialism)

and the PhD theses of:
- Sarah Gamble (on the cultural models of women in contemporary British and American fantasy by women writers; 1992; since published as *Angela Carter*, Edinburgh University Press, 1997)
- Robert Miles (on the aesthetics of Gothic fiction; 1992; since published as *Gothic Writing, 1750–1820: A Genealogy*, Routledge, 1993)
- Jonathan Rayner (on genre in the films of Peter Weir; 1995; since published as *Peter Weir*, Cassell, 1998)
- Fiona Hannant (on religious thinking in the poetry of Shelley; 1995; since partly published in *The Most Unfailing Herald: P.B.Shelley, 1792-1992*, University of South Africa Press, 1996)
- Gillian Banner (on Holocaust remembrance; 1998; since published as *Remembrance and Holocaust Literature*, Valentine Mitchell, 2000; co-supervised with Dr Sue Vice)

I have also supervised a large number of MA dissertations.

Dr Gamble is now Senior Lecturer in English at the University of Sunderland, Dr Miles is Professor of English Literature at Sheffield Hallam University and Dr Rayner is senior Lecturer in Film Studies at Sheffield Hallam University.

COMPLETE LIST OF PUBLICATIONS:

Books-in print:

- *The Novels of Thomas Love Peacock*, 245 pp., Croom Helm, London and Sydney, 1985. Comments in reviews include: 'A study which subtly and revealingly qualifies the traditional view' (*The Year's Work in English Studies*, 1985, p.361), 'A stimulating book, in short, with a keen sense of Peacock's humanity' (*Critical Quarterly*, Vol.27, No.3, 91), 'The author has a gift for sharp and pithy phrases that strike cogently to the roots of the general premisses of his arguments ... the quality of the argument is persuasive' (*British Book News*, July, 1985, 437) and '[T]he scope and the critical acumen of Bryan Burns's study ... give it the force of a general estimate...notably successful in discriminating both the development of Peacock's literary art through the seven novels and the rich particularity of individual texts' (J.P. Donovan, in O'Neill, Michael, [ed.], *Literature of the Romantic Period*, Clarendon Press, Oxford, 19998, p. 4)

- *World Cinema: Hungary*, 234 pp., Flicks Books, Trowbridge and Fairleigh Dickinson University Press, Madison, 1996. Comments in reviews include: 'Goes far in filling in the critical gaps around its subject' (*Sight and Sound*, Vol. 7, No. 2, Feb., 1997), 36. Other reviews are being written, especially for Hungarian periodicals.

Book-in press:
Angi Vera; to be published by Flicks Books

Articles-in print:
- 'Ray's Party Girl', *Kingfisher*, pp.31–5, 1979
- 'Thomas Love Peacock', *Makers of 19th Century Culture, 1800–1914*, ed. Justin Wintle, pp.481–2, 1982
- 'The Storytelling in *Joseph Andrews*', *Henry Fielding: Justice Observed*, ed. K G Simpson, pp.119–136, 1985
- 'The Classicism of Peacock's *Gryll Grange*', *Keats-Shelley Memorial Bulletin*, XXXVI, pp.89–101, 1985
- Review Article on criticism of Gothic Fiction, *Romanticism*, Vol.4, No.1 (1998), pp.147–52
- '"The Approaching Storm": The Goskinds on Jewish Life in Poland', *When Joseph Met Molly: A Reader In Yiddish Film*, ed. Sylvia Paskin, pp.273–87, 1999

The following comprehensive review articles, each dealing with the prose fiction of the Romantic period, generally discussing 10 or more books and up to 100 articles, and amounting to 4,000–5,000 words on average, appeared in *The Year's Work in English Studies* volumes covering the years 1978–87:

- for 1978, pp. 282–7, 1980
- for 1979, pp. 280–87, 1981
- for 1980, pp. 293–302, 1982
- for 1981, pp. 298–302, 1984
- for 1982, pp. 299–304, 1985
- for 1983, pp. 346–50, 1986
- for 1984, pp. 403–11, 1987
- for 1985, pp. 356–63, 1988
- for 1986, pp. 363–9, 1989
- for 1987, pp. 391–9, 1990

RESEARCH IN PROGRESS:

I am working on a series of articles on ghetto journals in Eastern Europe, based on my paper given at CCUE, and will presently develop these into a book, to be offered to Routledge.

Notes on Contributors

Gillian Banner was employed as a social worker by Derbyshire County Council during the 1980s, but returned to full-time study in the Department of English Literature at Sheffield University in 1990 where she completed a BA, a Masters, and a Ph.D., awarded in 1997. Since then, Gillian has taught English Literature at Sheffield University, worked for the MP for High Peak, and was the lay member for the High Peak and Dales Primary Care Group. Her Ph.D. formed the basis for a book, *Holocaust Literature: Schulz, Levi, Spiegelman and the Memory of the Offence* (2000). She has been employed full time teaching English at The King's School in Macclesfield since September 2000.

Donald Bloxham is Lecturer in History at the University of Edinburgh. He is the author of *Genocide on Trial: War Crimes Trials in the Formation of Holocaust History and Memory* (2001) and of numerous articles on the Holocaust, war crimes trials, and on his current research project concerning the Armenian genocide.

Bryan Cheyette is Chair in Twentieth-Century Literature in the English Department, University of Southampton. He is the author of *Constructions of 'the Jew' in English Literature and Society* (1993) and *Muriel Spark* (2000) and has edited *Between 'Race' and Culture* (1996) and, with Laura Marcus, *Modernity, Culture and 'the Jew'* (1998). He is currently completing *Diasporas of the Mind* for Yale University Press.

Robert Eaglestone works on contemporary and twentieth century literature, literary theory and philosophy in the Department of English, Royal Holloway, University of London. His publications include *Ethical Criticism: Reading after Levinas* (London, 1997), *Doing English* (1999, Second Edition 2002), *Postmodernism and Holocaust Denial* (2001) and articles on contemporary European philosophy, Samuel Beckett, Angela Carter, ethics, science, the Holocaust, archaeology and historiography. He is currently working on *The Holocaust and the Postmodern*, on literature, history and philosophy after the 'Final Solution'. He is the series editor of *Routledge Critical Thinkers*. The research for the present contribution was completed during leave funded by the Leverhulme Trust.

Rachel Falconer is Senior Lecturer in the Department of English Literature at the University of Sheffield. She has published *Orpheus Dis(re)membered* (a monograph on John Milton's writing), *Face to Face* (an edited collection of essays on Mikhail Bakhtin), and articles on contemporary fiction and Renaissance epic. She is presently writing a book about the descent to Hell in contemporary narrative, to be published by Edinburgh University Press in 2004.

Tony Kushner is Marcus Sieff Professor of Jewish/non-Jewish relations in the Department of History, University of Southampton. Amongst his recent work is the book *Refugees in an Age of Genocide* (1999) and he is joint editor of *Disraeli's Jewishness* (2002). He is currently completing a book on Mass-Observation.

David Renton studied at Oxford and Sheffield Universities and is now a Senior Research Fellow at Sunderland University. His most recent book is *The History of the Communist Party of Great Britain since 1920* (with James Eaden, 2002). His webpage is www.dkrenton.co.uk.

J.M. Ritchie has published widely in the field of German Studies from the Baroque era to the present day. Apart from his five-volume series on the *Theatre of German Expressionism* (1968 onwards), his main publications are his books *German Literature under National Socialism* (1983) and *German Exiles: British Perspectives* (1998). Since retirement from the chair of German at the University of Aberdeen, Hamish Ritchie has been Emeritus Professor and Chairman of the Research Centre for German and Austrian Exile Studies, University of London. He has been awarded the *Großes Verdienstkreuz der Bundesrepublik Deutschland* (the German Grand Cross of the Order of Merit).

Ben Smith studied English and History at the University of Southampton. He recently completed his doctoral thesis on cinematic representations of the Holocaust in the Department of English Literature, University of Sheffield.

Avram Taylor is Lecturer in History at the University of Northumbria at Newcastle. His thesis is to be published by Palgrave in November 2002 as *Working Class Credit Since 1918*. He is currently writing a joint-authored book with Don MacRaild, *Social Theory and Social History*, to be published in the 'Theory and History' series by Palgrave. He is also carrying out further research into the Jewish community in Glasgow for another piece on this topic.

Sue Vice is Reader in English Literature at the University of Sheffield. She is the author of *Introducing Bakhtin* (1997) and *Holocaust Fiction* (2000), and is currently working on a study of children's-eye views of the Holocaust.

Index

Aberdeen, 65, 66, 69
Aborigines, 29
Adelson, Alan, and Kathryn Taverna, *Łódź Ghetto* (1988), 4, 112
Adorno, Theodor, 102
Aichinger, Ilse, *Herod's Children*, 259
Alderman, Geoffrey, 155
Améry, Jean, 105; *At the Mind's Limits*, 122–3, 131
anti-Semitism, 14, 21, 24, 48, 52, 53, 68, 143, 156, 164, 186, 189
Ashton, T.A., 188, 189
Auerhahn, Nanette C., 250, 261, 266
Australasia, 20, 42; *see also* Aborigines
Austria, 63–77 *passim*, Graz, 72; Vienna 66, 186, 197

Bakhtin, Mikhail, 209, 217; the chronotope, 204, 207–26 *passim*, 227 n. 17, 228 nn. 24, 25, 31
Ballin, Neville David, 64
Banner, Gillian, 139 n. 70
Bardgett, Suzanne, 23
Bauman, Zygmunt, 178; *Modernity and the Holocaust*, 42
Beer, Judith Hahn, *The Nazi Officer's Wife*, 122, 123, 128, 135
Begley, Louis, *Wartime Lies*, 230 n. 46, 251
Berenbaum, Michael, 23
Bernstein, Michael André, 134
Blair, Tony, 52, 57, 59
Blunkett, David, 58
Booth, Alan, 191, 198
Borowski, Tadeusz, *This Way for the Gas, Ladies and Gentlemen*, 238
Bratu Hansen, Miriam, 95
Brink, Cordelia, 17
Brinson, Charmian, 65, 67, 70, 75
Britain, Britishness, 23, 28, 41–62, 63–77, 129, 134, 143–83, 184–200; *see also* Aberdeen, Glasgow, Sheffield, York
Browning, Christopher, 48, 60 n. 20
Burchill, Julie, 15
Butler, Judith, 118

Calvino, Italo, 205, 207
camps, concentration and death: Auschwitz-Birkenau,18, 19, 20, 23, 25, 27, 34, 41, 81, 119, 120, 123–4, 127, 129, 132–4, 203–30 *passim*, 249, 253, 255–6, 266; Belzec, 19, 29; Bergen-Belsen, 17, 18, 19, 22, 27, 31, 120; Buchenwald, 19, 33, 119, 129, 259; Chelmno, 82, 85, 86, 87; Dachau, 33; Majdanek, 19, 25, 249, 255, 260; Mauthausen, 24, 29; Ohrdruf, 19; Opole, 187; Sobibor, 19, 28; Treblinka, 19, 48, 82
Camus, Albert, 56
Caruth, Cathy, 135
Casetti, Francesco, 99
Cavani, Liliana, *The Night Porter* (1974), 31
Cayrol, Jean, 87
Celan, Paul, 107 n. 21, 129, 237
Centre for German and Austrian Exile Studies, London, 63–77 *passim*
Cesarani, David, 154
Chapman, Dinos, 25, 27
Chapman, Jake, 25, 26, 27
Charlesworth, Andy, 47
Cheyette, Bryan, 14
children, child psychology, *see* Gampel, Yolanda; Hemmendinger, Judith; Wilkomirski, Binjamin
Cole, Tim, 98, 134
Coleridge, Samuel Taylor, *The Rime of the Ancient Mariner*, 220, 224, 238
Colley, Linda, 58
Coppola, Francis Ford, *Apocalypse Now* (1979)
Czechoslovakia, 63, 69, 75; Prague, 129
Czerniakow, Adam, 113

Dante Alighieri, 204, 222, 227 n. 18; *Inferno*, 206, 209, 213, 223–4, 225, 229 n. 41
Darville, Helen, *The Hand that Signed the Paper*, 266 n. 4
Davidson, Shamai, 106
Davies, Andrew, 148
defamiliarization, 254–5, 256, 260–61, 263, 265
Delbo, Charlotte, 118, 123, 128, 129, 130, 132, 137; *Auschwitz and After*, 123–4; *Days and Memory*, 126;*The Measure of Our Days*, 125–6
De Man, Paul, 121
Demidenko, Helen, *see* Darville, Helen
Derrida, Jacques, 137
diaries, 113; *see also* journals
Dismore, Andrew, 43, 57

documentary film, 4, 81–8 *passim*, 105
Douglas, Lawrence, 18–19
Dove, Richard, 67, 70, 71–2, 74
drama, plays, 143–83 *passim*
Dunkirk, 24, 54

Eichmann, Adolf, 107 n. 20, 239
Einsatzgruppen, 20, 29
Eliot, T.S., 235
Elkes, Elkhanan, 112
Elsom, John, 148, 149, 155
exile, 63–77 *passim*

Fénelon, Fania, *Playing for Time*, 122, 129
Fforde, Cressida, 29
film, 3–4, 81–8 *passim*; 89–107 *passim*; *see also* under individual directors' names
Fink, Ida, *The Journey*, 251
Finkelstein, Norman, 6
Foley, Barbara, 132
Foucault, Michel, 122
France, the French, 15, 58, 59, 125
Frank, Anne, 113
Frankel, Neftali, 119, 132
Freud, Sigmund, 223, 256, 264
Friedlander, Saul, 91, 105; *When Memory Comes*, 262–3, 264
Friedman, Carl, *Nightfather*, 261
Friesner, Susan, 145, 156, 170
Frister, Roman, *The Cap*, 122, 129
Fuentes, Carlos, 133
Fuss, Diana, 117–18

Gabor, Pal, *Angi Vera* (1978), 3
Gampel, Yolanda, 264
Garret, Jim, 26, 30
Gartner, Lloyd P., 144
Gazdag, Gyula, *That was a Hungarian Fairy Tale* (1987), 4
gender, 30–32, 95, 233–5
Genette, Gérard, 135
genocide, 21, 30, 34, 35, 43–5, 50, 60 n. 25, 107 n. 21; Armenia, 21, 35, 54, 56; Bosnia, 35; Cambodia, 21, 35, 56; Rwanda, 21, 35, 56; Tasmania, 42
Genocide Memorial Day, 44
Geras, Norman, 258
Germans, Germany, 14–16, 17, 21, 22, 28, 33, 36 n. 11, 46, 54, 57, 59, 84, 120, 194–5, 228 n. 29, 244; Bielefeld, 189, 191
Geve, Thomas, *Guns and Barbed Wire*, 256–9
ghettoes, 3, 24; *see also* under individual cities
Glasgow, 71, 163–6, 171, 179
Glasser, Ralph, 162, 163, 177

Goldhagen, Daniel, 21, 60 n. 21
Gordon, Harry, *The Last Sunrise*, 258–9
Goskind, Shaul and Yitzhak, 4
Greenspan, Henry, 96
Grenville, Anthony, 74, 75
Grossman, Chajka, 93–4
Grynberg, Henryk, *Birthplace*, 35
Gyöngyössy, Imre, and Bárna Kabay, *The Revolt of Job* (1983), 3
Gypsies, 28, 54, 55

Hague War Crimes Trials, 21
Hart, Kitty, *Return to Auschwitz*, 120, 121, 129, 133, 134
Hartman, Geoffrey, 90, 97
Hayek, F.A. von, 188
Hayman, Ronald, 148–9
Helbling, Hanno, 254
Hemmendinger, Judith, 259, 265
Hilberg, Raul, 46, 81–2
Himmler, Heinrich, 129
Hitler, Adolf, 42, 64, 70, 73, 105, 234
Hobsbawm, Eric, 91, 188
Hoggart, Simon, 15
Holmes, Colin, 188, 189, 191, 197, 198
Holocaust Memorial Day (Britain), 26, 41–59 *passim*
homophobia, 56, 61 n. 43
homosexuality, 56, 57
Horowitz, Sarah, 125
Hughes, Ted, 235
Hungary, 3, 25, 69; Budapest, 4

identification, 255; in testimony, 117–38 *passim*
imperialism, 30
India, 42
Israel, 82, 155
Isaacson, Judith Magyar, *Seed of Sarah*, 120, 122

James, Henry, 132
Jancsó, Miklós, 4
Jews, Judaism, 5, 14, 23, 29, 33, 43, 46, 54–5, 66, 91, 105, 115, 160–83 *passim*, 192–4, 198, 233, 241, 242, 265
journals, ghetto, 111–16 *passim*
Judt, Tony, 86, 229 n. 43

Kafka, Franz, 223
Kapp, Yvonne, 64–5
Karpf, Anne, 23, 57
katabasis, 203–26 *passim*; 226 n. 3
Katan, Alphons, 29
Kindertransports, 185
King, Martin Luther, 52

Index

Klimov, Elem, *Come and See* (1985), 89–107
Kovner, Abba, 93, 96
Kristallnacht, 186
Kristeva, Julia, 232, 233
Kuczynski, Jürgen, 190
Kushner, Tony, 53

Lafitte, François, 64
Lamont, Rosette, 123
Langer, Lawrence L., 96, 115, 123, 131
Lanzmann, Claude, *Shoah* (1985), 3, 6, 8, 81–8 *passim*, 89, 90, 92
Latvia: Riga, 116, 159, 249
Laub, Dori, 250, 261, 266
Lawrence, Stephen, 27, 49
Lawrie, Steven, 66
Leitner, Isabella, *Fragments of Isabella*, 127, 129
Lengyel, Olga, *Five Chimneys*, 120, 121
Leo Baeck Institute, 63, 66
Levi, Primo, 20, 122, 131, 136, 203–30 *passim*, 237–8; *The Drowned and the Saved*, 133–4, 203, 211, 215–16, 221–2, 229 n. 44, 237, 246; *If This is a Man*, 120, 127, 205, 211–26, 240; *The Mirror Maker*, 220–21, 223–4; *The Periodic Table*, 205, 219–20; *The Search for Roots*, 203, 217, 222, 225; *The Truce*, 132, 133, 210, 218, 225–6; *The Voice of Memory*, 203
Levene, Mark, 50
Lindsey, Rose, 32
literature, literary effects, *see* Bakhtin, Mikhail; defamiliarization; Levi, Primo; Plath, Sylvia; testimony; Wilkomirski, Binjamin
Lithuania, 97, 115; Kovno, 3; Vilna, 111
Loshitzky, Yosefa, 96

MacKinnon, Catherine, 32
McLaughlin, Donal, 66, 69
McMillan, Joyce, 149
Maechler, Stefan, 249, 262
Malet, Marian, 67, 74, 75
Malvern, Sue, 16, 24, 33, 34
Marx, Karl, Marxism, 69, 119, 146, 169, 190, 193
Mathias, Peter, 191
memorials, memorialization, 13, 22, 27, 58, 59, 89–107 *passim*, 236, 242
Millu, Liana, *Smoke over Birkenau*, 227 n. 20
Mishell, William W., 113
Müller, Filip, 132
museums: Imperial War Museum, London, 13–40 *passim*, 41, 58, 60 n. 2, 60 n. 17; Liverpool Maritime Museum, 34; Manchester Jewish Museum, 26; Manchester Pump House Museum, 30; Pitt Rivers Museum, Oxford, 18, 19, 25, 34, 35; United States Holocaust Memorial Museum, Washington, 13, 19, 25, 35, 41
Mussolini, Benito, 220
Mynatt, Margaret, 64–5

Nazism, Nazis, 17, 18–19, 22, 24, 27, 29, 30, 31, 32, 33, 43, 45, 46, 51–7, 63, 64, 67, 88, 90, 92, 100, 103, 105, 111, 112, 116, 128, 130, 185, 217, 234, 243, 260
Novick, Peter, 134
Nuremberg Trials, 18, 19

Oliver, Cordelia, 159, 165, 172

pathos, and the Holocaust, 47, 59, 252, 256, 264, 265
Paucker, Arnold, 66
Peacock, Thomas Love, 2
Perec, Georges, *W or the Memory of Childhood*, 256, 264
Plath, Sylvia, 231–47 *passim*; *Collected Poems*, 239–40; 'Daddy', 234, 235, 241, 242; 'Little Fugue', 241, 243–5; 'The Thin People', 240–43
plays, *see* drama
poetry, 231–47 *passim*
Poland, 19, 52, 69, 81, 83, 86, 236, 250; Krakow, 2, 95; Łódź, 3, 111, 112, 115; Lvov, 30, 32, 111; Stryjj, 186; Tarnow, 119; Warsaw, 24, 111
Pollard, Sidney, 184–200 *passim*; *The Development of the British Economy*, 189; *The Genesis of Modern Management*, 189; *Marginal Europe*, 184, 191–2, 194
Postan, Michael, 190
Pulzer, Peter, 185

Rabelais, François, 206
racism, 14–16, 48, 49, 57–8, 61 n. 43, 187; *see also* anti-Semitism
Rapoport, Nathan, 22
refugees, 51, 63, 184–200 *passim*
Reiter, Andrea, 118
Resnais, Alain, *Night and Fog* (1955), 4, 81, 86, 87, 89, 92, 101–2
Riefenstahl, Leni, *The Triumph of the Will* (1934), 102
Ringelblum, Emanuel, 111
Ritchie, J.M., 63, 65, 72, 74
Robertson, Ritchie, 66
Roma, *see* Gypsies
Rose, Jacqueline, 231, 232–5, 240, 245

Rosenfeld, Alvin, 135
Rousset, David, *L'Univers concentrationnaire*, 119
Rumkowski, Chaim, 111
Russia, 64, 155, 159; Grodno, 156; *see also* USSR

Said, Edward, 14
Saunders, Frances Stonor, 260
Semprun, Jorge, *The Long Voyage*, 118, 128, 129, 133, 135
September 11 2001, 50, 237
Sereny, Gitta, 48
Sheffield, 64, 65, 184, 189, 190, 196–7
Simpson, Moira, 13, 18
Slade, Joseph, 31
slavery, 30, 59
Smith, Joan, 31
Smollett, Tobias, 3
Sobchack, Vivian, 89
Sokoloff, Naomi, 251
Spalek, John, 63
Spanish Civil War, 65, 68, 155
Spielberg, Steven, 57, 97; *Schindler's List* (1993), 89, 92, 95–6, 101, 102, 105
Stangl, Franz, 48
Steinberg, Paul, *Speak You Also*, 215, 229 n. 38
Stevenson, Anne, *Bitter Fame*, 232
Stone, Dan, 140 n. 81
Styron, William, *Sophie's Choice*, 31
Switzerland, the Swiss, 249, 250, 255, 260
Szabó, István, *Confidence* (1980), 3
Szeman, Sherri, *The Kommandant's Mistress*, 31

Taylor, C.P., 143–83 *passim*; *Aa Went Tae Blaydon Races*, 145, 150; *Bandits*, 152; *Bontsha the Silent*, 159; *Bread and Butter*, 144, 149, 166–71; *Bring Me Sunshine*, 147; *Good*, 145, 148, 152, 153, 164, 181 n. 41; *Happy Days Are Here Again*, 149; *The Killingworth Play*, 152; *Me*, 164–6; *Mr David*, 159; *And a Nightingale Sang*, 145, 152; *Oil and Water*, 164; *Operation Elvis*, 151; *The Plumber's Progress*, 145; *The Tie*, 147; *Walter*, 144, 149, 171, 173–9
Taylor, Jennifer, 67, 68, 70
Taylor, John, 27, 30, 32
Tec, Nechama, 52
testimony, oral history, 22, 29, 70, 73, 114, 117–38 *passim*
Thomas, D.M., *The White Hotel*, 31
Timms, Edward, 66
Tory, Avraham, 112, 113–16
trauma, 135–6, 255, 265
Ukraine, 20, 159
uniqueness, of Holocaust, 41–7, 50, 58, 61 n. 43
USSR, 20, 53, 54, 55, 71, 90, 100, 103

Vercel, Roger, *Tug-Boat*, 207
Vietor-Englander, Deborah, 67
Vrba, Rudolf, *I Cannot Forgive*, 120, 126, 129

Waletzky, Josh, *Partisans of Vilna* (1986), 89–107 *passim*
Wallace, Ian, 68, 73
war crimes trials, 37 n. 38; *see also* Hague; Nuremberg
Weiss, David, 25
Wiener Library, London, 72
Wiesel, Elie, 117, 128, 133, 135, 267 n. 20; *Night*, 107 n. 21
Wiesenthal, Simon, *The Sunflower*, 130–1, 135
Wilkomirski, Binjamin, *Fragments*, 135, 249–66 *passim*
Williams, Bill, 57
Wood, Marcus, 34
Wordsworth, William, 2
Wright, Richard, 20, 21, 29

Yad Vashem, 25
Yerushalmi, Yosef Hayim, *Zakhor*, 137
York, 28
Young, James, 24, 25, 33, 34, 136, 231–2, 235–9, 247
Yugoslavia, 21

Other Titles of Interest

Holocaust Historiography
Conceptualism, Terminology, Approaches and Fundamental Issues

Professor Dan Michman

While historical research on the Holocaust has been growing constantly, and in the last few decades almost exploded, the perspective of the targeted group – the Jews – as an active player in the historical arena of the Holocaust, a player with its own historical background, has not been seriously integrated into the larger fabric. In a series of treatises, some of which are based on articles previously published in several languages, this book tries to analyse existing research from these neglected perspectives.
The author also examines the ways in which 'The Holocaust' is conceptualised, and how different understandings of the same concept and the use of alternative terms lead to different, and even conflicting, conclusions. Looking at terms such as 'resistance', 'collaboration', 'Fascism', 'Judenrat', 'The Surviving Remnant', 'The Jewish People', etc. – the reader gets a variety of original introductions into the most fundamental issues of this event and the era in which it happened. On the basis of the insights gained from this 'X-ray' approach, the author provides both researchers and laymen with a better understanding of scholarly debates and research directions, while also proposing fresh historical explanations.

2002 224 pages
0 85303 436 2 cloth
0 85303428 1 paper
Parkes-Weiner Series on Jewish Studies

FRANK CASS PUBLISHERS
Crown House, 47 Chase Side, Southgate, London N14 5BP
Tel: +44 (0)20 8920 2100 Fax: +44 (0)20 8447 8548 E-mail: info@frankcass.com
NORTH AMERICA
920 NE 58th Avenue Suite 300, Portland, OR 97213-3786 USA
Tel: 800 944 6190 Fax: 503 280 8832 E-mail: cass@isbs.com
Website: www.frankcass.com

The Jewish Heritage in British History
Englishness and Jewishness

Tony Kushner, University of Southampton (ed.)

This volume of essays explores the way in which historians and manufacturers of British 'heritage' have represented the Jews and Jewish issues in the Middle Ages, early modern period and present day.

1992 234 pages illus
0 7146 3464 6 cloth
0 7146 4086 7 paper
A special issue of the journal Immigrants and Minorities   Frank Cass

FRANK CASS PUBLISHERS
Crown House, 47 Chase Side, Southgate, London N14 5BP
Tel: +44 (0)20 8920 2100 Fax: +44 (0)20 8447 8548 E-mail: info@frankcass.com
NORTH AMERICA
920 NE 58th Avenue Suite 300, Portland, OR 97213-3786 USA
Tel: 800 944 6190 Fax: 503 280 8832 E-mail: cass@isbs.com
Website: www.frankcass.com

Between Auschwitz and Jerusalem
Jewish Collective Identity in Crisis

Professor Yosef Gorny

This book analyzes the dialectic relations between the two major components of the collective Jewish identity – the Holocaust, and the state of Israel. The symbolic points for the beginning and the end of From Auschwitz to Jerusalem are: the Eichmann trial in Israel, and the founding of the Memorial Museum in Washington in 1993. At the first point the question was: has Israel the right to judge Eichmann in the name of the world Jewish people and at the second point, what is the Memorial representing: the unique Jewish tragedy or a universal problem? The research for the book was done on the basis of constant comparison between the discourses in Israel and the Diaspora, especially in the USA but also in England.

History, Jewish Studies

224 pages
0 85303 419 2 cloth
0 85303 421 4 paper
Parkes-Wiener Series on Jewish Studies

FRANK CASS PUBLISHERS
Crown House, 47 Chase Side, Southgate, London N14 5BP
Tel: +44 (0)20 8920 2100 Fax: +44 (0)20 8447 8548 E-mail: info@frankcass.com
NORTH AMERICA
920 NE 58th Avenue Suite 300, Portland, OR 97213-3786 USA
Tel: 800 944 6190 Fax: 503 280 8832 E-mail: cass@isbs.com
Website: www.frankcass.com

Holocaust Literature
Schulz, Levi, Spiegelman and the Memory of the Offence

Gillian Banner

Foreword by Colin Richmond

Holocaust Literature provides an evaluation of the dynamics of memory in relation to
representations of the Holocaust. It examines the compulsion to remember, the dilemmas of representation, and the relationship between memory, knowledge and belief in the works of Bruno Schulz, Primo Levi and Art Spiegelman. Holocaust Literature combines close readings of individual works, supported by a sound theoretical framework, with a consideration of the varieties of memory, and the particular problems of Holocaust memory. This approach reveals a 'hierarchy of remembrance' which exemplifies the changing nature of representations of Holocaust memory.

224 pages 2000 illus
0 85303 364 1 cloth
0 85303 371 4 paper
Parkes-Wiener Series on Jewish Studies

FRANK CASS PUBLISHERS
Crown House, 47 Chase Side, Southgate, London N14 5BP
Tel: +44 (0)20 8920 2100 Fax: +44 (0)20 8447 8548 E-mail: info@frankcass.com
NORTH AMERICA
920 NE 58th Avenue Suite 300, Portland, OR 97213-3786 USA
Tel: 800 944 6190 Fax: 503 280 8832 E-mail: cass@isbs.com
Website: www.frankcass.com